Communicating Interpersonally

A Reader

R. WAYNE PACE
University of New Mexico

BRENT D. PETERSON
Brigham Young University

TERRENCE R. RADCLIFFE
College of Great Falls

Charles E. Merrill Publishing Company
A Bell & Howell Company
Columbus, Ohio

Published by
Charles E. Merrill Publishing Company
A Bell & Howell Company
Columbus, Ohio 43216

ISBN: 0-675-09002-4

Library of Congress Catalog Card Number: 72-92574

2   3   4   5   6   7   8 / 77   76   75   74

Printed in the United States of America

Contents

Contents

Preface

Human beings have long sought after the ability to communicate effectively with others. Communicating interpersonally involves the qualities of being warm, genuine, supportive, accepting, and understanding. Through the processes of communication, we establish and maintain (or disrupt) relationships.

Understanding others and being understood involves a cooperative effort toward achieving a commonality of meaning. Instead of cooperating, however, as bunglers of relationships, we fight the meanings of one another. We hurt rather than help those who most demand our love and understanding. In reaching out for others, we jar their sensitivities; then we stare in wonder at their startled reactions. The consequence is often alienation, loneliness, and torn relationships.

Effectiveness in our relationships requires a genuine knowledge of and skill in communicating interpersonally — a skill we must learn. Being helpful to others in constructive ways, being warm, genuine, supportive, accepting, and understanding, expressing these qualities so others can recognize them, and accepting such expressions from others are all part of what it means to communicate with others. Having learned and acquired these skills, in good time, with practice and guidance, we might come to know each other — as true friends.

Communicating Interpersonally can help you learn what it means to communicate with others, what behaviors and other factors influence — positively and negatively — effective relationships, what you might anticipate as the consequence of changing your communicative style, and how you might achieve amelioration — improvement — in your interpersonal relationships through more effective communication.

In this book we have gathered together some provocative, interesting, and profound statements about communicative behavior. We have been able to provide you with essays and descriptions that are broad in scope, penetrating in depth, and straight from the original works of the most significant personalities in the field. That, it seems to us, is a good reason for this book.

The strength and true value of this compilation, however, lies in the powerful analysis of the communicative process as presented by the authors whose essays are included. We are deeply indebted to each author whose writings have been selected for inclusion. We express our gratitude to them, as we think you will also, for their singular and significant contributions to *Communicating Interpersonally*.

At the end of this beginning, we also wish to recognize and acknowledge the far-reaching influence that our colleagues in the Department of Speech Communication at the University of Montana have had upon us — in one word, BIG. We especially wish to thank Michelle Peterson for typing and editing the manuscript numerous times. Finally, our wives, Gae, Arlene, and Virginia, have provided the necessary incentives to bring this book to fruition.

R. Wayne Pace
Brent D. Peterson
Terrence R. Radcliffe

An Exchange

"HEY, WHAT ABOUT THIS COMMUNICATION STUFF? I WANT TO COMMU-NICATE WITH PEOPLE WHO DON'T SEEM TO COME THROUGH AT ALL, BUT, ABOVE EVERYTHING ELSE, I WANT TO BE ABLE TO DEVELOP MY OWN SKILLS IN ESTABLISHING AND MAINTAINING RELATIONSHIPS WITH OTHER HUMAN BEINGS. WHAT DO I NEED TO KNOW AND WHAT DO I NEED TO DO? HOW DO YOU GO ABOUT LEARNING TO COMMUNICATE BETTER? THIS WHOLE BUSINESS PUZZLES ME!"

"Aye, that's the rub. To know, to understand about understanding, to communicate about communicating. What to say?"

"Try this: Communication is a subject matter that is at the base of comprehending all human behavior, which may in fact be something that none of us can ever hope to achieve. We can understand some things about communicating, but we can never understand them fully or perfectly."

"THAT DOESN'T SEEM TO SOLVE THE WORLD'S PROBLEMS."

"True! We do believe, nevertheless, that through proper exposure to appropriate concepts and by experiencing interpersonal relationships in terms of the concepts, communication can be improved."

"To change interpersonal communication, we have to accept at least one significant assumption. That is, that interpersonal communication is a type of human behavior which is expressed in the form of certain kinds of learned skills. In other words, as with golf, brick laying, repairing electronic circuits, writing ads for television, playing a musical instrument, or creating a piece of pottery, communicating interpersonally involves a number of specific behaviors that can be learned. Naturally, the proficiency a person develops depends upon his ability to understand and acquire the behaviors. Integration of new communication behaviors often takes longer than those of other skills, but the rewards as well can be greater."

"WHAT ABOUT THIS BOOK? WHAT CAN IT DO?"

"*Communicating Interpersonally* provides theoretical explanations and practical guidance for understanding concepts of interpersonal communication. In addition, it will aid in developing the behaviors and skills necessary to establish and maintain effective interaction with others."

"Just reading this book isn't enough."

"WHAT ELSE MUST ONE DO?"

"While you learn about communication, you will want to deliberately engage in experimenting with the appropriate skills that produce effective interpersonal relationships. Since interpersonal communication, by definition and design, involves other people, you will want to study and practice new behaviors with one other person or even with a small group of people. The classroom will give you this opportunity; take advantage of the situation and plunge into the daily routine with vigor in an attempt to derive all the experience you possibly can in testing your own progress."

"THAT SOUNDS EASY."

"It may be for some, but occasionally your early communicative efforts may be a bit awkward and you may feel self-conscious. These feelings are natural, but they will diminish and you will begin to feel comfortable with your new patterns of behaving, just as a tennis player develops confidence and style as he practices. It will be up to you, of course, to read the materials and make applications in your daily interactions with those around you. The extent of your own development will depend rather fully on your own realization and commitment to follow up and engage in communicating interpersonally."

"WELL, IT LOOKS LIKE I MUST DO MORE THAN READ THE BOOK. HOW-EVER, WITH RESPECT TO READING THE BOOK, WHAT ARE THOSE GENERAL TOPICS AGAIN?"

"*Communicating Interpersonally* consists of four sections of readings. The sequence of the sections and the selections follow closely the order in which a course in interpersonal communication might be taught. That is, Section 1 deals with providing an understanding of the process or experience of engaging in person-to-person communication. Section 2 includes articles that review and explicate the major factors that influence interpersonal communication, such as perceptions and language, trust and credibility, feelings and non-verbal messages. Section 3 takes up the consequences of ineffective interpersonal relationships: alienation, rejection, demolished conversations, information loss, sabotaged meetings, and crossed transactions, among others. Section 4 explores the amelioration of interpersonal communication (i.e., how it might be changed in positive ways). Total listening, speaking personally, paraphrasing and other skills, new semantic and language techniques, and capacities for increasing understanding and widening emotional interchanges are among the methods explained and advocated."

"WHAT DO I DO NOW?"

"Read on!"

Note to the Instructor

Some consternation and a great deal of puzzled contemplation often precedes the selection of a book for use in teaching interpersonal communication. A few textbooks and an occasional collection of essays and articles are available for helping in the development of interpersonal communicative skills. We, too, have been perplexed by the ways in which books are utilized in courses in interpersonal communication. Buy the book, read a chapter, and talk about it in class. Read another chapter, talk about it, and take a test. For that approach, a textbook might be the easiest source to use. But what about teaching courses in that manner? Why even have a book for students to read? What does a book provide and accomplish in a course? We should like to dispel some misconceptions about how books ought to be employed in teaching interpersonal communication and suggest to you an approach that we think will excite both students and teachers.

Teaching and learning about interpersonal communication can best be approached from an experiential, process orientation. We have discovered that most people learn to adopt appropriate standards of behavior by experiencing the consequences of the behavior of others. Hence, an individual must be given opportunities to observe the behavior of others and then try out new styles of communicating for himself. This means that a substantial part of a course in interpersonal communication should be spent in experiencing the consequences of attempts at communicating interpersonally. That is, much of the time, the focus of classroom discussion should be on the behavior that takes place in the classroom itself. With an experiential approach, the instructor and the students talk about how they relate to each other, examine the experience of communicating in a classroom, explore those things that influence the process, and, especially, discover the consequences of various styles of communicating interpersonally. To facilitate these types of analyses, the instructor needs a number of "structured" experiences available to provide a stimulus for discussion. The students participate in the exercise, then they talk about what happened and why. Often they suggest alternative ways of responding to the situation. The discussion of the experience should be supplemented by reference to theories of interpersonal communication that provide sound explanations for what happened and why different alternatives might be reasonable.

A textbook for this approach should be used primarily for the purpose of providing information about interpersonal communication and explanations concerning why certain skills are important and how they might be implemented in establishing and maintaining effective relationships with others. Why, then, can this reader provide the necessary explanations as well, if not better than a traditional textbook? The answer depends in part upon the students using the readings and the teacher who facilitates the discussions.

Students must approach these readings and the course with the full understanding that a process style of teaching will be employed, and that they will be studying materials about interpersonal communication written originally for some other purpose. Among the readings they will find articles from popular magazines; chapters from textbooks on psychology, small groups, teaching, and consulting; mimeographed essays on interpersonal relationships; and provocative descriptions of aspects of interpersonal communication as viewed by psychiatrists, counselors, chemists, behavioral scientists, newspaper reporters, semanticists, professional educators, lawyers, and sociologists, as well as specialists in the field of interpersonal communication.

The readings in this collection need to be utilized somewhat differently from the chapters in a textbook. The uniqueness of a reader is that it provides the most cogent, understandable, provocative statements available on a given issue, written by the authors who originally created them. The special way in which the topic was initially treated has been preserved in the reader, whereas the author of a textbook must create a unique approach to each facet of a vast field of study, a task of which few, if any, individuals are capable. Each section of this reader contains the works of well-known and highly respected authors, each making his own distinctive contribution to the whole. Thus, each contribution in this reader should be studied for its unique point of view. It is possible for the teacher to judiciously select key contributions for in-depth study in a particular section, using the remaining selections as complementary readings for study by those students who are intrigued by the materials of the key readings. In this manner, the teacher actually builds the course around a core of readings that appeal most highly to him and his objectives, while having at his disposal additional references for more rapidly advancing students or for supplementary reading later in the course.

One obvious and apparent value of this book of readings is the availability of classic statements on topics that are out of print or for some other reason unavailable to students. Several such readings contained in this collection serve as cases in point. The article by Woodruff, "Learning from Experience," represents one of the most cogent explanations of how people process information, but it was originally printed as a chapter in a publication generally inaccessible to most students of interpersonal communication. The article by Hall and Hall on "The Sounds of Silence" appeared originally in *Playboy Magazine,* a publication that might very well be accessible to many, but one that might be overlooked as a source of information on this topic. The selection by Murray, Barnard, and Garland, "Semantic Disorders," appeared as a chapter in a book that is currently out of print but that was well ahead of its time in terms of insights about interpersonal communication. Finally, the article by Korzybski, entitled "The Role of Language in the Perceptual Process," appeared in a textbook on personality that has been unavailable for some time, but represents the clearest and most direct statement of some basic concepts of general semantics ever produced and written by the founder of the movement. It is considered a minor classic, and it is currently available only in this reader. Student exposure to the genuine understanding of several leaders in the field is available only through the facilities of this book of readings.

In this book, teacher and student alike may savor the wisdom of contemporaries and old masters. Brought together in a systematic treatment of interpersonal communication, the writings of friend and foe, protagonist and antagonist, behaviorist and humanist, educator and practitioner, communicator and communicatee may be examined, analyzed, criticized, and absorbed. Out of it may come a true learning experience, and, above all, an understanding of and facility in interpersonal communication.

THE EXPERIENCE OF
INTERPERSONAL COMMUNICATION

The experience of communicating with other human beings holds the potential for happiness and self-fulfillment unparalleled by any other facet of life. Climbing mountains is exhilarating, playing basketball is exhausting, building an intricate machine is fascinating, solving a puzzle is intriguing, and preparing a meal is exciting. Establishing a truly genuine communicative relationship with another human is falling in love, not in a physical sense but in the sense of caring and helping and cooperating with others. Interpersonal communication is at the foundation of all civilized activity. The way in which people relate to each other governs the extent to which they can feel concern, warmth, and trust for one another. The degree to which our relationships with others express respect, acceptance, kindness, consideration, and helpfulness is really the degree to which we reveal our humanness.

Communication, as Barnlund suggests in our first selection, represents an effort to find meaning in behavior, objects, and relationships. Meaning, as you will learn, represents the pivotal concept in a theory of communication and interpersonal relationships. How do we learn meanings? Woodruff identifies physical experience as the genesis of meaning. That is, the personal perception of something in life is at the base of all learning. Through the accumulation of perceptual experiences, each of us develops specific concepts that form general concepts, and, ultimately, comprehensive conceptions of life. Although intellectual conceptions are at the center of all learning activity, we do have feelings about those things we perceive. As Woodruff observes, when we disregard this fact, we begin to misunderstand human behavior.

Korzybski writes about concept learning as the process of abstracting. He describes what happens when our nervous system perceives an event, and distinguishes between first-order psychological direct experiences and verbal statements about those experiences.

1

As he notes, "statements are verbal; they are never the silent 'it'."
Korzybski's analysis of the relationships between perception, language,
and conceptualization can serve as a primary rationale for developing
"new" ways of talking to and about others in an effort to produce
more accurate meanings.

Understanding the processes of perception, as you can no doubt
tell, is one of the keys to understanding communication. Such
understanding may also help us to develop more effective communicative skills. The basic problems may be stated something like this:
Nearly all of us go through our lives firmly convinced that we see, hear,
and touch that which is truly there to be seen, heard, or felt. We think
of ourselves as inside observers of outside reality. Ordinarily, we
think we see what is really there. We say, "There are four chairs," or
"Here we are standing on this floor." We become incensed if somebody
suggests that statements beginning with "there are . . ." merely reflect
beliefs we have about those realities rather than certainties. After all,
we can go and sit on a chair and prove that it is indeed a chair.

Unfortunately, we can know the things out there only through our
senses, working with concepts we have developed in the manner
described by Woodruff. We cannot get outside of ourselves to check on
the accuracy of our perceptions to see if we are really seeing what is
actually there. This means that we cannot properly separate the
"things" in our environment from ourselves as observers, since we see
those things only in terms of our perceptions, conceptions, or, more
accurately, our memories of past perceptions.

Each experience, each new percept, helps to provide us with
expectations about the reality out there. We expect the world and the
people in it to behave in accord with our beliefs about them. We are
usually more sure of what to expect in relatively simple physical matters
than in more complex social relationships. We know as "true facts"
those things with which we have had a great deal of highly consistent
experience. The ground is solid (until we step in quicksand). Water is
liquid (at certain temperatures and pressures). Joe acts toward us in
friendly ways (until he interprets something we do as an insult).

For most of our day-to-day communicating, our common human
background and cultural common sense allow us to do well enough.
This degree of acceptable predictability seems to lull us into assuming
that we are doing adequately in more crucial situations. We assume that

we as communicators are being well understood, that we as communi-catees are understanding all that we need to. In crucial situations, it is useful for individuals in a relationship to spend some time exploring each other's beliefs, assumptions, and expectations concerning the matters at hand. In informal situations, this can often be handled by raising questions and listening and observing carefully, and by trying to put oneself "in the shoes of the other," to see things from his point of view. Formal situations, where there are many individuals involved, may require more formal techniques such as interviewing, or perhaps even large-scale surveys. We can help our receivers to perceive things more as we do by emphasizing, highlighting, and silhouetting those aspects we consider important. Again, we can do this more effectively where we know the ways our receivers see things and what their expectations are.

Dean C. Barnlund

INTRODUCTION: INTERPERSONAL COMMUNICATION

THE PROBLEM OF DEFINITION

Communication is universally regarded as the essential social process, the means by which man achieves his individual humanity and maintains social relationships. Without the capacity to use symbols and to interact, men would be forced to live out their lives in isolation, cut off from human contact, deprived of the advantages of library and laboratory, without resources for survival or growth. But when one attempts to discover precisely what is meant by "communication," one finds it surrounded by vagueness and contradiction.

Part of the difficulty lies in the widespread use of the word — there are few disciplines that cannot claim the term as their own. The idea of communication has been a recurring theme in the arts, philosophy, and engineering. The word occupies an important place in the technical vocabulary of sciences devoted to the study of human behavior, such as psychology, sociology, and psychotherapy. The term has acquired further connotation as a result of recent discoveries in information theory, cybernetics, speech pathology, and psycholinguistics. While all of this may underscore the critical place of communication in human experience, it complicates the problem of fixing its meaning.

Some would argue that it is unnecessary to define communication — that everyone understands what it means. Others would hold that so slippery a term must have some boundaries if it is to fulfill its conceptual promise. This is not the place, however, to undertake an exhaustive review of the many definitions of communication to be found in the literature. They are too numerous, and reviewing them in detail is tangential to our purpose. Communication has been conceived structurally (sender-message-receiver), functionally (encoding-decoding), and in terms of intent (expressive-instrumental). It has been defined with reference to source (production of messages), channel (signal transmission), receiver (attribution of meaning), code (symbolizing), effect (evoking of response), and in ways that combine several of these criteria. To some, communication is "the process of transmitting stimuli" (Schramm), "the establishment of a commonage" (Morris), "conveying meaning" (Newcomb), or "all the procedures by which one mind affects another" (Weaver). To others, it is "interaction by means of signs and sym-bols" (Lundberg), "the sharing of activity, excitement, information" (Hefferline), or "the signals that individuals make to each other or which they detect in each other and which may be conscious or unconscious" (Cameron). Nearly every communicative element, function, or effect has been made the focus of some defini-tion at some time.

COMMUNICATION AS DISCRIMINATION

A useful point of departure in clarifying the word *communication,* and one widely adopted by communicologists, is offered by S. S. Stevens:

> Communication is the discriminatory response of an organism to a stimulus. This definition says that communication occurs when some environmental disturbance (the stimulus) impinges on an organism and the organism does something about it (makes a discriminatory response). If the stimulus is ignored, there has been no communication. The test is a differential reaction of some sort. The message that gets no response is not a communication. (15, p. 689)

This is a global definition, of course, broad enough to encompass all types of chem-ical, electrical, and physical change. Assuming a liberal interpretation of "organism," one could apply it equally well to the action of a thermostat, a barking dog, or an armistice negotiator. Even after restricting its reference to living organisms and specifically to man, some further qualification may be desirable.

The word "stimulus" in the definition above sometimes carries the implication that meaning is to be found in the message or object, rather than in the interpreter of it. Clouds and crosses, draft cards and traffic signs do not *contain* meanings, or they would evoke identical reactions from everyone (in which case there would be little need to communicate at all). Instead, a stimulus or cue only places constraints upon the actions of those who perceive it, these constraints deriving from standards of adequacy or appropriateness internalized through experience with others.

A second qualification is needed with regard to the word "response," which suggests to some that man is an involuntary or passive reactor to external signs rather than an active creator of meanings. While cues have "response potential," to borrow a phrase from Roger Brown, it is the perceiver who decides upon the specific values they will have for him. It is he who constructs his world and decides how he is going to use it. The potency of any cue, verbal or nonverbal, is found in our capacity to use it in altering or supporting cognitive structures, affective states, or physical activities.

It is difficult in any discussion of communication to avoid the word "meaning." Because of its mentalistic connotations, scientists sometimes dismiss it altogether. But the word often reappears in their work, or is replaced by another term with no clearer referent. If all the changes that accompany communication were reflected in observable behavior, say a clenched fist or verbal profanity, there would be no problem, for the meaning of any symbol would be the response it evokes. But the discrimination of cues, at least in man, is not always manifest in outward behavioral changes, or else is reflected in changes of such subtlety that they elude scientific analysis. The meaning of any event may be implicit as well as explicit, that is, it may take the form of a change in attitude or information without providing any external manifestations. If the term "meaning" is used consistently to include the chemical, electrical, and physical changes that accompany the discrimination of cues in man, it can serve its technical function without forcing users into questionable mentalistic assumptions.

Communication, then, is an "effort after meaning," a creative act initiated by man in which he seeks to discriminate and organize cues so as to orient himself in his environment and satisfy his changing needs.

> While we are born into and inhabit a world without meaning, we rapidly invest it with significance and order. That life becomes intelligible to us—full of beauty or ugliness, hope or despair—is because it is assigned that significance by the experiencing being. Sensations do not come to us, all sorted and labeled, as if we were visitors in a vast, but ordered, museum. Each person, instead, is his own curator. We learn to look with a selective eye, to classify, to assign significance. (3)

It is individual communicators who make an event frightening, frustrating, or rewarding in its meaning. The cues potentially available to man in his search for meanings include those that belong to his physical environment (natural or manipulated), those he provides himself through action or introspection, and those arising out of the verbal and nonverbal acts of others. In describing communication as "discriminatory response" Stevens seems close to formulating an irreducible definition of the communication process.

The complexity of human communication should be readily apparent to anyone who reflects on the implications of this broad definition. It is clear that the acquisition of meaning is not limited to a single environmental circumstance; men make discriminatory responses when they are alone, when engaged in face-to-face interaction, and when participating in larger collective units. Nor is communication a discrete act — something that begins at one moment and ends at another — but a process that continues without serious interruption throughout life. The drives that may be satisfied through communication extend from the overcoming of physical and psychological isolation, through the settling of social and political differences, to the reorganization of the personality. The discrimination of cues may occur at many levels, both conscious and unconscious, and there appear to be channels of crosstalk that link these levels. The verbal cues that comprise a message may be displayed against a background of nonverbal elements that contradict, reinforce, or elaborate them. And most messages are likely not only to reflect external realities, but to illuminate internal states as well. Consideration of the many levels and forms of human communication may suggest some of the complications that surround it as a subject of research.

SCOPE OF HUMAN COMMUNICATION

If communication is to be regarded as a discriminatory act on the part of an organism, there is a sense in which it is accurate to speak of all communication as intrapersonal (or intraorganismic if not limited to man.) That is to say, all meaning evolves within people as they make sensory-motor adjustments to their environment. "When we respond to others," writes Coutu (8, p. 59), "actually we respond to our own responses as stimulus, not to the stimulus itself." While we are accustomed to refer to communication as a social process, an interaction between men, it may be technically miseading to do so. As Colin Cherry points out:

> We use signs when communicating with others, as we can but observe our own signs. Thinking to oneself is, in this view, a colloquy carried on in signs, mostly in language. "We" can argue with "ourselves" or with our "conscience": "we" can search "our hearts". Such arguings and searchings have the nature of a dialogue, expressed in signs, just as though we were holding an internal conversation. (7, p. 263)

In this instance, man constitutes what one behavioral scientist has called a "self-contained communicating system." Whether the adjustment is to cues arising within the organism, such as fatigue or fear, or to cues provided by the physical environment, such as lightning and thunder, or to cues that are a consequence of the acts of others, such as a greeting or insult, the perception of stimuli, no matter what their origin, is always confined to the nervous system of a single organism.

Yet some distinctions regarding the various settings in which men communicate will be found to be psychologically valid and scientifically useful. The encoding-decoding process that occurs while a man waits alone outside an operating room or introspects about some personal tragedy is a sufficiently distinctive type of communication to require separate analysis. For this reason it is desirable to restrict "intrapersonal communication" to the manipulation of cues within an individual that occurs in the absence of other people (although they may be symbolically present in the imagination). As such, its locus is confined to a single person transacting with his environment. He sees what his purposes require, senses what his organism will admit, associates signs according to the dynamics of his own personality.

While it may be accurate to speak of communication as something that is always intrapersonal in the sense that meanings are always private neutral adjustments, the presence of others adds immeasurably to the complexity of this act. The process of differentiating cues goes on in such a variety of social settings and these settings exert so profound an influence upon the process that it is necessary to treat separately communication in interpersonal, group, and collective settings.

Interpersonal Communication

What, then, characterizes the interpersonal communicative setting? First and most obvious would seem to be the presence of two or more individuals in physical proximity. But mere presence alone is not enough; people who occupy the same building or who pass on the street are often oblivious to each other. There must be some sort of "perceptual engagement." People who are attending to their physical surroundings or who are lost in reverie must begin to observe the actions of those about them. A movement or mannerism may be noted and become the basis for categorizing or making predictions about the other, or one may become aware that he is "exposed," that others are using his stance or gestures to form impressions of him. This kind of interpersonal scanning is identified as "unfocused interaction" by Goffman (9, p. 7): "Unfocused interaction consists of those interpersonal communications that result solely by virtue of persons being in one another's presence, as when two strangers across the room from each other check up on each other's clothing, posture, and general manner. . . ." As each perceives the other, he becomes aware of being perceived. This sort of rudimentary social contact is prerequisite to interpersonal communication, but it is an incomplete basis for identifying the inter-active process.

Second, as people become aware of each other they may go beyond simple monitoring of their own appearance and the appearance of others. Each begins to provide cues that are a direct consequence of the cues supplied by others. One speaks because a reply is sought, one plays a card because it is his turn, one laughs because a witty remark has been made. The behavior of each depends on that of the other. The reciprocal nature of this relationship is described by Newcomb (13, pp. 11-12) as "the fact that what one person notices and does is at the same time a response to what others have noticed and done (or to the symbols thereof) and also, potentially at least, a stimulus to what others will notice and do." The acknowledgment of communicative interdependence provides the base for creating and maintaining a common theme or activity. A "focused interaction" is the consequence (9, p. 7): "Focused interaction occurs when people effectively agree to sustain for a time a single focus of cognitive and visual attention, as in a conversation, a board game, or a joint task sustained by a close, face-to-face circle of contributors." Involvement in an interpersonal engagement, then, requires that participants be able to supply cues for others to act on, be reasonably responsive to the cues provided by others, and be capable of weaving these two coding activities into an appropriate pattern.

Third, focused interaction proceeds through an exchange of messages. Despite its apparent simplicity, constructing a message involves a complex cognitive process. Coding requires the selection of appropriate verbal and nonverbal signs to express the internal state of the sender of the message. But to be effective, this must be accompanied by an imaginative interpretation of the probable meaning to be assigned to the cues by the receiver. Without the capacity to encode *and* the capacity to interpret from the vantage point of the receiver, the sender would not know what to put into a message. (In addition, a communicator usually observes the subsequent reactions of the receiver in order to compare the imagined and actual effects of his message.) Thus the manipulation of cues and the projection of interpretation appear to be criteria for identifying interpersonal messages. The study of interpersonal communication would seem, therefore, to require careful analysis of message forms and message effects.

Fourth, interpersonal communication usually occurs in face-to-face encounters that provide a rich source of communicative cues. All sense modalities may be exploited. People confront each other totally. Communication in other settings may restrict either the supply of cues or the character of the response to them. Radio, television, film, and press, for example, control the visual and auditory signs that reach the receiver, and prevent or delay reactions from him. Large assemblies of persons, such as crowds and audiences, are governed by social codes that prohibit some responses and channel others into relatively stereotyped forms so that their informative significance is greatly reduced. The larger cue resources of the interpersonal setting, while complicating the problem of scientific analysis, provide communicants with greater opportunity to verify their interpretive assumptions.

Finally, it should be noted that the interpersonal setting is largely unstructured. There are relatively few rules that govern the frequency, form, or content of interpersonal messages. Ritualistic exchanges, such as those Malinowski identified as "phatic communion," do occur. And recent sociological studies reveal more regularities in ordinary conversation than were suspected in earlier, somewhat naive views of it. Yet the degree of variability, of spontaneous expression, is substantial. Participants decide to speak when they choose, and to whom they choose. Each person edits his messages to conform to his changing needs, and each selectively responds to the messages of others. It is the episodic and elliptical character of interpersonal discourse, with its topical vacillations and alternating strategies, that is its most widely recognized feature.

The study of interpersonal communication, then, is concerned with the investigation of relatively informal social situations in which persons in face-to-face encounters sustain a focused interaction through the reciprocal exchange of verbal and nonverbal cues.

Group Communication

Interpersonal communication also has its institutionalized form in the small group or committee. Here, too, there is face-to-face engagement with persons able to respond to the entire spectrum of verbal and nonverbal signs. There is genuine interaction, with participants alternating in their communicative functions—now speaking, now listening, now observing.

But there are also differences. One of these is the larger size of the group. Although interpersonal communication usually refers to interaction among two to four persons, the small group often consists of five to fifteen members. This slight numerical difference, as early social psychologists often emphasized, produces rather profound qualitative differences in expectations and behavior.

Another feature of the group is its clearer and less permeable boundaries. One may move into or out of a focused interaction with little awareness of being "in" or "out." But one is usually aware of his membership in a group. Exclusion prevents communication altogether, while inclusion carries specific communicative rights and obligations. The problem of the "stranger," a group problem of long standing, testifies to the tendency toward rigid boundaries in group interaction.

Groups are also relatively more permanent; they survive for longer periods of time. This is due partly to their being formed to solve persistent environmental problems or to satisfy continuing psychological needs. As a result, groups tend to pursue long-term goals, follow agenda that connect one meeting with another, and develop recurrent themes that give coherence to interaction.

The size and permanence of groups, along with the complex tasks that occupy them, combine to produce an elaborate internal structure as well. Some patterns of action are rewarded and reinforced, others are stifled through disapproval. The norms that evolve out of early interaction provide group members with standards for assessing the appropriateness of later communicative acts. Differences in ability lead to specialization of functions so that some members repeatedly perform certain tasks; others are expected to refrain from these tasks and support the group in other ways. Communication is fairly predictable with regard to the direction, frequency, form, and even content of the messages exchanged.

It should be emphasized that these differences are differences of degree: informal interaction is often of sufficient duration or involves enough people to manifest many group properties, and groups are sometimes so small, so amorphous, and so short-lived that they can best be viewed as cases of interpersonal communication. However, we share with Cooley, Sullivan, Simmel, and many others the conviction that interpersonal communication, apart from the study of group processes, constitutes a distinctive and significant area of social study.

Collective Communication

A still sharper line can be drawn between interpersonal and collective communicative settings. In the latter, large numbers of people, perhaps hundreds or thousands, are involved so that the members of a collective are only vaguely aware of the unique identity of the others present. This anonymous relationship stands in contrast to the highly personalized character of interpersonal and group encounters. The members of collectives, whether crowds or audiences, are also physically organized to reduce interactive opportunity and to promote the co-acting relationship. There is usually a single major source of messages, and everything is done to focus attention exclusively on the cues this source provides. Except for ritualized responses, communication is predominantly one-way. The communicative roles of the participants are polarized in formal settings, with the vast majority of persons confined more or less permanently to interpreting messages and relatively few, usually a single person, to initiating them. Furthermore, these are highly calculated cues, organized in advance and presented with little spontaneity. The continuous, planned nature of discourse in public settings contrasts sharply with the episodic, impulsive, and fragmentary character of interpersonal interaction. The impersonality of collective settings, the rigid control of channels, the calculated use of message cues, and the restrictions on communicative roles contribute to a highly structured social situation in which there is the expectation of unidirectional influence. . . .

CONCLUSION

There is much to recommend the study of interpersonal communication. Cultural necessity and scientific interest combine to focus attention upon it. The interpersonal situation affords a microscopic view of social systems in operation and provides a fruitful perspective from which to study individual personality. Both are combined in a single matrix. The process of communication is at once the chief agency of social change and the most viable means of self-actualization.

It is now several decades since Elton Mayo warned that there is no "ism" that will save us, only a continuing search for the determinants of social cooperation. His prescription fits this enterprise well: "I believe," he wrote, "that social study should begin with careful observation of what may be described as communication: that is, the capacity of an individual to communicate his feelings and ideas to another, the capacity of groups to communicate effectively and intimately with each other. That is, beyond all reasonable doubt, the outstanding defect that civilization is facing today" (11, p. 22).

REFERENCES

1. Aristotle. *Rhetoric*. Cambridge: Harvard University Press, 1939.
2. Ayer, A., "What is Communication?" in *Studies in Communication*. London: Martin, Secker, and Warburg, 1955.
3. Barnlund, D., "A Transactional Model of Communication" (in press).
4. Bennis, W., E. Schein, D. Berlew, and F. Steele. *Interpersonal Dynamics*. Homewood, Illinois: Dorsey Press, 1964.
5. Berlo, D., *The Process of Communication*. New York: Holt, Rinehart and Winston, 1960.
6. Burke, K. *A Grammar of Motives*. New York: Prentice-Hall, 1945.
7. Cherry, C. *On Human Communication*. New York: Wiley, 1957.
8. Coutu, W. *Emergent Human Nature*. New York: Knopf, 1949.
9. Goffman, E. *Behavior in Public Places*. New York: Macmillan, 1963.
10. Langer, S. *Philosophy in a New Key*. New York: Mentor, 1955.
11. Mayo, E. *The Social Problems of an Industrial Civilization*. Cambridge: Harvard University Press, 1945.
12. Miller, G. *Language and Communication*. New York: McGraw-Hill, 1951.
13. Newcomb, T. *Social Psychology*. New York: Dryden, 1950.
14. Nilsen, T., "On Defining Communication," *Speech Teacher*, 1957, 6, 10-17.
15. Stevens, S., "A Definition Of Communication," *Journal of Acoustical Society of America*, 1950, 22, 689-690.

Asahel D. Woodruff

LEARNING FROM EXPERIENCE

MAIN CONCEPT

Our experiences with the world register within us in the form of concepts, values, and feelings for things, language, skills, and habits. They then become the controlling elements in determining what we try to do, and how well we do it.

SUPPORTING CONCEPTS

1. When through experience we get a mental picture in our minds of one of the objects or forces which make up our world, we have a concept, which immediately becomes our "set" for any further perception of that same thing.

2. While concepts are forming through experience, the individual is also learning what value each of the objects and forces has for him through his impressions of how each of them affects him. This sense of value becomes a part of each concept and determines how he feels about it. This tends to influence his behavior toward that thing.

3. As a concept forms in our minds we learn symbols for the whole concept and for each of its parts or qualities, and these symbols become part of the concept also. . . .

DISCUSSION OF THE SUPPORTING CONCEPTS

1. When through experience we get a mental picture in our minds of one of the objects or forces which make up our world, we have a concept, which immediately becomes our "set" for any further perception of that same thing.

The human mind is the depository for all of our experience. It has a way of storing experience something like a motion picture record. This stored record makes possible the recollection of past experience almost as if it were happening again. The record is a composite of meaning or understanding, feeling and the value and preference it produces, and the symbols or languages related to them. This combination of meaning, value and symbols is called a concept.

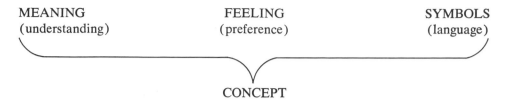

MEANING	FEELING	SYMBOLS
(understanding)	(preference)	(language)

CONCEPT

FIGURE 1. *The Composite Nature of a Concept*

The word concept is used in various ways by different people, such as a philosopher, theoretical scientist, psychologist, or nontechnical layman.[1] In all of these uses there is a common central characteristic, *a bit of meaning* which it at least partially organized into a recognizable and meaningful idea. All ideas are properties of a brain. That is where they originate, and where they are retained. Thus a concept is not an actual concrete entity in nature, it is a "construct," something *made by a brain,* in the effort of the person to understand something and cope with it. A concept cannot be literally handed from one person to another; but this is exactly what teachers often try to do! All a teacher can do to express his own concept of something is to talk about it. What he transmits to the other person is words. Those words may not give the other person a clear picture at all. In fact they may confuse him.

One of the working papers for a conference on teaching media, held in January, 1961, pointed out the limitations of words in the following way. We have expected radio, television, and other new media to do some things they cannot do. This overexpectation has been based on certain errors. One of the errors is the idea that communication is the transmission of meaning among people.

> "Meanings cannot be transmitted. Meaningful sets of symbols can. For our purpose, we can consider meaningful symbols as information, and we can assume that symbols are meaningful when there is consensus as to what they symbolize, and when the pattern of their presentation is consistent with established conventions. Some of our difficulties with extreme forms of modern art arise from the fact that there is a lack of consensus on what the symbols represent, aggravated by unaccustomed patterns of presentation of those symbols. . . . The essential point is that the transmission of meanings is an idealistic goal of communication, but a psychologically inaccurate description or definition of the process."[2]

Each person has to make his own concepts. The easiest way for him to make them is through directly perceiving the thing (referent) itself, not through listening to someone else's words. *Discussion* is a different thing from *telling,* as is explained later.

All learning begins with some form of personal contact with actual objects, events, or circumstances in life. The contacts occur through our sensory organs. The process by which the senses transmit meaning to the brain is known as perception. From these constantly occurring acts of perception we formulate our concepts which give us our understanding of life.

The act of perceiving something goes about as follows. The individual gives attention to some object (or event or circumstance) outside of his own mind. It might be a concrete object, a quality, an event, or any real thing. This object is our subject-matter, and it is often called "The Referent," meaning that it is the thing in the world to which one's mental concept refers.

Through a light wave, or a sound wave, or some form of direct contact with a sensory organ in the body, an impression is picked up and lodged in the mind. There is no literal picture in the mind. There is nothing there but some form of nervous tissue and its activities. However, for all practical purposes it is as if there is an actual picture. That picture is the person's recording of what he has seen or otherwise perceived. As continued perception of an object goes on and accumulates impressions, the meaning grows into a picture of increasing significance. The picture is called a concept. A concept, therefore, is nothing more than a mental image of something the person has experienced through his own sense organs. Figure 2 illustrates the process of perception.

The impression that registers in the mind is not at first accurate or complete. It tends to be immature and tentative. Concepts can change, and usually do with added experience. Children especially form fuzzy and subjective concepts because of their very limited background of experience. Even an adult, however, is likely to be rather inaccurate in his concept when he first perceives something. This is because he cannot comprehend all that lies before him in his first exposure to it. The more he looks, the more he will recognize and understand. His concepts will become more complete and more accurate in this way.

There is:
    (A_1) Something in the world (an event, object, condition, etc.). We call it the REFERENT.

There is:
    (A_2) A physical impression on a sensory nerve (sound, light, or other contact). We call it the STIMULUS.

There is:
    (A_3) An impression in the brain (some form of meaning). We call it the PERCEPT at first, or the CONCEPT when it becomes more complete.

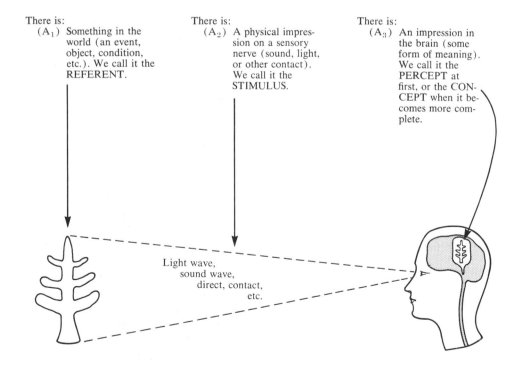

Light wave, sound wave, direct, contact, etc.

FIGURE 2. *A Concept and Its Referent*

We have referred to our senses. Just what are they and how do they serve as receivers of knowledge?

The most basic level of mental activity is called perception, or "seeing" actual objects directly. Of course it is more than eyesight. We often use the word "see" to include any process which gives us understanding, such as hearing, smelling, tasting, and touching. Note Figure 3. It indicates that the eye picks up visual sensations, but also warns us that this must not be confused with the use of the eye to see words on a printed page. Reading is something quite different from literal seeing, as a basic sensory process. The eye sees objects, colors, shapes, distances. These are first hand contacts with real things. Each such contact plants a bit of meaning in the mind, which is added cumulatively to all other related meanings the mind already has acquired.

Similarly, the ear picks up sounds, but this must not be confused with the use of the ear to hear words spoken by others. Conversation, or listening to lectures, is something quite different from literal hearing as a basic sensory process. The ear hears actual sounds of the world, a song, the wind in the pines, a rhythmic beat, the cry of a bird or other animal. These also are first hand contacts with real things. Each such aural (ear) contact plants a bit of meaning in the mind which is added cumulatively to all other related meanings the mind already has acquired.

The other senses do the same kind of thing. Odors, tastes, heat and cold, pressure, and other phenomena are picked up by the appropriate sense organs. Their various bits of meaning are all added together in the mind. Out of them all we construct our own concepts and thus have our own understandings of things around us. Since we have specifically excluded reading and talking from the basic sensory processes, however, a word needs to be said about them. They are literally part of the thinking process, not the perceiving process. A printed book is just a recorded talk. When one reads it he is having a silent conversation with the author. It is therefore a form of discussion. Like all discussions, it can discuss only what the person has already picked up through his personal experience and his own senses. It can of course help him elaborate on his existing store of knowledge. In some circumstances it can extend understanding greatly. Nevertheless it is excluded as not belonging among the basic perceptual processes, and will be treated with the thinking and discussion part of learning.

The final point of all this is that learning of all kinds *begins* with direct personal perception of something in life. When a person is having his first significant experience with any fact or truth, it should not be a second-hand experience such as a lecture, or any other form of verbal teaching. It should be a direct "seeing" of the actual referent itself. There is no possible substitute for the mental images we acquire through our senses. Once we get them, we can begin to discuss them and sort them out, but they have to be there first.

As a person looks at things, he thinks about them. That is, he recalls his past experiences with them and compares past experience with present experience. Something he perceives today may seem different from something he perceived earlier. If so, he will go back and take another look. He might do this physically by going back to the real subject. He might also do it mentally or internally, by just recalling the subject and trying to study his mental image of it more carefully. This is the process we call thinking. See level B in Figure 3. It is usually an effort to clear up an idea or concept of something. It is an extremely important process, because it

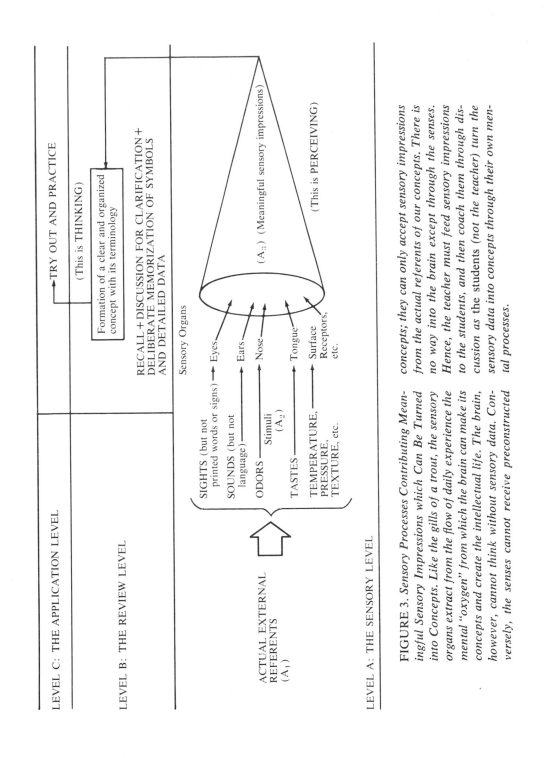

FIGURE 3. *Sensory Processes Contributing Meaningful Sensory Impressions which Can Be Turned into Concepts. Like the gills of a trout, the sensory organs extract from the flow of daily experience the mental "oxygen" from which the brain can make its concepts and create the intellectual life. The brain, however, cannot think without sensory data. Conversely, the senses cannot receive preconstructed concepts; they can only accept sensory impressions from the actual referents of our concepts. There is no way into the brain except through the senses. Hence, the teacher must feed sensory impressions to the students, and then coach them through discussion as the students (not the teacher) turn the sensory data into concepts through their own mental processes.*

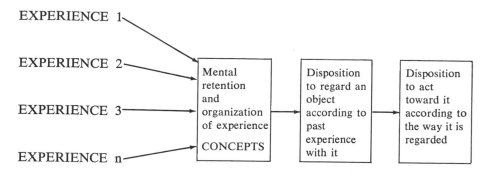

FIGURE 4. *How Concepts Form from Experience and Become Predispositions for Future Behavior*

leads to better understanding. It is the process which brings all of one's past experiences together and makes them have consistent meaning. A class discussion is a way of having the group engage in thinking together. The teacher can guide the thinking so it produces true interpretations of the truth being discussed. It is important to do this well, because the concept that forms this way is a strong influence in determining how we will see the same thing the next time we meet it, and the way we will act toward it.[3] Figure 4 indicates this tendency for past experience to form concepts and set up predispositions for future behavior.

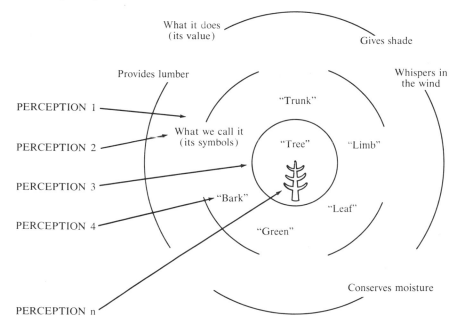

FIGURE 5. *Accumulating Perceptual Experiences Grow into Concepts*

Figure 5 presents the same the thing pictorially, showing the growing concept as a composite of an image in the mind, the parts of the whole object, the terms used to refer to it, and what it does or the effect it produces which is its value.

Now let us look at the intellectual part of this process, involving perception, conceptualization, thinking, evaluating, choosing, and the subconscious way in which much of it goes on. Figures 4 and 5 illustrate it rather simply as explained in the following set of statements, with the technical terms for those processes set at the side of them.

The Process	*What We Call It*
Through personal interaction with some thing in the world, the individual gets a mental impression of it.	
	Perception, Percept
As experience accumulates with this thing, the picture includes what it looks like, sounds like, smells like, tastes like (and so on), and what it does or produces.	
	Conceptualization, Concept
Each new mental picture of some thing is checked against the pictures already in the mind, and worked into them.	
	Thinking
Whenever a person has to choose a line of action, or make a response to any situation, he draws on his mental pictures of the things involved to determine what he should do,	
	Thinking or Evaluating
and	
he does the things his mental pictures show will bring about the results he wants.	
	Choosing
Much of this kind of learning, thinking, and choosing goes on without our awareness or realization of what we are doing.	
	Subconscious or Preconscious mental processes

In this way past experience tends to determine our behavior, or in other words, our concepts furnish the keys for our responses. Figure 6 shows how a concept of "weather" might develop.

A still larger concept of a culture is helped in its development by the concept of weather. Along with several other concepts such as geography, weather becomes part of a concept of physical living conditions, and finally a concept of a culture, as illustrated in Figure 7.

It is rather easy to illustrate this for yourself. Select some concept from your experience, such as banana, or dog, or speed. Recall experiences you had which provided the meaning you now have for this idea. On the basis of your experience, what could you use a banana for, or a dog? What does speed do? When would you speed? These questions help you see that the meanings you now have for these things

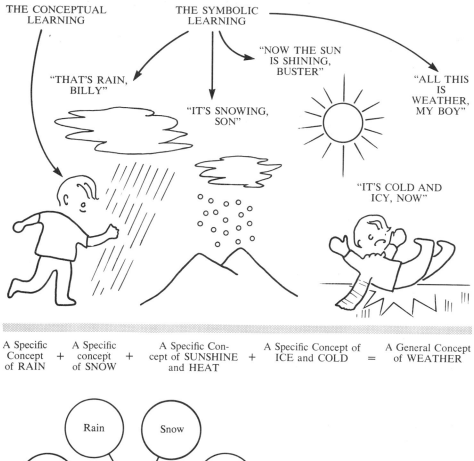

A Specific Concept of RAIN + A Specific concept of SNOW + A Specific Concept of SUNSHINE and HEAT + A Specific Concept of ICE and COLD = A General Concept of WEATHER

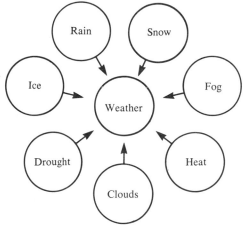

FIGURE 6. *How Specific Concepts Accumulate and Make General Concepts. As we run along life's path we have little experiences with parts of larger ideas. Each one is dropped into the mental storeroom as it comes along. After a time some experience serves to draw them out and get them combined into a larger concept.*

grew out of your past experience with them, and tell you how you might use them or behave toward them in various situations.

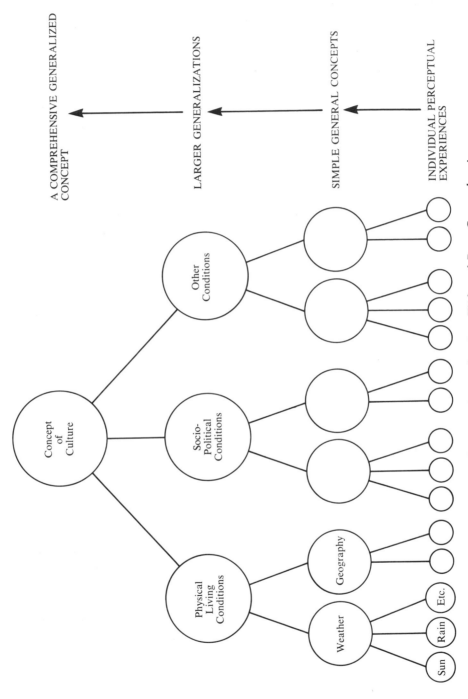

A COMPREHENSIVE GENERALIZED CONCEPT

LARGER GENERALIZATIONS

SIMPLE GENERAL CONCEPTS

INDIVIDUAL PERCEPTUAL EXPERIENCES

Concept of Culture

Other Conditions

Socio-Political Conditions

Physical Living Conditions

Geography

Weather

Sun   Rain   Etc.

FIGURE 7. *How Concepts Accumulate into Wide and Deep Comprehension*

The intellectual part of concept learning, that is, the formation of the mental image is the core of all the rest, for everything else about our concepts is something added to this intellectual or rational core. However, there are other important kinds of learning taking place right along with the intellectual, as described in the following clarifying concepts.

2. While concepts are forming through experience, the individual is also learning what value each of the objects and forces has for him through his impressions of how each of them affects him. This sense of value becomes a part of each concept and determines how he feels about it. This tends to influence his behavior toward that thing.

Man is a rational being, but he is also an emotional being. He not only thinks, he also feels. When he has a feeling, it is a feeling about something which he is also thinking about, and whenever he is thinking about something, he is also having some kind of a feeling about it. Remember that there is no such thing as a feeling which is not connected with some concept, and there is no such thing as a concept which does not have some element of feeling associated with it and part of it. Popular beliefs suggest that thoughts and feelings are separate and often opposed to each other. This is not really so.

The subject of all feelings is the self. It is the center point, the determining point in feelings. In human motives everything revolves around the self. When we disregard this fact or reject it, we begin immediately to misunderstand what we see going on in human behavior. Every person constantly keeps on eye on his self, as it were, more or less unconsciously. He judges everything in terms of what it seems to be doing to his self. When things are judged to be going well for the self, he feels good. When it is the other way he feels bad. This rather simple explanation is very sound, even though there are complications involved in explaining some of the ways in which this self-centered judgment operates.[4]

There is never an experience in which self judgment is not going on, and therefore there is never an experience which does not involve feeling. If the experience is accompanied by a good feeling, or is "satisfying," the individual tends to like that experience and its referent, and tends to turn *to* that thing rather than *away* from it when he meets it again. Conversely, if the experience is accompanied by a bad feeling, or is "annoying," the individual tends to dislike it and to turn away from the things involved in it when he meets them again. Of course some experiences are midway between satisfying and annoying, that is they are neutral, so the feeling is neutral and the individual is hardly conscious of the fact that such a feeling is going on.

This adds another dimension to each concept, that of value and emotional preference.[5] The first dimension discussed in this chapter was intellectual preference, which is based on intellectual recognition of the object and what it does. Emotional preference usually reinforces the intellectual preference, but not always. Sometimes we recognize that an object produces a result which we know to be valuable in some ways, but which we do not like because it annoys us or in some way frustrates us. The reverse is also true.

Figure 8 illustrates two elements of a complete concept, the intellectual core or meaning, and the self-centered value which produces the feeling. Under concept number 1 in this chapter the central mental process in concept formation was described with some appropriate terms. Here is a closely related process that goes on around the central one and helps to round out what we call "human" behavior.

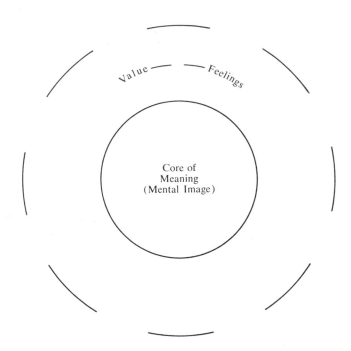

FIGURE 8. *Relationship between Meaning and Feeling in a Concept*

The Process	*What We Call It*
Everything the person experiences seems to him to have some effect on his own condition, either satisfying, or neutral, or annoying.	
	Value
A thing which seems to have a satisfying effect has usefulness to him, and intellectually he senses this usefulness.	
	Positive Value
The sense of usefulness becomes part of his mental picture or concept of the thing.	
	Concept of Value
When he feels satisfaction, he feels good, and he likes the thing.	
	Liking, or Preference
Those things which leave with him no sense of satisfaction or annoyance, have no value to him.	
	Neutral Value
He neither likes nor dislikes them.	
	Indifference
Those things that seem to have an annoying effect on him cause him to feel bad, and he dislikes them.	
	Annoyance, Dislike

The Process	*What We Call It*
Over the years we gradually develop well established feelings about things; and these feelings, based on their values, show up in the way we react toward things.	Attitudes
The feelings become inseparably interwoven with the mental pictures.	Emotionally charged concept
Much of this kind of learning goes on without our being fully aware of what is happening.	Subliminal emotional conditioning

Figure 9 illustrates the way in which meaning and feeling combine to create predispositions for or against things, and finally to affect our behavior toward them.

In addition to the intellectual and the emotional aspects of a concept, there is another which we must now learn about.

3. As a concept forms in our minds we learn symbols for the whole concept and for each of its parts or qualities, and these symbols become part of the concept also.

Language is one of the most distinctive features of human beings. Language is made up of symbols which stand for our thoughts. We turn most naturally to vocal symbols, because we can speak them easily ond others can hear them. This is the most direct way of communicating our thoughts. We also make up written symbols to stand for the vocal ones, so we can put our thoughts in writing and let others read them. Sometimes we use signs to stand for our thoughts. We have many of them, such as stop signs, dollar signs, arrows indicating direction, numbers, colors that stand for various things, and others.

As a teacher you must always remember that a symbol has no life or significance of itself. It simply stands for something in the mind of a person. The concept *always* comes first. After one has concept he needs a "handle" for it so he can manipulate

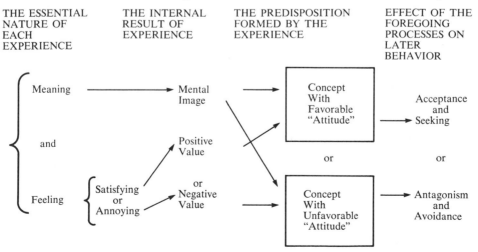

FIGURE 9. *How Experience Produces Feelings and So-Called Attitudes*

his idea. Therefore he invents or learns a symbol for it. No symbol has any meaning to him unless he learns the symbol in connection with an idea he already has.

This is a second mental process which goes on around the intellectual process of concept formation. Let's see how it works.

The Process	*What We Call It*
Because we can speak, hear, write, and read, we make up names for the things we perceive in the world.	
	Symbols
We use these names (symbols) to indicate to others what we are "seeing" in our minds (our concepts.)	
	Communication
We do this orally,	
	Speech
and in writing,	
	Writing
and also by the use of many kinds of signs.	
	Signs
We try to agree on what sign or name we will use for each thing, so we can understand each other.	
	Semantics
The process of learning these names consists of repeating them over and over until we can recall them easily.	
	Memorization

Look at these signs, and see if they have a meaning for you which is shared by other people:

$$\$ \qquad + \qquad -$$

These are rather well-known signs and everyone should easily agree on them. Here are some not so well known. See if you agree with others as to what they mean:

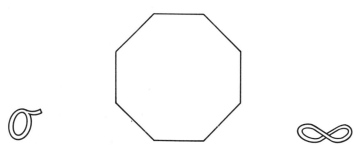

The first is the Greek letter sigma which is used in statistics. The second is an octagon, which is used for "stop" signs on the highway. The third is a sign standing for infinity in a number series.

Now see if you can identify any concepts in your own mind for which you do not have a name or symbol of some kind, even if it is your own private one. You will be exceptional if you can find any such unnamed concepts other than vague impressions which have not yet begun to take a part in your thinking.

Perhaps you have already remembered that the parts of speech are just classifications of verbal symbols of similar types. Nouns are names of objects. Verbs are names of actions. Adjectives are names of qualities of objects. Adverbs are names of qualities of actions, and so on. Since every idea has its words, and all words stand for ideas the person possesses, it is true to say that the size of one's vocabulary is a good index of his mental powers because it is a fair measure of the number of concepts he has and can use in his thinking.

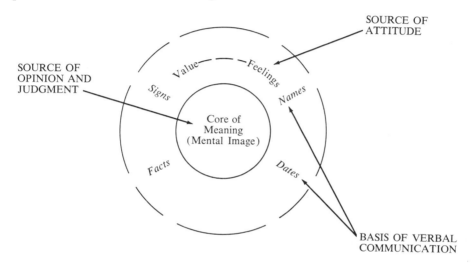

FIGURE 10. *Meaning, Feeling, and Knowledge of Symbols and Facts in a Concept*

Figure 10 presents a diagram of a complete concept. It has a core of meaning, it is colored with value, and it has a set of symbols for the various parts of the concept.

NOTES

1. See an unabridged dictionary; Warren, H. E., *Dictionary of Psychology*, Riverside Press, 1934; Good, Carter V., *Dictionary of Education*, McGraw-Hill Book Co., 1945; English, Horace B., *A Student's Dictionary of Psychological Terms*, Harper & Brothers, 1934.

2. Hoban, Charles F., Jr., "Research in New Media in Education," *Working Papers, National Conference on Teacher Education and New Media*, American Association of Colleges for Teacher Education, Washington, D.C., January, 1961.

3. Rhine, Ramon J., "A Concept-formation Approach to Attitude Acquisition," *Psych. Review*, Vol. 65, No. 6, 1958, pp. 362-370.

4. Sherif, Muzafer, and Cantril, Hadley, *The Psychology of Ego-Involvements*, New York, John Wiley & Sons, Inc., 1947. See particularly Chapter 5.

5. Broudy, Harry S., *Building a Philosophy of Education*, New York, Prentice-Hall, Inc., 1954. See Chapter 10.

Alfred Korzybski[1]

THE ROLE OF LANGUAGE IN
THE PERCEPTUAL PROCESSES

In my work I have found that there are some simple principles underlying the subject matter which I will attempt to convey here. More details may be found in the bibliography given, and the large amounts of other related literature available.

Not dealing with the problem of "perception" directly in my work, I shall use this term here in the vernacular sense. I do not consider myself qualified to define it, and so shall use quotation marks to indicate my nontechnical treatment of this type of human reactions. I cannot avoid dealing with the problems of "perception" indirectly but will do so from a different angle.

THE EFFECT ON PERCEPTUAL PROCESSES
OF THE LANGUAGE SYSTEM

Perhaps a story from the European underground under Hitler would be a good illustration. In a railroad compartment an American grandmother with her young and attractive granddaughter, a Romanian officer, and a Nazi officer were the only occupants. The train was passing through a dark tunnel, and all that was heard was a loud kiss and vigorous slap. After the train emerged from the tunnel, nobody spoke, but the grandmother was saying to herself, "What a fine girl I have raised. She will take care of herself. I am proud of her." The granddaughter was saying to herself, "Well, grandmother is old enough not to mind a little kiss. Besides, the fellows are nice. I am surprised what a hard wallop grandmother has." The Nazi officer was meditating, "How clever those Romanians are! They steal a kiss and have the other fellow slapped." The Romanian officer was chuckling to himself, "How smart I am! I kissed my own hand and slapped the Nazi."

Obviously it was a problem of limited "perception," where mainly "hearing" was involved, with different interpretations.

Another example of "perception" could be given which anyone can try for himself. In fact, I suggest that this simple demonstration should be repeated by all readers of this paper. The demonstration takes two persons. One, without the knowledge of the other, cuts out large headlines of the same size from different issues of a news-paper. The subject remains seated in the same position throughout. He is shown one of the headlines at a certain distance. If he is able to read it, it is discarded. Then he is shown another, different, headline at a somewhat farther distance away. Again, if he is able to read it, it is discarded. This process is repeated until the subject is unable to read the headline. Then the demonstrator tells him what is in the headline. The amazing fact is that the subject will then be able to *see and read* the headline the moment he "knows" what is there.

Such illustrations could be multiplied indefinitely. These examples are enough to illustrate the impossibility of separating sharply the "perceptual," "seeing," "hear-ing," etc., and "knowing," a division which cannot be made, except superficially on verbal levels.

In a non-Aristotelian orientation we take for granted that all "perceptual pro-cesses" involve abstracting by our nervous system at different levels of complexity. Neurological evidence shows the selective character of the organism's responses to total situations, and the papers in this symposium also corroborate the view that the mechanisms of "perception" lie in the ability of our nervous system to abstract and to project.

Abstracting by necessity involves evaluating, whether conscious or not, and so the process of abstracting may be considered as a *process of evaluating,* whether it be a "toothache," "an attack of migraine," or the reading of a "philosophical treatise." A great many factors enter into "perceiving," as suggested by the content of this symposium. As this seems to be a circular process, it is considered here on lower and higher levels of complexity (see page 48).

Processes of Abstracting

Our knowledge today indicates that all life is electro-colloidal in character, the functioning of the nervous system included. We do not as yet know the intrinsic mechanisms, but from an electro-colloidal point of view every part of the brain is connected with every other part and with our nervous system as a whole. With such a foundation, even though it becomes necessary to investigate different aspects of the processes of abstracting for purposes of analysis, we should be aware that these different aspects are parts of one whole continuous process of normal human life.

Let us consider what our nervous system does when we "perceive" a happening or event. The term "event" is used here in the sense of Whitehead as an instanta-neous cross-section of a process. Say we drop a box of matches. Here we have a first-order happening, which occurs on *nonverbal* or what are called the "silent" or "un-speakable" levels. The reflected light impinges on the eye, we get some sort of electro-colloidal configurations in the brain; then, since we are sentient organisms, we can react to those configurations with some sort of "feelings," some evaluations, etc., about them, on "silent" levels. Finally, on the verbal levels, we can speak about those organismal reactions. Newton may have said, about the falling matchbox, "gravitation"; Einstein may say "space-time curvature." Whatever we may *say* about it, the first-order happening remains on the silent levels. How we will *talk* about it may differ from day to day, or from year to year, or century to century. All our "feelings," "thinkings," our "loves," "hates," etc., *happen* on silent un-speakable levels, but may be affected by the verbal levels by a continuing interplay. We may

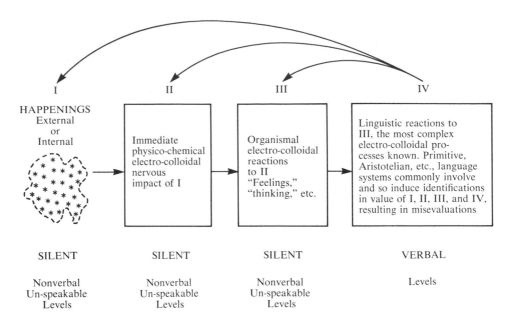

FIGURE 1. *The process of abstracting from an electro-colloidal*
non-Aristotelian point of view.

verbalize about them, to ourselves or others, intensify, decrease them, etc., but this
is a different problem.

In the diagram (Figure 1) is given an extensional analysis of the process of
abstracting from an electro-colloidal non-Aristotelian point of view. It is oversimpli-
fied and could be made more exhaustive. However, it is satisfactory for our purpose
of explaining briefly the most general and important points.

Most of us *identify in value* levels, I, II, III, and IV and react *as if* our verbalizations *about* the first three levels were "it" (see page 36 ff.). Whatever we may *say*
something "is" obviously *is not* the "something" on the silent levels. Indeed, as Wittgenstein wrote, "What *can* be shown, *cannot* be said." In my experience I found that
it is practically impossible to convey the differentiation of silent (un-speakable) levels
from verbal levels without having the hearer or reader pinch with one hand the finger
of the other hand. He would then realize organismally that the first-order psychological direct experiences are not verbal. The simplicity of this statement is misleading unless we become aware of its implications, as in our living reactions most of us
identify in value the entirely *different* levels, with often disastrous consequences.

Unfortunately, people in general, including many scientists, *disregard levels*
II and III completely, and react as if unconscious that IV "is not" I. In other words,
we do not take into account the mechanisms of the human nervous system or "think
electro-colloidally" about our reactions. Such a disregard leads to misunderstandings,
heated two-valued ("either-or") debates, hostilities, prejudices, bitterness, etc. In the
history of "philosophy," for example, the metaphysical fight about "solipsism" simply
ceases to be a problem when we become conscious that the only possible link between the inherently different silent (nonverbal) and verbal levels is found in their

similarity of structure, expressed in terms of relations, on which the present non-Aristotelian system is based.

An awareness of the processes of abstracting clarifies the *structure* of a great many of our interpersonal, professional, etc., difficulties, which may become trivial or nonexistent if we become conscious of the identifications involved. Self-made problems often turn out to be no problems.

Statements are verbal; they are never the silent "it." One may have a nightmare that he "is" a Stalin. That may be innocent enough. One may have daydreams of being a Stalin. That is more serious. One may proclaim consciously, "I am Stalin," and *believe it,* and begin to shoot people who disagree with him; usually such a person is locked up in a hospital, and he usually is a hopeless case.

We see how the above diagram indicates human semantic (evaluational) mechanisms in the average individual who is hovering between sanity and semantic illness. It is well known that what would be only a dream to a "normal" person, "is reality" to a dementia praecox patient, who lives and acts accordingly.

These mechanisms also function pathologically in infantile adults, who live in a fictitious world built upon identifications.

The verbal levels, in the meantime, are of unique human importance because we can abstract on higher and higher verbal levels from I, II, II, etc. In human life, IV represents means for intercommunicating and transmitting from individual to individual and generation to generation the accumulated experiences of individuals and the race. I call this human capacity the "time-binding" characteristic.

The symbolic levels of behavior differentiate most sharply *human* reactions from signal reactions of lower, less complex forms of life. If those accumulated experiences are not properly verbalized, it may seriously twist or even arrest human development.

This simple diagram represents most complex processes, involving "perception" on different levels, problems of interpretation, verbal formalism, etc. Every type of human reactions, from the lowest to the highest levels involves these mechanisms, the nonawareness of which may lead to disturbing, frustrating, or disastrous misevaluations and consequences. We will find later how this diagram applies to primitive and Aristotelian language structures.

I have stressed the serious or tragic aspect of our processes of abstracting here because I am attempting to convey the heavy life-value of what may otherwise appear too simple and obvious.

Verbal and Nonverbal "Thinking"

It will be noticed that I have put quotation marks around the word "thinking." This term usually implies a more "cortical" activity, indicating verbally some sort of a split between the functioning of the cortical and thalamic *regions* of our nervous system where there is actually no such split, but an interaction and integration on different levels.

"Is all thinking verbal?" Some say "yes," some say "no." If however, we limit ourselves to verbal "thinking," we are caught in our old linguistic ruts of bygone generations, socio-culturally trained and neurologically canalized in the inherited forms of representation. Under such conditions we are unable or unfit to see the outside or inside world anew, and so we handicap scientific and other creative work. We speak so glibly about "freedom," never considering Willard Gibbs' *degrees of freedom* on which all our advance depends. A non-Aristotelian system involves that new orientation which ultimately leads to creative "thinking." Thus, an automobile has indefinitely more degrees of freedom than a street-car, which is "canalized" in its rails. Unfortunately and perhaps tragically, the majority of us "think" verbally, so characteristic of the Aristotelian subject-predicate orientation, and thus are handicapped in or prevented from creative "thinking." The physico-mathematical and so scientific way of "thinking" broke through those handicaps, and thus is at the foundation of creative scientific work, which brings to mankind so many benefits.

There is a tremendous difference between "thinking" in verbal terms, and "contemplating," inwardly silent, on nonverbal levels, and then searching for the proper structure of language to fit the supposedly discovered structure of the silent processes that modern science tries to find. If we "think" *verbally,* we act as biased observers and project onto the silent levels the structure of the language we use, so remaining in our rut of old orientations which make keen, unbiased observations ("perception"?) and creative work well-nigh impossible. In contrast, when we "think" without words, or in pictures or visualizations (which involve structure and, therefore, relations), we may discover new aspects and relations on silent levels, and so may formulate important theoretical results in the general search for a similarity of structure between the two levels, silent and verbal. Practically all important advances are made in that way.

Jacques Hadamard, the great mathematician, has made a study of how some outstanding mathematicians and scientists "think." I refer to his valuable little book on *The Psychology of Invention in the Mathematical Field* (11). The majority of these creative men reported that they "think" in terms of visual structures. "Most generally images are used, very often of a geometrical nature," he found (11, p. 114). I may mention here one of the questions which Hadamard asked in his questionnaire, to which Einstein gave an answer of particular interest to us here:

> *Question:* It would be very helpful for the purpose of psychological investigation to know what internal or mental images, what kind of "internal word" mathematicians make use of; whether they are motor [kinesthetic], auditory, visual or mixed, depending on the subject which they are studying (11, p. 140).
>
> *Answer:* The above mentioned elements are, in my case, of visual and some of muscular type. Conventional words or other signs have to be sought for laboriously only in a secondary stage, when the mentioned associative play is sufficiently established and can be reproduced at will. . . . In a stage when words intervene at all, they are, in my case, purely auditive, but they interfere only in a secondary stage as already mentioned (11, p. 143).[2]

Personally, I "think" in terms of pictures, and how I *speak* about those visualizations later is a different problem. I also notice a severe strain on my eyes when doing creative work, due to that visualizing, which seems to be related somehow to "perception."

In this connection I may refer also to a most important essay on "Mathematical Creation" by the great mathematician, Henri Poincaré (34), which was delivered in the first years of this century as a lecture before the Psychological Society in Paris.

Language becomes then a *medium* through which we eventually talk to ourselves or to others, with its own definite limitations. "The relation between language and experience is often misunderstood," Sapir found (40). "Language is not merely a more or less systematic inventory of the various items of experience which seem relevant to the individual, as is often naively assumed, but is also a self-contained, creative symbolic organization, which not only refers to experience largely acquired without its help, but actually *defines experience for us* by reason of its formal completeness and because of our unconscious projection of its implicit expectations into the field of experience" (italics mine).

As Santayana said, "The empiricist . . . thinks he believes only what he sees, but he is much better at believing than at seeing" (21, p. 1).[3]

In *An Essay on Man,* Ernst Cassirer (7) discusses the "hunger for names" which every normal child shows at a certain age.

> By learning to name things a child does not simply add a list of artificial signs to his previous knowledge of ready-made empirical objects. He learns rather to form the concepts of those objects, to come to terms with the objective world. Henceforth the child stands on firmer ground. His vague, uncertain, fluctuating perceptions and his dim feelings begin to assume a new shape. They may be said to crystallize around the name as a fixed center, a focus of thought.

But herein lies an important aspect of "naming" or "labeling":

> The very act of denomination depends on a process of classification . . . they [the classifications] are based on certain constant and recurring elements in our sense experience. . . . There is no rigid and pre-established scheme according to which our divisions and subdivisions might once for all be made. Even in languages closely akin and agreeing in their general structure we do not find identical names. As Humboldt pointed out, the Greek and Latin terms for the moon, although they refer to the same object, do not express the same intention or concept. The Greek term *(men)* denotes the function of the moon to "measure" time; the Latin term *(luna, luc-na)* denotes the moon's lucidity or brightness. . . . The function of a name is always limited to emphasizing a particular aspect of a thing, and it is precisely this restriction and limitation upon which the value of the name depends. . . . in the act of denomination we select, out of the multiplicity and diffusion in our sense data, certain fixed centers of perception (7).[4]

A "name" (label) involves for a given individual a whole constellation or configuration of labeling, defining, evaluating, etc., unique for each individual, according to his socio-cultural, linguistic environment and his heredity, connected with his wishes, interests, needs, etc.

Cassirer makes some interesting comparisons between a child learning its first language and an adult learning a foreign language. I may add here that it happens that I was born into four languages (three different roots), and this has helped me not to be bound by words as I might have been if I had learned only one language as a child.

We see the seriousness of terminology, which is affected by *and also determines* our general *Weltanschauung.* In 1950, we must visualize the world in general as a submicroscopic, dynamic electronic process and life in particular as an electro-colloidal process of still much higher complexity (1, 2). What has made it possible for us to visualize an "object" and life in this way? Theories, verbalization, built up for thousands of years, up to the latest discoveries of modern science. Thus, we find again that ceaseless circularity (see pages 48 ff.). The fact that we can "perceive" happenings, objects, or persons in this way has very important bearings on that whole process, as we will find later in our discussion.

Primitive Language Structures

All languages have a structure of some kind, and every language reflects in its own structure that of the world as assumed by those who evolved the languages. Reciprocally, we read mostly unconsciously into the world the structure of the language we use. Because we take the structure of our own habitual language so much for granted, particularly if we were born into it, it is sometimes difficult to realize how differently people with other language structures view the world.

The *structure* of anything, whether it be a language, house, machine, etc., must be in terms of *relations*. To have "structure" we must have a complex or network of ordered and interrelated parts. The only possible link between the nonverbal and verbal levels is found in terms of relations; and, therefore, relations as factors of structure give the sole content of all human knowledge. Thus, we may realize the importance of the structure of a language, any language. Bertrand Russell and Ludwig Wittgenstein were the important pioneers in devoting serious attention to the problem of structure (38, 39, 51). I cannot go into this problem in more detail here, except to try to convey its fundamental importance.

Among primitive peoples with one-valued "pre-logical thinking" the "consciousness of abstracting" is practically nil. The effect upon an individual produced by something inside his skin is projected outside his skin, often acquiring a demonic character. The "idea" of an action or object is identified with the action of the object itself.

The "paralogical" state is a little more advanced. Here the identifications are based on *similarities*, and differences are neglected (not consciously, of course). Lévy-Bruhl describes this primitive evaluational level by formulating the "law of participation," by which all things which have *similar* characteristics *"are the same"* (29; 21, p. 514). A primitive "syllogism" runs somewhat as follows: "Certain Indians run fast, stags run fast; therefore, some Indians *are* stags." This evaluational process is entirely natural at this level and lays a foundation for the *building of language* and higher order abstractions. We proceeded by similarities, much too often considered as identities.

Primitive men do not discuss abstract "ideas." As Boas has found, "The Indian will not speak of goodness as such, although he may very well speak of the goodness of a person. He will not speak of a state of bliss apart from the person who is in such a state." However, Boas concludes, "The fact that generalized forms of expression are not used does not prove inability to form them, but it merely proves that the mode of life of the people is such that they are not required" (3 , pp. 64-67).

The use of abstract terms, such as a term for "goodness as such," made possible an enormous economy in communication, also a great increase in human time-binding progress, and ultimately it made modern science possible. In the meantime, the fact that we do abstract on higher orders becomes a danger if we are not conscious that we are doing so and retain the primitive confusions or identifications of orders of abstractions.

The following quotation[6] from "Being and Value in a Primitive Culture" by Dorothy D. Lee shows the extensional (by fact, rather than higher order verbal generalizations; see pages 41-43) type of language structure of the Trobrianders (25, p. 402):

> If I were to go with a Trobriander to a garden where the taytu, a species of yam, had just been harvested, I would come back and tell you: "There are good taytu there; just the right degree of ripeness, large and perfectly shaped; not a blight to be seen, not one rotten spot; nicely rounded at the tips, with no spiky points; all first-run harvesting, no second gleanings." The Trobriander would come back and say "Taytu"; and he would have said all that I did and more. Even the phrase "There are taytu" would represent a tautology, since existence is implied in being, is, in fact an ingredient of being to the Trobriander. And all the attributes, even if he could find words for them at hand in his own language, would have been tautological, since the concept of taytu contains them all. In fact, if one of these were absent, the object woud not have been a taytu. Such a tuber, if it is not at the proper harvesting ripeness, is not a taytu. If it is unripe, it is a bwabawa; if over-ripe, spent, it is not a spent taytu but something else, a yowana. If it is blighted it is a nukunokuna. If it has a rotten patch, it is a taboula; if misshapen, it is an usasu; if perfect in shape but small, it is a yagogu. If the tuber, whatever its shape or condition, is a post-harvest gleaning, it is an ulumadala. When the spent tuber, the yowana, sends its shoots underground, as we put it, it is not a yowana with shoots, but a silisata. When new tubers have formed on these shoots, it is not a silisata but a gadena. . . .
>
> As being is identical with the object, there is no word for *to be;* as being is changeless, there is no word meaning *to become.*

It is significant, also, to find that the *temporal* differentiations and *temporal* generalizations which we have are absent among the Trobrianders:

> Trobriand verbs are timeless, making no temporal distinctions. History and mythical reality are not "the past" to the Trobriander. They are forever present, participating in all current being, giving meaning to all his activities and all existence. A Trobriander will speak of the garden which his mother's brother planted, or the one which the mythical Tudava planted, in exactly the same terms with which he will refer to the garden which he himself is planting now; and it will give him satisfaction to do so . . . (25, p. 403).
>
> The Trobriander has no word for history. When he wants to distinguish between different kinds of occasions, he will say, for example, "Molubabeba in-child-his," that is, "in the childhood of Molubabeba," *not a previous phase of* this *time, but a different kind of time* (25, p. 405; italics mine).

Many excellent papers and books have been written by anthropologists, psychiatrists, linguists, etc., on how different primitive people or different nationalities dissect nature differently in accordance with the structure of their language.[7]

The main characteristics of primitive or "pre-logical" and "paralogical" language structures may be summarized in their identification of different orders of abstractions, and their lack of abstract terms. The "perceptions" of people on primitive levels are often different from ours, different in the degree to which higher order abstractions are confused, identified with, and projected on lower order abstractions. They identify or ascribe *one value* to essentially many-valued different orders of abstractions and so become impervious to contradictions with "reality" and impervious also to higher order experience.[8]

ARISTOTELIAN AND NON-ARISTOTELIAN LANGUAGE SYSTEMS

Aristotelian Language Structure

In mankind's cultural evolution, our current abstractions became codified here and there into systems, for instance the Aristotelian system. The term "system" is used here in the sense of "a whole of related doctrinal functions" (the doctrinal functions of the late Professor Cassius Keyser [17]. We are concerned with this structure here because of its still enormous influence on those of us whose language structure is of the Indo-European type.

I wish to emphasize here that in discussing the inadequacy of the Aristotelian system in 1950, I in no way disparage the remarkable and unprecedented work of Aristotle about 350 B.C. I acknowledge explicitly my profound admiration for his extraordinary genius, particularly in consideration of the period in which he lived. Nevertheless, the twisting of his system and the imposed immobility of this twisted system, as enforced for nearly two thousand years by the controlling groups, often under threats of torture and death, have led and can only lead to more disasters. From what we know about Aristotle and his writings, there is little doubt that, if alive, he would not tolerate such twistings and artificial immobility of the system usually ascribed to him.

Space limitations prevent my going into details here, and I can but refer the reader to my larger work on this subject, *Science and Sanity: An Introduction to Non-Aristotelian Systems and General Semantics* (21). A rough summary in the form of a tabulation of Aristotelian and non-Aristotelian orientations given in that volume (21, pp. xxv ff.) may help to convey to the reader the magnitude of this problem.

Here I will stress some of the main structural considerations of the Aristotelian system and their effects on our world outlook, evaluations, and, therefore, even "perceptions." Practically since the beginning of Aristotle's formulations, and particularly after their later distortions, there have been many criticisms of them, mostly ineffective because unworkable. One of their most serious inadequacies was very lately found to be the belief in the uniqueness of the subject-predicate form of representation, in the sense that every kind of relation in this world can be expressed in that form, which is obviously false to facts and would make science and mathematics impossible.

I will quote the following remarks[9] of Bertrand Russell, who did epoch-making work in his analysis of subject-predicate relations:

> The belief or unconscious conviction that all propositions are of the subject-predicate form—in other words, that every fact consists in some thing having some quality—has rendered most philosophers incapable of giving any account of the world of science and daily life . . . (37, p. 45; 21, p. 85).

Philosophers have, as a rule, failed to notice more than two types of sentence, exemplified by the two statements "this is yellow" and "buttercups are yellow." They mistakenly suppose that these two were one and the same type, and also that all propositions were of this type. The former error was exposed by Frege and Peano; the latter was found to make the explanation of order impossible. Consequently, the traditional view that all propositions ascribe a predicate to a subject collapsed, and with it the metaphysical systems which were based upon it, consciously or unconsciously (39, p. 242; 21, p. 131).

Asymmetrical relations are involved in all series—in space and time, greater and less, whole and part, and many others of the most important characteristics of the actual world. All these aspects, therefore, the logic which reduces everything to subjects and predicates is compelled to condemn as error and mere appearance (37, p. 45; 21, p. 188).

In this connection I may quote some remarks by Alfred Whitehead, who also did most important work on this subject:

... the subject-predicate habits of thought ... had been impressed on the European mind by the overemphasis on Aristotle's logic during the long mediaeval period. In reference to this twist of mind, probably Aristotle was not an Aristotelian (49, pp. 80-81; 21, p. 85).

The evil produced by the Aristotelian "primary substance" is exactly this habit of metaphysical emphasis upon the "subject-predicate" form of proposition (49, p. 45).[10]

The alternate philosophic position must commence with denouncing the whole idea of "subject qualified by predicate" as a trap set for philosophers by the syntax of language (48, p. 14; 21, p. 85).[11]

In his "Languages and Logic" Benjamin Lee Whorf makes an analysis of primitive and other language structures (50, pp. 43-52).

The Indo-European languages and many others give great prominence to a type of sentence having two parts, each part built around a class of words—substantives and verbs—which those languages treat differently in grammar.... The Greeks, especially Aristotle, built up this contrast and made it a law of reason. Since then, the contrast has been stated in logic in many different ways: subject and predicate, actor and action, things and relations between things, objects and their attributes, quantities and operations. And, pursuant again to grammar, the notion became ingrained that one of these classes of entities can exist in its own right but that the verb cannot exist without an entity of the other class, the "thing" class. ... Our Indian languages show that with a suitable grammar we may have intelligent sentences that cannot be broken into subjects and predicates.[12]

The subject-predicate structure of language resulted from the ascribing of "properties" or "qualities" to "nature," whereas the "qualities," etc., are actually manufactured by our nervous systems. The perpetuation of such projections tends to keep mankind on the archaic levels of anthropomorphism and animism in their evaluations of their surroundings and themselves.

The main verb through which these outlooks were structuralized in our language is the verb "to be." Here I will give a very brief analysis of some uses of the little word "is," and what important effect its use has had on our "thinking." A full investigation of the term "is" has been found to be very complex. The great mathematician and logician, Augustus de Morgan, one of the founders of mathematical logic, has justly said, in his *Formal Logic* (1847) (8, p. 56):

> The complete attempt to deal with the term *is* would go to the form and matter of everything in *existence,* at least, if not to the possible form and matter of all that does not exist, but might. As far as it could be done, it would give the grand Cyclopaedia, and its yearly supplement would be the history of the human race for the time.

Here, following Russell, we can only state roughly that in the Indo-European languages the verb "to be" has at least four entirely different uses (36, p. 64):

1. As an auxiliary verb: It is raining.
2. As the "is" of existence: I am.
3. As the "is" of predication: The rose is red.
4. As the "is" of identity: The rose is a flower.

The first two are difficult to avoid in English, and relatively harmless. The other two, however, are extremely pertinent to our discussion. If we say, "The rose is red," we falsify everything we "know" in 1950 about our nervous systems and the structure of the empirical world. There is no "redness" in nature, only different wave lengths of radiation. *Our reaction* to those light waves is only our individual reaction. If one is a Daltonist, for example, he will see "green." If one is color-blind, he will see "gray." We may correctly say, "We see the rose as red," which would not be a falsification.

The fourth, the "is" of identity, if used without consciousness of the identifications implied, perpetuates a primitive type of evaluation. In some languages—the Slavic, for instance—there is no "is" of identity. If we say, "I classify the rose as a flower," this is structurally correct, and implies that our nervous system is doing the classifying.

The importance of that "is" of identity embedded in the structure of our language can hardly be overemphasized, as it affects our neuro-evaluational reactions and leads to mis-evaluations in the daily life of every one of us which are sometimes very tragic.

Here let us recall the "philosophical grammar" of our language which we call the "laws of thought," as given by Jevons (12; 21, p. 749):

1. The law of identity. Whatever is, is.
2. The law of contradiction. Nothing can both be, and not be.
3. The law of excluded third. Everything must either be, or not be.

These "laws" have different "philosophical" interpretations, but for our purpose it is enough to emphasize that (*a*) the second "law" represents a negative statement of the first, and the third represents a corollary of the former two; namely, no third is possible between two contradictories; and (*b*) the verb "to be," or "is," and "identity" play a most fundamental role in these formulations and the consequent semantic reactions.

"Identity" as a "principle" is defined as "absolute sameness in 'all' ('every') respects." It can never empirically be found in this world of ever-changing processes, nor on silent levels of our nervous systems. "Partial identity" or "identity in *some* respects" obviously represents only a self-contradiction in terms. Identification, as the term is used here, can be observed very low in the scale of life. It may be considered the first organic and/or organismal relating of "cause" and "effect," order, etc., when lower organisms responded effectively to signals "as if" they were actualities. On lower levels such organismal identifications have survival value. Laboratory observations show that the amoeba will exhibit reactions to artificial stimulations, without food value, similar to its reactions to stimuli with food value. The amoeba as a living bit of protoplasm has *organismally identified* an artificial, valueless-as-food, laboratory stimulus with "reality." Thus, although the reaction was there, the evaluation was inappropriate, which does not change the biological fact that without such identifications, or automatic response to a stimulus, no amoeba could survive.

Advancing in the scale of life, the identifications become fewer, the identification reactions become more flexible, "proper evaluation" increases, and the animals become more and more "intelligent," etc. If identifications are found in humans, they represent only a survival of primitive reactions and mis-evaluations, or cases of underdevelopment or regression, which are pathological for humans.

Many of our daily identifications are harmless, but in principle may, and often do, lead to disastrous consequences. Here I give three examples of identification, one by a psychiatric hospital patient, another by a "normal" student of mine, and a third by a group of natives in the Belgian Congo.

When I was studying psychiatry in St. Elizabeth Hospital, a doctor was showing me a catatonic patient who was standing rigid in a corner. For years he had not spoken and did not seem to understand when spoken to. He happened to have been born and spent part of his life in Lithuania, where the people had been trained for several generations by the czar to hate the Poles. The doctor, without that historical knowledge, introduced me to the catatonic by saying, "I want you to meet one of your compatriots, also a Pole." The patient was immediately at my throat, choking me, and it took two guards to tear him away.

Another example is of a young woman who was a student in my seminar some years ago. She held a responsible position, but in her whole orientation she was pathologically fearful to the point of having daydreams of murdering her father because he did not defend her against her mother, who had beaten her and nagged her. During her childhood her brother, who was a number of years older and the favorite of their mother, patronized her, and she hated him for this attitude.

In this particular interview I was especially pleased with her progress and so I was speaking to her smilingly. Suddenly she jumped at me and began to choke me. This lasted only about five seconds. Then it turned out that she identified my smile with the patronizing attitude of her brother, and so she was choking "her brother," but it happened to be my neck.

There is another incident I want to tell you about that will indicate the problems we have to deal with (35, p. 52). We have all seen a box of Aunt Jemima Pancake Flour, with the picture of "Aunt Jemima" on the front. Dr. William Bridges of the New York Zoological Society has told this story about it: A United States planter in the Belgian Congo had some 250 natives working for him. One day the local chieftain called him and said he understood that the planter was eating natives, and that if he did not stop, the chief would order his men to stop work. The planter protested that he did not eat natives and called his cook as a witness. But the cook insisted that he did indeed eat natives, though he refused to say whether they were fried, boiled, stewed, or what not. Some weeks later the mystery was cleared up when the planter was visited by a friend from the Sudan who had had a similar experience. Between them they figured out the answer. Both had received shipments of canned goods from the United States. The cans usually bore labels with pictures of the contents, such as cherries, tomatoes, peaches, etc. So when the cook saw labels with the picture of "Aunt Jemima," they believed that an Aunt Jemima must be inside!

A structure of language perpetuating identification reactions keeps us on the level of primitive or prescientific types of evaluations, stressing similarities and neglecting (not consciously) differences. Thus, we do not "see" differences, and react *as if two* objects, persons, or happenings were "the same." Obviously this is not "proper evaluation" in accordance with our knowledge of 1950.

In analyzing the Aristotelian codifications, we have to deal also with two-valued, "either-or" types of orientation. Practically all humans, the most primitive peoples not excluded, who never heard of Greek philosophers, have some sort of "either-or" types of orientations. It becomes obvious that our relations to the world outside, and inside our skins often happen to be, *on the gross level,* two-valued. For instance, we deal with day *or* night, land *or* water, etc. On the living level we have life *or* death, our heart beats *or* not, we breathe *or* suffocate, are hot *or* cold, etc. Similar relations occur on higher levels. Thus we have induction *or* deduction, materialism *or* idealism, capitalism *or* communism, Democrat *or* Republican, etc. And so on endlessly on all levels.

In living life many issues are not so sharp; therefore, a system which posits the general sharpness of "either-or" and so objectifies "kind" ("properties," "qualities," etc.), is too distorted and unduly limited. It must be revised and made more flexible in terms of "degrees." The new orientation requires a physico-mathematical "way of thinking." Thus if, through our unconscious assumptions, inferences, etc., we evaluate the event, the submicroscopic process level, *as if it were the same as* the gross macroscopic objects which we perceive before us, we remain in our two-valued rut of "thinking." On the macroscopic level, if there are two apples side by side, for example, we perceive that they may "touch" *or* "not touch" (see Figure 2). This language does not apply to the submicroscopic process level, where the problem of "touch" or "not touch" becomes a problem of degree. There are continual interactions between the two on submicroscopic levels which we cannot "perceive." In accordance with the assumptions of science[1950], we must visualize a *process.*[13] It follows that this is the way we should "think" about an apple, or a human being, *or a theory.*

There is no "perception" without interpolation and interpretation (21, pp. xxviii ff.). We cannot stop it. But we can visualize the latest achievements of mathematical physics and other sciences and read these into the silent un-speakable processes going on around us and in us.

The Aristotelian language structure also perpetuated what I call "elementalism," or splitting verbally what cannot be split empirically, such as the term *mind* by itself and the terms *body, space, time,* etc., by themselves. It was only a few years ago (1908) that the outstanding mathematician Minkowski said in his epoch-making

MACROSCOPIC   SUBMICROSCOPIC

FIGURE 2. *Macroscopic view and submicroscopic process level of two apples, side by side.*

address entitled "Space and Time," delivered at the 80th Assembly of German Natural Scientists and Physicians at Cologne, "The views of space and time which I wish to lay before you have sprung from the soil of experimental physics, and therein lies their strength. They are radical. Henceforth space by itself, and time by itself, are doomed to fade away into mere shadows, and only a kind of union of the two will preserve an independent reality" (32, p. 75).

The "union" of what used to be considered distinct separate entities had to be accompanied by a change in the structure of the language, in this particular case by the formulation of Minkowski's new four-dimensional geometry of "space-time," in which "space" and "time" were permanently united by a simple grammatical hyphen, thus making the general theory of relativity possible.

The old elementalistic structure of language built for us a fictitious, anthropomorphic, animistic world not much different from that of the primitives. Modern science makes imperative a language structure which is non-elementalistic and does not split artificially what cannot be split empirically. Otherwise, we remain handicapped by neuro-evaluational blockages, lack of creativeness, lack of understanding, and lack of broad perspectives, etc., and disturbed by inconsistencies, paradoxes, etc.

The points I have touched upon here: namely, the subject-predicate type of structure, the "is" of identity, two-valued "either-or" orientations, and elementalism, are perhaps the main features of the Aristotelian language structure that molded our "perceptions" and hindered the scientific investigations which at this date have so greatly, in many instances, freed us from the older limitations and allowed us to "see the world anew." The "discovery of the obvious" is well known to be the most difficult, simply because the old habits of "thinking" have blocked our capacity to "see the old anew" (Leibnitz).

Non-Aristotelian Language Systems

As usually happens with humans, when we come to an impasse and find that revisions and new approaches are necessary, we do something about it. In this case, with the tremendous advances in science, a structure of language which did not falsify modern discoveries became imperative. As I do not know of any other non-Aristotelian system at this date, I must ask the reader's indulgence that I will have to speak rather exclusively about my own formulations. Many others have made applications, but here I will deal mostly with the theoretical side.

The new system is called "non-Aristotelian" since it includes the prevailing systems of evaluation as special cases within a more general system. Historically the Aristotelian system influenced the Euclidean system, and both underlie the consequent Newtonian system. The first non-Aristotelian revision parallels, and is interdependent with non-Euclidean and non-Newtonian developments in modern mathematics and mathematical physics. To satisfy the need to unify exact sciences and general human orientations was one of the main aims of the non-Aristotelian revision, historically the latest, because of its much greater complexities (21, esp. p. 97).

The non-Aristotelian system grew out of the new evaluation in 1921 of human beings as a time-binding class of life (18). This evaluation is based on a *functional* rather than zoölogical or mythological approach and considers "man" as an organism-as-a-whole-in-an-environment." Here the reactions of humans are not split verbally and elementalistically into separate "body," "mind," "emotions," "intellect," or different "senses," etc., by themselves, which affects the problems of "perception" when considered from a non-elementalistic point of view. With a time-binding consciousness, our criteria of values, and so behavior, are based on the study of human potentialities, not on statistical averages on the level of *homo homini lupus* drawn from primitive and/or un-sane evaluational reactions which are on record (23).

Common sense and ordinary observations make clear that the average so-called "normal" person is so extremely complex as to practically evade a nonsegmented, non-elementalistic analysis. In order to make such an analysis, it became necessary to investigate the main available forms of human reactions, such as mathematics, mathematical foundations, many branches of sciences, history, history of cultures, anthropology, philosophy, psychology, "logic," comparative religions, etc. It was found essential to concentrate on the study of two extremes of human psycho-logical reactions: (*a*) reactions at their best, because of their exceptional predictability, validity, and lasting constructiveness in the time-binding process, as in mathematics, the foundations of mathematics, mathematical physics, exact science, etc., which are manifestations of some of the deepest human psycho-logical reactions; and (*b*) reactions at their worst, as exemplified by psychiatric cases. In these investigations it became obvious that physico-mathematical methods have application to our daily life on all levels, linking science, and particularly the exact sciences, with problems of sanity in the sense of adjustment to "facts" and "reality."

In fact it was found that, to change the linguistic structure of our prevailing Aristotelian system, methods had to be taken bodily from mathematics. Thus, the structure of our language was changed through the use of extensional devices without changing the language itself. This will be expained briefly a little later.

When the premises of this new approach had been formulated, I found unexpectedly that they turned out to be a denial of the old "law of thought" and the foundation for a non-Aristotelian system, the *modus operandi* of which I have named "General Semantics." The premises are very simple and may be stated by means of an analogy:

1. A map *is not* the territory. (Words *are not* the things they represent.)
2. A map covers *not all* the territory. (Words cannot cover all they represent.)
3. A map is self-reflexive. (In language we can speak *about* language.)

We notice that the old prescientific assumptions violate the first two premises and disregard the third (20, pp. 750 ff.; 24).

The third premise turns out to be an application to everyday life of the extremely important work of Bertrand Russell, who attempted to solve self-contradictions in the foundations of mathematics by his theory of mathematical or logical types. In this connection the term *self-reflexive* was introduced by Josiah Royce. The theory of mathematical types made me aware of new kinds of linguistic perplexities to which practically no one, except a very few mathematicians, had paid attention before. The realization and analysis of such difficulties led me to the discovery that the principles of different orders of abstractions, multi-ordinality of terms, $\frac{over}{under}$ defined terms, second-order reactions ("thinking" about "thinking," doubt of doubt, fear of fear, etc.), thalamo-cortical interaction, the circularity of human knowledge, etc., may be considered as generalizing the theory of mathematical types.[14]

The degrees to which we are "conscious of abstracting," which includes, among others, the above, becomes a key problem in the way we evaluate and therefore to a large extent may affect the way in which we "perceive." If we can devise methods to increase our "consciousness of abstracting," this would eventually free us from the archaic, prescientific, and/or Aristotelian limitations inherent in the older language structures. The following structural expedients to achieve this I call the *extensional devices,* and the application of them automatically brings about an orientation in conformity with the latest scientific assumptions.

Extensional Devices. 1. *Indexes,* as in x_1, x_2, x_3 . . . x_n; chair$_1$, chair$_2$, chair$_3$ . . . chair$_n$; Smith$_1$, Smith$_2$, Smith$_3$ . . . Smith$_n$, etc. The role of the indexes is to produce indefinitely many *proper names* for the endless array of unique individuals or situations with which we have to deal in life. Thus, we have changed a *generic* name into a *proper* name. If this indexing becomes habitual, as an integral part of our evaluating processes, the psycho-logical effect is very marked. We become aware that most of our "thinking" in daily life as well as in science is hypothetical in character, and the moment-to-moment consciousness of this makes us cautious in our generalizations, something which cannot be easily conveyed within the Aristotelian structure of language. A generic term (such as "chair") deals with classes and stresses similarities to the partial exclusion or neglect or disregard of differences. The use of the indexes brings to consciousness the individual differences, and thus leads to more appropriate evaluation, and so eventually "perception," in a given instance. The harmful identifications which result from the older language structures are often prevented or eliminated, and they may become supplanted by more flexible evaluations, based on a maximum probability orientation.

2. *Chain-indexes,* as in chair$_{1_1}$ (in a dry attic), chair$_{1_2}$ (in a damp cellar) . . . chair$_{1_n}$; Smith$_{1_1}$ (under normal conditions) or, say (on the ground), Smith$_{1_2}$ (under extreme starvation conditions) or, say (in a place at extreme altitudes). Smith$_1$'s reactions are entirely different in many ways under the different conditions.

The role of the chain-indexes is to provide a technique for the introduction of environmental factors, conditions, situations, etc. On the human level, these would include psycho-logical, socio-cultural, etc., factors.

In a world where a given "cause" has or may have a multiplicity of "effects," each "effect" becomes or may become a "cause," and so on indefinitely. As we know from psychiatry, for instance, a single happening to an individual in childhood may start a chain-reaction series, and color and twist his psycho-logical or even psycho-somatic responses for the rest of his life. Chain-indexes also convey the general mechanisms of chain-reactions, which operate not only in atomic fission, but every-where in this world. We are particularly interested here that this includes organic processes, human interrelations, and also the processes of time-binding, as expressed in the "spiral theory" of our time-binding energy (18, 1st ed., pp. 232 ff.).

Chain-indexes (indexing an index indefinitely) are not new in mathematics. They have been used automatically, but to the best of my knowledge a general pattern was not formulated for their application in everyday life. For an example of their use in a scientific problem, see "On the Use of Chain-indexing to Describe and Analyze the Complexities of a Research Problem in Bio-chemistry" by Mortimer B. Lipsett (30).

To recapitulate, for better or worse, we are living in a world of processes, and so "cause-effect" chain-reactions, and we need to have linguistic means for ourselves and others to manage our evaluations in such a world. Perhaps the formulation of a linguistic chain-index pattern will help this.

3. *Dates,* as in $Smith_1^{1920}$, $Smith_1^{1940}$, $Smith_1^{1950}$ ... $Smith_1^t$. The use of dates places us in a physio-mathematical, four-dimensional (at least) space-time world of motion and change, of growth, decay, transformation, etc., yet the representations of the *process* can be *arrested* at any given point by linguistic means for purposes of analysis, clarity, communication, etc. This gives us techniques to handle dynamic actualities by static means.

Thus, it probably would make a good deal of difference whether a given auto-mobile is a 1930 or a 1950 model, if we are interested in buying one. We are not as a rule similarly conscious of "dating" our theories, creeds, etc., however, although it is "well known" to what extent dates affect science, theories, books, different customs and cultures, people and all life included.

As another example, if we read the *Communist Manifesto* by Karl Marx and Friedrich Engels (31) we find the word "modern" on many pages. It is easy to evaluate the "modern" as "1950," which apparently many readers do. My sugges-tion is that when we find that word we put on the margin by hand the date "1848." With that dating, many arguments become antiquated, and so obsolete, because we are living in the world of 1950, which is entirely different.

4. *Etc.* The use of "etc." as a part of our evaluating processes leads to aware-ness of the indefinitely many factors in a process which can *never* be *fully* known or perceived, facilitates flexibility, and gives a greater degree of conditionality in our semantic reactions. This device trains us away from dogmatism, absolutism, etc. We are reminded of the second premise (the map does *not* cover *all* the territory) and indirectly of the first premise (the map *is not* the territory).

Incidentally, in the "etc." we find the key to the solution of mathematical "in-finity," with important psycho-logical implications (21, chap. xiv).

5. *Quotes,* as in "body," "mind," "emotion," "intellect," etc., forewarn us that elementalistic or metaphysical terms are not to be trusted, and that speculations based on them are misleading or dangerous.

6. *Hyphens.* The use of hyphens links linguistically the actual empirical complex inter-relatedness in this world. There are most important structural implications in-volving the hyphen which represent recent advances in sciences and other branches of knowledge.

For example, the hyphen (*a*) in *space-time* revolutionized physics, transformed our whole world-outlook, and became the foundation of non-Newtonian systems;

(*b*) in *psycho-biological* marks sharply the difference between animals and much more complex humans (in my interpretation of it). This differentiation is also on the basis of the present non-Aristotelian system, where "man" as a "time-binder" is not merely biological, but psycho-biological. The hyphen (*c*) in *psycho-somatic* is slowly transforming medical understanding, practice, etc.; (*d*) in *socio-cultural* indicates the need for a new applied anthropology, human ecology, etc.; (*e*) in *neuro-linguistic* and *neuro-semantic* links our verbal, evaluational reactions with our neuro-physiological processes; (*f*) in *organism-as-a-whole-in-an-environment* indicates that not even an "organism-as-a-whole" can exist without an environment, and is a fiction when considered in "absolute isolation."

In regard to "psycho-biological" and "psycho-somatic," the original workers have missed the importance of the hyphen and its implications and used the terms as one word. This becomes a linguistic misrepresentation, and these pioneers did not realize that they were hiding an extreme human complexity behind an apparent simplicity of a single term. They did this on the unjustified, mistaken assumption that one word implies unity; in the meantime, it is misleading to the public because it conceals the inter-acting complexities.

Theoretical and Practical Implications. The simplicity of the extensional devices is misleading, and a mere "intellectual understanding" of them, without incorporating them into our living evaluational processes, has no effect whatsoever. A recanalization and retraining of our usual methods of evaluation is required, and this is what is often very difficult for adults, although comparatively easy for children. The revised structure of language, as explained briefly here, has *neuro-physiological effects,* as it necessitates "thinking" in terms of "facts," or *visualizing processes, before* making generalizations. This procedure results in a slight neurological delay of reaction, facilitating thalamo-cortical integration, etc.

The old Aristotelian language structure, with its subject-predicate form, elementalism, etc., hindered rather than induced such desirable neuro-physiological functioning. It led instead to verbal speculations divorced from actualities, inducing eventually "split personalities" and other pathological reactions.

We may recall the pertinent statement by the outstanding mathematician, Hermann Weyl, who wrote in his "The Mathematical Way of Thinking": "Indeed, the first difficulty the man in the street encounters when he is taught to think mathematically is that he must learn to look things much more squarely in the face; his belief in words must be shattered; he must learn to think more concretely" (47).

Healthy normal persons naturally evaluate to some degree in accordance with the extensional methods and with some "natural order of evaluation," etc., without being aware of it. The structural formulation of these issues, however, and the corresponding revision of our old language structure, make possible their analysis and teachability, which is of paramount importance in our human process of time-binding.

There are many indications so far that the use of the extensional devices and even a partial "consciousness of abstracting" have potentialities for our general human endeavor to understand ourselves and others. The extent of the revision required if we are to follow through from the premises as previously stated is not yet generally realized. Our old habits of evaluation, ingrained for centuries if not millenniums, must first be re-evaluated and brought up to date in accordance with modern knowledge.

In what way does a non-Aristotelian form of representation bring about a change in evaluating processes and effect deep psycho-logical changes? We have seen how the structure of a language often determines the way we look at the world, other persons, and ourselves. My experiences, and the experiences of many others, confirm that we can and do evaluate stimuli differently as the result of the application of the non-Aristotelian extensional methods.

In practically all fields of human endeavor there are indications that new, more flexible, etc., attitudes can be brought about, with resulting influences on the inter-relationships of the given individual with himself and others. A majority of these are in the field of education, but they include fields as diverse as psycho-somatic medicine, psychiatry, psychotherapy, law, economics, business, architecture, art, etc., political economy, politics, social anthropology, reading difficulties, etc.

The non-Aristotelian principles have been utilized in the United States Senate Naval Committee in connection with extremely important national problems such as "Establishing a Research Board of National Security" (45, p. 6), "A Scientific Evaluation of the Proposal that the War and Navy Departments be Merged into a Single Department of National Defense" (46), "Training of Officers for the Naval Service" (42, pp. 55-57). To the best of my knowledge today even on some ships in active duty the personnel are trained in some principles of general semantics (see also 33, esp. chap. i).

One of the main characteristics of the differences in orientation is that the Aristotelian language form fosters evaluating "by definition" (or "intension"), whereas the non-Aristotelian or physico-mathematical orientation involves evaluating "by extension," taking into consideration the actual "facts" in the particular situation confronting us.

For example, some older physicians still attempt to cure " a disease" and not the actual patient in front of them whose psycho-somatic malfunctioning and manifestations, observed or inferred from the patient's behavior or record, involve a multiplicity of individual factors not covered by any possible definition of "a disease." Fortunately, today the majority of physicians try to cure the patient, not "a disease."

In his paper on "The Problem of Stuttering" Professor Wendell Johnson (13) speaks of the significance of the diagnosis of a child as "a stutterer":

> Having *called* the child a "stutterer" (or the equivalent), they react less and less to the child and more and more to what they have called him. In spite of quite overwhelming evidence to the contrary, they assume that the child either cannot speak or has not learned. So they proceed to "help" him speak. . . . And when, "in spite of all their help" he "stutters worse than ever," they worry more and more. . . . There has been and still is a great deal of controversy among speech pathologists as to the most probable cause of stuttering. . . . But no one outside of general semantics has ever suggested that *the diagnosis* of stuttering was a cause of it, probably because no one outside of general semantics has appeared to realize the degree to which two persons talking about "stuttering" could be at variance in what they were talking about, and could be influencing what they were talking about. The uncertainty principle which expresses the effect of the observer on what he observes can be extended to include the effect of the speaker on what he names (pp. 189-93).[15]

Changes in *attitudes*, in our ways of evaluating, involve intimately "perceptual processes" at different levels. Making us *conscious* of our *unconscious assumptions* is essential; it is involved in all psychotherapy and should be a part of education in general. In this connection the extremely important and relevant work of Dr. Adelbert Ames, Jr., at the Hanover Institute and Princeton University, etc., is very useful in bringing about such consciousness. For example, Dr. J. S. A. Bois (4), consulting psychologist in Montreal and past president of the Canadian Psychological Association, in his report on "Executive Training and General Semantics" writes of his class in a basic training course in the non-Aristotelian methodology to seven key men of an industrial organization:

> I proceeded to disequilibrate their self-assurance by demonstrating that our sensory perceptions are not reliable. . . . We ended by accepting the fact that the world which each one of us perceives is not an "objective" world of happenings, but a "subjective" world of *happenings-meanings.*
>
> They were quite ready to accept these new views, but I felt that it was necessary to make them conscious of the fact that it is not sufficient to "understand" certain principles and to accept them "intellectually." It is imperative to change our habitual methods of thinking, and this is not so easy as it seems. To bring this last point home, I explained to them the senary number notation system, and gave them some homework on it: making a multiplication table, long additions, subtractions, multiplications and divisions. The following day they were conscious that it is annoying, irritating, and not so easy to pass from one method of thinking to another. They realized that keeping accounts in the senary system would mean a revolution in the office and the factory, would demand new gears in the calculating machines, etc., etc. I felt the stage was set for the main part of the course. . . . It is impossible to evaluate quantitatively the success or failure of such a course. The fact that the top group wanted it to be given to their immediate subordinates is already an indication that they found it helpful.[16]

Bois reported further that the men made their own evaluations in terms of increased efficiency, better "emotional" control and maturity, better techniques of communication among themselves and with their subordinates, etc.

Observations made of a formalized group procedure at Northwestern University by Liston Tatum suggest that when people are forced to follow the "natural order of evaluation" (evaluating by facts first, then making generalizations) they talk to each other differently (43).

The effect of language on our visual evaluations is shown in a study reported by L. Carmichael, H. P. Hogan, and A. A. Walter (5, pp. 74-82) entitled "An Experimental Study of the Effect of Language on the Reproduction of Visually Perceived Form." It was investigated whether the reproduction of visual forms was affected when a set of twelve figures was presented with a name assigned to each figure. The subjects were to reproduce the figures as accurately as possible after the series was over. The same visual figure was presented to all subjects, but one list of names was given to the figures when they were presented to one group of subjects, and the other list of names accompanied the figures given to a second group. For example: kidney bean   ⬭   canoe. The results indicated that "the present experiment tends to confirm the observations of previous experimenters in this field, and to show that, to some extent at least, the reproduction of forms may be determined by the nature of words presented orally to subjects at the time that they are first perceiving specific visual forms."

Professor Irving Lee has been trying out the procedures on students in his classes in general semantics at Northwestern University and reports (in a personal communication to me) that so far his students do *not* react as the subjects in the above experiment did, but that his students "drew the pictures far less influenced by the labels applied."

Of his teaching of non-Aristotelian methodology to policemen, Lee has written a preliminary report of a three-year pilot study with 140 policemen, from patrolmen to captains, enrolled in the Traffic Police Administration Course in the Northwestern University Traffic Institute (27). From the reports of the instructors and interviews and information from a cross-section of the students after completion of the course, Lee writes, the results indicate that the policemen saw themselves and their work in the school in quite different light after advice on the extensionalizing processes.

Psychologists and others may be interested in the following personal communication giving preliminary data which indicate new fields of investigation in criminology, personality development, etc. Dr. Douglas M. Kelley, professor of criminology at the University of California at Berkeley, has recently written me:

> At present I am concerned with the introduction of general semantics into two areas—interrogation and personality development. The first field is covered in a course which I give for 3 units, Detection of Deception, which consists to begin with of a half semester of straight general semantics, beginning with a discussion on the futility of words in communication and carrying right through to the various devices. The latter half of the course is concerned with the emotional relation of words as demonstrated by various types of lie detectors, and with report writing, where again the problems of multi-ordinality, etc., are dealt with at great length. A survey of all the existent literature indicates a complete lack of information in this area, and this approach purely based on your work reports an entirely new notion and opens up interrogative techniques and vistas hitherto unknown. It is my opinion from talking with a number of police officers that this approach will yield one of the most valuable results achieved from application of general semantics. In addition, I am teaching the same material to the Berkeley police force.
>
> In my course on the Psychiatric Aspects of Criminology, a large amount of discussion is included, based upon your work, as a method of indicating how and why people behave like human beings, and what possibly can be done about it. The students are all most favorably inclined toward the general semantics orientation, and I expect within a year or so to have a real program developed.[17]

During the Second World War Kelley[18] employed the basic principles of non-Aristotelian methodology with over seven thousand cases in the European Theater of Operations, reported on in his article "The Use of General Semantics and Korzybskian Principles as an Extensional Method of Group Psychotherapy in Traumatic Neuroses" (15). The principles were applied (as individual therapies and as group therapies) at every treatment level from the forward area to the rear-most echelon, in front line aid stations, in exhaustion centers, and in general hospitals. "That they were employed with success is demonstrated by the fact that psychiatric evacuations from the European Theater were held to a minimum," Dr. Kelley states (16, pp. vi-vii). "[The] other techniques are, of course, of value but these two simple devices [indexing and dating] proved remarkably potent in this type of neurotic reaction" (15, p. 7).

An example of the effect of indexing and dating, the main devices by which the structure of our language is made similar in structure to the world, may be seen by the reactions of a veteran from the Pacific Theater of War. This veteran was a student of Professor Elwood Murray at the University of Denver. I quote from the veteran's report:

> An example of pure identification comes out in the veteran's dislike for rice. His first view of the enemy dead was that of a Jap soldier which was in the process of deterioration. The bag of rice the soldier had been carrying was torn open and grains of rice were scattered over the body mixed in with maggots. When the veteran, to this day, sees rice, the above described scene is vivid and he imagines grains of rice moving in his dish. To overcome this, he has eaten rice several times trying to remember the rice before him is not the same as that on the body. Though the food is not relished, he has succeeded in overcoming the vomiting reflex at the sight of rice (19, p. 262).

These mechanisms of evaluating or "perceiving" *similarities* and neglecting, or not being fully aware of, the differences are potentially present in every one of us, but usually not in such extreme degrees. This involves the lack of differentiation between the silent and verbal levels and nonawareness of our processes of abstracting. The different orders of abstractions are identified, an inference is evaluated *as if* it were a description, a description *as if* it were the nonverbal "object" our nervous system constructed, and an "object" *as if* it were the nonverbal, submicroscopic, dynamic process.

In our non-Aristotelian work we deal very little, if at all, with "perceptions" as such. As our attitudes, however, are bound to be involved with our "perceptions," it would appear that the investigation of the structure of language becomes relevant indeed.

A great deal of work has been and is being done on struggling with the problem of prejudices. Analyses show that the mechanisms of prejudices involve identifications of verbal with nonverbal levels. That is, an individual or group is evaluated by the label and not by the extensional facts (26, pp. 17-28; 28). In a discussion of mechanisms of prejudice and a report on his teaching of general semantics to approximately six hundred people where he stressed the confusion of observation and inferential statements, the response to labels as if they labeled more than aspects, etc., Lee reports one of his findings as follows:

> Teachers reported greatly reduced tension when students came to apply what they heard to differences of opinion in the class discussions. The questions "Could they be called anything else?" "Is that an inference?" "Is that what could be observed?" put to a member making a sharp statement created a kind of game atmosphere. An example typical of many occurred in one discussion concerned with what people say about Negroes. Two of the participants most vocal in their assertions that "Negroes won't take advantage of education even if made available" were brought to scrutinize those assertions without the antagonism that results in the usual pro and con debating (28, p. 32).

It is of particular interest to consider the methods of the magicians, who have highly developed their art and even science for purposes of entertainment. Their methods of magic, however, have a deep underlying psychology of deception, self-deception, and misdirection. They have their own literature, so important for psychology, psychiatry, and daily life.

I quote from the paper by Dr. Douglas Kelley[19] entitled "The Psycho-logical Basis of Misdirection: An Extensional Non-aristotelian Method for Prevention of Self-deception" (14, pp. 53-60):

> While the artist in conjuring never hypnotizes his audience, not even in India, he accomplishes much the same results by his ability to create illusions by giving a wrong direction to their expectations and assumptions. By this means he can make his public fail to see what is in front of their very eyes, or believe that they see what is not there (p. 53).... A general though unconscious belief in the three aristotelian "laws of thought" plays a part of major importance in the success of such misdirection, since there is a general tendency to react in terms of those "laws."

For instance, Dr. Kelley explains,

> If a hat is faked with a false bottom, it may be shown to be apparently empty by the camouflaged lining in the bottom. If it is then tossed about in a reckless fashion, it simulates an empty hat since nothing drops out. Since according to the two-valued "law of the excluded middle," an existent thing has certain "properties" or does not have them, and since most people following this law expect to see objects if they are present in a hat and expect them to fall out when it is inverted, they are easily fooled by the misdirection employed and consequently are unable to predict the appearance of the rabbit which is eventually drawn forth by the conjurer (p. 57).

Magicians find that children are much more difficult to deceive than adults, as the structural implications of our language have not yet to such an extent put their limitations on the ability of children to "perceive."

THE CIRCULARITY OF HUMAN KNOWLEDGE

The electronic or electro-colloidal processes are operating on submicroscopic levels. From the indefinitely many characteristics of these processes, our nervous system abstracts and integrates a comparatively few, which we may call the gross or macroscopic levels, or the "objective" levels, all of them not verbal. The microscopic levels must be considered as instrumentally aided "sense data" and I will not deal with them here. Then, abstracting further, first on the labeling or descriptive levels, we pass to the inferential levels, and we can try to convey to the other fellow our "feeling about feeling," "thinking about thinking," etc., which actually happen on the silent levels. Finally, we come to the point where we need to speak about speaking.

Scientifically it is known that the submicroscopic levels are not "perceptible" or "perceptual." We do not and cannot "perceive" the "electron," but we observe actually the results of the eventual "electronic processes." That is, we observe the "effects" and assume the "causes." In other words, as explained before, our submicroscopic knowledge is hypothetical in character. The world behaves *as if* its mechanisms were such as our highest abstractions lead us to believe, and we will continue to invent theories *with their appropriate terminologies* to account for the intrinsic mechanisms of the world we live in, ourselves included. We read into nature our own latest highest abstractions, thus completing the inherent circularity of human knowledge, without which our understanding of nature is impossible.

Because of what was explained in the first part of this chapter (pages 27-29), and aided by the extensional methods and devices, we must come to the conclusion that inferential knowledge is often much more reliable *at a date, after cross-verification*, than the original "sense data," with which historically we had to start and which have been found to be wanting.

In scientizing, the inferential data must converge. If they do not, we usually have to revise our theories. It is well known that when a new factor is discovered our older generalizations have to be revised for the sake of the integration of our knowledge (21, pp. xxviii ff.) [20]

Our inferences, as abstractions on other levels than the "sense data," may also be on lower or higher orders of abstractions. The structure of our recent knowledge is such that we read into, or project onto, the silent, submicroscopic process levels the highest abstractions yet made by man, our hypotheses, inferences, etc.

Thus, all our fundamental deeper knowledge must be, and can never be anything but, hypothetical, as what we see, hear, feel, speak about, or infer, is never *it*, but only our human abstractions *about* "it." What kind of linguistic form our inferential knowledge is cast in thus becomes of utmost importance. As Edward Sapir has put it, "We see and hear and otherwise experience very largely as we do because the language habits of our community predispose certain choices of interpretation" (41, p. 245).

This circular process of our nervous systems in inter-action with the environments turns out to be a "feedback system," a most happy term which has been introduced lately and which exactly depicts the situation. According to Lawrence Frank (10):

> We are shifting our focus of interest from static entities to dynamic processes and the order of events as seen in a context or field where there are inter-reactions and circular processes in operation. . . . The concept of teleological mechanisms, however it may be expressed in different terms, may be viewed as an attempt to escape from these older mechanistic formulations that now appear inadequate, and to provide new and more fruitful conceptions and more effective methodologies for studying self-regulating processes, self-orienting systems and organisms, and self-directing personalities. . . . Thus, the terms *feedback, servomechanisms, circular systems*, and *circular processes* may be viewed as different but equivalent expressions of much the same basic conception (10, pp. 190, 191). [21]

The mechanisms of "feedback" have been brought to their culmination in humans, and the process of time-binding itself may be considered as an unprecedented, unique organic spiraling of feedbacks. In the exponential "spiral theory" given in my *Manhood of Humanity* (18, pp. 232 ff.), our time-binding capacity is obviously based on feedback mechanisms, chain-reactions, etc., without which humans as humans could not exist. The new understanding of humans as a time-binding class of life, free from the older crippling mythological or zoölogical assumptions, is one of the pivotal points toward a new evaluation of the unique role of humans in this world. It encourages or sponsors better understanding of ourselves, not only in relation to the world at large, but also toward ourselves.

I believe it is essential to begin with an entirely new functional formulation, with the implications which this involves for the study of "man" as "an organism-as-a-whole-in-an-environment," including our neuro-semantic and neuro-linguistic environments as environment.

In closing, I can find no more fitting summary than to quote the passages given below, which so beautifully and profoundly express the foundation of human knowledge.

It was Cassius J. Keyser who said:

> . . . for it is obvious, once the fact is pointed out, that the character of human history, the character of human conduct, and the character of all our human institutions depend both upon what man *is* and in equal or greater measure upon what we humans *think* man is (17, p. 424).[22]

This inescapable characteristic of human living has been formulated differently, but just as aptly, by Dr. Alexis Carrel:

> To progress again, man must remake himself. And he cannot remake himself without suffering. For he is both the marble and the sculptor (6, p. 274).

Arthur S. Eddington expresses himself in different words:

> And yet, in regard to the nature of things, this knowledge is only an empty shell—a form of symbols. It is knowledge of structural form, and not knowledge of content. All through the physical world runs that unknown content, which must surely be the stuff of our consciousness. Here is a hint of aspects deep within the world of physics, and yet unattainable by the methods of physics. And, moreover, we have found that where science has progressed the farthest, the mind has but regained from nature that which the mind has put into nature.
>
> We have found a strange foot-print on the shores of the unknown. We have devised profound theories, one after another, to account for its origin. At last, we have succeeded in reconstructing the creature that made the foot-print. And Lo! it is our own (9, p. 200).[23]

BIBLIOGRAPHY

1. Alexander, J. "Successive Levels of Material Structure." In J. Alexander (ed.), *Colloid Chemistry*. New York: Reinhold Publishing Corp., 1944, Vol. V.

2. Alexander, J. *Life: Its Nature and Origin*. New York: Reinhold Publishing Corp., 1948.

3. Boas, F. "Introduction." In Smithsonian Institute, U. S. Bureau of American Ethnology, *Handbook of American Indian Languages*. Part I. Washington, D.C.: U.S. Government Printing Office, 1911.

4. Bois, J. S. A. "Executive Training and General Semantics." Lakeville, Conn.: Institute of General Semantics, 1949. (Mimeographed.)

5. Carmichael, L., Hogan, H. P. & Walter, A. A. "An Experimental Study of the Effect of Language on the Reproduction of Visually Perceived Form." *J. exp. Psychol.*, 1932, 15, 73-86.

6. Carrel, A. *Man the Unknown*. New York: Harper & Bros., 1935.

7. Cassirer, E. *An Essay on Man.* New Haven, Conn.: Yale University Press, 1944.

8. De Morgan, A. *Formal Logic or the Calculus of Inference, Necessary and Probable.* London: The Open Court Co., 1926.

9. Eddington, A. S. *Space Time and Gravitation: an Outline of the General Relativity Theory.* Cambridge: Cambridge University Press, 1920.

10. Frank, L. K. "Foreword." In L. K. Frank, G. E. Hutchinson, W. K. Livingston, W. S. McCulloch, & N. Wiener, "Teleological Mechanisms." *Ann. N. Y. Acad. Sc.,* 1948, 50, 189-96.

11. Hadamard, J. S. *An Essay on the Psychology of Invention in the Mathematical Field.* Princeton, N. J.: Princeton University Press, 1945.

12. Jevons, W. S. *The Elements of Logic.* New York: American Book Co., 1883.

13. Johnson, W. "The Problem of Stuttering from the Point of View of General Semantics." In M. Kendig (ed.), *Papers 2nd Amer. Cong. General Semantics.* Lakeville, Conn.: Institute of General Semantics, 1943.

14. Kelley, D. M. "Mechanisms of Magic and Self-deception: The Psycho-logical Basis of Misdirection; An Extensional Non-Aristotelian Method for Prevention of Self-deception." In M. Kendig (ed.), *Papers 2nd Amer. Cong. General Semantics.* Lakeville, Conn.: Institute of General Semantics, 1943.

15. Kelley, D. M. "The Use of General Semantics and Korzybskian Principles as an Extensional Method of Group Psychotherapy in Traumatic Neuroses." Lakeville, Conn.: Institute of General Semantics, 1948. (Mimeographed.)

16. Kelley, D. M. Report in "Preface." On A. Korzybski, *Science and Sanity: An Introduction to Non-Aristotelian Systems and General Semantics* (3d ed.). Lakeville, Conn.: International Non-Aristotelian Library Publishing Co., 1948.

17. Keyser, C. J. *Mathematical Philosophy: A Study of Fate and Freedom.* New York: E. P. Dutton & Co., Inc., 1922.

18. Korzybski, A. *Manhood of Humanity: The Science and Art of Human Engineering* (1st ed.). New York: E. P. Dutton & Co., Inc., 1921. Same (2d ed.). Lakeville, Conn.: International Non-Aristotelian Library Publishing Co., 1950.

19. Korzybski, A. "A Veteran's Re-adjustment and Extensional Methods." *Etc.: A Review of General Semantics,* 1946, 3, 254-64.

20. Korzybski, A. "A Non-Aristotelian System and Its Necessity for Rigour in Mathematics and Physics." In *Science and Sanity: An Introduction to Non-Aristotelian Systems and General Semantics* (3d ed.) by the same author. (Supplement III, first edition of *Science and Sanity,* 1933.) Lakeville, Conn.: International Non-Aristotelian Library Publishing Co., 1948. Supplement III, pp. 747-61.

21. Korzybski, A. *Science and Sanity: An Introduction to Non-Aristotelian systems and General Semantics* (1st ed., 1933; 2d ed., 1941; 3d ed., 1948). Lakeville, Conn.: International Non-Aristotelian Library Publishing Co.

22. Korzybski, A. *Time-Binding: The General Theory, Two Papers: 1924-1926.* Lakeville, Conn.: Institute of General Semantics, 1949.

23. Korzybski, A. "What I Believe." In *Manhood of Humanity* (2d ed.) by the same author. Lakeville, Conn.: Institute of General Semantics, 1950.

24. Korbybski, A., & Kendig, M. "Foreword." In *A Theory of Meaning Analyzed: Critique of I. A. Richard's Theory of Language* by Thomas C. Pollock, and J. Gordon Spaulding, "Elementalism: the Effect of an Implicit Postulate of Identity on I. A. Richards' *Theory of Poetic Value.*" Gen. Semantics Monogr. No. III. Lakeville, Conn.: Institute of General Semantics, 1942.

25. Lee, Dorothy. "Being and Value in a Primitive Culture." *J. Philos.,* 1949, 13, 401-15.

26. Lee, I. J. "A Mechanism of Conflict and Prejudice." In M. Kendig (ed.), *Papers 2d Amer. Cong. General Semantics.* Lakeville, Conn.: Institute of General Semantics, 1943.

27. Lee, I. J. "The Assumptions of the Arrogant." *Education,* 1950, 70, 509-11.

28. Lee, I. J. *How Do You Talk about People?* ("Freedom Pamphlets.") New York: American Education Fellowship, 1950.

29. Lévy-Bruhl, L. *Primitive Mentality.* New York: The Macmillan Co., 1923.

30. Lipsett, M. "On the Use of Chain-Indexing to Describe and Analyze the Complexities of a Research Problem in Bio-Chemistry." *General Semantics Bull.,* 1949-50, 1 & 2, pp. 8, 9.

31. Marx, K., & Engels, F. *Manifesto of the Communist Party.* Translated by S. Moore. New York: International Publishers Co., Inc., 1932.

32. Minkowski, H. "Space and Time." In H. A. Lorentz, A. Einstein, H. Minkowski, and H. Weyl, *The Principle of Relativity: A Collection of Original Memoirs on the Special and General Theory of Relativity.* New York: Dodd, Mead & Co., Inc., 1923.

33. Naval Leadership. Annapolis, Md.: U.S. Naval Institute, 1949.

34. Poincaré, H. "Mathematical Creation." *Sci. American,* 1948, 179: 2, 54-57.

35. *Reader's Digest,* March, 1947.

36. Russell, B. *Principles of Mathematics.* Cambridge: Cambridge University Press, 1903.

37. Russell, B. *Our Knowledge of the External World as a Field for Scientific Method in Philosophy.* La Salle, Ill.: The Open Court Publishing Co., 1915.

38. Russell, B. *Introduction to Mathematical Philosophy* (2d ed.). New York: The Macmillan Co., 1920.

39. Russell, B. *The Analysis of Matter.* New York: Harcourt, Brace & Co., Inc., 1927.

40. Sapir, E. "Conceptual Categories in Primitive Languages." *Science,* 1931, 74, 578.

41. Sapir, E. As quoted in I. J. Lee, *The Language of Wisdom and Folly.* New York: Harper & Bros., 1949.

42. Saunders, J. A. "Memorandum: The New Science of General Semantics." In *Training of Officers for the Naval Service: Hearings before the Committee on Naval Affairs, U.S. Senate,* on S. 2304. June 13 and 14, 1946.

43. Tatum, G. L. *Preliminary Investigation of a Procedure for Conditioning for Discussion.* Unpublished master's thesis, School of Speech, Northwestern University, Evanston, Ill., 1948.

44. Thompson, L. "In Quest of an Heuristic Approach to the Study of Mankind." *Phil. Sci.,* 1946, 13, 53-66.

45. U. S. Senate Calendar No. 549, Report No. 551, July 28, 1945. *Establishing a Research Board for National Security,* submitted by Senator Byrd.

46. U. S. Senate Committee on Naval Affairs. *A Scientific Evaluation of the Proposal that the War and Navy Departments Be Merged into a Single Department of National Defense, March 13, 1946.* Washington, D. C.: U. S. Government Printing Office, 1946.

47. Weyl, H., "The Mathematical Way of Thinking." *Science,* 1940, 92, 437-46. (See also H. Weyl in *Studies in the History of Science.* Philadelphia: University of Pennsylvania Press, 1941.)

48. Whitehead, A. N., *The Principle of Relativity with Applications to Physical Science.* Cambridge: Cambridge University Press, 1922.

49. Whitehead, A. N. *Process and Reality.* New York: The Macmillan Co., 1929.

50. Whorf, B. L. "Languages and Logic." *The Technology Review* (Mass. Inst. of Technology), 1941, 43, No. 6. Also in M. Kendig (ed.), *Papers 2d Amer. Cong. General Semantics*. Lakeville, Conn.: Institute of General Semantics, 1943.

51. Wittgenstein, L. *Tractatus Logico-Philosophicus*. New York: Harcourt, Brace & Co., Inc., 1922.

ADDITIONAL READINGS

Cantril, H., Ames, A., Jr., Hastorf, A. H., & Ittelson, W. H. "Psychology and Scientific Research." *Science*, 1949, 110, 461-64, 491-97, 517-22.

Cassirer, E. *Substance and Function and Einstein's Theory of Relativity*. Translated by W. C. Swabey and Marie C. Swabey. La Salle, Ill.: The Open Court Publishing Co., 1923.

Farrington, B. *Greek Science: Its Meaning for Us (Thales to Aristotle)*. Harmondsworth, England: Penguin Books, 1944.

Frank, P. *Einstein: His Life and Times*. New York: Alfred A. Knopf, Inc., 1947.

Frank, P. *Modern Science and Its Philosophy*. Cambridge, Mass.: Harvard University Press, 1949.

George, W. H. *The Scientist in Action: A Scientific Study of His Methods*. New York: Emerson Books, Inc., 1938.

Hall, R. A., Jr. *Leave Your Language Alone!* Ithaca, N. Y.: Linguistica, 1950.

Keyser, C. J. *The Human Worth of Rigorous Thinking*. New York: Columbia University Press, 1925.

Keyser, C. J. *Mathematics as a Culture Clue: And Other Essays*. New York: Scripta Mathematics, Yeshiva University, 1947.

Lee, I. J. *The Language of Wisdom and Folly*. New York: Harper & Bros., 1949.

Lévy-Bruhl, L., *How Natives Think*. Translated by Lilian A. Clare. New York: Alfred A. Knopf, Inc., 1923.

Meyers, R. "The Nervous System and General Semantics. III. Perceptual Response and the Neurology of Abstraction." *Etc.: A Review of General Semantics*, 1949, 6, 169-96.

Wiener, N. *Cybernetics*. New York: John Wiley & Sons, Inc., 1948.

NOTES

1. Alfred Korzybski died on March 1, 1950, while doing the final editing of this paper. Miss Charlotte Schuchardt, his editorial secretary, in a letter made the following statement regarding the final form of the manuscript :"It should be stated that he did not complete the final editing of this paper. The editing which I did after his death was minor, and I am grateful for the assistance of some members of the Institute staff. Yet I must assume the responsibility both for the slight editing, and also, particularly, for not making editorial changes which he might have made."

2. By permission of Princeton University Press.

3. Arabic-numbered page references to Korzybski's *Science and Sanity* are correct for all editions. References in Roman numerals are to the third edition; for corresponding pages in the second edition, subtract five.

4. By permission of Yale University Press and Mrs. Toni Cassirer.

5. For the research supporting this theory, see Korzybski's *Science and Sanity*.

6. Reprinted from Dorothy Lee, "Being and Value in a Primitive Culture," *Journal of Philosophy* 46, no. 13 (June 23, 1949): 401-15, by permission of the *Journal of Philosophy*.

7. Among the documentations of this are (25) and other works by Dorothy D. Lee; also (44).

8. The following note was supplied by Miss Schuchardt: "It may be clarifying to elaborate briefly on some of Korzybski's views on primitive types of orientation and his use of the term 'primitive,' as I interpret them. It seems to me that he refers to certain complex socio-cultural, psycho-logico-linguistic, etc., levels of development and their attendant orientations found in different areas in the world. Considering our human class of life as a whole, we may assume that developments from 'primitive' to more advanced types of 'pre-scientific,' to 'scientific 1950' orientations, proceeded in degrees here and there, not linearly but, rather, 'spirally' in accordance with our understanding of ourselves and our environments (see pages 49-50). The developments of one culture were usually eventually intermingled with and carried along with transformations by other cultures.

"The reader is referred to (18), in which Korzybski first formulated his new definition of human beings as a 'time-binding class of life,' unique in that one generation can (potentially) begin where the former left off. This process can be handicapped or stifled in many ways. Korzybski stated in another context that 'The human understanding of time-binding as explained here establishes the deductive grounds for a full-fledged "science of man," where both inductive and deductive methods are utilized.... I had to include neuro-linguistic and neuro-semantic (evaluational) environments as environments, and also had to consider geographic, physico-chemical, economic, political, ecological, socio-cultural, etc., conditions as factors which mould human personalities, and so even group behaviour' (23).

"So far the highest orders of abstractions made by man, and those giving the greatest degree of predictability, may be observed in mathematical forms of representations (such as the tensor calculus). To bring to fuller expression the constructive potentialities of man in his ethical, socio-economic, etc., activities, and so keep pace with the achievements in mathematics, science, etc., and their technological consequences, was one of the main aims of Korzybski beginning with *Manhood of Humanity* in 1921.

"There seems no doubt that some primitive types of evaluation still survive in the orientations of most people in present-day Western cultures (and perhaps other cultures also, of which I feel incompetent to speak), involving dichotomies and conflicting premises, as in 'science *versus* religion,' etc. (23).

"I am aware that there are some who take exception to the findings of Lévy-Bruhl, Bois, and others. Korzybski, as far as I know, felt that they conveyed something of value in the analysis of these problems which still remain problems, and will continue to be analyzed with different interpretations and terminologies.—C.S."

9. By permission of Harcourt, Brace & Co., Inc.

10. From A. N. Whitehead, *Process and Reality*. Copyright 1929 by The Macmillan Co., and used with their permission and that of Mrs. A. N. Whitehead.

11. By permission of Cambridge University Press and T. North Whitehead.

12. Reprinted from *The Technology Review*, April 1941, edited at the Massachusetts Institute of Technology.

13. For the significance of the date in small figures, see page 42.

14. In this connection see the following from Korzybski's paper on *Time-binding: The General Theory* (1926): "In my independent inquiry I came across difficulties and had to solve them or quit. My solution is given in the G. T. [General Theory] and the A. [Anthropometer or Structural Differential]. It is found that this theory covers the theory of mathematical types invented by Russell.... I knew about the theory of types long before.... I could not *accept* the theory of types because it is not general enough and does not fit in my system; as far as my work is concerned I had to dismiss it. Scientific method led automatically to a solution of my difficulties; and perhaps no one was more surprised and happy than myself when I found that the G. T. covers the theory of types" (22, second paper, p. 7).

See also *Science and Sanity*, p. 429: "The author was pleasantly surprised to find that after his *A*-system was formulated, this... *non-el* [non-elementalistic] theory covers the theory of mathematical types and generalizes it" (21). C.S.

15. By permission of M. Kendig, editor, *Papers from the Second American Congress on General Semantics* (Lakeville, Conn.: Institute of General Semantics, 1943), and of the author.

16. By permission of J. S. A. Bois.

17. By permission of Douglas M. Kelley, M.D.

18. During the war Dr. Kelley was Chief Consultant in Clinical Psychology and Assistant Consultant in Psychiatry to the European Theater of Operations; also Chief Psychiatrist in charge of the prisoners at Nuremberg.

19. By permission of M. Kendig, editor, *Papers from the Second American Congress on General Semantics* (Lakeville, Conn.: Institute of General Semantics, 1943), and of the author.

20. See (21 pp. xxviii ff.).

21. By permission of *Annals of the New York Academy of Sciences* and the author.

22. By permission of Mrs. C. J. Keyser.

23. By permission of Cambridge University Press.

Section 2

INFLUENCERS OF
INTERPERSONAL COMMUNICATION

Various factors contribute to the way we perceive our worlds of
reality. Around us we have an infinity of stimuli in different forms,
patterns, intensities, rates, and wave lengths that impinge on our
senses—eyes and ears, for example. The accuracy of our perceptions
depends in part, therefore, on the quality and condition of our sense
organs, and, to some degree, on the strength of the stimuli. The
selection by Deese analyzes a number of factors that influence how we
perceive forms and create order out of our perceptions, how we
perceive space relations, and how we perceive sounds. We are suggesting that our visual and auditory perceptions form the bulk of the
sensations that we take into account in interpersonal communication.
Nevertheless, even silence, as described by Hall and Hall, evokes
meaning and aids in the creation of messages in communicating.

Misperception may be said to occur when details are *omitted* (we
fail to perceive all the characteristics of the situation), *added* (we
perceive something that is not actually part of the situation), and/or
distorted (some aspect of the situation is altered to fit expectations,
special interests, motives, or to make the situation consistent
with past perceptions of similar situations).

Problems or difficulties in evaluating a situation are, it is no
doubt true, directly related to misperceptions. Whorf suggests, however,
that our language habits also encourage faulty judgments that lead
to serious consequences. He describes a number of situations in
which the name of the situation affected the behavior of those involved.
The incident of the "empty" gasoline drums and careless tossing of
cigarette stubs may be a familiar experience. His explanation of the
Hopi language as one that analyzes reality in terms of the "eventings"
that occur, rather than in terms of substances and what-we-call-things,
demonstrates the solemn impact of language on how we behave.

Bettinghaus outlines the influence of the source—the communicator himself—on the meaning created by the receiver. Although he couches his analysis in terms of persuasive communication, the principles hold true for any communicative relationship. The key term is "credibility"—that is, the receiver's perception of the communicator's importance in producing change in the situation. If the communicator is perceived as important, he is regarded as having more influence. A careful study of the dimensions of credibility may help to explain why some individuals have more difficulty being understood and accepted than others.

Egan explores the influence of feelings on interpersonal relationships. He is critical of contemporary attitudes toward the expression of feelings when he says, "the best symbol of man as emotional today is the polyethylene bag. Nothing gets in. Nothing gets out." Nevertheless he introduces the concept of "poiesis" to represent the fusion of language and feeling in human communication and recommends its implementation to enrich human dialogue. He deplores the use of meaningless words and unverbalized feelings, charging both as sins against human communication.

Salomon introduces a topic which many of us have experienced but to which few of us have been introduced theoretically and systematically. In our own lives, we are well aware that "while the bulk of the vocabulary doubtless consists of words that carry little or no perceptible emotional charge (lamp, book, read, subtract, through), there are nevertheless a good many that produce reactions of various colors and shades, with voltages ranging from mild to knockout force." The high voltage terms are more often than not taboo. Salomon recognizes the volatile nature of some responses to some words when he states that "at almost any time and place, however, there will be found a few words so heavily frowned upon that by large elements of the population their use, whether in speech or in writing, is regarded as a gross breach of decorum or morals, or both." If, as Korzybski has suggested, words are simply symbols of things and not the things themselves, we have in taboo words a somewhat unique demonstration of the magic of words in evoking responses that suggests words are the things.

The Halls and Julius Fast treat the interesting subjects of silence and body language. "Few of us realize," the Halls assert, "how much we all depend on body movement in our conversation or are aware of the hidden rules that govern listening behavior." You will want to look into the intricacies of nonverbal communication and especially the language of the body in greater depth than we are able to cover it here. Study the unconscious signals you and your friends send each other. You will find something out about yourself, but you will also begin to understand the responses of others to you and you to them.

Perception, language, credibility, feelings, taboo words, gestures and body language, and silence have the capacity and power to influence interpersonal communication. Each of these factors produce unpredictable effects in human reactions. Because we cannot systematize the various influencers of communicative behavior, effective interpersonal relationships depend on a constant awareness of the impact the factors discussed in this section have on the way we relate to others.

James Deese

PERCEPTION

What we see of the world comes through our sense organs—those peep-holes on the swirling energies outside us. But we tell only part of the story when we describe the way in which the sense organs make experience available. The simple fact of seeing cannot be described by saying that we see bits of color which differ in saturation and brightness and which distribute themselves in changing kaleidoscopic patterns across the retina. We see people, trees, houses and mountains.

The basic fact of perception is that we see and hear *things,* not visual and auditory dimensions. That fact is so obvious to the student that he is apt to think the point scarcely needs elaboration or explanation. However, the psychologist makes a distinction between sensing and perceiving. Sensing has to do with the way in which the various sense systems work. Perceiving has to do with how we sense *things.* If we think carefully about the things we see and hear, and compare them with what happens in our sense organs, we face a great intellectual and scientific problem. A simple example illustrates the nature of the problem. . . .

FIGURE 1. *Even though the figure is an unfamiliar and meaningless one, figure-ground relations are well defined. There is no doubt whatever where the figure begins and ends.*

THE PERCEPTION OF FORM

Figure and Ground

All of our perceptual fields can be divided into figure and ground. The identification of the things we see as objects is a consequence of the perception of figure and ground. If this were not so, our perceptual worlds would be undifferentiated mosaics varying in hue, saturation, and brightness, but they would not consist of distinct objects and parts of objects seen against a general background (Koffka, 1935). Likewise, the occasional call of a songbird outside the window would not have the character of a unique sound from a unique source; it would be only a momentary change in the pitch and intensity of the general background of sound assaulting our ears continuously, as our eyes are assaulted by patterns of light and dark as long as we have them open.

Figure 1 shows a form—however meaningless and unnameable—which is clearly seen as a single form against a background. But Figure 2a and Figure 2b are ambiguous; each can be seen not as one form but as two. In Figure 2a, you see the central figure as a vase, or you can see the peripheral figure as two faces in profile. A figure or form is something that appears to stand out. In both Figures 1 and 2, the contour dividing the figure from the ground appears to be a property of the figure or form; but depending upon how you see Figure 2a, the contour will either be a vase or the profiles. The ground is more or less undifferentiated, and it appears to extend behind the figure. In further treatment of ambiguous figure-ground relationships, we shall continue to refer to the vase/profiles figure (Figure 2a) since it is one of the simplest and best known examples.

Why is the figure in 2a ambiguous? Certainly, some of the conditions for the perception of form would favor the vase rather than the two profiles, and, indeed, this is usually the *first* figure seen by a viewer. On the other hand, the contour can belong either to the vase or to the profiles. Here our experience helps, for if the vase were not in the shape of the familiar human profile, reversibility of the contour would be difficult to achieve. Indeed, it would be impossible for some people. Therefore, experience plays some role in determining where the contour belongs and which is figure and which ground. Experience, however, is not the only determiner of contour, and if we are to understand the figure-ground relationship we must know what does determine the contour (Rubin, 1921).

Contour. Contour is a sudden change in brightness or color. It is virtually impossible for a large change in brightness to occur over a short distance without producing the impression of a sharp line—a contour. In Figure 3 you see two square areas in which the shading changes from a light to a dark gray. One of these changes produces a vague, indefinite effect like the deepening of the sky at twilight. In the other square, however, the same amount of change occurs over a very small distance; the result is that the figure is sharply divided in the middle (see Woodworth and Schlosberg, 1954).

Whenever a change is gradual, a form is hard to see. In some experiments figures were prepared that were in between the two figures in Figure 3. These produced contours that could be seen at one moment but not at the next. If you look at such a barely perceivable contour for a long time, it will disappear. Such a result is an example of the tendency of the whole visual system to adapt to steady stimula-

FIGURE 2. *Two famous examples of reversible figure-ground relationships. In the top figure,* a, *you can see either a vase or two faces in profile. In the bottom figure,* b, *you can see either the head and neck of a young woman or the face of an old woman. With both of these examples, if you continue to gaze at the figure for a while, the figure-ground relation will spontaneously change back and forth.*

After W. E. Hill, from *Foundations of Psychology*, 1948, by Boring, Langfeld, and Weld. Reprinted by permission of the publisher, John Wiley & Sons, Inc.

tion. If, in fact, the visual image of a scene were to be held perfectly steady on your retina for a period of time, you would soon lose the ability to perceive that scene.

If your eye then shifted a tiny bit, you could once more see the image projected on your retina. We cannot, under ordinary conditions, hold an image perfectly steady because there are tiny, uncontrollable movements of the eyes and of the head. These movements make a continuously shifting pattern of light and dark across the retinal sense cells. At one moment a given cell may be stimulated by light reflected from a bright surface, and at the next moment may not be stimulated because a tiny movement of the eye has brought a dark surface into position to cast its image on that cell.

 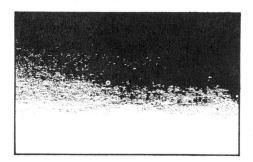

FIGURE 3. *The abrupt change produces a contour and, therefore, a figure. The gradual change does so less easily if at all. A contour is produced whenever there is a rapid rate of change in brightness, hue, or saturation across a limited space. The goodness of a contour depends upon the magnitude of the change and its rapidity.*

The perception of a clear, sharp contour depends upon these tiny eye movements. That is because individual receptors in the eye adapt very rapidly. The dependence of contour upon tiny eye movements can be demonstrated by an experiment in which all movement of the visual image ceases. Such a situation is described as a stopped-image experiment.

FIGURE 4. *The Yang and Yin Figure. There is no clear figure-ground relation in the form. The contour dividing the form belongs indifferently to either half.*

In the stopped-image experiment, a pattern is projected into the eye (Riggs, *et al.,* 1953). Attached to the eye by a contact lens is a small mirror. The mirror reflects the image of the pattern back to another reflecting surface. It is the image from that surface that the eye actually sees. The image is absolutely stationary with respect to the retina, for every time the eye moves, the image also moves.

If a ring of light is projected on a dark background with this device, it will be easily seen at first. As the same retinal elements are continuously stimulated by the ring of light, they adapt. The contour will gradually fade so that the ring of light can no longer be seen. Partial recovery may happen and the ring may momentarily reappear.

This experiment suggests that the perception of a sharp contour depends on some interaction between neighboring receptor cells. Because the eyes are continuously in movement, new elements are being stimulated by the same image. Such movement makes it possible for us to see fine lines, such as a black thread suspended against a light background.

Contour defines shape. Things that have weak contours have vaguely defined shapes. While contour defines shape, it is not the same as shape. The contour is merely a point of division; shape is determined by what is perceived as a figure. If you inspect the reversible figures in Figure 2a you can see that the contour sometimes defines the shape of a vase, and it sometimes defines the human profiles.

Part of the perception of a figure is determined by the continuity of contour. A nonsense figure will be best perceived as a figure when the contour is seen as completely enclosing it. Forms like the Yang and Yin symbol (a traditional Chinese religious symbol) have no figure-ground relationship (Figure 4). That is because no one part is more enclosed by contour than another. It is, perhaps, this property that yields some of the symbolic value of the diagram. Also, the vase is easier to see in Figure 2a because it makes a continuous contour; we can easily imagine the background to extend behind the figure. The continuity of contour is not so obvious for the profiles.

The Nature of Forms. Some forms are meaningful and others are not. Familiar forms that outline well-known objects are meaningful; they are meaningful if they match the schematic shapes of things we have experienced and remember. Nearly all outlines can be said to resemble something in a fanciful way, but the fussier and more elaborate the contour, the more difficult it is to match the form with the remembered schema.

Forms vary in their simplicity and these variations have interested psychologists because they seem to be fundamental to perception. There are some properties of forms which appear that way just because our eyes and brains are built the way they are.

In order to describe the organization that produces the shapes and forms of things in perception, we need to turn to the description of the organization of the entire field. If we can describe the organization of the entire visual field in a sensible way, we can understand how parts of the field go together to form objects in perception.

The Principles of Organization

Contours and figure-ground relationships are important to perceptual organization, but they do not tell us how different forms are seen as belonging in a group or as similar to one another. That aspect of organization has been most intensively studied by the Gestalt psychologists (Köhler, 1947).

The Gestalt psychologists, who were originally a group of German students of visual perception, took as their principal approach to the study of perception what has come to be known as **phenomenalism.** The word phenomenalism has many subtle meanings, but in the psychological sense it means the description of things as they are in sensory experience. Phenomenal description should be divorced, as far as possible, from preconceived ideas about the dimensions of experience or about the underlying causes of sensory experience. It should be the simple description of how things actually appear in experience.

From their phenomenal study of perception, the Gestalt psychologists were able to state a number of descriptive principles of perceptual organization. These principles are sometimes called the *Gestalt laws of perception.*

Proximity and Resemblance. The first principle is proximity. Things located together or close to one another in the visual (or auditory) field tend to be grouped together. Proximity is the basis for the obvious and compelling organization in Figure 5.

Proximity occurs in auditory experience, though here it takes the form of a temporal grouping. Regular, repetitive sounds become grouped into rhythmic patterns on the basis of temporal separation. In fact, such grouping is the basis of many familiar musical motives—such as, for example, the opening four notes of Beethoven's Fifth Symphony.

Objects also tend to be grouped by resemblance. The repetitive patterns you see in Figure 6 resolve themselves into groups of figures based upon similarity between the parts. The cross in Figure 6 is made insistently perceptible by the identity of the closed dots which contrast with the open dots. Even when open dots intervene between closed dots, as they do in Figure 6, the closed dots are unified into a pattern.

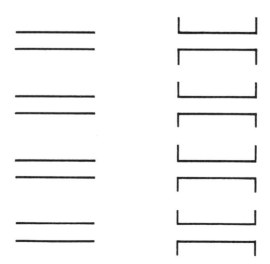

FIGURE 5. *Perceptual grouping by proximity. In the first set of figures simple proximity produces a grouping. In the second set, the direction of the added lines reverses the pattern of grouping.*

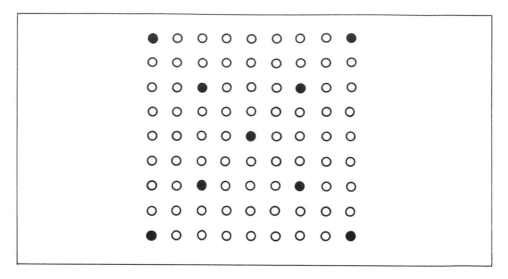

FIGURE 6. *The filled circles group themselves to form a figure (the cross). The grouping occurs even though the closed circles are separated by open figures.*

Good Form. What induces us to see the cross in Figure 6? The resemblance of the closed dots to one another is only part of the answer, for if they were randomly arranged (to make a randomly shaped form) we would not necessarily see them as belonging together. The cross, in the language of the Gestalt psychologists, is a *good form* and good forms are inevitably and naturally perceived as such.

The Gestalt psychologists have developed elaborate theories about good forms; they believe such forms are determined by innate organization in the perceptual system. Here are some of the criteria of good form.

CONTINUATION. Elements, such as the dots in Figure 6, tend to continue lines. The continuation will go on as long as the forms made by the elements are regular and simple. As long as the eye can easily sweep along a line, continuation exists. There is no continuation in Figure 7. If the eye fixates on any one of the dots, it is just as likely to move one way or another. There is no particular direction that provides good continuation.

SYMMETRY. Symmetry is another principle of good form. Simple forms may generally be completed by making one part a mirror image of another. The simplest form is the circle which not only is symmetrical but is everywhere the same. Symmetrical figures are redundant; it is possible to reconstruct the whole from some part.

A complicated form, like the one in Figure 8, cannot be reconstructed from one of its parts. It is not symmetrical and it is not, in the Gestalt sense, a good form.

CLOSURE AND COMMON FATE. Two other Gestalt principles, which are perhaps less important, are closure and common fate. *Closure* refers to a tendency to close or complete a figure, or to more easily perceive a figure that is closed or completed. *Common fate* refers to the selection and perception of parts of a figure that seem to

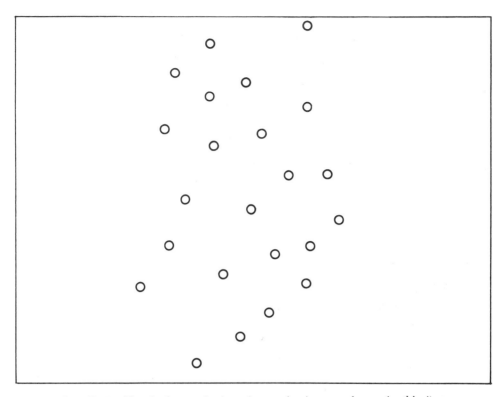

FIGURE 7. *No single continuity of organization stands out in this figure.*

FIGURE 8. *An asymmetrical figure. It is difficult to predict what one part of the contour of this figure will be from other parts.*

move in some common direction. Perhaps these principles have more to do with the aesthetics of visual perception than with principles of organization.

The Search for Order. What do these Gestalt principles of organization mean? Perhaps what they emphasize the most is the importance of our need and search for order, regularity, and correlation in what we perceive. We perceive more easily (and

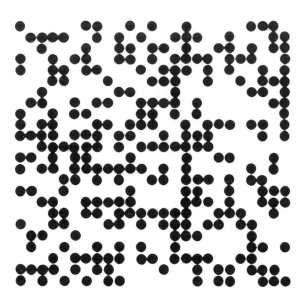

FIGURE 9. *A random arrangement. The figure was made from a table of random numbers. Circles were filled in if they carried even numbers. Despite the randomness, perceptual patterns emerge.*

remember, for similar reasons) those things which are simple and well oganized. Chaos, indeed, is difficult to perceive as such. Figure 9 is the result of a completely random, chaotic selection of small dots in the field. Notice, however, how difficult it is to avoid selecting parts of the field to organize and perceive as relatively good forms.

Good forms are simple forms. They are also complicated forms in which the parts are regular, redundant, symmetrical, or correlated with one another (see Garner, 1962). Simple forms are forms in which one part of the figure is predictable from another part of the figure. Any regular contour implies predictability, for you can easily fill in the missing part of any regular contour when some small part is missing. That is what enables us to perceive a simple and familiar form in the chaotic pattern found in Figure 10.

Illusions. The connection between the physical stimulus, the image it casts upon the retina, and conscious perception is not so simple as we sometimes think. In the last chapter we saw some of the complications in the relations between the stimulus and the retinal image, and in this chapter we shall find examples of puzzling relations between perception and the physical stimulus as well as between the perception and the image.

The Gestalt psychologists have argued that the physical stimulus, the retinal image, and perception are connected by nothing more elaborate than a kind of isomorphism (Köhler, 1947). *Isomorphism* means "similarity of form," and in the study of perception the term refers to the fact that for every region or point in the physical stimulus there is a corresponding point or region in the image and in percep-

FIGURE 10. *The predictability of familiar contours enables us to perceive a familiar object even though few details are given. Reprinted by permission of the publisher from Roy F. Street,* A Gestalt Completion Test *(New York: Teachers College Press, 1931), p. 41. Copyright 1931, by Teachers College, Columbia University.*

tion. There may be, however, considerable "distortion" between the regions or points. For example, a very peculiar trapezoid may project an even more peculiar outline (with, perhaps, curved edges) on the retina and yet be perceived as a square.

Even a simple straight line produces complications. A straight line does not project a straight line on the retina. For one thing, the retina is curved. For another, the lens of the human eye is not corrected for spherical aberration. Thus, every straight line projects a slightly curved line onto the retina, though that image is transformed into a straight line in perception. Furthermore, by virtue of the aberrations in the lenses and other optical media of the eyes, the visual world should wobble and change shape as we shake our heads. Except under rare circumstances it does not. Thus, in normal perception there is correction for such distortion. That correction depends upon perceptual adaptation, but the main point at present is that there is seldom a simple correspondence between the physical world and perception (see experiments by Köhler, 1962).

All of this leads us to the topic of illusions. In view of the fact that there is not a perfect correspondence between external reality and our perception of it, it is difficult to define some special case of faulty correspondence as illusory. Illusions are indeed special cases, but they are not simply cases in which there is a lack of correspondence between reality and perception—there are many examples of that. Illusions are cases in which the distortion is such that a particular perception is inconsistent wtih or incongruous with respect to some other perceptions. Something is perceptually out of kilter in an illusion. A very nice example is the continuous staircase illusion in Figure 11. Other illusions have to do with distortions in plane figures. A celebrated example is the Müller-Lyer illusion. Still others are illustrated in Figure 12.

Most illusions depend upon the apparent displacement of contours or lines by the presence of other contours or lines. Therefore, they serve to illustrate spatial interactions in the visual system. Illusions make it clear that what happens at one particular location in the perceptual field depends upon what happens at other points.

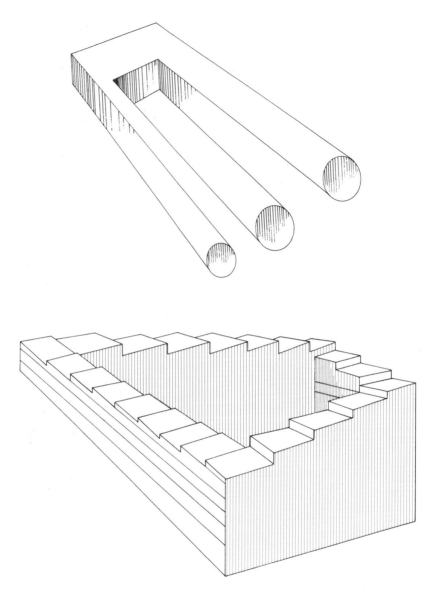

FIGURE 11. *Two well-known illusions. In the continuous staircase the impression is created that the stairs descend (or ascend) continuously, and yet they form a continuous, closed path. The illusion is so insistent that even a detailed following of the design (which is difficult to do) does not destroy it. A similar effect holds with the strange forked figure. This one has been widely reproduced.*

Most illusions, then, are special cases of spatial interactions in the visual system. We are not always certain whether that interaction takes place within the central nervous system or at the level of the retina, but for most illusions we expect the central nervous system to be the most important locus. An exception may be the dynamic illusion in Figure 13. If you shake the page while examining this figure, you

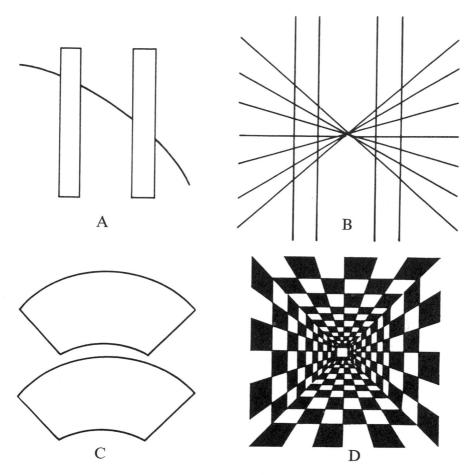

FIGURE 12. *A variety of distortions that can be introduced into the perception of figures in planes. A: Where the interrupted line emerges from the rectangles, it appears to be a different line from the one that entered on the other side. B: The straight lines appear to bow outward in the middle. C: The bottom figure appears to be larger than the top one. D: The two-dimensional figure appears to have depth.*

will notice the "creation" of rotary motion. Also, after you inspect this figure for twenty seconds or so you will notice that it distorts the lines of print when you look at them. Therefore, some illusions produce and are produced by temporal as well as spatial interactions. . . .

VISUAL SPACE PERCEPTION

Our visual world is a space filled with objects at various orientations and at different distances from one another. The problem of how this space is perceived has fascinated thinkers from the beginning of reflective thought. Projective geometry, as an intellectual exercise, had its origin in the problem of the projection of a three-dimensional world on a two-dimensional surface, such as the eye. Painters have

FIGURE 13. *A dynamic illusion. These effects are by now familiar through the fad of op art. If you jiggle the figure, the effect is even more striking.*

thought about, experimented with, and written about the problems of representing the three-dimensional space of the world upon the flat surface of a picture. Psychologists have speculated about how it is that a retinal image, a slightly curved two-dimensional projection of objects in space, can produce, in our perception, such an immediate and spontaneous feeling of depth.

We can readily identify a picture as a picture. No matter how skilled the artist at representing the world, a picture is but a two-dimensional representation of something that has three dimensions. The eye does something more than see a projection like the artist's picture. The naive man on the street sees his visual world as a real world; he sees objects in motion, not a series of motion-picture stills projected on his retina and transmitted by nerve cells acting as a kind of television cable to the brain.

The immediate reality of the visual world sometimes makes the psychologist's discussion of cues to depth perception seem unrealistic. We don't, in our everyday life, get cues that enable us to make judgments about the distances of things, as if we were playing a game of hide and seek. We see things as they are. When, however, the psychologist attempts to understand how it is that we see things this way, he resorts to analysis of the conditions that are responsible for the way in which we see things. When he studies depth perception, he tries to find which aspects of visual perception are important by removing them one at a time or in combination to see what happens to the ability to perceive and judge depth. Out of such work, he arrives at scientific rules and principles that describe the conditions necessary for human beings to perceive their visual worlds in the way they do. The mistake is in supposing that the scientific principles so discovered are cues or clues to visual depth, and that these allow us to make judgments such as "that building is farther away than the tree." We don't ordinarily make such judgments; we simply accept our perception of the greater distance of the building. The way things are to a naive observer, however, is the result of the operation of man's perceptual system; the kind of scientific principles of space perception that we shall describe are accounts of how that system works.

Monocular Conditions

The conditions that contribute to the normal perception of three-dimensional space are traditionally divided into two classes; those conditions available to an individual with only one functioning eye, and those conditions available to an individual with two eyes. The former are monocular conditions and the latter binocular.

There is little in the way of such a division in visual experience. It takes some sophistication and practice to become directly aware of the difference between the perception of space with one eye and with two (try it by comparing the world around you examined first by one eye then by two). The ability to make fine *judgments* of distance, however, depends most critically on the use of both eyes.

The Perspective Conditions. The most primitive aspect of our visual world is that there is a kind of gradient of texture across it (Gibson, 1950). As the ground, the floor, or any surface (railway tracks, for example) recedes into the distance, the large-grained pattern of the foreground gives way to a finer grained pattern and finally to indistinctness. All geometric lines that are, in the external world, parallel, converge in the distance. The whole world seems to be drawn to a point somewhere on the horizon.

This texture of the world is immediately given (what students of visual perception describe as "phenomenally"), though we are likely not to notice it unless someone calls our attention to it. The effects of texture and perspective are provided by the optical laws of visual projection. Any object projects an image to the eye which varies inversely in size with the square of the distance of the object from the eye.

The conditions of perspective are frequently broken down into several separate aspects. Among these are texture, size, and linear perspective. Texture and size are clearly related to one another, for it is the size of the bits and particles in the visual field which determines texture. Likewise, size and linear perspective are related. Phenomenally, however, each of these conditions is a bit different, and it is psychologically justifiable to discuss them separately.

TEXTURE. Texture describes the fine structure of the visual field, and it is closely related to what is called *microstructure*. The microstructure of objects is that property which enables us to perceive objects as having surfaces (Katz, 1935).

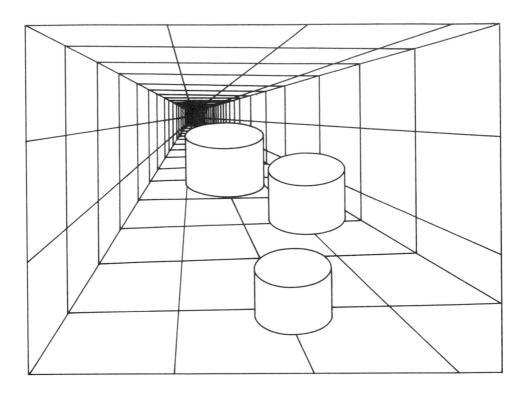

FIGURE 14. *The dependence of apparent size on the perception of receding surfaces. The cylinders are all the same size. (From Gibson, 1950.)*

A quite simple demonstration reveals the importance of microstructure in the perception of surface. A color wheel is set up a short distance away from the viewer, and under good illumination. A color wheel is a vari-colored disc mounted on a motor (like an ordinary fan). When the motor is going at high speed, the disc revolves so fast as to wash out all detail (minor blemishes, etc.) on the surface. It is viewed through a small aperture which can be made by rolling a piece of paper or by using a screen with a hole in it. When a bit of the surface of the color wheel is viewed through an aperture when the disc is stationary, it appears to be pretty much what it is—a bit of uniformly colored cardboard. When the color wheel is set in rotation, however, something else happens. Now the color wheel takes on a filmy and indefinite quality. It is not like a surface at all; it is rather like the sky. That is because the rotation of the wheel washes out the tiny imperfections and marks on the surface of the wheel. When the wheel is still these blemishes mark a surface as a surface; they are the microstructure. Microstructure is needed to perceive a surface as a surface. That is why a very high ceiling (as in a church) sometimes looks like the sky—it is too far away to see the microstructure. If a very smooth wall is viewed through an aperture under low illumination from some distance, the same indefinite filmy quality will result. The wall is smooth enough and far enough away not to present any discriminable surface imperfections to the eye (Katz, 1935).

A field that is perfectly flat (a sandy desert) may present a continuous gradation of microstructure all the way from the rough-grained foreground to the distant

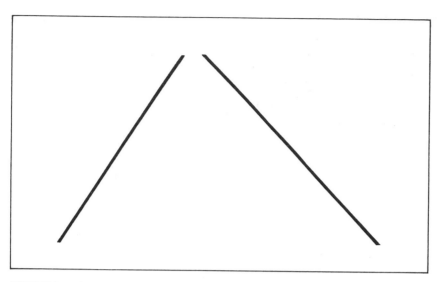

FIGURE 15. *Two lines that meet on a plane surface can suggest either a gradient of receding distance or a triangle in a plane that is perpendicular to the line of sight.*

surface which may have the filmy quality of the color wheel in rotation. Such a texture gradient is phenomenally perceived in conscious experience as depth.

SIZE. Size yields depth only by relation. There is a principle of size constancy. Therefore, we are able to perceive the distance of objects (and their sizes) only in other objects around them. Familiar objects can yield absolute interpretations of depth because we know how big they are and can bring judgment into play. Size illusions are common because we can vary the relations between the sizes and distances of familiar objects to produce illusory perception. Figure 14 (Gibson, 1950) is a good example.

LINEAR PERSPECTIVE. Linear perspective is just another way of interpreting size. The railroad tracks converge in the distance, though through size constancy we see them as simply receding, not as set at angles to one another. A simple triangle (Figure 15) can be interpreted as two lines converging in the distance or as just an upright triangle.

THE BASIS OF PERSPECTIVE. These effects—change of size with distance, linear perspective, and the texture gradient—are all conditions of perspective. They result from the projection of the three-dimensional world onto the two-dimensional surface of the retina. In this respect, the visual image on the retina is like a photograph. From the point of view of projective geometry, there is no need to distinguish among the aspects of perspective; they all follow mathematically from the principles of projective geometry. However, J. J. Gibson (1950) has argued that one of them, texture, is psychologically more fundamental. It is responsible, Gibson has argued, for the phenomenal impression—the immediate experience—of depth in our visual perception of the three-dimensional world. We may well perceive a small image of an automobile as being distant and a large image of a similar automobile as being near because of our past experience with automobiles. In a sense, then, thought or cogni-

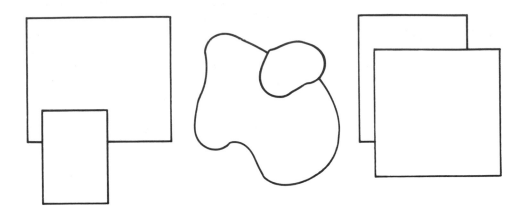

FIGURE 16. *Interposition. A contour that is interrupted places the figure made by that contour in the background.*

tion may be as much a determiner of perception as is the use of size as a cue for depth. Texture, however, is much more fundamental. In fact, we may not have to learn to interpret texture at all. If this is the case, the impression of depth that comes from a texture gradient from top to bottom in the visual field is innate. Thus, even though size, linear perspective and texture are all geometrically identical cues of depth, the peculiar phenomenal characteristics of texture may make it psychologicaly more fundamental.

Other Monocular Conditions. Much of our visual perception of space is the result of motion in the visual field. Imagine what can be seen from a railroad car. Telephone poles and other structures near the tracks fly by so fast you barely can see them, while a barn a mile or so from the tracks barely seems to move at all.

The apparent motion of objects in the visual field when you move your head is called **movement parallax.** You can produce movement parallax just by fixating some object across the room and moving your head back and forth. Objects in the foreground seem to move relative to the background. Hold your fingers a few inches from your face and observe how your fingers move relative to something on the wall. If you can hold your finger steady enough, you will be able to see that even a very tiny movement of the head produces a perceptible movement of the finger.

Movement parallax provides easy precise cues for *judgments* of depth in space, and people sometimes use movement parallax for exactly that purpose. If a one-eyed person moves his head while aligning two objects at the same distance from the eye, he will align about as accurately as a person with two eyes. So far as accuracy of discrimination is concerned, movement parallax is about the most precise of the monocular conditions of depth perception.

Movement of the whole visual field is important to the perception of movement in depth. If you walk along a narrow hallway looking straight ahead, you will notice that the walls and ceiling near you rush back of your head at a fast rate, but you can scarcely detect any change near the end of the hall. Such an effect is most important to the illusion of motion, and it is the main feature of the spectacular illusions of motion in motion pictures such as Cinerama.

Other aspects of the monocular perception of depth are complicated and depend upon our perception of forms. For example, there is an effect called interposition. That is a condition in which our view of one object is partially obscured by something else. Out of my window I can see two buildings. One is farther away than the other, and a corner of that building is obscured by the nearer building. My perception of the relative position of these buildings is influenced by my knowledge that the farther building is complete—in a sense it is part of the ground that is continuously behind the figure of the nearer building.

Interposition can be seen with abstract figures on a plane surface (see Figure 16). This has led to the notion that interposition is a direct result of the interruption of contours, and that it has little or nothing to do with our experience (which tells us that buildings and other things cut off by objects in the foreground are complete). Such an idea may be true in part, but experience does play an important role in our normal perception of interposition.

Shadows, or more specifically light and shade, are also responsible for the perception of depth. Consider the two circles in Figure 17. One is uniform in shade

FIGURE 17. *Shading and highlighting produce a perception of depth. (After Gibson, 1950.)*

and appears to be flat. The other has a gradient of brightness which gives it the appearance of a ball on which the light falls. Such an effect is much like the texture gradient, except that the gradient is not with respect to the eye but with respect to a source of light. The brightness gradient shows where an object is relative to the source of light. In the real world we perceive objects relative to their sources of illumination. How we perceive depth depends upon how we perceive the illumination (see Figure 18). . . .

AUDITORY PERCEPTION

Most of the study of auditory perception has centered around speech and music, two of the more interesting kinds of sounds to human beings. There has also been a lively interest in auditory space perception, and we shall examine that topic also.

The Perception of Speech

It is almost remarkable that we understand one another. Our speech is a pattern of different sound energies produced by the vocal cords and the vocal resonators. Speech varies through time and it varies in the pattern of frequencies and intensities it contains.

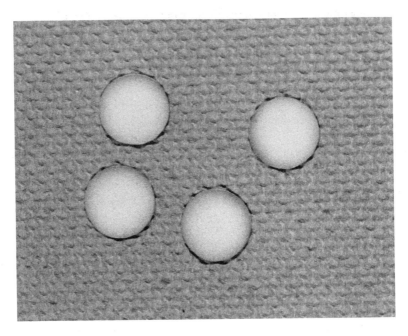

FIGURE 18. *The perception of depth depends upon the perceived source of illumination. The round objects in this photograph are flat pieces of paper that have been shaded. The shading gives the impression that light is striking three-dimensional objects.*

For example, the characteristic which differentiates the vowel sound in "bees" and "buys" is a different range of frequencies produced by the voice. Figure 19 (Licklider and Miller, 1951) shows the pattern of frequencies produced as some words are spoken. Notice that the voice is not sharply tuned. Each vowel, and even more, each consonant produces a broad range in frequency, each of which lasts for a short period of time. The frequency pattern for the "ee" sound in "bees" is not very different from the "eye" sound in "buys." Vowels are mainly distinguished by two or more resonant frequencies called *formants*. These are produced by the shape of the mouth. The mouth resonates at different frequencies when it is in different shapes. Consonant sounds are noisy, and they differ mainly in whether the noise is continuous, interrupted or abruptly stopped. There are also some sounds, such as "l" and "r" that are intermediate between vowels and consonants.

Small differences create problems and, in addition, speakers are not alike in the way in which they produce various speech sounds. For one thing, everyone has more or less characteristic voice qualities produced by the fundamental frequencies of the vocal cords and by the resonating cavities of the mouth. Each person's speech is different from occasion to occasion, though we are able to recognize certain features as constant.

The features of speech that we recognize as constant are the *phonemes*. Within any language, a phoneme is the smallest element that serves to distinguish between utterances in the language or in dialects of it. Even though the exact pattern of frequencies varies from occasion to occasion when we say a given vowel (the "ah"

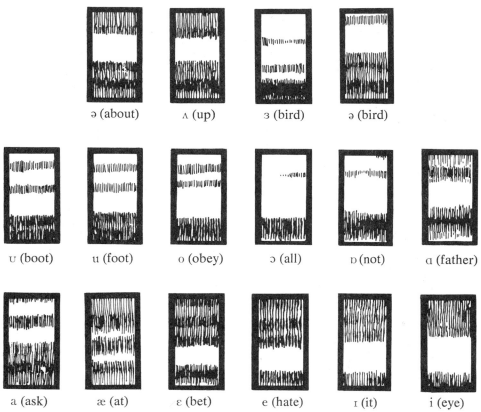

ə (about)   ʌ (up)   ɜ (bird)   ə (bird)

ʊ (boot)   u (foot)   o (obey)   ɔ (all)   ɒ (not)   ɑ (father)

a (ask)   æ (at)   ɛ (bet)   e (hate)   ɪ (it)   i (eye)

FIGURE 19. *Some spectrograms of vowel sounds. Each frame is a time-frequency graph. The frequency of the various sounds is given by the dark bands (higher frequencies on top). The duration of the sound is given by the base. (From Licklider and Miller, 1951.)*

sound in "lot," for example), there is something stable enough in the vowel sound to make it clear that the word is "lot" and not "let."

Listening to speech is rather like reading something poorly printed in which the Q's and O's are sometimes indistinguishable. No matter how poor the quality of the print, however, there is not a continuous variation between Q and O. There is no letter "somewhere in between." Therefore, we can decide that it is one letter or the other, even though sometimes we decide erroneously. Thus it is with phonemes. Even though the individual phonemes of a language vary from occasion to occasion, we perceive each variation of a given phoneme as that phoneme or possibly mistake it for another, but we never hear it as something in between.

We learn the sounds of our own native language. When we learn a new language, we find it hard to hear many new sounds, new phonemes. Our inability to reproduce the sounds used by a native speaker means that we speak the new language with an accent. Even though our accent varies from the accepted pattern of the new language, our speech is assimilated by those who speak the language; they hear the phonemes of the language—even though we do not speak them. In fact, our listeners *construct* in part what they *think* we said.

Redundancy in Speech

Fortunately, we do not have to perceive each sound in speech in order to understand it. Speech is redundant, and even when someone speaks carelessly, so that the distinction between different speech sounds is poor, we can understand that speech. Information is transmitted by other sounds which we can hear accurately (Miller, 1951).

In English, the consonants and vowels are not equally important. The vowels last longer than the consonants, and they constitute more of our speech than do the consonants. Nevertheless, it is the consonants that provide most of the information that allows us to discriminate one word from another. That is also true of printed language. Here is an example: *th prcptn f spch dpnds mr pn cnsnnts* (the perception of speech depends more upon consonants). You could probably puzzle out much of that example correctly, but you would make little headway with *e eeio o ee ee oe uo ooa.*

Vowels are both low and high in frequency, though most of the energy in the sounds of vowels is produced in lower frequencies. As we go through the series *e, i, u, o,* the contribution of low frequencies increases. Consonants are largely high-frequency sounds; that is particularly true of the unvoiced consonants. Unvoiced sounds are produced without the vocal cords vibrating. The hissing "sh" or the little explosion of sound in "tee" are unvoiced, high-frequency consonants.

All this means that the higher frequencies of speech—which occur in consonants —are more important to understanding, even though most of the energy in speech is concentrated in the lower regions of the speech-frequency spectrum (see Licklider and Miller, 1951), As a practical matter, speech can easily be understood in a communication system that cuts out or filters the low frequencies. Such speech seems different, but it is intelligible. The change in a person's voice when he speaks over the telephone is the result of the relatively poor quality of reception on a home telephone; it filters out the low frequencies which give a certain body to speech. Nevertheless, you seldom have real difficulty in understanding someone on the telephone (unless there is a masking sound).

Auditory Space Perception

The auditory world, as well as the visual world, is special. Sounds have location— direction and distance. The ear, however, is functionally very different from the eye, and the means by which it detects direction and distance are very different.

For one thing, the detection of direction of sound is almost entirely dependent upon perception through two ears (Woodworth and Schlosberg, 1954). If you have only one good ear, it is still possible to locate the direction of continuous sound, but you must move your head to do so. It is not possible to tell the direction of a sound with one ear if you hold your head perfectly still.

It is possible, of course, to tell direction with but one eye. That is because the retina itself detects the spatial location of objects in the visual field. The spatial mechanism in the ear, however, is given over to the differential perception of pitch, and there is no way for one ear alone to tell the direction of a sound without changing position. We locate sounds by comparing the input from the two ears.

Time Differences and the Perception of Direction. Figure 20 shows a sound source radiating sound to the human ear under a number of circumstances. Consider the

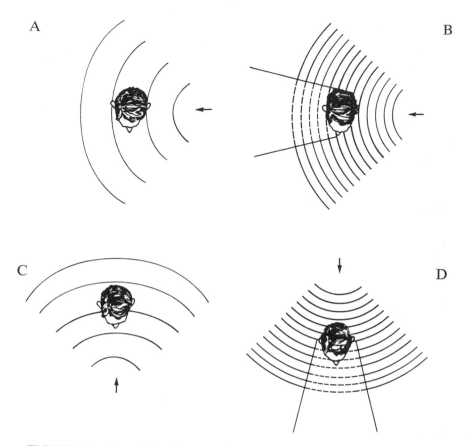

FIGURE 20. *The relation between the two ears and source of sound. In diagram A there is no sound shadow. One ear, however, gets the leading edge of the sound before the other. In diagram B, the small waves cannot bend around the head, therefore one ear is in a sound shadow. In diagram C, both ears receive the sound at the same time and there is no sound shadow. In diagram D, the pinnae of the ears create weak sound shadows for very high-frequency sounds.*

first case in Figure 20. Here the sound comes from the side of the head. Any given wave (including the initiation of the sound) reaches one ear before it reaches the other. Sound travels at approximately one thousand feet per second, and the distance between the two ears is much less than one foot. There is, then, a difference of less than 1/1000 of a second in the arrival time between the two ears, and, incredible as this may seem, such a difference can be detected (Woodworth and Schlosberg, 1954). This detection ability is, in part, responsible for perception of direction of a sound source.

The perception of direction by the time difference of sound reaching the two ears can be demonstrated by means of an experiment in which a person listens to two short clicks over two earphones. If the clicks are delivered to the two earphones simultaneously, the resulting single click seems to have no location—indeed, the subject may say that it seems to come from the middle of his own head.

If a click is delivered to one ear at something less than 1/1000 of a second before it is delivered to the other, the subject will report the click as coming from (located on) the side of the leading click. If the second click is delayed too much— as much as 1/100 of a second after the first—the subject will report two clicks, one on each side. Thus, clicks with extremely short intervals separating them are *perceived as the same sound,* and the source of the sound is perceived as being on the side of the leading click.

Intensity Differences and the Perception of Direction. There are other ways in which a sound coming from the side of head can be localized. Look again at Figure 20, this time at the second example. Here the sound source is again to the side of the head. This time, however, there is a "sound shadow" drawn on the side of the head opposite the source. Why is there a sound shadow in this figure and not in the first? Because the first example illustrates the effect of the head on *low-frequency* waves. Large waves bend around a small object like the head quite easily, so there is no sound shadow for low frequencies. High-frequency waves, however, do not bend around the head, and so the head creates a sound shadow.

The sound shadow makes an intensity difference between the two ears. Such an intensity difference can be perceived, and it yields sound localization. The source of the sound is located on the side of the greater intensity.

An experiment similar to that of the clicks separated by short intervals can be made using two different intensities. When the intensity differences are above threshold values, the subject will report the sound as located on the side of greater intensity (Stevens and Davis, 1958).

Accuracy of Sound Localization. The two remaining examples in Figure 20 illustrate the localization of sound sources directly behind the head. For sources located behind or in front of the head, there is no difference in the time of arrival at the two ears. Therefore, time differences cannot be the basis for the perception of location.

There is a very slight sound shadow for high-frequency sounds located behind the head; it is created by the pinnae of the ears. The shadow is about the same for both ears, however, and, since we cannot independently move the pinnae of our ears, we cannot use such a shadow (unless we move our heads). Many animals can use such shadows created by the pinnae. Observe a cat attending to some auditory stimulus. It may move its ears quite independently; in this way, it is able to produce sharp sound shadows for high-frequency sounds.

Figure 20 implies that the localization of sound should be best when the sound source is lateral and worst when the sound source is in the front or back of the head. Such is actually the case. Of course, under most circumstances we are free to move our heads, and if we wish to localize the source of some mysterious sound, that is exactly what we do. We orient our heads in different directions until we can detect the direction of the sound.

In the ordinary course of things, there is continuous interplay between the senses of sight and sound. Observe a television screen in which the loudspeaker is placed at the side or extreme bottom of the set. With no picture visible, the sound may be clearly perceived as emanating from the loudspeaker. Turn the picture on, however, and the sound of voices will now irresistibly be seen to come from the people on the screen. Past experience operates to fuse the localization coming to the separate senses.

When we listen to live music, we are usually aware that the music comes from a spread-out source. That is particularly the case with a symphony concert or a musical play in which the separate sound sources are far apart. Such perception is based upon the differences in the patterns of time and intensity of the separate sounds arriving at the ears.

It is possible to recapture completely the spatial locations of musical instruments by setting two microphones on either side of a dummy head. The output from these two microphones, suitably amplified, is led separately to appropriate earphones. The result is complete fidelity to the perception of spatial location; it is true stereophonic reproduction (Stevens and Davis, 1958).

What is ordinarily called the stereophonic effect, however, is only an approximation of this situation. In the familiar case, the output from two channels is fed separately to two speakers. Both ears hear both speakers, of course, but one ear is dominated by the speaker on its side (if the hearer is properly located—ask a hi-fi addict) and the other ear by its speaker. The result is a fair approximation of the perception of spread-out sound sources.

Auditory Motion Perception. Essentially the same conditions responsible for the perception of auditory location are responsible for the perception of a sound source that is moving. If the first click in a series of clicks, for example, arrives at the two ears simultaneously and subsequent clicks arrive at one of the ears a few milliseconds before they arrive at the other, the sound source will be perceived as having moved, even though the clicks are delivered separately by means of earphones.

In addition, there are a number of curious features about auditory perception. Movement with respect to the observer may be detected by the **Doppler principle.** As we approach a continuous sound source (or it approaches us), the pitch of the sound will appear to rise. That is because the distances between successive waves emitted by the source are shorter. When the sound source recedes, the pitch falls because the wave-lengths of the successive waves gradually increase. Of course, the velocity of movement must be great in order for a change of pitch to be detected. The familiar zoom of an approaching racing car and the noticeable change in the sound of a railroad crossing signal as the train speeds are good examples....

CONCLUSION

What we perceive at any time is the result of the intrinsic, innate organization of our nervous systems and the result of our past experience. The perceptual experience of people the world over is very much the same, but where we find differences in experiences we are apt to find differences in modes of perception.

REFERENCES

Garner, W. R. (1962) *Uncertainty and Structure as Psychological Concepts.* New York: Wiley.

Gibson, J. J. (1950) *The Perception of the Visual World.* Boston: Houghton Mifflin.

Katz, D. (1935) *The World of Color* (translated by R. B. MacLeod and C. W. Fox). London: Kegan, Paul.

Koffka, K. (1935) *Principles of Gestalt Psychology*. New York: Harcourt, Brace.

Kohler, I. (1962) Experiments with Goggles. *Scientific American*, Vol. 204, No. 5.

Kohler, W. (1947) *Gestalt Psychology* (2nd ed.). New York: Liveright.

Licklider, J. R., and Miller, G. A. (1951) "The Perception of Speech." In S. S. Stevens (Ed.), *Handbook of Experimental Psychology*. New York: Wiley.

Miller, G. A. (1951) *Language and Communication*. New York: McGraw-Hill.

Riggs, L. A., Ratliff, F., Cornsweet, J. C., and Cornsweet, T. (1953) "The Disappearance of Steadily Fixated Visual Test Objects." *Journal of Opt. Soc. Amer.*, Vol. 43, 495-501.

Rubin, E. (1921) *Visuell Wahrgenomme Figuren*. Copenhagen: Gyldenalska.

Stevens, S. S., and Davis, H. (1938) *Hearing*. New York: Wiley.

Woodworth, R. S., and Schlosberg, H. (1954) *Experimental Psychology*. (Rev. ed.) New York: Holt.

Benjamin Lee Whorf

THE RELATION OF HABITUAL THOUGHT
AND BEHAVIOR TO LANGUAGE

Human beings do not live in the objective world alone, nor alone in the world of social activity as ordinarily understood, but are very much at the mercy of the particular language which has become the medium of expression for their society. It is quite an illusion to imagine that one adjusts to reality essentially without the use of language and that language is merely an incidental means of solving specific problems of communication or reflection. The fact of the matter is that the "real world" is to a large extent unconsciously built up on the language habits of the group. . . . We see and hear and otherwise experience very largely as we do because the language habits of our community predispose certain choices of interpretation.
—Edward Sapir, "The Status of Linguistics as a Science," *Language*, V (1929), pp. 209-210.

There will probably be general assent to the proposition that an accepted pattern of using words is often prior to certain lines of thinking and forms of behavior, but he who assents often sees in such a statement nothing more than a platitudinous recognition of the hypnotic power of philosophical and learned terminology on the one hand or of catchwords, slogans, and rallying cries on the other. To see only thus far is to miss the point of one of the important interconnections which Sapir saw between language, culture, and psychology, and succinctly expressed in the introductory quotation. It is not so much in these special uses of language as in its constant ways of arranging data and its most ordinary everyday analysis of phenomena that we need to recognize the influence it has on other activities, cultural and personal.

THE NAME OF THE SITUATION AS AFFECTING BEHAVIOR

I came in touch with an aspect of this problem before I had studied under Dr. Sapir, and in a field usually considered remote from linguistics. It was in the course of my professional work for a fine insurance company, in which I undertook the task of analyzing many hundreds of reports of circumstances surrounding the start of fires, and, in some cases, of explosions. My analysis was directed toward purely physical

Excerpted from *Language, Culture, and Personality: Essays in Memory of Edward Sapir*, edited by Leslie Spier, A. Irving Hallowell, and Stanley S. Newman (Menasha, Wisconsin, 1941). Reprinted by permission of the Sapir Memorial Publication Fund.

conditions, such as defective wiring, presence or lack of air spaces between metal flues and woodwork, etc., and the results were presented in these terms. Indeed it was undertaken with no thought that any other significances would or could be revealed. But in due course it became evident that not only a physical situation, *qua* physics, but the meaning of that situation to people was sometimes a factor, through the behavior of the people, in the start of the fire. And this factor of meaning was clearest when it was a *linguistic meaning*, residing in the name or the linguistic description commonly applied to the situation. Thus around a storage of what are called "gasoline drums" behavior will tend to a certain type, that is, great care will be exercised; while around a storage of what are called "empty gasoline drums" it will tend to be different—careless, with little repression of smoking or of tossing cigarette stubs about. Yet the "empty drums" are perhaps the more dangerous, since they contain explosive vapor. Physically the situation is hazardous, but the linguistic analysis according to regular analogy must employ the word "empty," which inevitably suggests lack of hazard. The word "empty" is used in two linguistic patterns: (1) as a virtual synonym for "null and void, negative, inert," (2) applied in analysis of physical situations without regard to, e.g., vapor, liquid vestiges, or stray rubbish, in the container. The situation is named in one pattern (2) and the name is then "acted out" or "lived up to" in another (1), this being a general formula for the linguistic conditioning of behavior into hazardous forms.

In a wood distillation plant the metal stills were insulated with a composition prepared from limestone and called at the plant "spun limestone." No attempt was made to protect this covering from excessive heat or the contact of flame. After a period of use the fire below one of the stills spread to the "limestone," which to everyone's great surprise burned vigorously. Exposure to acetic acid fumes from the stills had converted part of the limestone (calcium carbonate) to calcium acetate. This when heated in a fire decomposes, forming inflammable acetone. Behavior that tolerated fire close to the covering was induced by the use of the name "limestone," which because it ends in "stone" implies noncombustibility.

A huge iron kettle of boiling varnish was observed to be overheated, nearing the temperature at which it would ignite. The operator moved it off the fire and and ran it on its wheels to a distance, but did not cover it. In a minute or so the varnish ignited. Here the linguistic influence is more complex; it is due to the metaphorical objectifying (of which more later) of "cause" as contact or the spatial juxtaposition of "things"—to analyzing the situation as "on" versus "off" the fire. In reality the stage when the external fire was the main factor had passed; the overheating was now an internal process of convection in the varnish from the intensely heated kettle, and still continued when "off" the fire.

An electric glow heater on the wall was little used, and for one workman had the meaning of a convenient coat hanger. At night a watchman entered and snapped a switch, which action he verbalized as "turning on the light." No light appeared, and this result he verbalized as "light is burned out." He could not see the glow of the heater because of the old coat hung on it. Soon the heater ignited the coat, which set fire to the building.

A tannery discharged waste water containing animal matter into an outdoor settling basin partly roofed with wood and partly open. This situation is one that ordinarily would be verbalized as "pool of water." A workman had occasion to light a blowtorch nearby, and threw his match into the water. But the decomposing waste matter was evolving gas under the wood cover, so that the setup was the reverse of "watery." An instant flare of flame ignited the woodwork, and the fire quickly spread into the adjoining building.

A drying room for hides was arranged with a blower at one end to make a current of air along the room and thence outdoors through a vent at the other end. Fire started at a hot bearing on the blower, which blew the flames directly into the hides and fanned them along the room, destroying the entire stock. This hazardous setup followed naturally from the term "blower" with its linguistic equivalence to "that which blows," implying that its function necessarily is to "blow." Also its function is verbalized as "blowing air for drying," overlooking that it can blow other things, e.g., flames and sparks. In reality a blower simply makes a current of air and can exhaust as well as blow. It should have been installed at the vent end to *draw* the air over the hides, then through the hazard (its own casing and bearings) and thence outdoors.

Beside a coal-fired melting pot for lead reclaiming was dumped a pile of "scrap lead"—a misleading verbalization, for it consisted of the lead sheets of old radio condensers, which still had paraffin paper between them. Soon the paraffin blazed up and fired the roof, half of which was burned off.

Such examples, which could be greatly multiplied, will suffice to show how the cue to a certain line of behavior is often given by the analogies of the linguistic formula in which the situation is spoken of, and by which to some degree it is analyzed, classified, and allotted its place in that world which is "to a large extent unconsciously built up on the language habits of the group." And we always assume that the linguistic analysis made by our group reflects reality better than it does.

GRAMMATICAL PATTERNS AS INTERPRETATIONS OF EXPERIENCE

The linguistic material in the above examples is limited to single words, phrases, and patterns of limited range. One cannot study the behavioral compulsiveness of such material without suspecting a much more far-reaching compulsion from large-scale patterning of grammatical categories, such as plurality, gender, and similar classifications (animate, inanimate, etc.), tenses, voices, and other verb forms, classifications of the type of "parts of speech," and the matter of whether a given experience is denoted by a unit morpheme, an inflected word, or a syntactical combination. A category such as number (singular vs. plural) is an attempted interpretation of a whole large order of experience virtually of the world or of nature; it attempts to say how experience is to be segmented, what experience is to be called "one" and what "several." But the difficulty of appraising such a far-reaching influence is great because of its background character, because of the difficulty of standing aside from our own language, which is a habit and a cultural *non est disputandum*, and scrutinizing it objectively. And if we take a very dissimilar language, this language becomes a part of nature, and we even do to it what we have already done to nature. We tend to think in our own language in order to examine the exotic language. Or we find the task of unraveling the purely morphological intricacies so gigantic that it seems to absorb all else. Yet the problem, though difficult, is feasible; and the best approach is through an exotic language, for in its study we are at long last pushed willy-nilly out of our ruts. Then we find that the exotic language is a mirror held up to our own.

In my study of the Hopi language, what I now see as an opportunity to work on this problem was first thrust upon me before I was clearly aware of the problem. The seemingly endless task of describing the morphology did finally end. Yet it was evident, especially in the light of Sapir's lectures on Navaho, that the description of the *language* was far from complete. I knew for example the morphological formation of plurals, but not how to use plurals. It was evident that the category of plural in Hopi was not the same thing as in English, French, or German. Certain things that were plural in these languages were singular in Hopi. The phase of investigation which now began consumed nearly two more years.

The work began to assume the character of a comparison between Hopi and Western European languages. It also became evident that even the grammar of Hopi bore a relation to Hopi culture, and the grammar of European tongues to our own Western or European culture. And it appeared that the interrelation brought in those large subsummations of experience by language, such as our terms "time," "space," "substance," and "matter." Since with respect to the traits compared there is little difference between English, French, German, or other European languages with the *possible* (but doubtful) exception of Balto-Slavic and non-Indo-European, I have lumped these languages into one group called SAE, or Standard Average European.

That portion of the whole investigation here to be reported may be summed up in two questions: (1) Are our own concepts of "time," "space," and "matter" given in substantially the same form by experience to all men, or are they in part conditioned by the structure of particular languages (2) Are there traceable affinities between (a) cultural and behavioral norms and (b) large-scale linguistic patterns? I should be the last to pretend that there is anything so definite as " a correlation" between culture and language, and especially between ethnological rubrics such as "agricultural," "hunting," etc., and linguistic ones like "inflected," "synthetic," or "isolating."[1] When I began the study the problem was by no means so clearly formulated and I had little notion that the answers would turn out as they did.

PLURALITY AND NUMERATION IN SAE AND HOPI

In our language, that is SAE, plurality and cardinal numbers are applied in two ways: to real plurals and to imaginary plurals. Or more exactly, if less tersely, perceptible spatial aggregates and metaphorical aggregates. We say "ten men" and also "ten days." Ten men either are or could be objectively perceived as ten, ten in one group-perception[2]—ten men on a street corner, for instance. But "ten days" cannot be objectively experienced. We experience only one day, today; the other nine (or even all ten) are something conjured up from memory or imagination. If "ten days" be regarded as a group it must be as an "imaginary," mentally constructed group. Whence comes this mental pattern? Just as in the case of the fire-causing errors, from the fact that our language confuses the two different situations, has but one pattern for both. When we speak of ten steps forward, ten strokes on a bell, or any similarly described cyclic sequence, "times" of any sort, we are doing the same thing as with "days." *Cyclicity* brings the response of imaginary plurals. But a likeness of cyclicity to aggregates is not unmistakably given by experience prior to language, or it would be found in all languages, and it is not.

Our *awareness* of time and cyclicity does contain something immediate and subjective—the basic sense of "becoming later and later." But in the habitual thought of us SAE people this is covered under something quite different, which though mental should not be called subjective. I call it *objectified,* or imaginary, because it is patterned on the *outer* world. It is this that reflects our linguistic usage. Our tongue makes no distinction between numbers counted on discrete entities and numbers that are simply counting itself. Habitual thought then assumes that in the latter case the numbers are just as much counted on *something* as in the former. This is objectification. Concepts of time lose contact with the subjective experience of "becoming later" and are objectified as counted *quantities,* especially as lengths, made up of units as a length can be visible marked off into inches. A "length of time" is envisioned as a row of similar units, like a row of bottles.

In Hopi there is a different linguistic situation. Plurals and cardinals are used only for entities that form or can form an objective group. There are no imaginary plurals, but instead ordinals used with singulars. Such an expression as "ten days" is not used. The equivalent statement is an operational one that reaches one day by a suitable count. "They stayed ten days" becomes "they stayed until the eleventh day" or "they left after the tenth day." "Ten days is greater than nine days" becomes "the tenth day is later than the ninth." Our "length of time" is not regarded as a length but as a relation between two events in lateness. Instead of our linguistically promoted objectification of that datum of consciousness we call "time," the Hopi language has not laid down any pattern that would cloak the subjective "becoming later" that is the essence of time. . . .

HABITUAL THOUGHT IN SAE AND HOPI

The comparison now to be made between the habitual thought worlds of SAE and Hopi speakers is of course incomplete. It is possible only to touch upon certain dominant contrasts that appear to stem from the linguistic differences already noted. By "habitual thought" and "thought world" I mean more than simply language, i.e., than the linguistic patterns themselves. I include all the analogical and suggestive value of the patterns (e.g., our "imaginary space" and its distant implications), and all the give-and-take between languages and the culture as a whole, wherein is a vast amount that is not linguistic yet shows the shaping influence of language. In brief, this "thought world" is the microcosm that each man carries about within himself, by which he measures and understands what he can of the macrocosm.

The SAE microcosm has analyzed reality largely in terms of what it calls "things" (bodies and quasi-bodies) plus modes of extensional but formless existence that it calls "substance" or "matter." It tends to see existence through a binomial formula that expresses any existent as a spatial form plus a spatial formless continuum related to the form as content is related to the outlines of its container. Nonspatial existents are imaginatively spatialized and charged with similar implications of form and continuum.

The Hopi microcosm seems to have analyzed reality largely in terms of *events* (or better "eventing"), referred to in two ways, objective and subjective. Objectively, and only if perceptible physical experience, events are expressed mainly as outlines, colors, movements, and other perceptive reports. Subjectively, for both the physical and nonphysical events are considered the expression of invisible intensity-factors, on which depend their stability and persistence, or their fugitiveness and proclivities. It implies that existents do not "become later and later" all in the same way; but some do so by growing, like plants, some by diffusing and vanishing, some by a procession of metamorphoses, some by enduring in one shape till affected by violent forces. In the nature of each existent able to manifest as a definite whole is the power of its own mode of duration; its growth, decline, stability, cyclicity, or creativeness. Everything is thus already "prepared" for the way it now manifests by earlier phases, and what it will be later, partly has been, and partly is in act of being so "prepared." An emphasis and importance rest on this preparing or being prepared aspect of the world that may to the Hopi correspond to that "quality of reality" that "matter" or "stuff" has for us.

HABITUAL BEHAVIOR FEATURES OF HOPI CULTURE

Our behavior, and that of Hopi, can be seen to be co-ordinated in many ways to the linguistically conditioned microcosm. As in any fire casebook, people act about situations in ways which are like the ways they talk about them. A characteristic of Hopi behavior is the emphasis on preparation. This includes announcing and getting ready for events well beforehand, elaborate precautions to insure persistence of desired conditions, and stress on good will as the preparer of right results. Consider the analogies of the day-counting pattern alone. Time is mainly reckoned "by day" (taⳑk, -tala) or "by night" (tok), which words are not nouns but tensors, the first formed on a root "light, day," the second on a root "sleep." The count is by *ordinals*. This is not the pattern of counting a number of different men or things, even though they appear successively, for even then they *could* gather into an assemblage. It is the pattern of counting successive reappearancs of the *same* man or thing, incapable of forming an assemblage. The analogy is not to behave about day-cyclicity as to several men ("several days"), which is what *we* tend to do, but to behave as to the successive visits of the *same man*. One does not alter several men by working upon just one, but one can prepare and so alter the later visits of the same man by working to affect the visit he is making now. This is the way the Hopi deal with the future— by working within a present situation which is expected to carry impresses, both obvious and occult, forward into the future event of interest. One might say that Hopi society understands our proverb "Well begun is half done," but not our "Tomorrow is another day." This may explain much in Hopi character.

This Hopi preparing behavior may be roughly divided into announcing, outer preparing, inner preparing, covert participation, and persistence. Announcing, or preparative publicity, is an important function in the hands of a special official, the Crier Chief. Outer preparing is preparation involving much visible activity, not all necessarily directly useful within our understanding. It includes ordinary practising, rehearsing, getting ready, introductory formalities, preparing of special food, etc. (all of these to a degree that may seem overelaborate to us), intensive sustained muscular activity like running, racing, dancing, which is thought to increase the intensity of development of events (such as growth of crops), mimetic and other magic, preparations based on esoteric theory involving perhaps occult instruments like prayer sticks, prayer feathers, and prayer meal, and finally the great cyclic ceremonies and dances, which have the significance of preparing rain and crops.

From one of the verbs meaning "prepare" is derived the noun for "harvest" or "crop": na'twani "the prepared" or the "in preparation."[3]

Inner preparing is use of prayer and meditation, and at lesser intensity good wishes and good will, to further desired results. Hopi attitudes stress the power of desire and thought. With their microcosm it is utterly natural that they should. Desire and thought are the earliest, and therefore the most important, most critical and crucial stage of preparing. Moreover, to the Hopi, one's desires and thoughts influence not only his own actions, but all nature. This too is wholly natural. Consciousness itself is aware of work, of the feel of effort and energy, in desire and thinking. Experience more basic than language tells us that if energy is expended effects are produced. *We* tend to believe that our bodies can stop up this energy, prevent it from affecting other things until we will our *bodies* to overt action. But this may be only because we have our own linguistic basis for a theory that formless items like "matter" are things in themselves, malleable only by similar things, by more matter, and hence insulated from the powers of life and thought. It is no more unnatural to think that thought contacts everything and pervades the universe than to think, as we all do, that light kindled outdoors does this. And it is not unnatural to suppose that thought, like any other force, leaves everywhere traces of effect. Now when *we* think of a certain actual rosebush, we do not suppose that our thought goes to that actual bush, and engages with it, like a searchlight turned upon it. What then do we suppose our consciousness is dealing with when we are thinking of that rosebush? Probably we think it is dealing with a "mental image" which is not the rosebush but a mental surrogate of it. But why should it be *natural* to think that our thought deals with a surrogate and not with the real rosebush? Quite possibly because we are dimly aware that we carry about with us a whole imaginary space, full of mental surrogates. To us, mental surrogates are old familiar fare. Along with the images of imaginary space, which we perhaps secretly know to be imaginary only, we tuck the thought-of actually existing rosebush, which may be quite another story, perhaps just because we have that very convenient "place" for it. The Hopi thought-world has no imaginary space. The corollary to this is that it may not locate thought dealing with real space anywhere but in real space, nor insulate real space from the effects of thought. A Hopi would naturally suppose that his thought (or he himself) traffics with the actual rosebush—or more like, corn plant—that he is thinking about. The thought then should leave some trace of itself with the plant in the field. If it is a good thought, one about health and growth, it is good for the plant; if a bad thought, the reverse.

The Hopi emphasize the intensity-factor of thought. Thought to be most effective should be vivid in consciousness, definite, steady, sustained, charged with strongly felt good intentions. They render the idea in English as "concentrating," "hold it in your heart," "putting your mind to it," "earnestly hoping." Thought power is the force behind ceremonies, prayer sticks, ritual smoking, etc. The prayer pipe is regarded as an aid to "concentrating" (so said my informant). Its name, na'twanpi, means "instrument of preparing."

Covert participation is mental collaboration from people who do not take part in the actual affair, be it a job of work, hunt, race, or ceremony, but direct their thought and good will toward the affair's success. Announcements often seek to enlist the support of such mental helpers as well as of overt participants, and contain exhortations to the people to aid with their active good will.[4] A similarity to our concepts of a sympathetic audience or the cheering section at a football game should not obscure the fact that it is primarily the power of directed thought and not merely sympathy or encouragement, that is expected of covert participants. In fact these latter get in their deadliest work before, not during, the game! A corollary to the power of thought is the power of wrong thought for evil; hence one purpose of covert participation is to obtain the mass force of many good wishers to offset the harmful thought of ill wishers. Such attitudes greatly favor co-operation and community spirit. Not that the Hopi community is not full of rivalries and colliding interests. Against the tendency to social disintegration in such a small, isolated group, the theory of "preparing" by the power of thought, logically leading to the great power of the combined, intensified and harmonized thought of the whole community, must help vastly toward the rather remarkable degree of co-operation that in spite of much private bickering the Hopi village displays in all the important cultural activities.

Hopi "preparing" activities again show a result of their linguistic thought background in an emphasis on persistence and constant insistent repetition. A sense of the cumulative value of innumerable small momenta is dulled by an objectified, spatialized view of time like ours, enhanced by a way of thinking close to the subjective awareness of duration, of the ceaseless "latering" of events. To us, for whom time is a motion on a space, unvarying repetition seems to scatter its force along a row of units of that space, and be wasted. To the Hopi, for whom time is not a motion but a "getting later" of everything that has ever been done, unvarying repetition is not wasted but accumulated. It is storing up an invisible change that holds over into later events.[11] As we have seen, it is as if the return of the day were felt as the return of the same person, a little older but with all the impresses of yesterday, not as "another day," i.e., like an entirely different person. This principle joined with that of thought-power and with traits of general Pueblo culture is expressed in the theory of the Hopi ceremonial dance for furthering rain and crops, as well as in its short, piston-like tread, repeated thousands of times, hour after hour.

NOTES

1. We have plenty of evidence that this is not the case. Consider only the Hopi and the Ute, with languages that on the overt morphological and lexical level are as similar as, say, English and German. The idea of "correlation" between language and culture, in the generally accepted sense of correlation, is certainly a mistaken one.

2. As we say, "ten at the *same* time," showing that in our language and thought we restate the fact of group-perception in terms of a concept "time," the large linguistic component of which will appear in the course of this paper.

3. The Hopi verbs of preparing naturally do not correspond neatly to our "prepare"; so that na'twani could also be rendered "the practised-upon," "the tried-for," and otherwise.

4. See, e.g., Ernest Beaglehole, Notes on Hopi Economic Life (Yale University Publications in Anthropology, No. 15, 1937), especially the reference to the announcement of a rabbit hunt, and on p. 30, description of the activities in connection with the cleaning of Toreva Spring—announcing, various preparing activities, and finally, preparing the continuity of the good results already obtained and the continued flow of the spring.

Erwin P. Bettinghaus

THE INFLUENCE OF
THE COMMUNICATOR

Some communicators are better at persuasion than others. Most people can agree easily that this is true and can cite some of the reasons why. These reasons could include better preparation on the part of some communicators, better delivery of a speech, better writing, more effective use of gestures to carry ideas, and similar reasons. Some people, however, when asked why they think the statement is true, may decline to cite specific reasons. They may say something like, "I don't know why! But I do know that some people have it, and some don't." The intent of this chapter is to examine the communicator, the source of persuasive messages, and attempt to pinpoint what the quality is that some people have and some apparently do not have.

The notion that the source of communication is extremely important in understanding the entire process can be found at least as far back as the ancient Greeks. Aristotle looked on the speaker as a force just as important as the receivers or the message itself. His words translate in a manner difficult to disagree with today:

> Persuasion is achieved by the speaker's personal character when the speech is so spoken as to make us think him credible. We believe good men more fully and more readily than others: This is true generally whatever the question is, and absolutely true where exact certainty is impossible and opinions are divided. . . . It is not true, as some writers assume in their treatises on rhetoric, that the personal goodness revealed by the speaker contributes nothing to his power of persuasion: on the contrary, his character may almost be called the most effective means of persuasion he possesses.[1]

Telling the communicator that to be effective he must be a good man, is of little help to him unless he is also told how to go about becoming a more effective source. To aid the source in being more effective, it is necessary to examine source characteristics relevant to receiver perceptions.

The influence that a source might exert on the outcome of any persuasive communication situation cannot be examined solely by identifying physical or social characteristics of varying sources. Such characteristics will influence the behavior

of a receiver only to the extent that they are perceived by the receiver as being important. In the research literature there are three strains that look at the same problem
of source influence: source credibility, status, and opinion leadership. In addition
to these areas, which emphasize differences between receiver perceptions of the
source and of the self, there is a research strain that looks at similarities between
source and receiver. Finally, this chapter will examine *charisma,* a set of characteristics possessed by some sources that seems to defy analysis.

SOURCE CREDIBILITY RESEARCH

The literature relating to the importance of the source in persuasive communication
stems from many origins. The Greeks referred to the *ethos* that the speaker had.
Early theologians talked about charisma. Management trainers and small-group
theorists have talked about leadership. Other terms which have seen wide application
include image, status, prestige, and source credibility. Regardless of the term used,
the variable being referred to is the same. For the sake of simplicity, the term "source
credibility" will be used here to refer to the communicator's importance in the persuasive communication situation.

A hypothetical example will help in arriving at a definition of credibility. Imagine that a speech is prepared calling for fair housing legislation. The speech is put
into the form of a tape recording by someone. Then researchers collect two audiences
randomly drawn from a city and find out what their attitude toward fair housing is.
The investigators determine that there are no apparent differences between the two
groups of people with respect to their prespeech attitude toward fair housing. Then
the investigators let the two groups listen to the speech, but with a difference between
the two presentations. For one presentation they announce the playing of the tape
by saying that the speaker is the mayor of East Lansing, Michigan. For the other
presentation they announce that the speaker is a member of the Junior Chamber of
Commerce of East Lansing. After the tape is finished, the investigators again ascertain
the attitudes of the two groups. Imagine that they find the group which thought they
heard the Mayor had changed significantly more in favor of fair housing than did
the group which was told they were hearing the Junior Chamber of Commerce member. Since the tapes are exactly the same, and since the groups were similar in their
original attitudes, the only conclusion to be drawn is that the differences between
the two groups must be due to a difference in perceived *credibility* between the two
sources. This example represents the basic paradigm under which much credibility
research has been conducted. The experimenter holds the message constant, uses
equivalent audiences, and then systematically varies the characteristics of the communicator in his effort to find out what factors attributable to the source are
persuasive.

There are a number of studies that establish credibility as an important factor
in communication. Haiman[2] used a design almost exactly like our hypothetical
example, with the topic of the speech being socialized medicine and the supposed
speakers being the Surgeon General of the United States and a student at Northwestern University. The results of the study showed more attitude change for the
group hearing the Surgeon General of the United States. Hovland, Janis, and Kelley[3]
report a study in which written messages were used and the sources included both

individuals and institutions, for example, J. Robert Oppenheimer and *Pravda*. Again the results of this study suggested that individuals or institutions possessing more credibility are also more effective in persuasion.

In these two studies the assumption is made that credibility is a variable much like sex; that is, that people either do or do not have credibility and that it is relatively easy to determine who has it and who does not. For many situations, in which it is possible to compare the probable credibility of two individuals, accurate predictions as to the relative credibility of two individuals are possible. Most people would have little trouble in agreeing that the Surgeon General of the United States, the Secretary of State, and a United States senator will have more credibility than will a high school senior, a plumber, and a television repairman. Will these people always be evaluated as having high credibility on the one side and low credibility on the other? Probably not. Imagine that the topic concerns the way in which the plumbing has been installed in the new city hall. The mayor of the city makes a speech defending the installation. He is opposed by one of the city's master plumbers, who holds that the job was badly done and that the city paid too much for the job. Will the mayor possess more credibility in this situation than the master plumber? Many people may not be sure of their answer in such a situation.

The problem is that credibility is not a single characteristic of an individual, such as age or sex. Neither is it a set of characteristics, such as socio-economic position. Credibility is a set of perceptions by the receiver. Characteristics of the source like age, sex, or socio-economic status may affect the perceptions that the receiver has, and thus such characteristics become relevant to the study of credibility. In the example the difference between the Secretary of State and a television repairman is a difference of role position as it might be perceived by a receiver. The difference between the mayor and the master plumber is also a difference in role position, but if the plumber is viewed as more credible in the particular situation described, credibility must be assumed to come from perceived competence differences between the two sources.

Hovland, Janis, and Kelley[4] in the study already mentioned suggest that credibility seems to depend on two factors: the *competence* or *expertness* ascribed to the source by the receiver and the *trustworthiness* ascribed to the source by the receiver. Expertness or competence is seen more specifically as a task-related variable, while trustworthiness is a more general characteristic. Other studies have tended to treat credibility as either a single-factor variable that is general in nature, and will carry over from one situation to another, or as a factor that is specific only to a given situation. Thus Marple[5] makes the assumption that credibility is based on some factor of general trustworthiness and that it will remain relatively constant over a number of subjects. Lorge,[6] on the other hand, suggests that credibility will vary from topic to topic and that the influence of the source will be different in different situations and for different topics.

The most careful examination of source credibility has been given by Berlo, Lemert, and Mertz.[7] They followed procedures developed by Osgood, Tannenbaum, and Suci[8] to measure connotative meaning and applied their procedures as an analogous methodology to the systematic rating of varying sources. Essentially, the method consisted of developing a set of polar adjectives like good–bad, right–wrong, clear–unclear, and competent–incompetent, placing the adjectives at either end of a seven-point scale, and having groups of subjects rate a number of sources on each scale. An illustration (Figure 1) shows the appearance of the kind of rating scale used by Berlo and his associates.

FIGURE 1. *An Example of a Rating Scale*

Lyndon B. Johnson

Pleasant_____:_____:_____:_____:_____:_____:_____Unpleasant

Skilled_____:_____:_____:_____:_____:_____:_____Unskilled

Active_____:_____:_____:_____:_____:_____:_____Passive

Safe_____:_____:_____:_____:_____:_____:_____Dangerous

Sincere_____:_____:_____:_____:_____:_____:_____Insincere

    In their preliminary studies as many as eighty-three different scales were used. The preliminary analysis showed that some of the scales did not seem to apply to the sources being rated, and they were discarded. In their final study a total of thirty-five different scales were used, and twelve different sources were rated. The sources included public figures, who were placed within a situational context that seemed relevant to the individual and within another, irrelevant complex — for example, James R. Hoffa as a source on abstract art — as well as a series of interpersonal sources selected by the receiver. Each respondent was asked to rate all twelve sources on each of the thirty-five different scales. The ratings were then analyzed by the methods of factor analysis to find out whether there seemed to be common ways of judging sources and whether there were similar intensities of judgment recorded by the receivers for each of the sources.

    The results of the Berlo, Lemert, and Mertz research indicate that there are three dimensions, or factors, which people use in judging the credibility of various sources. The first factor that they identify is termed a *safety* factor. It seems analogous to the trustworthiness factor hypothesized by Hovland, Janis, and Kelley. A second was labeled a *qualification* factor, which seems much like the expertness factor suggested by Hovland and his associates. The third factor isolated by Berlo can be identified as a *dynamism* dimension. This third factor accounts for less variance than the first two dimensions but does stand out as a separate and independent judgment dimension. Each of these three dimensions needs more discussion.

Safety

The safety dimension seems to be characterized by the use of scales having some relation to general personality traits. Thus a communicator who would score *high,* or very safe, on this dimension could be characterized as kind, congenial, friendly, agreeable, pleasant, gentle, unselfish, just, forgiving, fair, hospitable, warm, cheerful, sociable, ethical, calm, and patient. A given source may not be rated with high intensity on each and every one of these scales, but he would have been rated high on the majority of the scales for the group of subjects. An individual considered *low,* or very dangerous, by the group would be characterized by high intensity loadings on a set of scales that are the opposite of the safe scales. These include cruel, dangerous, quarrelsome, unfriendly, disagreeable, unpleasant, harsh, selfish, unjust, unforgiving, unfair, inhospitable, cool, gloomy, unsociable, unethical, upset, and impatient. Again, a particular source need not be rated unsafe on each of these terms, but the over-all pattern of rating would be in the direction of the unsafe terms.

Qualification

The qualification dimension consists of scales that are related to the impression the receiver has of the source's competency or training for the topic with which the source is associated. It is an independent dimension from either dynamism or safety, which means that knowing how an individual marks scales on the safety dimension for a variety of sources does not help in predicting what he will mark on the qualification dimension for the same group of sources. There is no necessary correlation between the dimensions. A person rated high on qualification would be considered to be trained, experienced, qualified, skilled, informed, authoritative, able, and intelligent. A source rated low on the qualification dimension might be characterized by some or all of the following terms: untrained, inexperienced, unqualified, unskilled, uninformed, unauthoritative, inept, and unintelligent.

Dynamism

Dynamism accounts for less variance than either safety or qualification, and many receivers apparently do not make use of the qualities of dynamism in judging source credibility. The majority of receivers, however, seem to judge the credibility of a communicator, in part, by the appearance he makes as either a dynamic or undynamic person. A source rated high on the dynamism factor would be described as aggressive, emphatic, frank, forceful, bold, active, energetic, and fast. A communicator rated as low on the dynamism factor would be described as meek, hesitant, reserved, forceful, timid, passive, tired, and slow. Although there was some evidence that the dynamism factor is not as stable as the other two factors, Berlo and his associates concluded that it is a meaningful factor that receivers use in judging message sources.

Each of the three dimensions of source credibility has been discussed in detail. For each one there is a set of perceived characteristics that receivers use to describe highly credible or less credible sources. If an individual communicator was rated by each of his receivers as possessing all of the characteristics of the highly credible source, the supposition would be that such an individual would have, *because of his perceived personal characteristics,* great persuasive abilities. One hypothesis would be that the topic the source was talking about would not make much difference, because his personality would be the deciding force in producing attitude change. Similarly, an individual who was rated on all of the scales as having low source credibility would be unsuccessful in persuasion, no matter what his subject was. Thus, if the leader of the Communist People's party in Communist China were to give a speech advocating Chinese withdrawal from Southeast Asia, most Americans would probably express great doubt and suspicion about the speech as a result of the low credibility that the leader of the Communist party in China would have for them. The same speech by the Secretary General of the United Nations might be much better received by many Americans, although there are others who would be suspicious even of that individual's credibility.

The cases cited above represent extremes. For most sources, credibility is a matter of being rated high or low on only a few characteristics. Furthermore, although almost all Americans may perceive the leader of Communist China in much the same way, most sources are not perceived in the same way by different people. The local congressman will be perceived differently by strong Democrats and strong Republicans. The PTA president will be seen as safe and qualified by some people and as unqualified and lethargic by others. The Berlo, Lemert, and Mertz study also suggested that the topic on which an individual is communicating is important to the credibility that an individual is seen to possess. The ways of judging a source in terms of the three dimensions do not change when the source turns from one topic to another, but the perceived credibility of the source does change. Thus, when James R. Hoffa testifies before a United States Senate committee on auto and truck safety, he may be perceived as qualified. When he is associated with fair labor-management practices, he is not seen as qualified by many people.

The author once asked a group of students to list the five people they thought best able to deal with labor-management practices in the United States.[9] The answers showed the varying concepts of credibility that individuals had. The time was 1953, when there was great discussion about the growing influence of labor in the United States. The individuals receiving the largest number of votes were the late Senator Robert A. Taft and John L. Lewis, then president of the United Mine Workers. Others receiving large numbers of votes included Dwight D. Eisenhower, who had been elected but had not taken office as President; Harry S Truman, who was still the President, and Adlai Stevenson, who had just been defeated for the presidency. Individuals receiving more than ten votes included Eleanor Roosevelt; Eugene Hartley, cosponsor of the Taft-Hartley Bill; Walter Reuther, and George Meany. Other people who could have been listed as high on the qualification scale, such as Cyrus Ching, received very few votes. One conclusion, of course, is that college students do not know much about labor-management problems. A closer look at the names suggested by the students reveals the use of the three dimensions that Berlo and his associates suggest. Some of the individuals listed are not listed for their close association to labor problems but for their perceived safety, or general trustworthiness. Others certainly are greatly trusted individuals for many Americans but were selected by the students because they were considered competent or qualified to work in this particular area. This was demonstrated by comparing the people listed for their ability to deal with labor-management problems with a similar request to the same student group to list those people they considered best able to deal with foreign affairs. Neither Robert A. Taft nor John L. Lewis were mentioned on that list. But Eisenhower, Truman, and Stevenson appeared very high on the second list, along with the Secretary General of the United Nations. Taft and Lewis were apparently chosen for the first list for their perceived competence, while Eisenhower, Truman, and Stevenson were chosen for their perceived trustworthiness.

Source credibility has been shown to be a significant variable in persuasive communication situations. An individual who is not perceived as credible will not produce the same kinds of significant attitude change in a receiver as a communicator who is perceived as credible. Source credibility, however, is not an absolute or fixed characteristic of any communicator. The amount of credibility that an individual is seen to have is a function of who the receiver is, what the topic is, and what the situation is. Since the influence that the source possesses depends on the relationship between the source and the receiver, there are relatively few fixed characteristics of any source that either increase or decrease his credibility and thus his influence on persuasion. The scales utilized by Berlo and his colleagues are all receiver-oriented descriptions. To the extent that it is possible to find out how various receivers rate a communicator, the possible influence that the receiver might have on the effects of persuasion can be predicted. But when predictions can not be made about the ways in which a receiver or a group of receivers perceive a particular source, researchers must turn to whatever knowledge is available about the relationship between the souce and the receiver.

STATUS RESEARCH

Every individual occupies a number of role positions as he goes about his daily life. The same individual may be a husband and father early in the morning, a boss as well as a subordinate during the day, a husband and father again in the house before dinner, and perhaps a church steward or a lodge member in the evening hour. Another person may be a mother and wife during the morning, become a PTA president during the early afternoon, a Cub Scout den mother before supper, and play first violin in the local symphony orchestra during the evening. Each role that is played or occupied by an individual demands a particular kind of behavior. Each person brings some unique personal characteristics to any given role, but the role demands certain behavior of any person occupying the position. Look at the role behavior associated with being a high school teacher. The teacher is expected to meet her classes on time each day. She is expected to teach a subject in such a way that her students will be able to pass standardized tests at the end of the year. She is not expected to teach exactly as do all other teachers, but her role demands that there be similarities. There are kinds of behavior associated with other roles that are not associated with the teacher's role. For example, the dentist frequently will have soft music piped into his office for his patients. The teacher would not be allowed to do that. The point is clear. Particular roles demand certain behavior on the part of the individuals occupying them. Some of the roles a person plays are central to much of his behavior, such as his job role or those roles associated with being a father or husband. Others arc secondary and are assumed only on rare occasions, such as the role of voter, which an individual assumes only once a year or less frequently. But when an individual is occupying a particular role, his behavior is to some extent predictable from the behavior prescribed for that role.

In persuasion, what is important is not the actual role that any communicator or receiver is occupying but the relationship between the role occupied by a source and that occupied by a receiver. Each role can be described in terms of the *status* or the *prestige* associated with the role. The President of the United States has higher prestige because of his role position than does the governor of a state. The foreman within an automobile plant has more status than does the worker on the production line. The college teacher has more prestige than does the high school or grade school teacher. When any two role positions are compared, one can usually determine which position would be accorded higher prestige by a group of receivers. In Table 1 a number of pairs of role positions are compared. The position that will be perceived to be the more likely to have the higher prestige is listed first. Note that it is possible for an individual to occupy more than one position and to be perceived as higher in one role relative to a given receiver and lower in another role relative to that same receiver.

TABLE 1. *Relative Role Position Rankings*

Higher Position	*Lower Position*
President of the United States	United States Congressman
Mayor of New York City	Chief of Police, New York City
President of General Motors Corporation	Colonel, United States Army
President of Stanford University	Professor, University of Michigan
Policeman, City of Detroit	Fireman, City of Detroit
Master plumber	Carpenter
Boy Scout scoutmaster	Usher, Methodist Church
President, Parent-Teachers' Association	Secretary, League of Women Voters
President, Chamber of Commerce	Chairman, Building Committee of Methodist Church

At the top of the list in Table 1 the relative prestige is easier to determine, and more people would agree on the position given. Toward the bottom of the list it is harder to determine which position would actually be rated higher by the majority of the people, but the chances are that most individuals would produce a list very similar to that in Table 1.

The importance of the differential status attached to different role positions is that the higher the prestige attached to a given position, the more likely is an individual occupying such a position to be influential in a persuasive situation. Or to put it in another way, the role position occupied by an individual is one major indicator of his potential influence as a source. In the Haiman study already cited the difference between a college sophomore and the Surgeon General of the United States is at least partly a perceived difference in the status of the two role positions.

A few years ago the U.S. Public Health Service published a report dealing with the relationship between smoking and lung cancer. Many of the items of the report were not new and had been the subject of messages by a number of doctors. There was, however, little decrease in smoking behavior by most individuals as a result of these messages. Then the Surgeon General of the United States held a news conference at which he released the service's report. A large number of individuals stated that they had stopped smoking (at least temporarily) as a result of this report. Many things may help explain the apparent persuasiveness of the Surgeon General's report over the messages of the many other individuals who have talked about the relationship between smoking and lung cancer. The timing of the message, the length, the language used, the amount of publicity given the report are all factors that may have helped the reception of the report. But doubtless the status accorded the Surgeon General was an important factor.

The status that an individual is seen to possess is not itself responsible for the persuasibility of any given receiver. But the perceived prestige differences between sources and receivers may well lead to one individual's being perceived as more worth listening to, as more believable, or as more influential. Thus it becomes important for a communicator who wishes to engage in persuasive communication to attempt to ascertain where he stands with respect to the role position he will be perceived as occupying and with the role position that his receiver will be occupying.

OPINION LEADERSHIP RESEARCH

The status attached to any given role position is not the sole determining factor that is related to the influence of the source in persuasive situations. Imagine that there is a group of housewives collected within a large room. They are listening to a speech by another housewife regarding the beautification of the neighborhood. Here there are no status differences that can be ascertained. Each of the women in the room is a housewife and is in that particular role position as she listens to the speech. Or imagine that there is a group of farmers discussing the merits of a particular weed spray. One farmer speaks in favor of a particular brand. He does not occupy a position that is seemingly any different from the positions occupied by the other farmers. Yet after the housewife speaks and after the farmer speaks, there seems to be general agreement with what is said, and significant attitude change in favor of the side advocated by the speaker. What has happened? Was the message so well prepared and delivered? Or is it necessary to examine some other characteristics of sources than those of the role position that they occupy?

One such characteristic may be whether a source is regarded as an *opinion leader* by other members of his peer group. The pioneering study pointing to the importance of opinion leadership was made by Katz and Lazarsfeld.[10] They examined the effects of the mass media of communication on attitudes and behavior of those who listened to radio and television or read the daily newspaper. Their initial conclusion, after presenting a message over one of the mass media and then measuring the effects of the message, was that there is little effect from most messages presented over mass media. But when they measured some weeks later, they found that there had been significant shifts in attitude. In looking for an explanation of the unexpected, later shifts, they suggested that the original message had been received by people but those people changed their attitudes only after they had talked to others in whom they had confidence. They then referred to these later individuals as *opinion leaders*. Since the Katz and Lazarsfeld study a number of studies have tended to show that certain people seem to exercise more influence in persuasive situations than others.

The opinion leader is not an individual of noticeably higher status than those he influences. He does not necessarily have a better job. He may not be a formal leader in any group. But he does influence opinion formation and attitude change. This chapter will not consider the first part of the situation which Katz and Lazarsfeld were studying, that is, the transference of information from the mass media. This will be considered in examining the effect of varying channels of communication. But this chapter will look closely at the second part of the process and attempt to see whether particular individuals can be identified as opinion leaders and thus as influential in persuasive communication.

Berelson, Lazarsfeld, and McPhee[11] suggest that there are a number of characteristics of the opinion leader that can be identified. Only those that seem of use to the persuasive communicator will be discussed. The most general characteristic of the opinion leader is that he serves as a *model* for the members of his group. He is asked for his opinions by members of the group, and the group listens to his advice. There seem to be few characteristics that all opinion leaders possess, but there are some characteristics that are useful in predicting opinion leadership. They usually have slightly higher social status. They tend to be somewhat better informed about those subjects in which they are considered to be opinion leaders. They attend to the mass media to a greater degree than nonleaders and are better informed about the content of the mass media when it concerns the subjects on which they are influential. Berelson and his associates were concerned with an election study and the determination of opinion leaders in a political situation. They report these leaders to be more interested in the election than nonleaders, to be better informed about the election, to have stronger opinions about the election, and to feel that they had more concern about the progress of the election.

Opinion leaders differ with the topic under consideration. The opinion leader for the political arena is not too likely to be the opinion leader for the latest in sports nor perhaps for the latest in stock market activities. The housewife in the neighborhood who is looked to for her opinions and influence about the latest recipes may not be the opinion leader for childrearing practices. Furthermore, opinion leaders cannot be detected entirely by the amount of education or social status they have, since this variable is a relative one. For a neighborhood where the average education is one year of high school, the opinion leader may have had three years of high school. Ten blocks away there may be a neighborhood where the average number of years of schooling is one year of college, and the opinion leader may be a college graduate. The two opinion leaders probably cannot trade positions and still remain as opinion leaders with their new groups. Opinion leadership is another variable that is defined by the receivers. Within the group, the variables of education, social status, mass media usage, information level, and intensity of opinions will help to identify the opinion leaders.

Source credibility, status, and opinion leadership are similar concepts. Each of these research strains emphasize the point that sources can be influential in determining the outcome of persuasive communication when they are perceived by the receiver as possessing high credibility or high status, or as being an opinion leader. These areas further emphasize that it is not what the source is but what he is perceived to be that determines the influence he will have.

SIMILARITY RESEARCH

The three research areas examined in the preceding sections emphasize the fact that certain types of differences between source and receiver may be influential in determining the outcome of persuasion. Another research strain suggests that the source may be influential in affecting the outcome of persuasion when the receiver perceives some degree of similarity between himself and the communicator. In order to show how such similarity may affect persuasibility, it is first necessary to look at such variables as age, sex, and education.

Part 1 of this book studied the persuasibility of various kinds of receivers. Age, sex, social status, and other factors were examined as indicators of the ways in which any receiver might be expected to behave. Communicators also possess characteristics like age, sex, race, and similar variables. It should be possible to look at such characteristics of communicators and ask what their effect might be on an audience of receivers. Very little of this kind of research has been reported, and much of the research is completely inconclusive. The problem is that the influence of the source is highly dependent on the nature of the topic that the source is communicating about and on the relationship of the receiver to the topic.

An example will illustrate the problem. Imagine that a man and a woman deliver exactly the same speech. Two different but matched audiences listen to the speech and record the amount of attitude change that is shown. The results show that the male speaker was more influential than the female. Is it justified to conclude that men are more influential than women? Certainly not. If the topic had happened to be the importance of increased intramural athletic programs in high school, the difference may have been caused by the fact that men are considered more credible on that subject. If the subject had been the importance of sex education for preteen-age girls, the result might well have been reversed.

The close link between source, topic, and receiver is present for many variables. Education, age, sex, occupation, income level, and social status are all variables that may well be significant in many communication situations but that are highly dependent on the nature of the topic or the makeup of the audience. Individuals possessing the characteristics that were discussed in the consideration of source credibility, status, and opinion leadership do influence persuasion when they act as sources, but there is also a large body of information that points to the importance of the topic in persuasion.

Baker and Redding[12] report a study in which they examined the differences in persuasive effects produced by a source perceived as "tall" and one perceived as "short." The study tended to show that the height of a source was not a significant variable. The author, in collecting data for another purpose, measured attitudes toward individuals with "normal" dress, that is, regular college clothes and suits, and "abnormal" clothes, that is, overalls and sweatshirts. The results showed that the poorly dressed individuals were rated lower than the more normally attired individuals. There were no significant differences due to dress in the amount of attitude change produced when the individuals later delivered persuasive speeches.[13]

There are a number of studies that examined the race of the communicator as a factor in persuasion. Berg[14] reports no significant differences between the agreement of whites with Negroes and the agreement of whites and whites in an autokinetic situation. Aronson and Golden[15] report that there were differences in the influence of white communicators over Negro communicators but that the differences were small and may depend on the role position of the two individuals. Both white and Negro engineers were more effective than was a Negro dishwasher, but a Negro engineer was not significantly more effective than a white dishwasher. However, the authors suggest that race is not the most useful factor for making predictions, that more discriminating results can be obtained when the receiver's initial racial prejudice level is taken into account. Kraus[16] found that having two communicators, one white and one Negro, was more effective in a filmed situation than having two whites or two Negroes. Rokeach has suggested that individuals will choose to associate with Negroes rather than with whites if they see the Negro as more like them than the white person is.[17] Apparently, race can be an important factor in persuasive communication. But it becomes important only when other factors are operating in such a way as to render the communicator's race relevant to the particular situation.

A careful examination of the research in this area suggests a general hypothesis about the role of the source. A communicator may have significant influence on persuasion when he is seen as *similar* to the receiver. The converse of this hypothesis would be that whenever the source is seen as extremely different from the receiver, the influence of the source on the outcome of the persuasive situation will diminish and other factors will become decisive. Similarity between source and receiver can take place on any dimension. Attitudinal similarity may become important. Similarity of age or sex may be important. Educational similarity may be important. Any of the characteristics that have been looked at in detail may become important to the outcome of the interaction between source and receiver.

The research suggests that perceived similarity between source and receiver on such demographic variables as age, sex, race, and education are not as important as is attitudinal similarity. Even variables like opinion leadership and status differential can be profitably examined in terms of the probable attitudinal similarity between an opinion leader and the members of his group or between individuals occupying similar role positions. Similarity must, of course, be defined in terms of the receiver. It is the similarity between the source and the receiver that is perceived by the receiver which is responsible for the effect of the source, not the similarity between source and receiver as it might be defined by the source.

CHARISMATIC RESEARCH

The reader may have reached the point in this discussion of the influence of the source, where he is saying to himself, "Knowing that kind of information is not going to make me into a Winston Churchill." Winston Churchill and other tremendously influential communicators need to be discussed apart from the study of variables relevant to communicator influence. There is a term for such individuals. They are said to possess *charisma*. The charismatic leader is one whose ability at persuasion and leadership seems to transcend any of the usual abilities that individuals seem to possess. Winston Churchill, Adolf Hitler, Franklin D. Roosevelt have all been called charismatic leaders. The late President Kennedy had an effect on many audiences that might be called charismatic. Originally, the term was used to ". . . refer to the qualities of those who claim or are believed to possess powers of leadership derived from some unusual sanction — divine, magical, diabolic — or merely exceptional individuals."[18] Today the term is usually removed from the realm of magic, but it is still used to refer to unusual credibility or to the unique personal influence of an individual that is relatively constant over many topics and for many different audiences. To say that an individual possesses charisma is to say that he seems to possess characteristics which cannot be easily defined or explained.

Throughout history, individuals have appeared who seem to have possessed a charisma that led them to leadership of large groups of individuals. Demosthenes of Greece, Cicero of Rome, Gautama Buddha of the Far East, Disraeli of England, and Gandhi of India can all be added to the leaders mentioned above. In each of these cases the abilities of the individuals to affect attitude and behavior changes through persuasive communication appear almost magical. The research literature examined in preparing this book did not attempt to deal with charisma. The best guess as to the nature of charisma is that it is the possession of many of the dimensions of credibility by a single individual and possession of those factors to a greater extent than is usual for the persuasive communicator. The PTA president, the Chamber of Commerce leader, the state senator, the factory foreman, and the local physician can all improve their effectiveness at persuasive communication through improving the credibility they display. It is doubtful, however, that charismatic leaders can be so easily produced. They remain as individuals whose effect on audiences and history is not explained by research literature.

ADVICE TO THE COMMUNICATOR

The research on source credibility suggests that the source does indeed play an important part in determining the effect of any persuasive message. But the research also suggests that there are no single characteristics of communicators which are universally important in affecting the performance of the source in attitude-change situations. Source credibility appears to be a fragile factor, important in many communication situations but extremely difficult to pinpoint as to which communicator characteristics are actually responsible for credibility.

As indicated, it is impossible to give the persuasive communicator advice on how to become a charismatic leader. But it is possible to make some suggestions about the ways in which communicators could raise their effectiveness in the persuasive communication situation:

1. The dimensions of source credibility have been examined, and also the characteristics of communicators who possess high source credibility. A communicator can help improve his credibility by the way in which he is introduced to his receivers. Are there activities in which the source has participated that would make him appear more qualified? Has he participated in decision-making activities that imply trustworthiness on his part? Even the suggestion that a communicator has appeared before many groups may help to improve the perception of dynamism that an audience begins to have. Obviously, an introduction, no matter how laudatory, cannot compensate for a poor performance. But it can help to enhance a good performance.

2. Most persuasive communication situations occur under conditions in which the communicator is not suddenly made known to his audience. Before the listener starts to listen, before the reader starts to read, and before the viewer starts to view, they are beginning to make judgments about the source to which they are about to expose themselves. This suggests that it is not the momentary exposure to the source at the time of message transmission which is important, but the total set of impressions from the time the receiver first becomes aware of the source. The individual who wishes to become persuasive must act accordingly during his daily activities, not merely during the communication situation. This background may be mentioned during an introduction of a speaker, but it will have made its greatest impact before the particular communication situation ever takes place.

3. Status level has been shown to relate to persuasion. Most sources cannot raise their social status for a specific speech or for a letter to the editor. Yet a receiver may associate a source with one organization and be completely unaware of the level that the source has reached in another organization. For example, imagine that a group of social workers listen to Danny Kaye talk about the problems of orphan children in Europe. The social worker may well wonder just why she, a professional, should be listening to an actor, no matter how good, talk about a subject that has no connection with acting. But if the introduction mentioned the international commissions dealing with children that Kaye has served as chairman and described the work he has been doing for the United Nations Educational, Scientific, and Cultural Organization (UNESCO), the status of Danny Kaye as perceived by the social worker might well be improved and his influence increased.

4. The concept of opinion leadership is important to persuasion for two reasons. First, the persuasive communicator who must communicate to a large group of individuals may find his task easier if he can concentrate on the opinion leaders in

the group. They serve to channel communication from outside a group to the members of the group. They can take the message of a communicator who has little effective contact with the members of one social stratum and make that message an effective personalized message for the members of the group. When the opinion leaders can be reached and persuaded as to the rightness of a particular position, many other members of the group will also be affected.

The second reason that the concept of opinion leadership is important is that the persuasive speaker himself will frequently serve as an opinion leader for a group. His chances of doing so are increased when he exhibits the characteristics of an opinion leader, that is, when he attends to the mass media, exposes himself to many different kinds of information, and shows a willingness to talk to others and to answer questions about those areas that interest him. The opinion leader must digest information and then pass along the information as attitudes and beliefs to the members of his group.

An individual who wishes to serve as an opinion leader cannot get himself elected to that office. It is not the formal kind of leadership that requires elections and terms of office. Individuals serve as opinion leaders at the whim of the group, and they may move in and out of such an influential position as the group changes or as the situation changes. However, a communicator can enhance his chances of being regarded as an opinion leader, and thus his persuasive influence, by behaving as an opinion leader would.

5. The voluntary membership groups that a receiver belongs to can indicate the kinds of attitudes that an individual holds. If the source can suggest that there is some similarity of membership groups, the receiver is likely to make the assumption that there is also similarity of attitude. For example, the speaker who begins his speech to a group of union members by announcing, "I come from a family long active in union affairs," is likely to be more effective than a speaker who begins his speech to the same group by saying, "I have employed union labor for years, and therefore I understand your problems."

6. The communicator can make an effort to ascertain what beliefs and attitudes the members of his audience are likely to have in a particular area and build into his speech statements that indicate his support of those beliefs and attitudes. The age, sex, race, social background, and other variables indicate the kind of beliefs that a group is likely to have in general, even if they do not indicate specific beliefs on a particular topic. The communicator whose intent is to change a set of attitudes will find it easier if he can indicate to an audience that he is in agreement with audience members on attitudes other than those associated with the specific topic of the speech.

7. The communicator can make use of authorities who carry considerable credibility to bolster his own presentation. Most people possess some credibility of their own. But well-known individuals, such as the President, Cabinet members, well-known scientists, congressmen, and public officials, carry far more credibility for the average receiver. The communicator who can associate authorities carrying high credibility with his own message will improve his own position.

8. In situations in which the communicator is transmitting a message to a number of receivers, he must adapt his message to the largest number of audience members. This means that he has no opportunity to explore carefully what attitudes a particular receiver may hold. But in interpersonal situations, in which there is opportunity for give-and-take between source and receiver, the source can use the

statements of a receiver to ascertain more precisely what attitudes are held by a receiver and adapt his message to show the similarity between himself and the receiver. Again, the communicator improves his chances of being influential in his own right.

SUMMARY

Receivers are clearly not guided in their attitude formation or changes in attitude as the sole result of the impact that the source makes on the receiver. But this examination of source-connected variables suggest that the source is important to an understanding of the process of persuasion. A concluding statement might be that sources can either impede persuasion when their perceived credibility is low or help to facilitate belief when credibility is high.

NOTES

1. W. R. Roberts, "Rhetorica," in W. D. Ross, ed., *The Works of Aristotle*, New York: Oxford University Press, vol. 11, p. 7.

2. F. S. Haiman, "The Effects of Ethos in Public Speaking," *Speech Monographs*, vol. 16 (1949), p. 192.

3. C. I. Hovland, I. L. Janis, and H. H. Kelley, *Communication and Persuasion*, New Haven, Conn.: Yale University Press, 1953, pp. 19-53.

4. C. I. Hovland, I. L. Janis, and H. H. Kelley

5. C. H. Marple, "The Comparative Susceptibility of Three Age Levels to the Suggestion of Group versus Expert Opinion," *Journal of Social Psychology*, vol. 4 (1933), pp. 176-86.

6. I. Lorge and C. Curtiss, "Prestige Suggestion and Attitudes," *Journal of Social Psychology*, vol. 7 (1936), pp. 386-402.

7. D. Berlo, J. Lemert, and R. Mertz, "Dimensions for Evaluating the Acceptability of Message Sources," mimeographed report, Michigan State University, 1966, pp. 22.

8. C. Osgood, P. Tannenbaum, and G. Suci, *The Measurement of Meaning*, Urbana, Ill.: University of Illinois Press, 1957.

9. E. Bettinghaus, "An Experimental Study of the Effectiveness of the Use of Testimony in an Argumentative Speech," unpublished Master's thesis, Bradley University, 1953.

10. E. Katz and P. F. Lazarsfeld, *Personal Influence*, New York: The Free Press of Glencoe, Inc., 1955.

11. B. Berelson, P. F. Lazarsfeld, and W. N. McPhee, *Voting: A Study of Opinion Formation during a Presidential Campaign*, Chicago: University of Chicago Press, 1954.

12. E. Baker and C. Redding, "The Effects of Perceived Tallness in Persuasive Speaking: An Experiment," *Journal of Communication*, vol. 12 (1962), p. 51.

13. E. Bettinghaus, "The Operation of Congruity in an Oral Communication Situation," unpublished Ph.D. dissertation, University of Illinois, 1959.

14. K. Berg, "Ethnic Attitudes and Agreement of White Persons with a Negro Person in the Autokinetic Situation," *Dissertation Abstracts*, vol. 23 (1962), p. 334.

15. E. Aronson and B. W. Golden, "The Effect of Relevant and Irrelevant Aspects of Communicator Credibility on Opinion Change," *Journal of Personality*, vol. 30 (1962), pp. 935-46.

16. S. Kraus, "An Experimental Study of the Relative Effectiveness of Negroes and Whites in Achieving Racial Attitude Change via Kinescope Recordings," *Speech Monographs*, vol. 27 (1960), pp. 87-88.

17. M. Rokeach and L. Mezie, "Race and Shared Belief as Factors in Social Choice," *Science*, vol. 151 (January 1960), pp. 167-72.

18. J. Gould and W. L. Kolb, eds., *A Dictionary of the Social Sciences*, New York: The Free Press of Glencoe, Inc., 1965, p. 84.

Gerard Egan

THE ELEMENTS OF HUMAN DIALOGUE: PATHOS, LOGOS, POIESIS

PATHOS: MAN AS THE SUBJECT OF FEELINGS AND EMOTIONS

The Flight from Emotion

There is growing concern—and perhaps it may also be said that there is growing evidence, though it is the fruit of observation rather than experimentation—over the inability of some people to engage in a free and constructive expression of emotion. The hypothesis might be stated: many men in our society, especially those in the middle and upper classes, are constricted in their ability to experience emotion and to give expression to their emotions; for one reason or another, they have not faced up to their possibilities in these areas. . . .

Formal education is overloaded in the area of intellect, impoverished in the area of emotion. As Neill (1968) notes:

> Today our schools educate the head and leave the emotions to the crowd-compellers — the press, the radio, the TV, the churches, the commercial exploiters with their lying advertisements. Our pop heroes and film stars have become our leading schoolmasters dealing with real emotions. . . . The danger today is under-developed emotion, perverted emotion, infantile emotion [p. 37].

Paperback novels, movies, and the ubiquitous television set all constitute a two-edged sword in the emotional life of man. If used with imagination and discretion, they can complement a person's emotional life, enhance and enrich it by broadening his emotional experience, and provide the beginnings of some kind of insight or vision into a wide variety of human experiences. But too many people misuse these media, with the result that the media are not complements to emotional living but rather substitutes for it; and, for many, this vicarious emotional living is sufficient.

Fromm (1941) decries the general tendency of society to discourage emotion, and the resulting "cheap and insincere sentimentality with which movies and popular songs feed millions of emotional-starved customers [p. 271]." He sees the child developing a "pseudo character," not because he has to learn to control his feelings, but because he must deny that he even experiences them. Lynd (1958) notes the same trends: "In our society 'emotional' is frequently used as a derogatory term. Developing emotional maturity is more often conceived in terms of training a child in what he should *not* feel and in controlling the expression of his feelings than in extending the range and depth of his emotions and their expression [p. 236]." Fromm goes so far as to suggest that bad dreams result from the fact that people force their true feelings out of consciousness because these feelings do not fit in with the social self.

In a recent book, Schutz (1967) describes the joy that he experienced watching his newborn son being totally absorbed in the experience, both happy and unhappy, of growing. He describes what he sees as unbounded joy, but also begins to wonder: "But will something happen to Ethan as it does to us all? Where will his joy go? In most of us it becomes depleted, distorted, contorted. Guilt and fear begin to defile it. Somehow the joy of Ethan goes, never to fully return [p. 10]." The rest of the book is an engaging essay on some ways and means of winning back the joy that too many men forfeit as the price of security, socialization, and productivity.

Keniston's Hypothesis. One way of looking at the emotional parasitism of society—men become parasites to television, movies, and the other things mentioned above—is that it is an essential or at least unavoidable phenomenon in a technocratic society such as ours. Keniston (1965) suggests that two phenomenon of our society converge to create an emotional dilemma for the working man. First of all, many men find little emotional satisfaction in the work they do to earn a living. Work, instead of satisfying emotional needs, intensifies them. Breadwinners come home, then, hungering for emotional satisfaction and expecting to find it with their families. But today's family—and this is the second phenomenon—is a smaller unit than yesterday's. Family no longer means a complex of grandparents, aunts, uncles, and children living in the same at least relatively circumscribed geographical area. Family today means wife and two or three children, too geographically or psychologically separated from close relatives to constitute an interactional unit with any direct emotional meaning or impact. Keniston claims that, given the emotional constriction or frustration of the breadwinner at work, the family, especially so small a family, cannot satisfy his intensified or exaggerated emotional needs at home. Obviously, the wife faces analogous emotional frustrations, and then husband's and wife's intensified emotional needs become interactive.

There are no ready-made solutions for these emotional binds. Ideally, husband and wife, without abandoning their obligations to work and children, will move out into the community, into such things as church and civic activities, thus broadening the bases of emotional fulfillment. However, other less responsible solutions tend to destroy the equilibrium of the family: tension and fighting in the home, extramarital adventures, emotional constriction and insulation, and the vicarious emotional living mentioned above, made easy, for instance, by the proliferation of engaging but undemanding sports events on television.

Man's struggle for freedom has been the theme of much of his literature from the very beginning of recorded history. While this freedom is conceived of in more or less political terms, there has been a concomitant or parallel struggle for more interior forms of freedom such as emotional freedom. Today, even if men have been freed from the emotion-constricting slavery of Jansenism, Puritanism, and Victorianism (and certainly not all have), many have managed to shackle themselves with new bonds. While the prior slavery was enjoined in the name of morality and religion, the new slavery is imposed in the name of technocracy, progress, and production. Many have been duped into thinking that they are emotionally free, when all that has happened has been a change in the facade of their bondage. It is as if men were afraid to allow men to experience either themselves or their environment in an unfettered way and to institute communication with one another based on this experiencing. Rather, this is the unknown, the unknown is dangerous, the dangerous is to be feared, and the feared is to be resisted.

Some men are relieved when they are told that "feelings get in the way," for it justifies an already determined mode of interpersonal acting. Men who are guarded in their feelings toward others do not particularly want to become aware of these feelings. They would also prefer that others not feel strongly about them. It is thought uncivil, rude, unconventional, unwarranted, and even obscene to express feelings toward others. Emotional insulation parades under such euphemisms as "respect for others" and the "dignity of privacy." Sometimes the mentally ill are feared, not because they express too little but because they express too much. Men who are afraid of feelings and emotions to begin with are utterly terrified when these are expressed without restraint. Perhaps the best symbol of man as emotional today is the polyethylene bag. Nothing gets in. Nothing gets out. He remains encased in interpersonal asepsis. . . .

LOGOS: MAN'S TRANSLATION OF HIMSELF INTO LANGUAGE

Introduction

Logos, when used as a generic term, refers to man's interaction with man in terms of human language, the way a man translates himself into language. . . . More attention must be given to such molar dimensions of language as the quality of man's verbal expression in his interpersonal contacts.

As Wiener and Mehrabian (1968) note, it is too fruitful an area of interpersonal discovery to ignore:

> Anyone who listens carefully to the way people say things quickly learns that the particular words a speaker uses to describe an event or experience can be a rich source of information about his feelings and attitudes. The bases for making these kinds of inferences are not usually explicit, although members of a communication group appear to respond regularly to these subtle variations in word usage [p. 1].

The Problems and Potential of Language

Problems. There are various ways in which people underuse or abuse language in interpersonal situations and many reasons why they do so. Some language problems stem directly from, and reflect varying degrees of, psychopathology. Bettelheim (1967) discusses children who have surrendered the use of language because of parental disapproval, their mutism being an indication that they have given up any hope of influencing their world. This surrender of speech closes a vicious circle:

Once the child has even stopped communicating with others, his self becomes impoverished, the more so the longer his mutism lasts, and the more so the longer his personality remains underdeveloped at the time of the onset of withdrawal [p. 56].

If this [mutism] happens before he has fully learned to manipulate symbolic forms, before the age of three or four, then the child also fails to develop the higher intellectual processes [p. 57].

Erikson (1954) discovered that one of the outcomes of traumatic war experiences was a distrust and devaluation of language. Meerloo (1956) found neurosis manifested in language-use disturbances: "The insecure neurotic shrinks from free word-play; he tries to manipulate words mechanically, like machinery. He fears the adventure of communication [p. 87]." Ruesch (1957) sees the origin of communication problems in parents' inability to adapt themselves to the maturation level of their children. According to Ruesch, three types of language are learned in succession: somatic, action, and verbal. If parents do not adapt their language to the developmental stage of their children, while at the same time offering encouragement to improve verbal-language proficiency, then communication disturbances may arise in their children.

Language problems arise from and reflect not only psychopathology in the strict sense; they reflect also the psychopathology of the average. Many normal men fear the communication process because of more or less normal fears of involving themselves deeply with others. They neither pour themselves into their language in interpersonal situations nor expect others to do so. Language must remain on a safe level. They habitually put filters between what they really think and feel and what they say. This results in exsanguinated or muddied, but safe, communication. Some men engage in language that is overly precise—they ask too much of language while others engage in language that is too vague—that is, they ask too little of language. Both extremes are usually defensive measures, ways of keeping interpersonal contacts at acceptable levels of intensity. Some men are victims of poor education in language. They have lived in families or societies that are afraid of open communication, with the result that patterns of language are not available to them to express what they would like to express. This conversational or language anemia is recognized by the novel writer:

> Even in modern-novel dialogue the most real is not the most conformable to actual current speech. One has only to read a transcribed tape of actual conversation to realize that it is, in the literary context, not very real. Novel dialogue is a form of shorthand, an impression of what people actually say; and besides that, it has to perform other functions — to keep the narrative moving (which real conversation rarely does), to reveal character (real conversation often hides it), and so on [Fowles, 1968, p. 89].

Men read novels not only for vicarious *pathos* but also for vicarious *logos*, the meaningful talk that is missing from their lives.

In societies that subtly discourage or limit conversational freedom and deeper interpersonal contact through language, some men abandon language (at least in a relative sense) either because it is useless as an instrument of deep human communication or because the patterns of language allowed are identified with the establishment that is being rejected. In the case of the present "hippie" culture, this flight from a language involves both (1) the creation of an argot reflecting a break from the values of society seen as useless or oppressive, while emphasizing the values of the subculture and (2) an often irresponsible immersion in the *pathos* dimensions of living. A counter language evolves, and a counter *pathos* society is established, parallel to or outside the confines of the society being rejected.

Potentialities. Despite the problems involved in using exsanguinated language and communication, language is still one of the most dramatic ways in which man differs from other animals. Stout (1902) sees language as an instrument by means of which man examines the world around him. If he is afraid of this world, his language will be anemic and feeble, but if he loves the world and is challenged by it, his language will be strong and searching. To adapt a phrase from Wittgenstein (1922), the limits of a person's language are the limits of his world. Cioran (1968) sees silence as unbearable and says he would find it easier to renounce bread than speech. He claims that one cannot withdraw one's confidence from words "without setting one's foot in the abyss." Language exposes, reveals both individuals and societies: "Words, at least in traditional societies, often express far more than feelings or ideas. The way words are used — in tales, riddles, proverbs, and typical modes of address and conversation—can reveal a great deal about the structure and values of a society [Abrahams, 1968, p. 62]."

Novelists and writers frequently have, if not deeper insights, at least more striking, distinctive, and challenging insights into the nature and force of human language than do behavorial scientists. Writers continually try to enlarge the possibilities. D. H. Lawrence, Virginia Woolf, and James Joyce never hesitated to experiment with verbal symbols that would most fully convey what they experienced. As Burgess (1968) notes: "Language, of its very nature, resists tautology; it wants to launch out, risk lies, say the thing which is not."

Brian Friel's entire play *Philadelphia Here I Come* is based on the distinction between what the leading character really thinks, feels, and would like to say and what he actually says. In the play, there are two levels of conversation—the vague, hesitant, compliant, failed bravado of the son about to leave his father in Ireland to seek a new way of life in the United States, and the vigorous speech of the son's "inner core" (played by a separate character). The pity of it all is that, although the audience is electrified by what the "inner man" says, it knows that his speech really dies (and in a sense the son dies with it) because it is never spoken. The man who chains his language chains himself. . . .

Different Kinds of Language

In keeping with the consideration of language from a molar, interactional point of view, the following distinctions—again, despite the fact that they are somewhat abstractive—might give direction to the discussion that follows.

Logos. Logos, in the strict or restricted sense, refers to man's ability to translate his real self into language. Logos is language filled with the person who is speaking, and therefore refers to his ability to use speech to express his identity. It also refers to the use man makes of speech in order to establish some kind of growthful interpersonal contact. Negatively, it is the refusal to use speech merely to fill interactional space and time or as a smoke screen or shield behind which to hide.

Just as there are different kinds of truly human contact and various degrees or levels of such contact, so there are different kinds of *logos*. If a man talks meaningfully about his political or religious beliefs, this is *logos*. . . .

Logos must be clearly differential from the ability to speak fluently and elegantly, for both fluency and elegance are at times used to camouflage, rather than reveal, one's identity. It also seems necessary to distinguish *logos* from the ability to speak with insight about oneself. This ability has traditionally been seen as a favorable condition, if not a prerequisite, for effective participation in psychotherapy—an hypothesis that is being seriously challenged today (Carkhuff & Berenson, 1967; London, 1964). *Logos* here means translating oneself, or handing oneself over the others, through the medium of speech, whatever the esthetic value of the language used.

Logos implies a respect for language as a form of communication and contact. It implies dialogue, and, as Matson and Montagu (1967) point out, for certain contemporary existentialist thinkers, authentic existence *is* communication, life *is* dialogue. . . .

Dialogue, in the sense in which it is used here, is opposed to "game" communication. Dialogue is game-free, or at least an attempt to make communication game-free. Rapoport (1964) and Wiener (1950), both of whom have made significant contributions to the mathematical theory of games, caution against the use of game theory as a basis for human communication. Rapoport finds dialogue with the "strategist" impossible, for the basic question in the strategist's mind is: In a conflict, how can I gain an advantage over my opponent? Rapoport thinks that the much more basically human question is: If I can gain an advantage over another, *what sort of person* will I become? The "cybernetic" man is basically monological, not dialogical, and for him, communication is intimately wedded to control—the control of the other.

Berne (1966) uses "game" in a somewhat different sense. The "games people play" are ways of avoiding intimacy in human relationships. The game prevents dialogue.

Commercial Speech. "Commercial speech" refers to the language of the marketplace the use of language in the commercial transactions of men. Such language is lean, utilitarian, pragmatic; it deals with objects rather than persons, for it is a medium of exchange rather than of interpersonal contact. Much of such language today is left to computers. It would be of no interest to us here were it not for the fact that there are people who use commercial speech as their principal mode of speech in interpersonal transactions. They see people as objects to be manipulated, rather than persons to be contacted, and this is reflected in the quality of their speech.

If speech is principally commercial, then, as McLuhan (1964) suggests, it can be dispensed with: "Electric technology does not need words any more than the digital computer needs numbers [p. 80]." However, the utopia he envisions, characterized by a "speechlessness that could confer a perpetuity of collective harmony and peace" arising from a "collective awareness that may have been the preverbal condition of man [P. 80]," is antithetical to man himself. Speech defines man. It is just strange that he makes such poor use of it in his effort to humanize himself.

Cliché Talk.   "Cliché talk" refers to anemic language, talk for the sake of talk, conversation without depth, language that neither makes contact with the other nor reveals the identity of the speaker (except negatively, in the sense that he is revealed as one who does not want to make contact or does not want to be known). Cliché talk fosters ritualistic, rather than fully human, contact ("Do you think that it is really going to rain?"—"The way they're playing, they'll be in first place by the first of September!"). Cliché talk fills interactional space and time without adding meaning, for it is superficial and comes without reflection. . . .

People usually listen to cliché talk, especially when it is pseudo-*logos*—that is, dressed up or doctored to sound important:

> When a conversation fails to capture the spontaneous involvement of an individual who is obliged to participate in it, he is likely to contrive an appearance of being involved. This he must do to save the feelings of the other participants and their good opinion of him, regardless of his motives for wanting to effect this saving [Goffman, 1967, p. 126].

If the needs of the listener are such that he is willing to put up with the boredom of cliché talk in order to enjoy the safety that is found in ritual, then the circle is complete and the field is wide open for such conversation.

One of the most common forms of cliché talk in our culture (and perhaps this is a transcultural phenomenon) is "griping," a more or less superficial communication of dissatisfaction with persons, institutions, or things outside oneself. It is one of the few verbal expressions of feeling allowed in public, and it is probably allowed because it is a ritual and most rituals are safe. The trouble with chronic griping is that it is a fixative. As Ellis (1962) points out, a person's verbalizations to himself and others often stand in the way of change: "Forces outside me control me"; "I can do nothing to change."

Cliché talk is just words, while *logos* always connotes human contact. Some people speak endlessly about themselves and say nothing (if they were really disclosing themselves, others would not find it boring). They say nothing about themselves because they have no real feeling for themselves—they are deficient in the *pathos* dimension of life—and could hardly be expected to relate what they do not experience. Such people simply are not using speech as a mode of contact. For them, speech is solipsistic, self-centered, centripetal. It is monologue rather than dialogue.

Anti-logos.   When language is actually used to destroy growthful interpersonal contact rather than to foster it, then it is *anti-logos*. There are a number of forms of speech that are really violations, rather than uses, of language. For instance, in the heat of anger, language can be used as a weapon, a tool of destruction rather than an instrument of growthful encounter. When a married couple stand shouting at each other (often saying things they do not really mean), language becomes completely swallowed up in emotion; it loses its identity as language. At such times it has more in common with a sledgehammer than with speech. Lying, too, can be a form of *anti-logos,* for deception cannot be the basis of growthful interpersonal contact. The speech of the psychopath, for example, is frequently, if not continually, *anti-logos,* for he uses speech to create situations, to manipulate others rather than to engage in growthful encounters with them. Finally, the language of the psychotic, while it might have its own peculiar logic (and without discounting the possibility that a psychosis may be a desperate form of revolt against a sick family or society—see Laing, 1967), is frequently *anti-logos.* The psychotic, at least at times, appears to use language to drive others away. He fears human contact so deeply that he reverses the function of language, making it a barrier instead of a bridge. . . .

Most men engage in all four kinds of speech at one time or another. They not only use commercial speech in strictly commercial transactions, but also allow it to slip occasionally into interpersonal encounters. Indeed, life without some cliché talk would be intolerably intense for most men. It is a question, however, of proportion, and most men need to find ways of increasing the amount of *logos* (in the restricted sense) in their lives. . . . .

The Extra-Linguistic Dimensions of Speech

Much can be learned about a person, not only from the verbal content of his communications (the content can be strong, cliché-ridden, ambiguous, weak, etc.), but also from the quality of the voice in delivery, or as Wiener and Mehrabian (1968) put it, from "variations in tonal qualities, patterns of stress, pitch, and pauses which are not dictated by the required linguistic form [p. 51]." For example, a person may claim that he is not anxious but betray his anxiety quite openly in the tone, pitch, and timbre of his voice: "An insecure person . . . may speak in complex, involved or even unfinished sentences, with poor pitch and volume control, and with frequent nervous mannerisms [Mahl & Schulze, 1964, p. 51]." Voice quality, rhythm, continuity, speech rate, and verbal output all communicate something to the listener, or, from a more active point of view, the speaker has all of these extralinguistic factors at his disposal, to use, as he sees fit, to increase the effectiveness of his communication. In a sense, there are two kinds of extralinguistic phenomena: (1) those related to speech itself (e.g., pitch, tone, etc.) and (2) those forms of behavior which, although they communicate, are more or less separable from speech in the strict sense. . . .

Logos: Nonverbal Communication

The Scientific Study of Nonverbal Communication.   Although it is a truism that nonverbal behavior plays an extremely important part in the entire communication process, some have suggested that its scientific study is not worth pursuing. La Barre (1964) takes strong exception to such a suggestion:

> It is easy to ridicule kinesiology as an abstruse, pedantic, and unimportant study by pure scientists. But I believe that kinesiology is, on the contrary, one of the most important avenues for better understanding internationally. Consider, as one small example, how Chinese hate to be touched, slapped on the back, or even to shake hands; how easily an American could avoid offense by merely omitting these intended gestures of friendliness! Misunderstanding of nonverbal communication of an unconscious kind is one of the most vexing and unnecessary sources of international friction. (Consider, for example, the hands-over-the-head self-handshake of Khrushchev, which Americans interpreted as an arrogant gesture of triumph, as of a victorious prize-fighter, whereas Khrushchev seems to have intended it as a friendly gesture of international brotherhood.) [p. 218].

Birdwhistell (1952, 1961, 1963a, 1963b) and Hall (1959, 1963a, 1963b, 1964, 1966) have both elaborated categories which relate body movements, including gestures and facial expressions, to the process of communication. Davitz (1964) has reviewed the literature on the interpretation of emotions from facial expressions, and researchers such as Ekman (1965) and Ekman and Friesen (1967) continue to do research in this area. Dittmann (1963) is another who studies the relation of bodily movement to communication. La Barre (1964) discusses (not without humor) a wide variety of nonverbal communicative behavior—greetings, kissing, sticking out the tongue (in China "a quick, minimal tongue-protrusion and -retraction signifies embarrassment and self-castigation [p. 200]"), gestures of contempt (Neapolitans click the right thumbnail off the right canine in a downward arc [p. 201]"), gestures of *politesse* ("a Shan may bend over and snuff the sleeve of the benefactor's coat [p.202]"), conventionalized motor acts (e.g., in both Oriental and Occidental acting), and conversational gestures (e.g., "the shaken right forefinger of accusation, sharp criticism, and threat [p. 203]")—on a cross-cultural basis. . . .

Poiesis: Words Made Flesh

When *pathos* finds expression in human language, when *logos* is suffused with human feeling and emotion, a new term is needed to describe the communication that takes place. The term used here is *poiesis,* which comes from the Greek verb meaning "to do, to make." The English word "poetry" comes from the same stem. When meaning and feeling become artfully one in language, the result is poetry. In human dialogue, when words are meaningfully filled with human emotion, when feelings and emotions find creative expression in human language, the result is *poiesis.* Forrest (1965) uses the same term with somewhat negative connotations. For him, *poiesis* is a "making" almost in the sense of "making up" or "contriving." The schizophrenic, for instance, uses language not just to describe or communicate something, but to "make" something. In the schizophrenic's language, wishes are not merely uttered but fulfilled. In fact, fulfillment of his wishes occurs only in the world of words. Be that as it may, in the present context, *poiesis* has only positive connotations. It is too rich a term to be wasted on pathology. *Poiesis* is word made flesh in human dialogue.

Men seem to feel safer when they compartmentalize their experiences. Feelings are all right, and language is all right, but they are to be kept apart, if possible. Lynch (1967) recognizes in movies a similar movement—that is, toward immediate, private, and wordless experience. He deplores such a movement: "Words and ideas have been given a hard time; they have been pushed into a polarized state, devoid of contact with images and things. They need to be allowed to re-enter the world and re-establish their relation to things and their own power as a human art [p. 79]." Meaningless words and unverbalized feelings both sin against human communication. Lynch suggests that even brutal language is better than either emasculated words or silences that hide hate and bitterness:

> . . . The words in *Who's Afraid of Virginia Woolf* are, on the surface, ordinary human words that say something. On the second level they turn out to be words describing games being played at, unrealities, fictions. On the third and final take they have inflexibly human rules behind them and are the only forms of salvation and *contact,* cruel though they might be, between George and Martha [p. 83, emphasis added].

Language, then, can be strong medicine, if it is made strong by becoming the vehicle of the speaker's experience. . . .

Failed Poiesis: Action Divorced from Language. While perhaps the primary failure to achieve *poiesis* consists in an inability or a refusal to include emotion in verbal expression, there is also another, even more dramatic, form of failed *poiesis*. It involves what Bloch (1968) calls "an inability to substitute and utilize language for action and activity [p. 178]." When a married couple stand screaming at each other, a kind of communication through action is taking place, but the use of language is really incidental to the whole process. This dumping of raw emotion on each other is an action or an activity devoid of both *logos* and *poiesis*. But if a marriage begins primarily on the level of *pathos* so that, although each experiences the other, neither is capable of translating that experience into language, and if the marriage continues principally on the level of *pathos,* with commercial speech alone used in the necessary transactions between partners, then trouble is almost unavoidable. The couple turns up in some marital-counseling situation and it is discovered that their problem is, predictably, a lack of communication. From the beginning, their feelings toward each other have been strong and turbulent, but strength and turbulence do not imply depth. They have never really questioned their feelings. They eschew *logos:* they never speak meaningfully about their core, their values, their goals, the interlaced meanings of all phases of their lives. *Pathos,* therefore, is not modified, stimulated, and matured by effective *logos*. There has never been any "need" for words. When ephemeral feeling dies away, however, and the inevitable problems of living together arise, communication fails because it has never really been a part of the relationship. The *pathos* level on which the relationship has been based is not sufficient to handle the problems. When undiscussed problems mount too high, irresponsible *pathos* runs wild, with words becoming the lackeys of feeling. Then the conversation that does exist is nothing but a caricature of communication. The sooner a couple realize the potential of human language and make mature verbal interactional systems part of their relationship, the better prepared will they be to handle problems that arise, and, more important, the greater will be their potential for interpersonal growth.

REFERENCES

Abrahams, R. D. "Public Drama and Common Values in Two Caribbean Islands." *Trans-Action*, 1968, 5 (8), 62-71.

Berne, E. *Principles of Group Treatment*. New York: Oxford University Press, 1966.

Bettelheim, B. *The Empty Fortress*. New York: Collier-Macmillan, 1967.

Birdwhistell, R. L. "Paralanguage: 25 Years after Sapir." In H. W. Brosin (Ed.), *Lectures in Experimental Psychiatry*, Pittsburgh: University of Pittsburgh Press, 1961.

Birdwhistell, R. L. "Body Signals: Normal and Pathological." Paper read at Annual Meeting, American Psychological Association, Philadelphia, August-September, 1963a.

Birdwhistell, R. L. "The Kinesic Level in the Investigation of Emotions." In P. H. Knapp (Ed.), *Expression of the Emotions in Man*. New York: International Universities Press, 1963b. Pp. 123-139.

Bloch, H. S. "An Open-Ended Crisis-Oriented Group for the Poor who are Sick." *Archives of General Psychiatry*, 1968, 18, 178-185.

Burgess, A. "The Future of Anglo-American." *Harper's*, 1968, 236, 53-56.

Carkhuff, R. R., and Berenson, B. G. *Beyond Counseling and Psychotherapy*. New York: Holt, Rinehart and Winston, 1967.

Cioran, E. M. *The Temptation to Exist*. R. Howard (Trans.). Chicago: Quadrangle, 1968.

Davitz, J. R. *The Communication of Emotional Meaning*. New York: McGraw-Hill, 1964.

Dittmann, A. T. "Kinesic Research and Therapeutic Process: Further Discussion." In P. H. Knapp (Ed.), *Expression of the Emotions in Man*. New York: International Universities Press, 1963.

Ekman, P. "Differential Communication of Affect by Head and Body Cues." *Journal of Personality and Social Psychology*, 1965, 2, 726-735.

Ekman, P., and Friesen, W. V. "Head and Body Cues in the Judgment of Emotion: A Reformulation." *Journal of Perceptual and Motor Skills*, 1967, 24, 711-724.

Ellis, A. *Reason and Emotion in Psychotherapy*. New York: Lyle Stuart, 1962.

Erikson, E. H. "On the Sense of Inner Identity." In R. P. Knight and C. R. Friedman (Eds.), *Psychoanalytical Psychiatry and Psychology: Clinical and Theoretical Papers*. Vol. I. New York: International Universities Press, 1954.

Forrest, D. V. "Poiesis and the Language of Schizophrenia." *Psychiatry*, 1965, 28, 1-18.

Fromm, E. *Escape from Freedom*. New York: Farrar and Rinehart, 1941.

Goffman, E. *Interaction Ritual: Essays on Face-to-Face Behavior*. Garden City, New York: Anchor Books (Doubleday), 1967.

Hall, E. T. *The Silent Language*. New York: Fawcett, 1959.

Hall, E. T. "Proxemics: The Study of Man's Spatial Relations." In I. Goldston (Ed.), *Man's Image in Medicine and Anthropology*. New York: International Universities Press, 1963 a. Pp. 422-445.

Hall, E. T. "A System for the Notation of Proxemic Behavior." *American Anthropologist*, 1963b, 65, 1003-1026.

Hall, E. T. "Silent Assumptions in Social Communication." *Disorders of Communication*, 1964, 42, 41-55.

Hall, E. T. *The Hidden Dimension*. Garden City, New York: Doubleday, 1966.

Keniston, K. *The Uncommitted: Alienated Youth in American Society*. New York: Harcourt, Brace and World, 1965.

LaBarre, W. "Paralinguistics, Kinesics, and Cultural Anthropology." In T. A. Sebeok, A. S. Hayes, and M. C. Bateson (Eds.), *Approaches to Semiotics*. The Hague: Mouton, 1964. Pp. 191-220.

Laing, R. D. *The Politics of Experience*. New York: Pantheon Books (Random House), 1967.

London, P. *The Modes and Morals of Psychotherapy*. New York: Holt, Rinehart and Winston, 1964.

Lynch, W. F. "Counterrevolution in the Movies." *Commonweal*, 1967, 87, 77-86.

Lynd, H. M. *On Shame and the Search for Identity*. New York: Science Editions, 1958.

Mahl, G. F., and Schulze, G. "Psychological Research in the Extra-Linguistic Area." In T. A. Sebeok, A. S. Hayes, and M. C. Bateson (Eds.), *Approaches to Semiotics*. The Hague: Mouton, 1964. Pp. 51-125.

Matson, F. W., and Montagu, A. (Eds.) *The Human Dialogue*. New York: Free Press, 1967.

McLuhan, M. *Understanding Media: The Extensions of Man.* New York: McGraw-Hill, 1964.

Meerloo, J. *The Rape of the Mind.* Cleveland: World, 1956.

Neill, A. S. "Can I come to Summerhill? I hate my school." *Psychology Today*, 1968, 1 (12), 34-40.

Rapoport, A. *Strategy and Conscience.* New York: Harper and Row, 1964.

Ruesch, J. *Disturbed Communication.* New York: Norton, 1957.

Schutz, W. C. *Joy.* New York: Grove Press, 1967.

Stout, G. F. *Analytic Psychology.* Vol. 2. New York: Macmillan, 1902.

Wiener, N. *The Human Use of Human Beings.* New York: Discus Books (Avon), 1967 (originally Houghton Mifflin, 1950).

Wiener, M., and Mehrabian, A. *Language within Language: Immediacy, a Channel in Verbal Communication.* New York: Appleton-Century-Crofts, 1968.

Wittgenstein, L. *Tractatus Logico-Philosophicus.* London: Routledge and Kegan Paul, 1955 (originally published in 1922).

Louis B. Salomon

EMOTIVE ASSOCIATION, EUPHEMISM, TABOO

THE EMOTIVE COMPONENT OF MEANING

If the human mind were a strictly logical device like a calculating machine, it would deal with words simply as names of categories, and with categories as essential tools for imposing order and system on a universe which otherwise presents itself as an unsorted chaos of sense stimuli. But human reaction to words, like much other human behavior, is also motivated by irrational impulses such as those we label *love, hate, joy, sorrow, fear, awe,* and so forth; and, whenever the users of a language evince a fairly uniform emotional response to a given word, that response becomes part of the connotation, therefore part of the standard meaning of the word in that language. While the bulk of the vocabulary doubtless consists of words that carry little or no perceptible emotional charge (*lamp, book, read, subtract, through*), there are nevertheless a good many that produce reactions of various colors and shades, with voltages ranging from mild to knockout force.

Not that is is always easy to distinguish the emotional response to a word itself from the emotional response to the class of things or concepts the word names. A rose or a skylark's song by any other names would smell or sound as sweet, and a dungheap or a subway train's wheel-screech by any other names would be a stench in the nostril or a pain in the eardrum; but many words are undoubtedly "loaded" with the speaker's or hearer's feelings, independent of any observable attributes in the class of objects named. When someone says "Watch your language!" he is usually not attacking your right to refer to the thing(s) you are referring to, but only urging you to abstain from an expression that in itself, quite apart from its denotation and linguistic connotation, is offensive to his ear or eye. There are, as Professor Hayakawa puts it, words that snarl and words that purr—and, of course, there are innumerable gradations in between. An informer and an informant deliver the same confidential information; selective service and the draft impose identical duties on young male citizens; sweat and perspiration produce the same demand for deodorant —but the different words have different odors too, and the nose that is insensitive to their scent is apt to end up a punched nose; the ear that does not hear their harmonies and discords, a cauliflower ear.

In *Romeo and Juliet,* for example, when hot-blooded Tybalt meets Mercutio and Benvolio, the friends of the man he is seeking, he might say to Mercutio, "Thou knowest [*or* art a friend of, *or* often accompaniest] Romeo;" instead, he begins, doubtless maliciously, "Mercutio, thou consort'st with Romeo——." Mercutio immediately bridles in anger at the choice of a word which, being then associated with bands of wandering minstrels, could only in contempt be applied to noblemen: "Consort! What, dost thou make us minstrels? . . . Zounds, consort!" A few moments later Tybalt has "made worm's meat" of Mercutio, Romeo has slain Tybalt, and the train of circumstances leading to the tragic deaths of the two young lovers has been irrevocably set in motion. Today, although the minstrel connection no longer operates to arouse such a violent sense of insult, the word *consort* still has a somewhat derogatory flavor (compare the phrase "consorting with known criminals") as compared with the almost completely neutral *associate,* though both terms have the same denotation and the same linguistic connotation.

Sometimes even slightly different forms of the same basic verbal symbol will carry widely variant emotive charges, as, for example, *informer* and *informant,* already cited. If you wanted to compliment a man on his virility of appearance or behavior you would speak of him as *manly,* certainly not as *mannish* (a derogatory term applied mostly to women) or *manlike* (usually a neutral term divorced from value judgement, as in "The carvings included several manlike figures"). The same emotive distinctions are to be found in the usage of *womanly, womanish, womanlike;* the form *childly* never appears, but *childish* and *childlike* convey respectively denigration and mild praise.

At first glimpse it might appear that this emotive component occurs only in the passion-sullied vocabulary of common speech, that judiciously selected diction— above all, scientific terminology—carries no such inflammatory charge. While this is hopefully true of the use of terms in technical discussion among trained scientists, there is nothing whatever to prevent a "scientific" word from being taken into the popular vocabulary, or, once there, from developing an aura of feeling that may all but obliterate its original denotion and linguistic connotation. The word *science* itself furnishes a striking instance: one of the most potent bits of ritual incantation in the repertoire of present-day spellbinding is "Science says. . . ." This being the case, as people with things or ideas to sell are well aware, any word that even sounds or looks like a scientific term carries a quasi-magical charge that makes blood tingle and cash register tinkle. You have probably never seen, and hopefully never will see, an advertisement reading "This mouthwash contains megatherium"; but if you look at the "Atomic" entries in the 1964-65 Manhattan telephone directory you will find, along with Atomic Energy Commission, such other nuclear-oriented enterprises as Atomic Cleaners and Dryers, Atomic Dress Co., Atomic Handbag Co., Atomic Music Co., Atomic Neckwear Mfg. Co., Atomic Trucking Corp., and Atomic Undergarment Co.

"SHADES" OF MEANING

Since the emotive component of meaning reflects so much of the current technological-sociological-moral climate, it is subject to more rapid and unpredictable change than are the denotation and linguistic connotation—so much so, indeed, that in extreme cases observation on particular specimens may sound as dated as last year's slang.[1] Even at any one time the emotive connotation of a given term may vary a great deal in both kind and intensity from one group of speakers to another, or among the same group in different circumstances. Some words acceptable at stag smokers cause raised eyebrows in mixed company in a drawing room; some that are appropriate in addressing a college class will sound pompous or stuffy in haranguing the same college students at a campus football rally; some are allowable in printed books and on the stage but not in radio or television broadcasts or in "family" magazines. Perhaps this kaleidoscopic shiftiness becomes most painfully apparent when you try to acquire a real working knowledge of a foreign language, that is, a mastery of the subtle nuances that make one phrase courteous and another, perhaps only slightly different, offensive. Even in your own language you may run into problems enough, particularly if you move from one social or cultural milieu to another—as many young men have found on entering the armed services, and then again on reentering civilian life.

The term *nuances* may be misleading, since it suggests that two or more terms really mean the same thing apart from a trivial shade of feeling they arouse. But we have defined symbolic meaning as the totality of what is conveyed by a symbol; hence, no two words are exactly synonymous, regardless of what they denote or what defining qualities they connote, as long as any tinge of emotive association, however minuscule, differentiates them. Consider, for example, the supply of simple adjectives at your disposal for indicating that a person's figure is noticeably below the national norm in weight. If it is someone whose feelings you particularly want to spare (yourself, for instance), you might use *slender;* if you want to sound patronizing, even a trifle acid, you might say *thin* or *lanky;* if you really want to leave a sting you might try *skinny* or *scrawny*—leaving still, for intermediate shades, *slim, spare, delicate, underweight, lean, emaciated.* For the opposite weight pattern, you could make your selection among *plump, well-rounded, portly, fleshy, over-weight, stout, pudgy, chubby, fat, corpulent, obese,* and *bloated.* The abundance of such word choices makes possible an instructive little exercise, proposed many years ago by Bertrand Russell under the name "conjugation of adjectives." Examples (playing the game without too rigid adherence to rules) might go: "I am careful, you are timid, he is afraid of his shadow"; "I am interested, you are inquisitive, he is a snooper"; "I am a social drinker, you may be overindulging, he is a lush."

In the rough-and-tumble of actual use, however, synonym-juggling is anything but a game—unless Russian roulette is also a game. The differences between a fair trade practices law and a minimum price law, between senior citizens and old people, between underprivileged areas and slums, between extra crews and feather-bedding, between a quarantine and a naval blockade: these are differences measurable in such units as sales figures, votegetting, and bloodletting. The bloody draft-law riots of 1863 may or may not have been avoidable, but it is sobering to reflect that there have never been any selective-service-law riots. The modern public relations specialty known as motivation research has a heavy stake in identifying the hidden, perhaps subconscious resonances of contempt or reverence, aggression or longing, archetypal dread or narcissistic self-love which are likely to be stirred by verbal symbols at a given time and place, because without this information an advertising program or a political campaign might founder on an insidiously loaded synonym like a ship on a submerged reef.

TABOO AND EUPHEMISM

The dyslogistic connotations of a good many words, to be sure, are matters openly acknowledged and widely agreed upon, and whenever a common word gathers so heavy a load of taboo or social disapproval that many speakers hesitate to use the word at all, a process known as euphemism sets in. Most people, that is, employ another expression (either a new coinage or a new application for one already familiar) to symbolize the class to which the taboo word normally refers. Some speakers, on the other hand, resist such substitutions as semantically unjustifiable, and speak with pride of "calling a spade a spade," implying that the symbol *spade* is the one and eternally right name for the well-known digging tool, hence any other must be a shilly-shallying evasion. Without taking sides, this book will merely observe that for certain classes of objects, actions, and ideas (not, ordinarily, including spades) there are often two or more expressions with the same denotation and the same linguistic connotation, and that in general the shortest, simplest (and, historically, oldest) word tends to be more or less taboo, while a longer word or phrase, often originally metaphorical as a substitute for the taboo word, has gentler overtones or is socially more acceptable. Naturally this phenomenon occurs oftenest in connection with concepts that in themselves produce a sense of uneasiness in the minds of the users of the language—whether because of religious or sociological pressures peculiar to a certain culture or because of deep-rooted psychological impulses common to virtually the entire human race.

A few examples of this gentling-down process will suffice to suggest many others:

1. The idea of death is so painful that most speakers (including undertakers and life insurance salesmen, who of all people have occasion to talk about it most matter-of-factly) shun the three-letter verb in favor of euphemisms like *pass away, pass on, pass out of the picture, be no longer with us,* and so on.

2. Serious diseases of the heart or the mind sound somehow less forbidding as *heart condition, mental case.*

3. Because the use of the deity's name and other theological terms, except in solemn and reverent discussions, is regarded as blasphemous by many religious sects, we have (for nontheological discourse) near approximations in sound: *gosh, golly, gad* for *God; darn, dang, dash* for *damn; heck* for *hell*—or, in writing, the omission of one or more letters, as in G–d for God.

4. Names of the physiological functions of sex and excretion, and of the external parts of the body most closely associated with these, of course have spawned an assortment of euphemistic expressions, the use of which reflects wide variation in level of taboo from one cultural epoch to another. In mid-Victorian England, even *legs* became *limbs,* and all articles of underclothing *unmentionables.*

It is worth noting that the law of diminishing returns governs the value of any given euphemism just as inexorably as it does that of a factory machine, and the more commonly the euphemistic term appears in speech and writing, the more it tends to gather to itself the same stigma of taboo that is associated with whatever word or words it displaced. The word *undertaker*, for example, though once about as neutral a term as could be found for a person whose professional *raison d'être* we prefer not to be reminded of, is now giving way to *mortician* or *funeral director* because *undertaker* sounds too callously frank. Or take the name of that ingenious bathroom fixture which disposes of the waste products of the human body: the nearest approach to a plain, direct name for it in present-day standard American English is *toilet*—originally a euphemism of a very metaphorical order, stemming from the French *toile* ("cloth"). Once this euphemism came into very general use, however, it became the name for a thing which many people still prefer to mention obliquely, and for which any reader can easily supply a half-dozen substitute expressions currently in vogue. The phrase *to make one's toilet*, referring to purely cosmetic activity, has all but been driven out of circulation, and the modern reader of *The Rape of the Lock* feels a sense of almost grotesque incongruity when, in a setting as urbane as any in English verse, he comes to the line introducing Belinda's dressing table: "And now, unveiled, the Toilet stands displayed."

From one culture or social stratum or chronological era to another, the kind and number of words subject to taboo, and hence generative euphemistic substitutes, swings between wide extremes. At almost any time and place, however, there will be found a few words so heavily frowned upon that by large elements of the population their use, whether in speech or in writing, is regarded as a gross breach of decorum or morals, or both. Indeed, many legal prosecutions for obscenity have been based not on the subject-matter of a book or play but merely on the fact that it employed one or more of these words.[2] Even in the relatively permissive linguistic climate of the time in which this book has been written, there is a small handful of short, pungent English words which, though they are found liberally scrawled on walls and sidewalks, even printed in works of fiction or poetry issued by highly reputable publishers, the present writer feels constrained to mention only by proxy, as it were, in order to avoid giving offense.

These words, all with pedigrees of great antiquity, are used in two very different ways. First, they have denotation and linguistic connotation related to sex or excrement, and are so employed, either simply and naturally by speakers to whom these are symbols untainted by taboo, or self-consciously by a sophisticated class of men and women bent on demonstrating their emancipation from middle-class standards of respectability. But taking a statistical rather than a normative view one finds that in the vast majority of their occurrences these highly charged words point to no referents and no defining qualities at all, but are called upon to serve merely as rhetorical intensifiers, attention-getters, corresponding in function to gestures, changes of vocal intonation, or writing-devices like italics or exclamation points. This is true to some extent of all taboo words, and hence may be illustrated with examples that, hopefully, will not bruise any reader's sensibilities. Consider the meanings of the following phrases: *a good-looking girl, a damned good-looking girl, a goddamned good-looking girl;* or, conversely, *a homely girl, a damned homely girl, a goddamned homely girl; a hell of a fine play, a hell of a flop; Who the hell do you think you are? Hi, there, how the hell are you?* Obviously, the taboo words in these contexts do not refer to anything, but are simply another way of saying "very" or "Listen to this" or "Hey, this is important!" or pounding on the table.

What is being made use of is the shock value of the taboo itself, and any expressions with a strong-enough dyslogistic charge would do equally well.

Two other curiosities may be observed about this divorcing of emotive connotation entirely from the other components of meaning. In the first place, it is not necessary that any of the highly taboo words themselves, or even near-homophones of them, be physically present as long as it is somehow suggested that their intensifying effect is what is intended. Devices traditionally used by the more finicky to produce the same effect include the spoken *so-and-so* or *blankety-blank*, the written asterisks or dashes, which permit the hearer or reader to supply his own verbal intensifiers or not, as he likes; the question of what is meant by the dashes has little to do with what words, if any, the reader chooses to imagine in their place.

Second, the law of diminishing returns operates here too in a way to give pause even to those who scorn to let social or moral pressures circumscribe their vocabulary. Setting aside any possible considerations deriving from squeamishness, and merely weighing the effect in the passionless scale of the efficiency expert, one can easily see that in a passage such as "How the ———— are you? I sure as ———— wish, ———— ———— it, you'd quit reading that ———— ———— book and give me the ———— low-down on what the ———— ———— you've been doing since I saw you at that ———— party at the boss's ———— ———— country place," and so forth, the attention-getting force of each successive three-em line, or whatever taboo expression it may replace, is less than that of the preceding one. If anyone speaks habitually in a shout, his decibels soon become merely monotonous, and only a sudden drop to a whisper will bring his audience up with a jolt.

Both points are well illustrated by H. L. Mencken's anecdote of a World War I drill sergeant who was accustomed to interlard his speech so liberally with forms of one especially taboo word that when he ordered his men, "Go get your ———— rifles!" they knew it was a routine command and took their time about obeying. One day, though, he called out, "Go get your rifles!" and every startled G.I. in the platoon "lit out" for the barracks on the double.

Since response to a command affords the best possible pragmatic test of what meaning, if any, has been conveyed, this little story demonstrates also: (a) that emotive connotation is indeed part of meaning; (b) that, like the other components of meaning, it is not inherent in any given verbal symbol but is imputed by the users of the symbol; and (c) that the speaker's intention and the hearer's inference do not necessarily coincide.

NOTES

1. Compare Shakespeare's Doll Tearsheet, disputing Pistol's claim to the title of captain: "A captain! God's light, these villains will make the word as odious as the word 'occupy,' which was an excellent good word before it was ill sorted."

2. The term *obscenity* usually is reserved for language that violates the sexual and excremental taboos, *blasphemy* for those that violate the religious taboos. *Profanity* seems to take in both categories. *Pornography*, commonly defined as writing designed to appeal to the prurient interest, often makes use of no words that in themselves are taboo; for example, consider the polished, even flowery diction of *Fanny Hill*, as contested with *Lady Chatterley's Lover*, the objection to which was based very largely on its use of taboo words.

Edward and Mildred Hall

THE SOUNDS OF SILENCE

actions do indeed speak louder than
words—and new interpretations
of nonverbal communications
tell us how to read them

Bob leaves his apartment at 8:15 A.M. and stops at the corner drugstore for breakfast. Before he can speak, the counterman says, "The usual?" Bob nods yes. While he savors his Danish, a fat man pushes onto the adjoining stool and overflows into his space. Bob scowls and the man pulls himself in as much as he can. Bob has sent two messages without speaking a syllable.

Henry has an appointment to meet Arthur at 11 o'clock; he arrives at 11:30. Their conversation is friendly, but Arthur retains a lingering hostility. Henry has unconsciously communicated that he doesn't think the appointment is very important or that Arthur is a person who needs to be treated with respect.

George is talking to Charley's wife at a party. Their conversation is entirely trivial, yet Charley glares at them suspiciously. Their physical proximity and the movements of their eyes reveal that they are powerfully attracted to each other.

José Ybarra and Sir Edmund Jones are at the same party and it is important for them to establish a cordial relationship for business reasons. Each is trying to be warm and friendly, yet they will part with mutual distrust and their business transaction will probably fall through. José, in Latin fashion, moved closer and closer to Sir Edmund as they spoke, and this movement was miscommunicated as pushiness to Sir Edmund, who kept backing away from this intimacy, and this was miscommunicated to José as coldness. The silent languages of Latin and English cultures are more difficult to learn than their spoken languages.

In each of these cases, we see the subtle power of nonverbal communication. The only language used throughout most of the history of humanity (in revolutionary terms, vocal communication is relatively recent), it is the first form of communication you learn. You use this preverbal language, consciously and unconsciously, every day to tell other people how you feel about yourself and them. This language includes your posture, gestures, facial expressions, costume, the way you walk, even your treatment of time and space and material things. All people communicate on several different levels at the same time but are usually aware of only the verbal dialog and don't realize that they respond to nonverbal messages. But when a person says one thing and really believes something else, the discrepancy between the two can usually be sensed. Nonverbal-communication systems are much less subject to the conscious description that often occurs in verbal systems. When we find ourselves thinking, "I don't know what it is about him, but he doesn't seem sincere," it's usually this lack of congruity between a person's words and his behavior that makes us anxious and uncomfortable.

Few of us realize how much we all depend on body movement in our conversation or are aware of the hidden rules that govern listening behavior. But we know instantly whether or not the person we're talking to is "tuned in" and we're very sensitive to any breach in listening etiquette. In white middle-class American culture, when someone wants to show he is listening to someone else, he looks either at the other person's face or, specifically, at his eyes, shifting his gaze from one eye to the other.

If you observe a person conversing, you'll notice that he indicates he's listening by nodding his head. He also makes little "Hmm" noises. If he agrees with what's being said, he may give a vigorous nod. To show pleasure or affirmation, he smiles; if he has some reservations, he looks skeptical by raising an eyebrow or pulling down the corners of his mouth. If a participant wants to terminate the conversation, he may start shifting his body position, stretching his legs, crossing or uncrossing them, bobbing his foot or diverting his gaze from the speaker. The more he fidgets, the more the speaker becomes aware that he has lost his audience. As a last measure, the listener may look at his watch to indicate the imminent end of the conversation.

Talking and listening are so intricately intertwined that a person cannot do one without the other. Even when one is alone and talking to oneself, there is part of the brain that speaks while another part listens. In all conversations, the listener is positively or negatively reinforcing the speaker all the time. He may even guide the conversation without knowing it, by laughing or frowning or dismissing the argument with a wave of his hand.

The language of the eyes—another age-old way of exchanging feelings—is both subtle and complex. Not only do men and women use their eyes differently but there are class, generation, regional, ethnic and national cultural differences. Americans often complain about the way foreigners stare at people or hold a glance too long. Most Americans look away from someone who is using his eyes in an unfamiliar way because it makes them self-conscious. If a man looks at another man's wife in a certain way, he's asking for trouble, as indicated earlier. But he might not be ill mannered or seeking to challenge the husband. He might be a European in this country who hasn't learned our visual mores. Many American women visiting France or Italy are acutely embarrassed because, for the first time in their lives, men really look at them—their eyes, hair, nose, lips, breasts, hips, legs, thighs, knees, ankles, feet, clothes, hairdo, even their walk. These same women, once they have become used to being looked at, often return to the United States and are overcome with the feeling that "No one ever really looks at me anymore."

Analyzing the mass of data on the eyes, it is possible to sort out at least three ways in which the eyes are used to communicate: dominance *vs.* submission, involvement *vs.* detachment and positive *vs.* negative attitude. In addition, there are three levels of consciousness and control, which can be categorized as follows: (1) conscious use of the eyes to communicate, such as the flirting blink and the intimate nose-wrinkling squint; (2) the very extensive category of unconscious but learned behavior governing where the eyes are directed and when (this unwritten set of rules dictates how and under what circumstances the sexes, as well as people of all status categories, look at each other); and (3) the response of the eye itself, which is completely outside both awareness and control—changes in the cast (the sparkle) of the eye and the pupillary reflex.

The eye is unlike any other organ of the body, for it is an extension of the brain. The unconscious pupillary reflex and the cast of the eye have been known by people of Middle Eastern origin for years—although most are unaware of their knowledge. Depending on the context, Arabs and others look either directly at the eyes or deeply *into* the eyes of their interlocutor. We became aware of this in the Middle East several years ago while looking at jewelry. The merchant suddenly started to push a particular bracelet at a customer and said, "You buy this one." What interested us was that the bracelet was not the one that had been consciously selected by the purchaser. But the merchant, watching the pupils of the eyes, knew what the purchaser really wanted to buy. Whether he specifically knew *how* he knew is debatable.

A psychologist at the University of Chicago, Eckhard Hess, was the first to conduct systematic studies of the pupillary reflex. His wife remarked one evening, while watching him reading in bed, that he must be very interested in the text because his pupils were dilated. Following up on this, Hess slipped some pictures of nudes into a stack of photographs that he gave to his male assistant. Not looking at the photographs but watching his assistant's pupils, Hess was able to tell precisely when the assistant came to the nudes. In further experiments, Hess retouched the eyes in a photograph of a woman. In one print, he made the pupils small, in another, large; nothing else was changed. Subjects who were given the photographs found the woman with the dilated pupils much more attractive. Any man who has had the experience of seeing a woman look at him as her pupils widen with reflex speed knows that she's flashing him a message.

The eye-sparkle phenomenon frequently turns up in our interviews of couples in love. It's apparently one of the first reliable clues in the other person that love is genuine. To date, there is no scientific data to explain eye sparkle; no investigation of the pupil, the cornea or even the white sclera of the eye shows how the sparkle originates. Yet we all know it when we see it.

One common situation for most people involves the use of the eyes in the street and in public. Although eye behavior follows a definite set of rules, the rules vary according to the place, the needs and feelings of the people, and their ethnic background. For urban whites, once they're within definite recognition distance (16-32 feet for people with average eyesight), there is mutual avoidance of eye contact — unless they want something specific: a pickup, a handout or information of some kind. In the West and in small towns generally, however, people are much more likely to look at and greet one another, even if they're strangers.

It's permissible to look at people if they're beyond recognition distance; but once inside this sacred zone, you can only steal a glance at strangers. You *must* greet friends, however; to fail to do so is insulting. Yet, to stare too fixedly even at them is considered rude and hostile. Of course, all of these rules are variable.

A great many blacks, for example, greet each other in public even if they don't know each other. To blacks, most eye behavior of whites has the effect of giving the impression that they aren't there, but this is due to white avoidance of eye contact with *anyone* in the street.

Another very basic difference between people of different ethnic backgrounds is their sense of territoriality and how they handle space. This is the silent communication, or miscommunication, that caused friction between Mr. Ybarra and Sir Edmund Jones in our earlier example. We know from research that everyone has around himself an invisible bubble of space that contracts and expands depending on several factors: his emotional state, the activity he's performing at the time and his cultural background. This bubble is a kind of mobile territory that he will defend against intrusion. If he is accustomed to close personal distance between himself and others, his bubble will be smaller than that of someone who's accustomed to greater personal distance. People of North European heritage—English, Scandinavian, Swiss and German—tend to avoid contact. Those whose heritage is Italian, French, Spanish, Russian, Latin American or Middle Eastern like close personal contact.

People are very sensitive to any intrusion into their spatial bubble. If someone stands too close to you, your first instinct is to back up. If that's not possible, you lean away and pull yourself in, tensing your muscles. If the intruder doesn't respond to these body signals, you may then try to protect yourself, using a briefcase, umbrella or raincoat. Women — especially when traveling alone — often plant their pocketbook in such a way that no one can get very close to them. As a last resort, you may move to another spot and position yourself behind a desk or a chair that provides screening. Everyone tries to adjust the space around himself in a way that's comfortable for him; most often, he does this unconsciously.

Emotions also have a direct effect on the size of a person's territory. When you're angry or under stress, your bubble expands and you require more space. New York psychiatrist Augustus Kinzel found a difference in what he calls Body-Buffer Zones between violent and nonviolent prison inmates. Dr. Kinzel conducted experiments in which each prisoner was placed in the center of a small room and then Dr. Kinzel slowly walked toward him. Nonviolent prisoners allowed him to come quite close, while prisoners with a history of violent behavior couldn't tolerate his proximity and reacted with some vehemence.

Apparently, people under stress experience other people as looming larger and closer than they actually are. Studies of schizophrenic patients have indicated that they sometimes have a distorted perception of space, and several psychiatrists have reported patients who experience their body boundaries as filling up an entire room. For these patients, anyone who comes into the room is actually inside their body, and such an intrusion may trigger a violent outburst.

Unfortunately, there is little detailed information about normal people who live in highly congested urban areas. We do know, of course that the noise, pollution, dirt, crowding and confusion of our cities induce feelings of stress in most of us, and stress leads to a need for greater space. The man who's packed into a subway, jostled in the street, crowded into an elevator and forced to work all day in a bull pen or a small office without auditory or visual privacy is going to be very stressed at the end of his day. He needs places that provide relief from constant overstimulation of his nervous system. Stress from overcrowding is cumulative and people can tolerate more crowding early in the day than later; note the increased bad temper during the evening rush hour as compared with the morning melee. Certainly one factor in people's desire to commute by car is the need for privacy and relief from crowding (except, often, from other cars); it may be the only time of the day when nobody can intrude.

In crowded public places, we tense our muscles and hold ourselves stiff, and thereby communicate to others our desire not to intrude on their space and, above all, not to touch them. We also avoid eye contact, and the total effect is that of someone who has "tuned out." Walking along the street, our bubble expands slightly as we move in a stream of strangers, taking care not to bump into them. In the office, at meetings, in restaurants, our bubble keeps changing as it adjusts to the activity at hand.

Most white middle-class Americans use four main distances in their business and social relations: intimate, personal, social and public. Each of these distances has a near and a far phase and is accompanied by changes in the volume of the voice. Intimate distance varies from direct physical contact with another person to a distance of six to eighteen inches and is used for our most private activities—caressing another person or making love. At this distance, you are overwhelmed by sensory inputs from the other person—heat from the body, tactile stimulation from the skin, the fragrance of perfume, even the sound of breathing—all of which literally envelop you. Even at the far phase, you're still within easy touching distance. In general, the use of intimate distance in public between adults is frowned on. It's also much too close for strangers, except under conditions of extreme crowding.

In the second zone—personal distance—the close phase is one and a half to two and a half feet; it's at this distance that wives usually stand from their husbands in public. If another woman moves into this zone, the wife will most likely be disturbed. The far phase—two and a half to four feet—is the distance used to "keep someone at arm's length" and is the most common spacing used by people in conversation.

The third zone—social distance—is employed during business transactions or exchanges with a clerk or repairman. People who work together tend to use close social distance—four to seven feet. This is also the distance for conversations at social gatherings. To stand at this distance from someone who is seated has a dominating effect (e.g., teacher to pupil, boss to secretary). The far phase of the third zone—seven to twelve feet—is where people stand when someone says, "Stand back so I can look at you." This distance lends a formal tone to business or social discourse. In an excutive office, the desk serves to keep people at this distance.

The fourth zone—public distance—is used by teachers in classrooms or speakers at public gatherings. At its farthest phase—25 feet and beyond—it is used for important public figures. Violations of this distance can lead to serious complications. During his 1970 U. S. visit, the president of France, Georges Pompidou, was harassed by pickets in Chicago, who were permitted to get within touching distance. Since pickets in France are kept behind barricades a block or more away, the president was outraged by this insult to his person, and President Nixon was obliged to communicate his concern as well as offer his personal apologies.

It is interesting to note how American pitchmen and panhandlers exploit the unwritten, unspoken conventions of eye and distance. Both take advantage of the fact that once explicit eye contact is established, it is rude to look away, because to do so means to brusquely dismiss the other person and his needs. Once having caught the eye of his mark, the panhandler then locks on, not letting go until he moves through the public zone, the social zone, the personal zone and, finally, into the intimate sphere, where people are most vulnerable.

Touch also is an important part of the constant stream of communication that takes place between people. A light touch, a firm touch, a blow, a caress are all communications. In an effort to break down barriers among people, there's been a recent upsurge in group-encounter activities, in which strangers are encouraged to touch one another. In special situations such as these, the rules for not touching are broken with group approval and people gradually lose some of their inhibitions.

Although most people don't realize it, space is perceived and distances are set not by vision alone but with all the senses. Auditory space is perceived with the ears, thermal space with the skin, kinesthetic space with the muscles of the body and olfactory space with the nose. And, once again, it's one's culture that determines how his senses are programmed—which sensory information ranks highest and lowest. The important thing to remember is that culture is very persistent. In this country, we've noted the existence of culture patterns that determine distance between people in the third and fourth generations of some families, despite their prolonged contact with people of very different cultural heritages.

Whenever there is great cultural distance between two people, there are bound to be problems arising from differences in behavior and expectations. An example is the American couple who consulted a psychiatrist about their marital problems. The husband was from New England and had been brought up by reserved parents who taught him to control his emotions and to respect the need for privacy. His wife was from an Italian family and had been brought up in close contact with all the members of her large family, who were extremely warm, volatile and demonstrative.

When the husband came home after a hard day at the office, dragging his feet and longing for peace and quiet, his wife would rush to him and smother him. Clasping his hands, rubbing his brow, crooning over his weary head, she never left him alone. But when the wife was upset or anxious about her day, the husband's response was to withdraw completely and leave her alone. No comforting, no affectionate embrace, no attention—just solitude. The woman became convinced her husband didn't love her and, in desperation, she consulted a psychiatrist. Their problem wasn't basically psychological but cultural.

Why has man developed all these different ways of communicating messages without words? One reason is that people don't like to spell out certain kinds of messages. We prefer to find other ways of showing our feelings. This is especially true in relationships as sensitive as courtship. Men don't like to be rejected and most women don't want to turn a man down bluntly. Instead, we work out subtle ways of encouraging or discouraging each other that save face and avoid confrontations.

How a person handles space in dating others is an obvious and very sensitive indicator of how he or she feels about the other person. On a first date, if a woman sits or stands so close to a man that he is acutely conscious of her physical presence —inside the intimate-distance zone—the man usually construes it to mean that she is encouraging him. However, before the man starts moving in on the woman, he should be sure what message she's really sending; otherwise, he risks bruising his ego. What is close to someone of North European background may be neutral or distant to someone of Italian heritage. Also, women sometimes use space as a way of misleading a man and there are few things that put men off more than women who communicate contradictory messages—such as women who cuddle up and then act insulted when a man takes the next step.

How does a woman communicate interest in a man? In addition to such familiar gambits as smiling at him, she may glance shyly at him, blush and then look away. Or she may give him a real come-on look and move in very close when he approaches.

She may touch his arm and ask for a light. As she leans forward to light her cigarette, she may brush him lightly, enveloping him in her perfume. She'll probably continue to smile at him and she may use what ethologists call preening gestures—touching the back of her hair, thrusting her breasts forward, tilting her hips as she stands or crossing her legs if she's seated, perhaps even exposing one thigh or putting a hand on her thigh and stroking it. She may also stroke her wrists as she converses or show the palm of her hand as a way of gaining his attention. Her skin may be unusually flushed or quite pale, her eyes brighter, the pupils larger.

If a man sees a woman whom he wants to attract, he tries to present himself by his posture and stance as someone who is self-assured. He moves briskly and confidently. When he catches the eye of the woman, he may hold her glance a little longer than normal. If he gets an encouraging smile, he'll move in close and engage her in small talk. As they converse, his glance shifts over her face and body. He, too, may make preening gestures—straightening his tie, smoothing his hair or shooting his cuffs.

How do people learn body language? The same way they learn spoken language —by observing and imitating people around them as they're growing up. Little girls imitate their mothers or an older female. Little boys imitate their fathers or a respected uncle or a character on television. In this way, they learn the gender signals appropriate for their sex. Regional, class and ethnic patterns of body behavior are also learned in childhood and persist throughout life.

Such patterns of masculine and feminine body behavior vary widely from one culture to another. In America, for example, women stand with their thighs together. Many walk with their pelvis tipped slightly forward and their upper arms close to their body. When they sit, they cross their legs at the knee or, if they are well past middle age, they may cross their ankles. American men hold their arms away from their body, often swinging them as they walk. They stand with their legs apart (an extreme example is the cowboy, with legs apart and thumbs tucked into his belt). When they sit, they put their feet on the floor with legs apart and, in some parts of the country, they cross their legs by putting one ankle on the other knee.

Leg behavior indicates sex, status and personality. It also indicates whether or not one is at ease or is showing respect or disrespect for the other person. Young Latin-American males avoid crossing their legs. In their world of machismo, the preferred position for young males when with one another (if there is no older dominant male present to whom they must show respect) is to sit on the base of their spine with their leg muscles relaxed and their feet wide apart. Their respect position is like our military equivalent; spine straight, heels and ankles together—almost identical to that displayed by properly brought up young women in New England in the early part of this century.

American women who sit with their legs spread apart in the presence of males are not normally signaling a come-on — they are simply (and often unconsciously) sitting like men. Middle-class women in the presence of other women to whom they are very close may on occasion throw themselves down on a soft chair or sofa and let themselves go. This is a signal that nothing serious will be taken up. Males on the other hand lean back and prop their legs up on the nearest object.

The way we walk, similarly, indicates status, respect, mood and ethnic or cultural affiliation. The many variants of the female walk are too well known to go into here, except to say that a man would have to be blind not to be turned on by the way some women walk—a fact that made Mae West rich before scientists ever studied these matters. To white Americans, some French middle-class males walk in a way that is both humorous and suspect. There is a bounce and looseness to the French walk, as though the parts of the body were somehow unrelated. Jacques Tati, the French movie actor, walks this way; so does the great mime, Marcel Marceau.

Blacks and whites in America—with the exception of middle- and upper-middle class professionals of both groups—move and walk very differently from each other. To the blacks, whites often seem incredibly stiff, almost mechanical in their movements. Black males, on the other hand, have a looseness and coordination that frequently makes whites a little uneasy; it's too different, too integrated, too alive, too male. Norman Mailer has said that squares walk from the shoulders, like bears, but blacks and hippies walk from the hips, like cats.

All over the world, people walk not only in their own characteristic way but have walks that communicate the nature of their involvement with whatever it is they're doing. The purposeful walk of North Europeans is an important component of proper behavior on the job. Any male who has been in the military knows how essential it is to walk properly (which makes for a continuing source of tension between blacks and whites in the Service). The quick shuffle of servants in the Far East in the old days was a show of respect. On the island of Truk, when we last visited, the inhabitants even had a name for the respectful walk that one used when in the presence of a chief or when walking past a chief's house. The term was *sulfan,* which meant to be humble and respectful.

The notion that people communicate volumes by their gestures, facial expressions, posture and walk is not new; actors, dancers, writers and psychiatrists have long been aware of it. Only in recent years, however, have scientists begun to make systematic observations of body motions. Ray L. Birdwhistell of the University of Pennsylvania is one of the pioneers in body-motion research and coined the term kinesics to describe this field. He developed an elaborate notation system to record both facial and body movements, using an approach similar to that of the linguist, who studies the basic elements of speech. Birdwhistell and other kinesicists such as Albert Sheflen, Adam Kendon and William Condon take movies of people interacting. They run the film over and over again, often at reduced speed for frame-by-frame analysis, so that they can observe even the slightest body movements not perceptible at normal interaction speeds. These movements are then recorded in notebooks for later analysis.

To appreciate the importance of nonverbal-communication systems, consider the unskilled inner-city black looking for a job. His handling of time and space alone is sufficiently different from the white middle-class pattern to create great misunderstandings on both sides. The black is told to appear for a job interview at a certain time. He arrives late. The white interviewer concludes from his tardy arrival that the black is irresponsible and not really interested in the job. What the interviewer doesn't know is that the black time system (often referred to by blacks as C. P. T.—colored people's time) isn't the same as that of whites. In the words of a black student who had been told to make an appointment to see his professor: "Man, you *must* be putting me on. I never had an appointment in my life."

The black job applicant, having arrived late for his interview, may further antagonize the white interviewer by his posture and his eye behavior. Perhaps he slouches and avoids looking at the interviewer; to him, this is playing it cool. To the interviewer, however, he may well look shifty and sound uninterested. The interviewer has failed to notice the actual signs of interest and eagerness in the black's behavior, such as the subtle shift in the quality of the voice—a gentle and tentative excitement—an almost imperceptible change in the cast of the eyes and a relaxing of the jaw muscles.

Moreover, correct reading of black-white behavior is continually complicated by the fact that both groups are comprised of individuals—some of whom try to accommodate and some of whom make it a point of pride *not* to accommodate. At present, this means that many Americans, when thrown into contact with one another, are in the precarious position of not knowing which pattern applies. Once identified and analyzed, nonverbal-communication systems can be taught, like a foreign language. Without this training, we respond to nonverbal communications in terms of our own culture; we read everyone's behavior as if it were our own, and thus we often misunderstand it.

Several years ago in New York City, there was a program for sending children from predominantly black and Puerto Rican low-income neighborhoods to summer school in a white upper-class neighborhood on the East Side. One morning, a group of young black and Puerto Rican boys raced down the street, shouting and screaming and overturning garbage cans on their way to school. A doorman from an apartment building nearby chased them and cornered one of them inside a building. The boy drew a knife and attacked the doorman. This tragedy would not have occurred if the doorman had been familiar with the behavior of boys from low-income neighborhoods, where such antics are routine and socially acceptable and where pursuit would be expected to invite a violent response.

The language of behavior is extremely complex. Most of us are lucky to have under control one subcultural system—the one that reflects our sex, class, generation and geographic region within the United States. Because of its complexity, efforts to isolate bits of noverbal communication and generalize from them are in vain; you don't become an instant expert on people's behavior by watching them at cocktail parties. Body language isn't something that's independent of the person, something than can be donned and doffed like a suit of clothes.

Our research and that of our colleagues has shown that, far from being a superficial form of communication that can be consciously manipulated, nonverbal-communication systems are interwoven into the fabric of the personality and, as sociologist Erving Goffman has demonstrated, into society itself. They are the warp and woof of daily interactions with others and they influence how one expresses oneself, how one experiences oneself as a man or a woman.

Nonverbal communications signal to members of your own group what kind of person you are, how you feel about others, how you'll fit into and work in a group, whether you're assured or anxious, the degree to which you feel comfortable with the standards of your own culture, as well as deeply significant feelings about the self, including the state of your own psyche. For most of us, it's difficult to accept the reality of another's behavioral system. And, of course, none of us will ever become fully knowledgeable of the importance of every non-verbal signal. But as long as each of us realizes the power of these signals, this society's diversity can be a source of great strength rather than a further—and subtly powerful—source of division.

Julius Fast

CAN YOU INFLUENCE PEOPLE
THROUGH "BODY LANGUAGE"?

The bus was crowded when Peter boarded it and he found himself close to a very pretty girl. Peter enjoyed the bus ride and admired the girl, in fact, he couldn't keep his eyes off her. Staring at her, he noticed that she had light blue eyes and dark brown hair, a pleasant combination.

His innocent enjoyment was shattered when the girl turned to him angrily before she left the bus and said loudly, "You should me ashamed of yourself!"

"What did I do?" Peter asked the driver in honest bewilderment. "I only looked at her."

"It takes all kinds . . ." the driver shrugged, but did he mean Peter or the girl? Peter spent a miserable evening wondering just what he had done that was wrong. He would have known what was wrong if he understood some of the rules of body language. Peter violated a very basic law. He looked at the girl beyond the proper looking time.

For every situation there is a proper looking time, a definite period during which you are allowed to meet and hold someone's eyes. In an elevator the time is so brief that it can hardly be considered looking at all. Your eye catches that of a stranger and you look away at once. In a crowded bus, a subway or train, you can look a little longer. But go beyond the proper time—some 10 seconds—and you violate the unwritten but rigid code of body language and take the chance of getting into the same situation that embarrassed Peter.

The girl Peter admired interpreted his stare as insolent or arrogant or insulting in the same way that a cripple interprets the stares of the curious. If we have any consideration, we look only briefly at a cripple or a deformed person, pretending not to look at all.

We look at celebrities in the same way, taking care not to catch their eyes, not to stare at them with too curious a look.

The unwritten laws of body language allow a longer time for staring when we talk to someone, but it is still a limited time. In all conversations we look away frequently and break eye contact. Only a lecturer or a politician addressing an audience can hold eye contact as long as he wishes.

Just what are these unwritten laws of body language? For that matter, just what is body language? Are the rules learned or are they acquired instinctively? Do we all know them, or are they something we must learn? If so, how do we learn them?

These questions have intrigued psychologists ever since they discovered that we communicate with more than the words we speak. Words are only one part of communication. How we use those words is another part. Are our voices loud, angry, overbearing, confident, soft, shy? The quality of a voice can communicate as much as the words. The same words can be tender, mocking, sarcastic or angry, depending on how they are said. We can signal our own authority by talking in a loud, overbearing way. We can use the same words to signal our humility by talking softly and hesitantly. But even beyond voice communication, there are the messages our bodies send out constantly. Sometimes the body message reinforces the words. Sometimes the messages are sent with no accompanying words and we speak in body language alone.

But what gestures make up body language? Most of us are familiar with the common hand gestures. Some people cannot talk without using their hands. They reach out as they explain, almost shaping the words, emphasizing and exaggerating and punctuating with their hands. Other people hardly use their hands at all when they talk. How people use their hands and whether they use them depends on their cultural background. Italians are great hand movers. So are Russians and Latin Americans. Englishmen are stingy about their hand movements; they appear as more controlled and rigid in their behavior.

In the United States, almost any type of hand movement can be found because we have a mixture of cultures. American etiquette books tell us that waving the hands and gesticulating is ill-mannered and distasteful. It is "unrefined." Refined behavior is always tight and formal. True etiquette can be equated with control and discipline. It can also be equated with an Anglo-Saxon, overcontrolled culture. But our cultural mix in the last century has been too much for books of etiquette.

It is just this cultural mix in America that makes some men more eloquent than others. When body language is used to emphasize the spoken language, to reinforce it, the man who cannot use it is crippled. Too many politicians, awkward with their hands, have learned this to their sorrow. Many have had their images revamped by a reeducation in body language.

A man who uses hand movements when he talks appears freer, more open and more honest to an audience than a controlled nonmover. At certain times, however, a limited amount of hand movement indicates things like solidity, reliability and confidence.

A good politician knows this instinctively and matches his hand movements to the image he wishes to project. Former President Johnson was apparently taught the proper hand movements because his image was too distant and withdrawn. There was a period, before he learned the gestures, when he appeared awkward and uncomfortable.

It seems obvious that President Nixon has had his body language changed and tailored to match his new image. He does not come across now as the same man who lost the election to John Kennedy in 1960, and the change is largely due to a more controlled, but not nearly so stiff, body movement.

Fiorello H. La Guardia, New York City's mayor in the '30's and early '40's, used to campaign in English, Italian and Yiddish. When he spoke Italian he had one set of hand gestures, another set for Yiddish and still a third for English. Each language demanded its own set of body-language gestures.

But body language is more than hand movements. The eyes play a large part, too. Try holding a fellow pedestrian's eye a bit longer than the proper time. You create an awkward situation and often the only solution is to smile and offer a casual remark, "How are you?" or "Nice day." You may find yourself in conversation with a complete stranger.

The eyes give hidden signals as well as obvious ones. Scientists have found that the pupils dilate unconsciously under pleasant circumstances. Show a man a naked lady, or show a woman a pretty baby, and their pupils dilate. Do the pupils also dilate when a man has a good hand at poker? If so, then perhaps the "natural" poker player is one who unconsciously reads this body-language sign.

What of the rest of the body? Does it also send out unconscious signals?

It does, and the fact that these signals are unconscious means that they are beyond our control. We are not aware that we are sending them out and, therefore, they are more honest than words. It is easy to lie with our voices, but harder to lie with our bodies.

Actors are the exception to this rule. They are trained to lie with their bodies. Recently I talked to Lily Tomlin, who plays a number of characters on "Laugh-In." One of them, a telephone operator, is a masterpiece of body language. The operator torments a customer as she plucks at her breast and twists her face and body. Discussing her movements I told Miss Tomlin that the breast-touching indicated loneliness and introversion; the foot-twisting, self-satisfaction.

"That's what she is," Miss Tomlin agreed. "Lonely and yet self-satisfied with what she is doing. The gestures? They just came naturally once I knew the character."

This is an unconscious adoption of body-language gestures by an actress who first created the character, then lived it and, in living it, naturally used the right body-language gestures.

In addition to the messages we send with our bodies, we also use the space around us to communicate. All of us have our own territories—comfortable distances that we like to keep between us and our friends. We stay closer to people we love, farther away from strangers. When a stranger intrudes on our territory—comes too close to us—we may find it uncomfortable. If the intruder is a wife or husband or lover, we may like the intrusion. It tells us, "I care for you. I love you."

Parents often use space to dominate a child. By looming over him, a parent proves her superiority. The child feels the parent as overpowering and himself as helpless. On the other hand, a parent can draw a child into the circle of her arms and by forcibly invading his space, communicate love and warmth. To do this more easily, the parent may kneel down to the child's level and do away with the looming quality of an adult-child encounter.

Teachers, too, can take a tip from body language in relating to their pupils. The teacher who sits behind a desk is placing an obstacle, the desk, between herself and her pupils. In body language she's saying, "I am your superior. I am here to teach you. You must obey me."

Many educators feel that this is an important and necessary attitude to establish if any "real" teaching is to be done. Other teachers, however, try to do away with the barrier of a desk. They perch on the edge of it and have nothing between them and their students. Still others feel that this is an elevated position, putting the teacher above the student and creating resistance to the teacher. They prefer a position in the center of the room, surrounded by the students, some of whom must turn in their seats to face the teacher.

"This," a teacher once explained to me, "puts me in the center of things. I never sit in a student's seat because I'd be too low. I'd be no better than a student, and a teacher has to be better or why be a teacher? I sit on a student's desk in the center of the room. I'm one of them and yet still a teacher. You'd be amazed at how well they respond."

She is using space to communicate a body-language message. "I'm one of you. I'm on your side even though I'm your teacher."

Which method is most efficient? It's hard to say, except that each teacher must adopt the method that works best for her. If her body language is restricted and tight, sitting on a student's desk may seem simply an affectation—false and unnatural.

The use of the desk as a protective device is familiar to everyone who has watched the Johnny Carson show. Carson uses a desk to separate himself from his guests and to achieve a certain formality. David Frost, when he interviews a guest, does away with a desk and sometimes even does away with chairs, sitting on the stage steps with his guest and using territorial invasion and touch to communicate closeness and warmth. Frost's interviews have a different quality from Carson's because of this different use of space. Perhaps not better, but surely more personal.

The quality of an interview depends not only on the body language of the interviewer, but on his personality as well, and every personality has its own characteristic body-language gestures, even as each culture has its own gestures. We shake our heads up and down for "yes." In India they use the same gesture for "no." To really understand a person's body language we must understand something of their personality, as well as something of their cultural background.

But there are some gestures, such as smiles, that seem to cut across cultural lines. In America there are many common gestures in spite of our cultural mix. Arm-crossing and leg-crossing are two of them. If someone is trying to persuade us and we cross our arms tightly, it is often a sign of resistance. Crossed legs can also be a sign of resistance. When a woman crosses them tightly at the knees and at the ankles, sort of intertwining them, it may indicate resistance to sexuality or a tight, closed personality. (However, it may also be a necessary pose because she's wearing a miniskirt.)

Women in pants tend to give better clues to their emotions by the positioning of their legs. They can sprawl out comfortably. If they sit with open laps they may indicate acceptance, not only sexually, but also intellectually. The well-organized woman may tend to run her legs parallel—as orderly as her life. But I say "tend" because these are still just tendencies. With a skirt, parallel legs are simply a model's pose. Girls are taught in charm schools that this is more graceful. They are also taught the proper arm-crossing.

If all this is true, can we ever really tell anything from a person's body language? Can we use it to control other people or to interpret the true meaning of the messages they send?

We can. We can learn certain tricks of domination to control a situation. We can arrange to be higher than our subordinates, or we can allow our boss to be higher than we are. We can be aware that we dominate our children when we hover

over them, that certain facial gestures should be matched to certain body gestures for a smoother appearance—but these are tricks and rather superficial. The real value of body language lies in the insight it can give to our behavior.

Are we tight and rigid about life in general? Our body language can give us a clue to how we are acting and allow us to change our behavior for the better. How a woman sits next to a man on a couch contains a dozen clues to her personality. Does she use her arms as a barrier? Does she cross her legs away from him? Does she turn her body toward him?

How we react to other people's zones of privacy, and how strong our territorial needs are, give other clues. Do we feel uncomfortable when people are close to us? Are we afraid of touching, of being touched? If we are, it might be a sign of our own insecurity, our own fear of revealing ourselves. Understanding this can allow us to take the first step toward dropping the barriers that stand between us and the world.

Only when these barriers begin to fall is it possible to realize not only our own potential as human beings, but the potential of the entire world around us.

Section 3

THE CONSEQUENCES OF
INTERPERSONAL COMMUNICATION

From effective interpersonal communication we gain lasting friendships, personal happiness, fulfillment in our relationships with others, and love for one another. Commitment, successful decision making, an increase in trust, and reduced conflicts all stem from the more effective use of skills related to maintaining interpersonal relationships. The pleasurable and productive consequences of effective interpersonal communication are reflected in the lives of those who have developed the appropriate and proper skills. The sad, despondent, disappointed and unfulfilled humans whose lives reek of distrust, lack of cooperation, conflict, and withdrawal from affection are experiencing consequences of ineffective interpersonal communication. Cruelty and destruction of others are true signs of the deadly results of disruptive human communication.

Alienation is probably at this time the term most frequently used to refer to a multitude of "gaps" between individuals and groups of people. When someone appears or feels separated from, or withdrawn from, or turned away from another, he refers to himself, or others call him, alienated. The striking feature of alienation in all of its many forms is the lack of communication. In alienation interpersonal relationships are estranged and suffer with tension and disaffection. The alienated are often quarrelsome, contentious, disagreeable, unharmonious, and pugilistic. Goffman describes the dimensions and forces that contribute to alienation from interaction. As he notes, "Joint involvement appears to be a fragile thing, with standard points of decay, a precarious, unsteady state that is likely at any time to lead the individual into some form of alienation." The sources of alienation take on particular significance to students of interpersonal communication since they gather their strength from the mismanagement of the communicative relationship itself. A sensitivity to the factors that engender inhibition, blocking, or withdrawal from interaction can lead us to confront the issue more quickly and more directly in an effort toward greater understanding.

Jernigan and Meyer report a series of incidents that illustrate in part how some human beings become alienated from interaction and how others promote alienation. How would you react if Jernigan had come to you with his questions?

Kaye Starbird has caught the essence of the consequence of communication problems when she describes her informal essay in terms of a "conversation being demolished." As much as you might try to avoid it, how often have you been led into the murky waters of conversations that have proceeded reasonably from the wrong premises? With a touch of light humor, Kaye Starbird illuminates some of the most frustrating instances of tangled interaction.

George A. Miller, prominent Harvard psychologist, explains some of the factors that influence the spread of information through both individual units and person-to-person-to-person or serial units. He identifies four basic reasons for social communication: to increase uniformity of information, to increase uniformity of opinion, to change status in the group, and to express emotions. He describes experiments investigating the effects of different types of networks on communication processes, and he looks at the different kinds of errors that occur when information is passed through four or five people in succession. You might want to experiment yourself with group communication by looking at the consequences of different networks and the serial reproduction of information. Miller provides a step-by-step description of an early investigation by Allport and Postman that can be used as a model for your own study.

"People usually know more about how to sabotage communication," Fleishman states, "than they do about how to promote it." He then identifies seven rules that, if applied judiciously, will effectively sabotage group action. While reading Fleishman's brief commentary, you may want to return to section 1 and study again the article by Korzybski, since they express similar theoretical points of view. As a serious attempt to begin the process of improving your own communicative behavior, you may want to carefully check your own methods of interaction to determine to what degree you have acquired the methods of the saboteur of interpersonal communication.

Of the many contemporary approaches to understanding interaction, transactional analysis has caught the imagination of professionals and practitioners alike. Lyman Randall has digested and synthesized the ideas and writings from a variety of significant figures in the field today, whom he recognizes with "some special strokes for special folks." Using Harris's "I'm O.K., You're O.K." paradigm for explaining the kinds of attitudes people can hold toward one another in a communicative relationship, Randall has taken the theory of transactions out of the specialized field of academics and applied it to the work situation. You'll be O.K. when you finish reading "P-A-C at Work" and reflect on its applications to your own relationships with others. As you begin to feel the conviction of being O.K. yourself, you will acquire the strength and ability to communicate to others that "You're O.K." From this you can build and maintain healthy relationships, the consequence of effective interpersonal communication.

Erving Goffman

ALIENATION FROM INTERACTION

I. INTRODUCTION

When the individual in our Anglo-American society engages in a conversational encounter with others he may become spontaneously involved in it. He can become unthinkingly and impulsively immersed in the talk and carried away by it, oblivious to other things, including himself. Whether his involvement is intense and not easily disrupted, or meager and easily distracted, the topic of talk can form the main focus of his cognitive attention and the current talker can form the main focus of his visual attention. The binding and hypnotic effect of such involvement is illustrated by the fact that while thus involved the individual can simultaneously engage in other goal-directed activities (chewing gum, smoking, finding a comfortable sitting position, performing repetitive tasks, etc.) yet manage such side-involvements in an abstracted, fugue-like fashion so as not to be distracted from his main focus of attention by them.

The individual, like an infant or an animal, can of course become spontaneously involved in unsociable solitary tasks. When this occurs the task takes on at once a weight and a lightness, affording the performer a firm sense of reality. As a main focus of attention talk is unique, however, for talk creates for the participant a world and a reality that has other participants in it. Joint spontaneous involvement is a *unio mystico,* a socialized trance. We must also see that a conversation has a life of its own and makes demands on its own behalf. It is a little social system with its own boundary-maintaining tendencies; it is a little patch of commitment and loyalty with its own heroes[1] and its own villains.

Taking joint spontaneous involvement as a point of reference, I want to discuss how this involvement can fail to occur and the consequence of this failure. I want to consider the ways in which the individual can become alienated from a conversational encounter, the uneasiness that arises with this, and the consequence of this alienation and uneasiness upon the interaction. Since alienation can occur in regard to any imaginable talk, we may be able to learn from it something about the generic properties of spoken interaction.

II. INVOLVEMENT OBLIGATIONS

When individuals are in one another's immediate presence, a multitude of words, gestures, acts, and minor events become available, whether desired or not, through which one who is present can intentionally or unintentionally symbolize his character and his attitudes. In our society a system of etiquette obtains that enjoins the individual to handle these expressive events fittingly, projecting through them a proper image of himself, an appropriate respect for the others present, and a suitable regard for the setting. When the individual intentionally or unintentionally breaks a rule of etiquette, others present may mobilize themselves to restore the ceremonial order, somewhat as they do when other types of social order are transgressed.

Through the ceremonial order that is maintained by a system of etiquette, the capacity of the individual to be carried away by a talk become socialized, taking on a burden of ritual value and social function. Choice of main focus of attention, choice of side-involvements and of intensity of involvement, become hedged in with social constraints, so that some allocations of attention become socially proper and other allocations improper.

There are many occasions when the individual participant in a conversation finds that he and the others are locked together by involvement obligations with respect to it. He comes to feel it is defined as appropriate (and hence either desirable in itself or prudent) to give his main focus of attention to the talk, and to become spontaneously involved in it, while at the same time he feels that each of the other participants has the same obligation. Due to the ceremonial order in which his actions are embedded, he may find that any alternate allocation of involvement on his part will be taken as a discourtesy and cast an uncalled-for reflection upon the others, the setting, or himself. And he will find that his offense has been committed in the very presence of those who are offended by it. Those who break the rules of interaction commit their crimes in jail.

The task of becoming spontaneously involved in something, when it is a duty to oneself or others to do so, is a ticklish thing, as we all know from experience with dull chores or threatening ones. The individual's actions must happen to satisfy his involvement obligations, but in a certain sense he cannot act *in order* to satisfy these obligations, for such an effort would require him to shift his attention from the topic of conversation to the problem of being spontaneously involved in it. Here, in a component of non-rational impulsiveness — not only tolerated but actually demanded—we find an important way in which the interactional order differs from other kinds of social order.

The individual's obligation to maintain spontaneous involvement in the conversation and the difficulty of doing so place him in a delicate position. He is rescued by his co-participants, who control their own actions so that he will not be forced from appropriate involvement. But the moment he is rescued he will have to rescue someone else, and so his job as interactant is only complicated the more. Here, then, is one of the fundamental aspects of social control in conversation: the individual must not only maintain proper involvement hmiself but also act so as to ensure that others will maintain theirs. This is what the individual owes the others in their capacity as interactants, regardless of what is owed in whatever other capacities they participate, and it is this obligation that tells us that, whatever social role the individual plays during a conversational encounter, he will in addition have to fill the role of interactant.

The individual will have approved and unapproved reasons for fulfilling his obligation *qua* interactant, but in all cases to do so he must be able rapidly and delicately to take the role of the others and sense the qualifications their situation ought to bring to his conduct if they are not to be brought up short by it. He must be sympathetically aware of the kinds of things in which the others present can become spontaneously and properly involved, and then attempt to modulate his expression of attitudes, feelings, and opinions according to the company.

Thus, as Adam Smith argued in his *Theory of the Moral Sentiments,* the individual must phrase his own concerns and feelings and interests in such a way as to make these maximally useable by the others as a source of appropriate involvement; and this major obligation of the individual *qua* interactant is balanced by his right to expect that others present will make some effort to stir up their sympathies and place them at his command. These two tendencies, that of the speaker to scale down his expressions and that of the listeners to scale up their interests, each in the light of the other's capacities and demands, form the bridge that people build to one another, allowing them to meet for a moment of talk in a communion of reciprocally sustained involvement. It is this spark, not the more obvious kinds of love, that lights up the world.

III. THE FORMS OF ALIENATION

If we take conjoint spontaneous involvement in a topic of conversation as a point of reference, we shall find that alienation from it is common indeed. Joint involvement appears to be a fragile thing, with standard points of weakness and decay, a precarious unsteady state that is likely at any time to lead the individual into some form of alienation. Since we are dealing with obligatory involvement, forms of alienation will constitute misbehavior of a kind that can be called "misinvolvement." Some of the standard forms of alienative misinvolvement may be considered now.

1. External Preoccupation

The individual may neglect the prescribed focus of attention and give his main concern to something that is unconnected with what is being talked about at the time and even unconnected with the other persons present, at least in their capacity as fellow-participants. The object of the individual's preoccupation may be one that he ought to have ceased considering upon entering the interaction, or one that is to be appropriately considered only later in the encounter or after the encounter has terminated. The preoccupation may also take the form of furtive by-play between the individual and one or two other participants. The individual may even be preoccupied with a vague standard of work-activity, which he cannot maintain because of his obligation to participate in the interaction.

The offensiveness of the individual's preoccupation varies according to the kind of excuses the others feel he has for it. At one extreme there is preoccupation that is felt to be quite voluntary, the offender giving the impression that he could easily give his attention to the conversation but is wilfully refusing to do so. At the other extreme there is "involuntary" preoccupation, a consequence of the offender's understandably deep involvement in vital matters outside the interaction.

Individuals who could excusably withdraw involvement from a conversation often remain loyal and decline to do so. Through this they show a nice respect for fellow-participants and affirm the moral rules that transform socially responsible people into people who are interactively responsible as well. It is of course through such rules, and through such reaffirming gestures, that society is made safe for the little worlds sustained in face-to-face encounters. No culture, in fact, seems to be without exemplary tales for illustrating the dignity and weight that might be given to these passing realities; everywhere we find enshrined a Drake who gallantly finishes some kind of game before going out to battle some kind of Armada, and everywhere an outlaw who is engagingly civil to those he robs and to those who later hang him for it.[2]

2. *Self-consciousness*

At the cost of his involvement in the prescribed focus of attention, the individual may focus his attention more than he ought upon himself—himself as someone who is faring well or badly, as someone calling forth a desirable or undesirable response from others. It is possible, of course, for the individual to dwell upon himself as a topic of conversation—to be self-centered in this way—and yet not to be self-conscious. Self-consciousness for the individual does not, it seems, result from his deep interest in the topic of conversation, which may happen to be himself, but rather from his giving attention to himself as interactant at a time when he ought to be free to involve himself in the content of the conversation.

A general statement about sources of self-consciousness ought to be added. During interaction, the individual is often accorded by others and by impersonal events in the situation an image and appraisal of self that is at least temporarily acceptable to him. He is then free to turn his attention to matters less close to home. When this definition of self is threatened, the individual typically withdraws attention from the interaction in a hurried effort to correct for the incident that has occurred. If the incident threatens to raise his standing in the interaction, his flight into self-consciousness may be a way of rejoicing; if the incident threatens to lower his standing and damage or discredit his self-image in some way, then flight into self-consciousness may be a way of protecting the self and licking its wounds. As a source of self-consciousness, threat of loss seems more common and important than threat of gain.

Whatever the cause of self-consciousness, we are all familiar with the vacillation of action and the flusterings through which self-consciousness is expressed; we are all familiar with the phenomenon of embarrassment.

Self-consciousness can be thought of as a kind of preoccupation with matters internal to the interactive social system, and as such has received more common-sense consideration than other kinds of internal preoccupation. In fact we do not have common-sense words to refer to these other kinds of improper involvement. Two forms of these I shall refer to as "interaction-consciousness" and "other-consciousness" to emphasize a similarity to self-consciousness.

3. *Interaction-consciousness*

A participant in talk may become consciously concerned to an improper degree with the way in which the interaction, *qua* interaction, is proceeding, instead of becoming, spontaneously involved in the official topic of conversation. Since interaction-consciousness is not as famous as self-consciousness, some sources of it may be cited by way of illustration.

A common source of interaction-consciousness is related to the special responsibility that an individual may have for the interaction "going well," i.e. calling forth the proper kind of involvement from those present. Thus, at a small social gathering the hostess may be expected to join in with her guests and become spontaneously involved in the conversation they are maintaining, and yet at the same time if the occasion does not go well she, more than others, will be held responsible for the failure. In consequence, she sometimes becomes so much concerned with the social machinery of the occasion and with how the evening is going as a whole that she finds it impossible to give herself up to her own party.

Another common source of interaction-consciousness may be mentioned. Once individuals enter a conversation they are obligated to continue it until they have the kind of basis for withdrawing that will neutralize the potentially offensive implications of taking leave of others. While engaged in the interaction it will be necessary for them to have subjects at hand to talk about that fit the occasion and yet provide content enough to keep the talk going; in other words, safe supplies are needed.[3] What we call "small talk" serves this purpose. When individuals use up their small talk, they find themselves officially lodged in a state of talk but with nothing to talk about; interaction-consciousness experienced as a "painful silence" is the typical consequence.

4. Other-consciousness

During interaction, the individual may become distracted by another participant as an object of attention—exactly as in the case of self-consciousness he can become distracted by concern over himself.[4]

If the individual finds that whenever he is in the conversational presence of specific others they cause him to be overly conscious of them at the expense of the prescribed involvement in the topic of conversation, then they may acquire the reputation in his eyes of being faulty interactants, especially if he feels he is not alone in the trouble he has with them. He is then likely to impute certain characteristics to those who are thus perceived, doing so in order to explain and account for the distraction they cause him. It will be useful to our understanding of interaction to list a few of the attributes imputed in this way.

By the terms "affection" and "insincerity" the individual tends to identify those who seem to feign through gestures what they expect him to accept as an uncontrived expressive overflow of their behavior. Affection, as Cooley suggests, ". . . exists when the passion to influence others seems to overbalance the established character and give it an obvious twist or pose." . . . "Thus there are persons who in the simplest conversation do not seem to forget themselves, and enter frankly and disinterestedly into the subject, but are felt to be always preoccupied with the thought of the impression they are making, imagining praise or depreciation, and usually posing a little to avoid the one or gain the other."[5] Affected individuals seem chiefly concerned with controlling the evaluation an observer will make of them, and seem partly taken in by their own pose; insincere individuals seem chiefly concerned with controlling the impression the observer will form of their attitude toward certain things or persons, especially toward him, and seem not to be taken in by their own pose. It may be added that while those who are felt to be self-conscious give the impression of being overly concerned with what will happen or has happened to them, those who are felt to be insincere or affected give the impression that they are overly concerned with what they can achieve in what is to follow and are willing to put on an act in order to achieve it. When the individual senses that others are insincere or affected he tends to feel they have taken unfair advantage of their communication position to promote their own interests; he feels they have broken the ground rules of interaction. His hostility to their unfair play leads him to focus his attention upon them and their misdemeanor at the price of his own involvement in the conversation.

In considering the attributes imputed to those who cause another to be conscious of them, we must give importance to the factor of immodesty. On analytical grounds overmodesty should equally count as a source of other-consciousness, but empirically, immodesty seems much the more important of the two. What the individual takes to be immodesty in others may present itself in many forms: immodest individuals may seem to praise themselves verbally; they may talk about themselves and their activity in a way that assumes greater interest in and familiarity with their personal life than the individual actually possesses; they may speak more frequently and at greater length than the individual feels is fitting; they may take a more prominent "ecological" position than he thinks they warrant, etc.

One interesting source of other-consciousness is to be found in the phenomenon of "over-involvement." During any conversation, standards are established as to how much the individual is to allow himself to be carried away by the talk, how thoroughly he is to permit himself to be caught up in it. He will be obligated to prevent himself from becoming so swollen with feelings and a readiness to act that he threatens the bounds regarding affect that have been established for him in the interaction. He will be obliged to express a margin of disinvolvement, although of course this margin will differ in extent according to the socially recognized importance of the occasion and his official role in it. When the individual does become over-involved in the topic of conversation, and gives others the impression that he does not have a necessary measure of self-control over his feelings and actions, when, in short, the interactive world becomes too real for him, then the others are likely to be drawn from involvement in the talk to an involvement in the talker. What is one man's overeagerness will become another's alienation. In any case we are to see that over-involvement has the effect of momentarily incapacitating the individual as an interactant; others have to adjust to his state while he becomes incapable of adjusting to theirs. Interestingly enough, when the impulse of the over-involved individual has ebbed a little, he may come to sense his impropriety and become self-conscious, illustrating again the fact that the alienative effect the individual has on others is usually one he cannot escape having upon himself. Regardless of this, we must see that a readiness to become over-involved is a form of tyranny practised by children, *prima donnas*, and lords of all kinds, who momentarily put their own feelings above the moral rules that ought to have made society safe for interaction.

A final source of other-consciousness may be mentioned. If the individual is to become involved in a topic of conversation, then, as a listener, he will have to give his aural and usually his visual attention to the source of communication, that is, to the speaker, and especially to the speaker's voice and face. (This physical requirement is underlined by social rules that often define inattention to the speaker as an affront to him.) If the speaker's communication apparatus itself conveys additional information all during the time that transmission is occurring, then the listener is likely to be distracted by competing sources of stimuli, becoming over-aware of the speaker at the expense of what is being said. The sources of this distraction are well known: the speaker may be very ugly or very beautiful; he may have a speech defect such as a lisp or a stutter; he may have inadequate familiarity with the language, dialect, or jargon that the listeners expect to hear; he may have a slight facial peculiarity, such as a hare lip, eye twitch, crossed or wall eyes; he may have temporary communication difficulties such as a stiff neck, a hoarse voice, etc. Apparently the closer the defect is to the communication equipment upon which the listener must focus his attention, the smaller the defect need be to throw the listener off balance. (It should be added that in so far as a speaker is required to direct his attention to his listener and yet not be overly conscious of him, defects in the appearance of the listener can cause the speaker to be uneasy.) These minor defects in the apparatus of communication tend to shut off the afflicted individual from the stream of daily contacts, transforming him into a faulty interactant, either in his own eyes or in the eyes of others.

In concluding this discussion of sources of alienating distraction, I should like to state an obvious caution. When the individual senses that others are unsuitably involved, it will aways be relative to the standards of his group that he will sense the others have behaved improperly. Similarly, an individual who would cause certain others to be unduly conscious of him because of his apparent insincerity, affectation, or immodesty would pass unnoticed in a subculture where conversational discipline was less strict. Hence, when members of different groups interact with one another, it is quite likely that at least one of the participants will be distracted from spontaneous involvement in the topic of conversation because of what appears to him to be unsuitable behavior on the part of the others.[6] It is to these differences in expressive customs that we ought to look first in trying to account for the improper behavior of those with whom we happen to be participating and not try, initially at least, to find some source of blame within the personalities of the offenders. . . .

IV. GENERALIZING THE FRAMEWORK

1. The Context of Involvement Obligations

One limitation we have set ourselves is to deal with situations where all those present to one another are officially obligated to maintain themselves as participants in conversation and to maintain spontaneous involvement in the conversation. This is a frequent enough condition to serve as a reference point, but there is no need to be ultimately bound by it. Involvement obligations are in fact defined in terms of the total context in which the individual finds himself. Thus there will be some situations where the main involvement of those present is supposed to be invested in a physical task; conversation, if carried on at all, will have to be treated as a side-involvement to be picked up or dropped, depending on the current demands of the task at hand. There will be other situations where the role and status of a particular participant will be nicely expressed by his right to treat a conversation in a cavalier fashion, participating in it or not, depending on his inclination at the moment. A father sometimes has this right regarding the mealtime conversation maintained by lesser members of the family, while they do not.

I should like to cite another way in which the individual may accept a different allocation of involvement for himself from that expected of others. In the teasing that the young receive from the old, or in the interrogations that employees receive from employers, loss of composure on the subordinate's part may be accepted by the superordinate as an expected and proper part of the involvement pattern. At such times the subordinate may feel he would like to be spontaneously involved in the talk but is in too much of a panic to do so, while the superordinate may feel that for him the appropriate focus of attention, and one he can sustain with comfort, is not the actual talk but the wider situation created by the humorous plight of the inferior as he struggles in the conversation.[7] In fact, if the subordinate shows composure on these occasions, the superior may feel affronted and embarrassed. Similarly there will be occasions when we feel an individual ought, out of respect for the difficulties he is in, to be preoccupied or over-involved. This misinvolvement may somewhat disrupt the interaction, but perfect poise on his part might so scandalize those present as to disrupt the interaction even more. Thus while it is true that sometimes an individual will be thought an interaction hero if he remains involved in a conversation under difficult conditions, at other times loyalty will be thought foolhardly

Differential obligations regarding the same spoken interaction may be seen most clearly in large-scale interactions, such as public speeches, where we are likely to find specialization and segregation of involvement roles, with a division between full participants, who are expected to talk or listen, and non-participating specialists, whose job is to move unobtrusively about and look after some of the mechanics of the occasion. Examples of these non-participants are domestics, ushers, doormen, stenographers, and microphone men. The special alignment these officials have to the interaction is their particular right and obligation; it is accepted openly by them and for them, and they would in fact cause uneasiness were they to become manifestly involved in the content of the talk. They show respect for the occasion by treating it as a side-involvement.

Participants, themselves, in large-scale interaction can have a license in regard to involvement that could not be afforded them in two- or three-person talk, perhaps because the more participants there are to sustain the proceedings, the less dependent the occasion will be on any one participant. In any case, we often find in large-scale interaction that it is permissible for a few participants to enter for a moment into by-plays and side-discussions, providing they modulate their voice and manner to show respect for the official proceedings. In fact, a participant may even leave the room for a moment and do this in such a way as to convey the impression that his main focus of attention is still held by the talk, even though his body is not present. On such occasions, main involvement and side-involvements may become fictions maintained officially in form while alternate involvement patterns are actually maintained in practice.

2. Pseudo-conversations

We have so far restricted our attention to interactions that have as their constituent communicative acts the turns at talking taken by participants. We can extend our view and consider conversation-like interactions in which the token exchanged is not speeches but stylized gestures, as in the interchange of non-verbal greetings,[8] or moves of some kind, as in card games. These unspoken yet conversation-like interactions seem to be similar, structurally, to spoken interaction, except that the capacities that must be mobilized in order to carry on such interaction seem to have more to do with muscular control of limbs than in the case of spoken interaction.

3. Unfocused Interaction

I have suggested that speech-, gesture-, and game-interactions are characterized by a single official focus of cognitive and visual attention that all full-fledged participants help to sustain. (The focus of visual attention may move, of course, from one participant to another as one speaker gives up his speaking-role and returns to the role of listener.) With this focused kind of interaction we must contrast the unfocused kind, where individuals in one another's visual and aural range go on about their respective business unconnected by a shared focus of attention. Street behavior and conduct at a large social party are instances.

When we examine unfocused interactions we find that involvement obligations are defined not in relation to a conjoint focus of cognitive and visual attention but in relation to a role that can be suggested by the phrase "decorous individual noninterferingly going about his proper business." Once we shift to this point of reference, however, we find that all the kinds of misinvolvement that occur during focused interaction also occur during unfocused interaction, though sometimes under a different name. Just as an adolescent may become self-consciously uneasy when talking to his teacher, so, in walking into a full classroom, he may feel that he is being critically observed and that his way of walking, which he feels is stiff and wooden, reveals his social anxiety. Just as we can have preoccupied persons in conversational interaction, so in unfocused interaction we can have "absent-minded" participants, who by their posture, facial expression, and physical movements suggest that they are momentarily "away," that they have momentarily let fall the expressive costume that individuals are expected to wear whenever they are in the immediate presence of others. And, of course, boredom, too, can occur during unfocused interaction, as we may observe in almost any queue of individuals waiting to buy a ticket. And just as agencies such as alcohol and marijuana may be employed to transform a conversation into something that is not embarrassing or boring, so these may function to put individuals at ease in the wider scene provided by unfocused interaction. Just as a witticism may do honor to the conversational moment, so the wearing of new or special clothing, the serving of rare or costly food, and the use of perishable flowers can draw attention to the unique value of a wider social occasion. Clearly, then, there are ways in which the perspective employed in this paper can be used for studying unfocused interaction.

We must not, however, expect the similarity between the two kinds of interaction to be complete. For example, it appears that individuals are more frequently unself-conscious in their capacity as participants in unfocused interaction than they are as participants in focused interaction, especially focused interaction of the spoken kind. In fact, in spoken interaction, spontaneous "normal" involvement seems to be the exception and alienation of some kind the statistical rule. That is understandable. On the one hand, participants are required to be spontaneously carried away by the topic of conversation; on the other hand, they are obligated to control themselves so that they will always be ready to stay within the role of communicator and stay alive to the touchy issues that might cause the others to become ill at ease. On the one hand they are obliged to adhere to all applicable rules of conduct, and on the other they are obliged to take enough liberties to ensure a minimum level of involving excitement. These obligations seem to be in opposition to each other, requiring a balance of conduct that is so delicate and precarious that alienation and uneasiness for someone in the interaction are the typical result. Unfocused interaction does not seem to require the same delicacy of adjustment.

NOTES

1. One of its heroes is the wit who can introduce references to wider, important matters in a way that is ineffably suited to the current moment of talk. Since the witticism will never again be as telling, a sacrifice has been offered up to the conversation, and respect paid to its unique reality by an act that shows how thoroughly the actor is alive to the interaction.

2. Yet different strata in the same society can be unequally concerned that members learn to project themselves into encounters; the tendency to keep conversations alive and lively may be a way in which some strata, not necessarily adjacent, are characteristically different from others.

4. The problem of safe supplies is further considered in my "Communication Conduct in an Island Community," Unpublished Ph.D. Dissertation, Department of Sociology, University of Chicago, 1953, ch. XV.

5. Other-consciousness is briefly but explicitly considered in James Baldwin, *Social and Ethical Interpretations in Mental Development* (London, 1902), pp. 213-14.

5. Charles H. Cooley, *Human Nature and the Social Order* (Charles Scribner's Sons, New York, 1922), pp. 196, 215.

6. For example, in social intercourse among traditional Shetlanders, the pronoun "I" tends to be little used; its greater use by individuals from the mainland of Great Britain, and especially its relatively frequent use by Americans, leads the Shetlander to feel that these non-Shetlandic people are immodest and gross. Shetlandic tact, it might be added, frequently prevents non-islanders from learning that their manner causes Shetlanders to be uneasy.

7. The plight of the self-conscious person is in fact so good a stimulus for calling forth spontaneous involvement on the part of those who witness it, that during conversations where there may be difficulty in capturing the involvement of those present, individuals may take turns both at committing minor infractions against propriety and at becoming embarrassed, thus ensuring involvement. Hence the paradox that if all the rules of correct social behavior are exactly followed, the interaction may become flaccid, stale, and flat.

8. The following is an instance of psychiatrist-patient interaction that is verbal on one side only: ". . . in the course of an analysis of a very disturbed schizophrenic with depressive features the patient hid herself within her only garment, a blanket, so that only the eyebrow showed; nothing daunted I continued the conversation from where we left off last time and noted changes in that eloquent but only visible member, which changes—a frown, scowl, surprise, a flicker of amusement, a softening of the curve—indicated the changes in her mood and thought. My surmises proved correct for when next she displayed her face and used her voice she corroborated the general trend of my guesses as to what had gone on in her mind. That session was no verbal *interchange*—it might even be called an eyebrow analysis—but there was an endeavour to verbalize, to conceptualize and make concrete 'in the here and now' what was occurring concurrently in her mind." (John Richman, "The Role and Future of Psycho-therapy with Psychiatry," *Journal of Mental Science*, 96 [1950], 189)

Duie R. Jernigan / James B. Meyer

A DAY IN
ANOTHER MAN'S MOCCASINS

As an Army chaplain for more than 10 years, I had often said to those who came to me for help, "Yes, I understand." And yet, I knew at the same time that it was impossible to understand how they really felt. I became interested in discovering a means by which I could actually experience the emotions and anguish of a person seeking the help of a clergyman. To do so, I realized that I must somehow become that person.

The most difficult part of this project was making up my mind to actually go through with it. When the creative project assignment came up, I settled on the plan of dressing up as a destitute person and visiting fellow pastors in a pretended effort to find a job. I had it in mind to ask the clergymen I visited two basic questions. The first was, "Do you feel there is any difference in killing a person in combat during war and killing a civilian, if both are your enemies?" I wanted to find out what the reactions would be to such a lead question. Would they give me advice, a rationalization, a sermonette? Or, would they try to understand *why* I was troubled by the question? I was also interested in how they would treat the confidentiality of the situation.

The second question was less complex: "Do you know where I might find a job?" I was interested to learn what sort of occupational information might be offered and what agencies thèy would refer me to. I also wanted to see if I would be judged on the basis of my unkempt appearance, or if they would view me as a *person* with a real need.

The project actually began when I dressed for my visits. To camouflage my identity, I wore paint-splattered trousers, an old wool Army shirt (minus name tag and insignia), and a pair of old tennis shoes with broken and untied laces. For authenticity I rolled the shirt in leaves and dirt, and I didn't shave for three days. The clergymen I selected to visit represented five different denominations and included Caucasian and Negro ministers. The churches were located in a city with a population of 300,000.

My first visit completely disarmed me. I entered the church in the early evening and noticed members of the congregation gathering for their weekly church dinner. I located the office area and spoke with the secretary, asking to talk with the pastor.

After a deliberate and demeaning visual appraisal of my clothes, the secretary answered that the pastor was not in. I asked if she might help me with my problem. She said that it depended on what my problem was. I entered her small office and sat down submissively. She asked my name, and then bluntly asked me if I had been drinking. My answer was, "No, why?" She said she could smell liquor. Apparently my appearance had misled her.

My impression was that she saw me as nothing more than a bum. When I said that I was not looking for a hand-out but was interested in finding a job, she picked up the phone and called someone in charge of "special ministries." After a hasty conversation she referred me to another person at a mission where they "took care of men like me." I asked the secretary what she meant by that phrase, and she had a difficult time explaining without referring to me directly as a bum or drunk.

I had intentionally not eaten since breakfast in order to understand how a hungry, destitute person feels. My stomach growled loudly several times during the brief interview. Although dinner was being served in the church dining area, I was not invited to eat. I was quickly ushered past the dining area without even an offer of a cup of coffee in the kitchen. As I left that church I began to realize how much my human dignity had suffered.

When I reached the next church my spirits were at a very low level. I walked into the elegantly furnished lounge area of the church and was acutely aware of my appearance. The church was very large and had many parlors, dining rooms, and offices. Again, people were gathering for their weekly church dinner. As I walked down the hallway toward the offices, most people moved deliberately to the other side of the hallway and took great care not to stare at me. (I must have looked worse than I thought I did!) I walked around for several moments in an effort to find someone who would direct me to the pastor, but the people studiously avoided me. No one seemed to care.

I walked down to the main dining room entrance and watched as people prepared for the church supper. An officious-looking person quickly walked toward me and introduced himself as pastor of the church. I asked if I could talk with him for a moment about some problems that were bothering me. He quickly reminded me that he was busy with the dinner. I apologized for bothering him, but indicated that I just needed to talk to someone. With this he moved me over to the side of the hallway and said, "OK, what's on your mind?"

After getting his assurance that our conversation would be held in confidence, I posed my first question about killing people if they were your enemies, whether in war or peace time. The pastor answered with philosophical statements about American involvement in the Vietnam war. He didn't seem interested in *why* I had asked the question or the fact that I might have some psychological guilt about having killed someone in combat. What if I had been contemplating killing someone I considered to be a civilian enemy?

After his statements about the Vietnam war, the pastor quietly focused his attention on my unsightly appearance. I hurriedly asked my second question about finding a job. His response was that he had no idea where I might secure help in finding a job. His nonverbal communication strongly indicated that he would be most pleased if I would leave his church and not bother him any further. I then asked if I could come back after the dinner was over to discuss my problems in a more complete manner. He told me that he was very busy and that it would not be possible to talk with me until the next day.

It is difficult to describe the de-personalized feeling I experienced as I stood listening to that pastor. Though he probably had no deliberate intention of doing so, he made me feel less worthy than my outer garments indicated. His comments indicated that he viewed me not as a person in need of his help, but as a useless derelict who was taking up his valuable time. As I left the church the building superintendent instructed the janitor to "keep an eye on me and be sure I left the premises." He did.

I drove across town to visit another church. A young man in clerical attire greeted me in the sanctuary and offered me a place to wait while the pastor finished his dinner. Thirty minutes later an elderly clergyman appeared and spoke to me. We went into his office and began our conversation. I asked if what we talked about would be held in strict confidence; he replied that it would and closed the door.

When he asked how he might help me, I posed my first question about killing people in combat. From his comments and nonverbal response, I felt that he thought I was a criminal. He began by describing the variety of ministries carried on by his church office. He said, "You'll be interested to know that I received a call today from the state penitentiary requesting that I find a job for a prisoner who is soon to be released." Realizing the implications of what he had said, he quickly recovered by adding, "Of course, I'm not suggesting that this is your problem."

When I turned the conversation to my second question regarding the possibility of a job, he asked what kind of work I could do. I told him that while in the service I had repaired tents, worked on jeeps, and pointed to my airborne jump badge which indicated I could jump out of airplanes. At this, the clergyman burst into laughter and commented that he didn't think there was a great demand for parachutists in the city! Then he added, "Perhaps you could become a delivery boy. You could sure make fast deliveries, couldn't you!" The absurdity of the situation allowed me to share a hearty laugh with him. It was the first time I had laughed since beginning my church visits. After a few more moments of conversation, however, he began directively to close our session. I sensed that he had become uneasy in my presence. His last suggestion was for me to check for employment with the Salvation Army. As I left his church I felt that he had not taken enough time to look beyond my shoddy outward appearance before deciding what the appropriate behavorial responses were to deal with me.

Fortunately, my reception at the next church was much different. When I first entered, I was told that the pastor had not arrived. During the interim wait I spoke with a young man who was assisting in the preparation for the meeting. He was warm and friendly and gave the impression he would like to help me. After a few moments the pastor came in. By this time I had become defensive about my intrusion on a busy evening. When I was introduced to the pastor I said that I needed to talk with him, but I could come back later. The pastor's reply was, "No problem! Give me a few minutes to get the meeting started and I'll be right back. Nothing is more important than talking to you!"

Suddenly I felt like a person again! This clergyman had accepted me as a person and apparently was not upset by my appearance. He returned shortly and led me into his small office. Again I posed my question about killing a person in combat or civilian circumstances. To my surprise he didn't seem shocked or suspicious. Instead, he encouraged me to discuss the problem with him. After a mutual discussion of the topic, he even showed me a scar on his shin that he had received in combat in Korea. Though he didn't probe the subject deeply, I could tell he was sincerely concerned about how I felt.

When I presented my question to him about finding a job, he immediately asked me if I had anything to eat and a place to stay for the night. I told him that I hadn't eaten, but that I felt maybe I should "look around" a little more before it got too late. As I prepared to leave, he excused himself for a moment and then returned and handed me a slip of paper with his name and phone number written on it. Folded inside the paper was a dollar bill. Noticing the money, I quickly handed it back to him, saying that I shouldn't take it. He handed it back, insisting it was something he wanted to do. As I left, he reminded me that if I didn't find something soon, I should call him and he would provide me with something to eat and a warm place to stay. As I left this man's church I felt that for the first time the clergyman had viewed me as a person and that he was sincerely interested in helping me.

My last church visit was different from all the others. As I approached the foyer I noticed the large number of well-dressed people. The mink stoles looked especially elegant, and the brilliance of diamond rings was quite noticeable. I felt more out of place than ever. Eventually I was able to talk with a man who said he was a lay minister. He indicated that we could hold our conversation in the lobby. In response to my first question, he gave me a six-to-eight-minute doctrinal lecture on war and peace. I was unable to get in a single phrase or question during the entire time. When he finished he turned to me and said in condescending tones, "Now if we can ever be of help to you again, feel free to call on us!" I looked puzzled and asked, "What do you mean?" The man stood speechless for a moment, and then hurriedly excused himself to attend to some people entering the foyer. I didn't get a chance to ask my question about finding a job.

In the center of the lobby was a luxuriously carpeted stairway leading into the sanctuary. I approached it and walked halfway up. From the vantage point I could see the whole congregation and they could see me. Directly behind the lectern, in brilliant gold-leaf lettering, were the words "God Is Love." I felt the questioning eyes of all those well-dressed people focused directly on me, but I just stood there and looked at those words. I wondered to myself, "What does love mean to these people?" Confused and stunned with emotion, I started to leave the church. As I opened the door, I read the inscription above it: "Come unto me all ye that labor and are heavy laden, and I will give you rest."

WHAT I LEARNED

What I learned from this creative project cannot be found in any textbook; the insights gained will be invaluable to me in my future work as a counselor. From my small study I learned how my fellow clergymen are dealing with people who are unfortunate. I was very surprised to witness the somewhat hypocritical role of these men; they seemingly wanted to help, but didn't want to become really involved with me or my problems. I was shocked that I never did get direct answers to my two questions; most of the churchmen I visited seem to get hung up on my physical appearance or their own self-importance and "role."

I was pleased to find at least one pastor who was willing to treat me as a human being with problems, rather than a problem human being. I'll always remember that pastor's quiet dignity as he offered me a place to stay and something to eat. The knowledge and insights gained from this project could not have been obtained in any other way; I learned a great deal about myself and my motivation to become a counselor.

Kaye Starbird

CAUTION!
CONVERSATION BEING DEMOLISHED

The first law of discussion,
it seems, is that if there's any
possible way to derail the train
of thought, somebody will

I like a good discussion as well as the next person. But over the years I have come to recognize that the premise of even the simplest oral exchange can get lost in a tangle of side issues and individual interpretations. On such occasions, I am reminded of the time I went to church as a child, and we sang that hymn entitled "Gladly the Cross I'd Bear." While the grown-ups in the congregation were picturing the long road to Calvary, I, like many another child before me, was visualizing a big furry animal with a strange name and an unfortunate ocular problem—Gladly, the cross-eyed bear.

I cite this incident to demonstrate how the spoken word can give rise to varying misconceptions, which often complicate further conversation to the point of absurdity. One classic example of this difficulty, which I call Proceeding Reasonably From a Wrong Premise, occurred shortly after World War II when a beau of mine named Homer Hoskins appeared at the house.

I came downstairs to find Homer talking with my father, a retired Army general, in the living room. They were discussing what everyone had done during the war. Somewhat defensively, Homer announced that he had been a conscientious objector. But he didn't use the term "conscientious objector." He simply said that he had spent the previous 19 months as a C.O. out on the West Coast.

There was a moment of silence. Then my father, delighted, slapped his knee and said he thought the occasion called for a drink. I couldn't understand his uncharacteristic reaction, until I suddenly remembered that C.O. meant Commanding Officer in Army parlance; my father had automatically accepted the abbreviation in the context familiar to him. "At your age," he kept saying approvingly. "At your age."

Somewhat puzzled at first, Homer gained confidence over a couple of congratulatory brandies and explained that each man had to do what he believed in and serve according to his own capacities and instincts to help attain peace. My father said: True, true; any army officer worth his salt knew that. Whereupon Homer said he was glad my father realized how trying his position had sometimes been; it wasn't easy for a man to isolate himself from the companionship of most of his friends and acquaintances. My father nodded. Being a C.O. was a damned lonely business, he agreed. Damned lonely.

I was perspiring profusely in my concern with what would happen when the two of them got down to details. In a flurry of fake femininity and contrived excuses, I whisked Homer off to the movies.

The People Who Proceed Reasonably From a Wrong Premise are not the only ones to muddy the crystal waters of conversation. There are also the Cute Kids, the Haters, the Monologuists, the Irrational Rationalizers and the Premise Shifters. The Cute Kids, Haters and Monologuists have a lot in common. They listen for words rather than meanings, restlessly waiting for an opportunity to thrust their own humor, vituperation or opinionated reminiscence into the first vocal opening. A Cute Kid will say anything for laughs. If everyone in the room is talking about whether or not Tennessee Williams is a great playwright, a Cute Kid will say that he always liked *A Streetcar Named Desire,* but there ought to be an Irish version of it called *The Rose Of Trolley.*

A Hater, on the other hand, is mainly on the alert for proper names that will give him a chance to vilify someone. He can make do with a limited vocabulary. The talk can be about Whistler's Mother, Albert Schweitzer or the high-school janitor, and he will suddenly pound his fist on whatever's handy and snort: "That s.o.b.!" There is no use trying to converse seriously with a Cute Kid or Hater present. Or a Monologuist either, for that matter.

My grandmother was a great Monologuist. In nothing flat, she could bring even the most well-channeled conversation around to the subject of the Old West. I remember one afternoon when she was serving tea to two elderly Monologuist contemporaries, a Mr. McDillip and his wife. My grandmother started off by saying what a cold winter it was, and Mr. McDillip said Yes, it was almost as cold as the winter of '81 when his house burned in Maine. My grandmother said she guessed she had been out in the Old West that year; and Mrs. McDillip said her rheumatism was bothering her again; it always did in cold weather. Mr. McDillip said it was 20 below zero when his house caught fire in Maine. At around 11 p.m. he had smelled smoke and had yelled like an Indian. My grandmother said she had got pretty accustomed to Indians out in the Old West, although she had to admit she'd been a bit leery of them when the Colonel first married her and took her to Fort Laramie. Sometimes, she was left alone in the house with Annie the cook and an orderly who was too crippled to be of much use. Mrs. McDillip sympathized with the crippled orderly. Some mornings she could scarcely move, she said. Of course, she had her new heating pad, but it was hard to regulate the heat. Heat! said Mr. McDillip. Nobody ever felt anything like the heat from the burning kitchen the night he and his parents and two younger brothers hurried through the hallway in their bathrobes out into the freezing weather. . . . And so it went, all afternoon, the three of them carrying on their monologues quite amicably in the naive belief that they were communicating with one another.

Monologuists are at least predictable. Unfortunately, the same thing can't be said for Irrational Rationalizers. Teen-agers are practiced Irrational Rationalizers and are inclined to take rather a patronizing attitude toward anyone who fails to comprehend. As a mother, I call this Oatmeal Logic.

When my oldest daughter, Kit, was 14, she used to fill her cereal bowl at breakfast with great mounds of cereal which she never ate. "Why do you take all that oatmeal every morning?" I asked her one day.

"If I don't have a lot of oatmeal," she answered, "I start to feel faint before noon."

"Yes, but you never eat it," I pointed out.

"I never have time," she said.

"Well, if you never have time to eat the cereal," I went on, refusing to let well enough alone, "why do you put so much in your bowl?"

"I told you," she replied witheringly. "If I don't have a lot of oatmeal in the morning, I start to feel faint before noon."

The Premise Shifters are another devious breed. I have a sister who is an accomplished one. The other night she was saying she couldn't understand why I had sent my daughters to the local Country Day School. Public school had been good enough for her, she said, and it was important for kids to be brought up in a democratic atmosphere and not be snobs. I explained that the school was excellent and had a well-endowed scholarship fund which enabled students from any social or economic background to attend. There was a plumber's daughter enrolled, a policeman's son, a hairdresser's son, and my cleaning woman's oldest girl, who was very talented musically. That was all very well, my sister said, but what baffled her was why I wanted my children in with that bunch of beatniks in the first place. When I suggested that we were talking about snobs, my sister said I was trying to evade the issue.

When you get an assortment of these types together, it's hopeless attempting to discuss *anything* in an orderly manner. Yesterday at a cocktail party, a friend of mine mentioned that he had recently got over a bad bout of Asian flu, which had affected his motor reflexes. A woman near him, Proceeding Reasonably from a Wrong Premise, said she had trouble driving a car, too. She added that she was going to have to take another driver's test soon, and she hoped the examiner wouldn't be too exacting. One of the Haters present happened to know the examiner — an s.o.b. if he'd ever met one—who held his job only because he was a nephew of the mayor (another s.o.b.). A lurking Premise Shifter managed to parlay the subsequent listing of the mayor's personality faults into an appraisal of the downtown traffic problem—a situation which a listening female Irrational Rationalizer seemed to feel was in some way responsible for the poor architecture on Main Street. The North Country bank was bad enough, she said, but the sight of the new bus terminal actually made her ill. A Cute Kid leapt on this statement to chortle something about "terminal illness"; and a sleepy-eyed Monologuist philosopher, abruptly coming alive, commented on the brevity of our sojourn in this vale of tears and commenced a rambling dissertation on the Life to Come.

As I disengaged myself from the group, I had one fleeting thought: I don't know much about the Eternal Life, but in a conversation like this Life Here and Now can sometimes *seem* eternal.

George A. Miller

THE SOCIAL APPROACH

The increase of communication may not only fail to give agreement in valuations and modes of conduct but may actually be used to increase conflict, competitiveness, and slavery. For sharing a language with other persons provides the subtlest and most powerful of all tools for controlling the behavior of these other persons to one's advantage—for stirring up rivalries, advancing one's own goals, exploiting others.

C. H. Morris

Social organization without communication is impossible. The influence of a group can extend only as far as the group has effective channels for communication. A person who does not talk to any of the members of a group is necessarily isolated from that group. A person who talks only to members of one group is necessarily dependent upon that group for all his information. The pattern of communication among members of various social groups is an important key to social structure. The relation between the pattern of communication and the eventual action of the group is quite complex. . . .

COMMUNICATION NETS

A social group is two or more people held together by a *social relation*. The relation among the members can be any interpersonal relation that we are able to define and recognize. The relation that we are most interested in is "talks to" or "communicates with." We can state the communicative organization of the group by a series of sentences of the form "A talks to B" or "A does not talk to B." Such a sentence is given for every pair of members in the group. In the same way, other relations can be used to show other organizational aspects of the group. "Is a friend of," "pays money to," "commands," "disagrees with," etc., are all recognizable social relations. Any one or more of these relations may play an important role in the functions of the group.

The Pattern of Channels

The structure of the group under the relation "talks to" forms a *communication net*. The communication net is described completely by the set of sentences that state whether the relation holds between every pair of members. These statements can be treated as a kind of algebra (Luce and Perry, 1949; Luce, 1950), but it is simpler to think of them in terms of diagrams. The different members of the group are designated in the diagram by letters. If the relation holds between any two, then an arrow is drawn from the first letter to the second. Two communication nets are diagrammed in Figure 1. The net on the left represents part of the net formed during a radio broadcast. The talker on the radio, A, can speak to all the other members, but none of the others can speak to him. C and D can communicate, but all the rest are isolated. According to some definitions this broadcasting net does not organize the members into a group. The net permits action, but not interaction, among the members. The diagram on the right in Figure 1 might represent the net formed by five people meeting face to face to discuss a topic. Every member can talk to every other member. This sort of organization in a face-to-face situation is sometimes called a *primary group*.

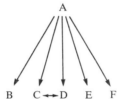 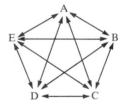

FIGURE 1. *Diagrams illustrating different communication nets. Letters represent members of the group, and the arrows indicate the directions in which messages can pass.*

According to our definitions, all the telephone subscribers in the world form a social group. Telephonic channels of communication exist whereby any one can talk to any other one. Ordinarily we would not refer to this collection of people as a social group because the fact is that they do not communicate. Only a tiny fraction of all the possible telephone connections is ever used. This fact suggests that we should modify our statement of the communicative relation. Instead of saying who *can* communicate with whom, we are more interested in who *does* communicate with whom. So we introduce the notion of *traffic density*. If a particular channel is frequently used, we say it has a high traffic density. If another channel is never used, we say it has zero traffic density. All channels with zero traffic density can be discarded in our study of a social group because they cannot affect the way the group functions. Any channel that exists but is not used might as well not exist; it can be deleted from the diagram of the communication net.

The traffic density over each of the arrows in the diagram can be indicated by a number that tells how many messages pass over the channel per unit of time. A high traffic density indicates that the particular channel is important in the functioning of the group. Analysis of the traffic densities can reveal bottlenecks in group communication that may decrease the group's efficiency.

It is sometimes necessary to modify the statement of the relation "talks to" still further. In primary groups any talker is necessarily heard by every other member, and yet his remarks may be addressed to a particular member of the group. If we wish to preserve this distinction in the description of a communication net, we can distinguish two nets. One net shows the traffic densities for *directed communications,* the other for *undirected communications.* The radio broadcast is almost necessarily undirected, whereas the telephone net carries nothing but directed communications.

The Pattern of Information

In addition to these qualifications of the basic relation, there are numerous qualifications that we may want to impose upon the description of the members. Suppose, for example, that the communication net exists for the sole purpose of spreading information to all members of the group. For any particular item of information, therefore, we would like to be able to say whether or not each member had received it. The statement of which members know which items is the *pattern of group information.* For example, in a three-member group all three may know the item, or only A and B, or A and C, or B and C, or only A, or B, or C, or none of the three members may know the item. In this example there are eight different patterns of information about a single item among the three members of the group. In general, there are 2^{mn} different patterns of information among m members with respect to n different items of information. Thus we see that the information patterns of the group are quite numerous and varied, even for relatively small groups.

The pattern of group information changes as the group communicates. One pattern exists if only A knows a particular item. As soon as A communicates this item to B, however, the pattern shifts. Therefore it is necessary to state the time at which any particular pattern of information existed. If we know the pattern at any particular time, and if we also know the order in which the different members communicated, we can reconstruct the pattern at any later point in time. A group continues to communicate until the pattern is one in which every member knows every item of information. When this uniform pattern is attained, there is no longer any need to communicate. Then the group activity stops until some new item of information is introduced.

This description raises the question, however, as to how the members of the group know when they are finished. How can one member know that all the other members know everything he has to say? Or, more generally, how do the members know the pattern of information at any time? If B knows a particular item, it is a waste of time for A to tell him that item again. What A knows that B knows must govern what A communicates to B. In other words, two kinds of information must be communicated. The *primary information* is the message that the group is attempting to circulate. The *secondary information* is knowledge about who knows what, knowledge of which pattern of information exists at the moment.

The particular primary information that the group is trying to communicate has little to do with the way the group operates. The secondary information, however, is determined by the structure of the net and can have a strong influence on the behavior of the members. Secondary information is given to the talker by the recipients' responses. If the talker says, "John has a black coat," he conveys primary information to the recipient. If a recipient then conveys this message to another person, the original talker can listen also to see that the message is relayed correctly. But he cannot check that his message got across if his recipient never repeats it or if it is repeated where he cannot hear it. The secondary information, that the recipient knows the item, must somehow return to the original talker. Thus in the functioning of the group the repetition of messages serves as a safeguard against mistakes. If the talker never hears his message repeated correctly, he must assume that a mistake was made somewhere. In that case he must try again. So he repeats his message until the recipients eventually show him that they have received his information correctly. Then he can proceed to the next item.

In normal conversation secondary information is conveyed by facial expressions, "yes," "what," etc., or the general relevance of subsequent behavior. These responses carry no primary information. They simply advise the talker about the recipient's state of information. . . . Thus every communication plays a double role, for it both lets the people know and also lets the people know that the people know.

Reasons for Social Communication

In the preceding example it is assumed that the purpose of the net is to provide information to the members. The group functions until the pattern of information is homogeneous over all members. The net may serve other purposes. If the group is organized for the purpose of taking some particular action, it may not be necessary to continue until everybody knows everything. It may be sufficient that a single person, the leader or the spokesman of the group, have all the information.

In many groups an important function of the net is to permit the members to reach a common opinion. In spontaneous groups, where members can join or resign freely, uniformity of opinion is often an important condition for the survival of the group. If the group is divided by a strong difference of opinion, members on the two sides of the argument communicate in order to change the opinions of the others. If the difference cannot be resolved, the group may split.

The analysis of the opinion-spreading group is not greatly different from the analysis of the information-spreading group. The question becomes, Who *believes* this item? instead of, Who *knows* this item? The primary information takes the form of arguments pro or con. The secondary information is carried by the recipient's reply. The reply tells the talker whether he has succeeded in changing the recipient's opinion. Instead of the pattern of information, we specify the *pattern of opinion* at successive instants in time. The group continues to function until it reaches unanimity or becomes exhausted.

The description of group communication can become still more complex if some additional relation is imposed upon the members. The most important additional relation is "dominates" or "is superior to." In most groups some members have higher status than others. Such groups are called *hierarchies*. The hierarchy structure is described completely by listing, for each member, every member who is his superior. In these groups it is well to keep track, not only of who talks to whom, but of the status level of both members. Differences of status influence the traffic density over the different channels and play an important role in determining which way opinions change.

We have assumed that the members of a group are motivated to communicate with one another in order to attain uniformity of information or of opinion within the group. Another reason for communicating is to change one's position in the group or to move from one group to another. A member may wish to change his status in a hierarchy or may wish to join some subgroup within the larger group. When a member cannot move in the desired direction, he wants to talk about it.

Still another important reason for communication is the desire on the part of the members to express their emotions. Festinger (1950) has pointed out that expressive messages are consummatory rather than instrumental. *Instrumental communication* requires feedback from the recipient. The talker wants to know whether or not his message had an effect. *Consummatory communication* does not depend upon the effect it has on others. The talker is usually not interested in secondary information about the effects of his consummatory communication. The expression of the emotion reduces his need to communicate regardless of its effects.

We have, therefore, four basic reasons for social communication, (1) to increase uniformity of information, (2) to increase uniformity of opinion, (3) to change status in the group, and (4) to express emotions. All four types of messages may travel over a net, and a single message may fall into more than one class. For example, a member may give information in the hope that it will lead the group to adopt his opinion and so prepare the way for his own promotion.

So much for the logic of social communication.

COMMUNICATION IN SMALL GROUPS

Problem Solving with Restricted Nets

Most of the studies of group communication do not try to control the arrangement of channels between the members. The conference or committee situation is of major practical interest, and most experiments adopt its face-to-face conditions. As soon as we begin to control the various channels, we must deprive some members of direct contact with others. The isolation so created tends to make the situation unnatural or artificial. The principal reason for imposing such restrictions is to gain better control over the group's operations and so permit a more careful exploration of the conditions necessary for efficient cooperation. Restricted nets are of more than purely theoretical interest, however. Such situations do arise occasionally in games, in telephone conversations, in military communications, etc.

In one experiment of this sort (Leavitt, 1951) five subjects were seated around a table, but separated from one another by vertical partitions. There were slots in the partitions through which written notes could be passed. By varying the slots that were open, the channels among the five could be manipulated into any desired

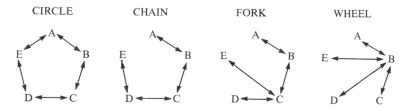

FIGURE 2. *Diagrams of four communication nets studied by Leavitt (1951).*

pattern. Four patterns were tested: (1) in the *circle* each person could pass notes to the person to his right or left; (2) the *chain* was identical to the circle except that one more slot was closed, and so the subjects on either side of this closed slot found themselves at the two ends of the chain; (3) the *fork* was a four-member chain, and the fifth subject could exchange notes with one of the inner members of this chain;

and (4) the *wheel* put one subject at the center of the net in such a way that he could exchange messages with all the other members, but the other four could not exchange information without passing it through the central member. These four nets are shown in Figure 2.

Each subject was given five different symbols out of a possible set of six. The task was for the entire group to discover as rapidly as possible the one symbol held in common by all five members. Each group completed 15 such tasks during the experimental session. Records were kept of speed, errors, and number of messages. At the end of the experimental session the subjects were given a questionnaire before they talked to each other.

The peripheral men in the wheel always sent their information to the central man (B), who arrived at the answer and sent it out. This plan of operation usually evolved by the fourth or fifth trial and was not changed. The fork also operated so that the most central man (C), got all the information and sent out the answer, but this organization evolved more slowly than it did in the wheel. The chain was not as stable as the wheel and the fork. Usually the center man (C) sent out the answer, but this function was occasionally performed by one of the men on either side of him (B or D). The organization evolved more slowly in the chain than it did in the wheel and the fork. The circle showed no consistent pattern of operation. Members of the circle simply sent messages until they received or could work out the answer for themselves.

The circle made the greatest number of errors. The fork and the wheel made the fewest errors. The different nets did not differ significantly, however, in the time it took them to finish the problem.

One of the questions asked at the end of the experimental session was "Did your group have a leader? If so, who?" In the circle there was no agreement as to who had been the leader. In the chain the central man (C) was recognized as the leader by about two-thirds of the members who thought there had been a leader, and no one recognized the most peripheral members (A and E) as the leader. In the fork 85 per cent of those members who thought there was a leader recognized C's leadership. In the wheel nearly everyone knew there was a leader and everyone agreed that the leader was B. Thus the emergence of recognized leadership (under the conditions of this experiment) was closely related to the centrality of the member's position in the communication net.

The subjects were also asked how well they enjoyed their jobs. Members of the circle liked the job better, on the average, than did the members of the other nets. The lowest morale was found among the members of the wheel. When the answers from the wheel, the fork, and the chain were analyzed, it was found that subjects in the most central positions were the best satisfied and subjects in the most peripheral positions were the most discontented.

If we contrast the circle with the wheel, we find the (1) the circle was unorganized, unstable, passed the greatest number of messages, was leaderless but satisfying to its members, and got the job done about as rapidly as any other net, whereas (2) the wheel was well organized, stable, passed relatively few messages, and had a clearly recognized leader but did not satisfy four of the five members. . . .

Bavelas (1950) has suggested that some communication nets may prevent the members from having insight into the group's problem. In order to explore this notion, he uses a problem that requires the formation of squares out of odd bits of cardboard. Five squares are cut up, and the pieces are distributed among the five members of the group. The members can pass pieces or messages over the communication channels. The task is to redistribute the pieces until all five members can form a square. There is only one distribution of the pieces that enables everybody to form a square, but there are many partial solutions where one member can form a square out of pieces the other members need so that the other members are completely blocked. When one member forms a square that blocks the group's progress, he must break up this square so that the pieces can be redistributed before the group effort can succeed. The member who has this false success is understandably reluctant to abandon it. The ease with which he can take this course of action away from his own goal depends to a large extent upon his knowledge of the total situation. Secondary information about the success or failure of the other members is absolutely essential for the group's success. When the communication among the members is restricted to any severe degree, the distribution of secondary information is usually more restricted than the distribution of primary information. Thus any severe restriction of the communication channels makes the solution almost impossible.

COMMUNICATION IN LARGE GROUPS

As long as the group is relatively small, it is possible to analyze the communication net in detail. When the group has as many as 10 members, however, the number of possible combinations is unwieldy. With 100 members a detailed analysis is practically impossible. When the problem gets this complex, we must search for short cuts.

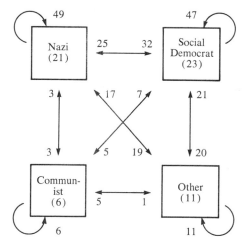

FIGURE 3. *Net of visiting relations among families in a small German town. Families are grouped by political affiliation. Numbers beside arrows indicate traffic densities. (After Loomis, 1946.)*

A possible short cut when the number of members begins to get out of hand is to look for subgroups within the larger group. These subgroups can then be treated as if they were the individual members of a small group. An example is provided by a study of the visiting relations among the 61 families in a small German village (Loomis, 1946). The heads of these families were grouped according to political affiliation as Nazi (21 families), Social Democrat (23 families), Communist (6 families), and other (11 families). This classification gives four subgroups within the larger social unit of the village. The observed frequencies of visiting between families are shown in Figure 3. The squares represent the four political groups, and the numbers in the squares represent the number of families. The numbers by the arrowheads represent the traffic densities for social visiting. Thus 49 visiting relations involve Nazis visiting Nazis, 32 involve Nazis visiting Social Democrats, 25 involve Social Democrats visiting Nazis, etc. All possible channels between the groups are used, but some are used more frequently than others. There is a tendency for visiting relations to be established between families of the same political affiliation, but the tendency is small.

The usual procedure with large groups is to use statistics. We may not be able to trace out the exact paths over which the information travels, but we can state certain average values. The averages are based on the assumption that channels exist more or less randomly and homogeneously throughout the group. Suppose we have a group of 1000 people who can exchange messages freely (so far as we know) in any direction. Since there are too many channels to consider each one in detail, we make a simplifying assumption. We assume that the frequencies with which messages originate or terminate at any member are distributed uniformly through the group. A given message is just as likely to go to one member as to any other; it is just as likely that the message originated with any one member as with any other; and a member is just as likely to send himself a message as he is to send a message to any other member. If there are 1000 members of this group who can send or receive the messages, then each person has one chance in 1000 of having sent or received any particular message. Now suppose we form subgroup A within the original group of 1000 members. There are, let's say, 100 members in subgroup A. What are the chances that a particular message will go to a member of this subgroup? Each member has 1 chance in 1000 of receiving it, and there are 100 members — thus there are 100 chances in 1000 that some member of A will receive the message. Similarly, the chances are 100 in 1000 that any particular message was sent by a member of A.

Consider now another subgroup, B, that has 10 members, none of them members of A. What is the chance that a message will both originate with subgroup A and terminate with subgroup B? Since we are asking for the probability of simultaneous events, the answer is obtained by multiplying the two probabilities together. The chance that A sent it is $100/1000$, or 0.1, and the chance that B received it is $10/1000$, or 0.01, so the chance that both A sent and B received the message is (0.1) (0.01), or 0.001.

The subgroups A and B can be identified with two cities, and the number of people living in the cities is the size of the subgroups. The chance that any message will originate in city A and go to city B is then proportional to the product of the populations of the two cities. If P_1 is the population of the first and P_2 is the population of the second city, the traffic density between them should be proportional to P_1P_2. The larger the two cities are, the greater the chance that messages will pass between them.

We know a little more about the situation than this equation indicates. If two people in a group find it difficult to exchange messages, the probability that they will communicate should be reduced. With 1000 people in the group a member on the easternmost fringe may find it much easier to send messages to his neighbor than to send them all the way to a man on the western fringe of the group. When a large number of people belong to the group, it is reasonable to assume that the likelihood of messages passing from one person to another is inversely proportional to the distance between them (Zipf, 1949; Stewart, 1947; Miller, 1947). The greater the distance, the lower the traffic density. . . .

RUMOR

When false information acquires wide acceptance and is passed along from person to person with no secure evidence offered, we call the phenomenon a rumor. In times of social crisis rumors can become dangerous to a community by spreading alarm or raising hopes needlessly. They may even be used deliberately by subversive groups to arouse hostility and dissension. Most of our rumors are idle gossip and serve little purpose but to pass the time of day or to avoid the embarrassment of dead silence. Most rumors reflect the motives of the people who spread them. Scandal appeals to sexual motives, malicious gossip and slander satisfy a dislike of some person or group, pipe dreams thrive where there is hope and desire.

Successive Reproductions

Inaccuracies have been observed in the reporting of simple testimony. Now suppose that this testimony is passed along through four or five people in succession. At each repetition there are new chances for error. Each participant imposes his own distortions on the account. After the story has passed through several hands, it may be completely unrecognizable as an account of the original event.

In order to study the successive distortions introduced along the rumor chain, Allport and Postman (1947) developed the following experimental procedure: Out of a college class or forum audience a group of six or seven people is selected. They are asked to leave the room. They are told only that when they return to the room they must listen carefully to what they hear and be able to repeat it as exactly as possible. A picture of some detailed situation is then shown, and some member of the audience is requested to describe it (while looking at it) to the first subject. He is asked to include about 20 details in his description. The members of the selected group are called back one at a time and placed where they cannot see the picture. The first subject hears the description. The second subject is called in, and the first subject repeats what he has heard. Then the third subject is called in, and the second repeats the account to him. So the account proceeds through several steps. The successive descriptions are recorded by the experimenter for more careful dissection later.

As an example of the kind of records obtained, examine the following sequence of reports. The picture used is shown in Figure 4.

Description from the Screen

This is a picture of an elevated train stopping at Dyckman Street. Evidently an Avenue Express. It shows the interior of the train with five people seated and two standing. There are the usual advertising signs above the windows. One is about smoking a certain cigarette, one is a soap ad, another about some camp, another is a political ad for a certain McGinnis for Alderman. Seated is a man with a hat on and a newspaper. He is a funny, rounded man engrossed in his newspaper.

Next to him is a woman with a shopping bag on her right arm, eyeglasses, and a funny hat. Then there is some empty space, and in front of it a Negro in a zoot suit, pork-pie hat and loud tie, talking with a defense worker wearing old clothes: overalls, high boots, sleeveless sweater, and cap. He seems to be a shipyard worker, has a razor in his left hand, and is evidently arguing with the Negro. Next person sitting is a woman with a small baby in her arms, watching the two men in their argument. She is commonly dressed and has long hair. Sitting next to her is a man in a cloak, a Jewish rabbi, reading a book, with a funny hat. He is wearing a long coat, not modern. Sitting next to him is a fat man, fast asleep, with his hands clasped.

First Reproduction.　A picture of a subway train, stopping at Dyckman Street. It shows the interior of the subway car, about five people sitting, two standing. There are the usual ads, one for cigarettes; one for a political candidate, McGinnis. The people sitting are a fat man interested in his newspaper, next to him a woman, then an empty seat, then a Negro in a zoot suit having an argument with a defense worker carrying a razor. It seems to be a serious argument. Then a woman holding a baby, then a man who appears to be a Jewish rabbi; a fat man fast asleep. The two men are standing; a fat woman is watching the two men standing.

Second Reproduction.　Scene is a subway train at Dyckman Street. This is the interior of the car with five people sitting and two standing. There are the usual ads, one for cigarettes, one political for a candidate named McGinnis. People sitting are a fat man very interested in his newspaper, a woman, then an empty space, then a Negro and a defense worker. The Negro is wearing a zoot suit, and one of them is carrying a razor. They are having a serious argument standing. Then there is a woman and child and another man.

Third Reproduction.　This is a scene inside a car at Dyckman Street. There are seven people in the car, five sitting and two standing. Among the signs is a political one for a man named McGinnis. People standing are a fat man and a woman with a baby. Sitting down are two men, then a space, then a woman and two defense workers having an argument. One is a colored man with a zoot suit who has a razor in his hand. The argument must be pretty heated.

Fourth Reproduction.　Scene is in a subway car. Five people are seated and two standing. Signs and ads are along the top of the car. One is for McGinnis for Congress. There are a man sitting and a woman, and two defense workers. One of them is a Negro in a zoot suit who is waving a razor. A woman is standing with a baby in her arms. There is a fat man standing.

Fifth Reproduction.　The scene is in a subway car, with five people sitting and two standing. In the car there are advertisements; one of the ads is for McGinnis for Congress. In the front of the car there are a man, a woman, and two defense workers, one a Negro with a razor, which he is waving in anger. One person is standing, woman holding baby. The man standing is a fat man.

Sixth Reproduction.　This is a picture of a typical subway scene. In the picture three people are standing. The subway has the usual characteristics. There are ads, one of McGinnis for Congress. Sitting down are a man and a woman. Two other men, one a Negro, are discussing the coming election. The Negro is waving a razor. In another part a woman is standing, holding a baby. You also see that in the subway.

FIGURE 4. *Picture used to study the distortions introduced into rumors. (From Allport and Postman, 1947.)*

The razor shifts, you will note, from the white hand to the Negro. The woman with the baby is soon standing. The number of people standing varies. And McGinnis grows in stature from a candidate for alderman to a candidate for Congress, while the other signs drop out.

Allport and Postman distinguish three types of distortion that occur. *Leveling* occurs when successive versions omit details, grow shorter and easier to grasp and remember. With *sharpening,* some detail that happens to be preserved gains in emphasis and importance. *Assimilation* occurs when the special interests, motives, expectations of the subject influence his interpretation of what he hears.

In most cases we receive information from several sources—newspapers, radios, conversations, magazines. We check one of these sources against the other and so perform, in a limited way, a kind of statistical comparison of the several versions. Because the network of communication channels in a social group permits each member to be connected with the source of information via several paths, the social situation provides its own kind of redundancy. By checking one path against another it is often possible to detect the errors and distortions. To illustrate how this might work, we can try to reconstruct the original from several distorted fragments. Allport and Postman give several protocols obtained from the same original picture. From their records we extract the following group of accounts. All of them are the third reproduction (fourth communicatee) in a series.

There are four colored men working, one holding a hand grenade. There is a church steeple with a cross on it. The time is ten minutes past two. There are also signs along the side of the road.

This is a battle scene. The scene is one of general ruin, evidently a village shot up pretty badly. In the left foreground is a lieutenant in charge. There is a soldier lying down and shooting over the stone wall of the ruins of a restaurant. There is a church steeple on which a clock says ten minutes to two. There is also an ambulance with a couple of fellows running away from it. In the distance is the enemy. Somewhere in the foreground there are a lot of fellows, one of them a lieutenant because you can see the bar on his shoulders. A Negro in the picture is apparently trying to urge the men on to fight.

The scene is in France. There are two soldiers in a trench and a wounded soldier. There is an ambulance in the picture, and a house in the background, also a church with a steeple; the time is . . . I don't remember. There is a signpost 'Cherbourg 21 miles, Paris 50 miles.' There is a Negro soldier in the picture.

The picture is a battle scene. There is a church in the background with a clock which shows ten minutes to two. There is an airplane and a bomb bursting. A road sign says 150 miles to Paris and 21 miles to Cherbourg.

Now catalogue the various items we have been told are in the picture. After a little work we construct a table that looks about like this:

Mentioned 4 times: Church, clock (or time)
Mentioned 3 times: Negro, several men, road signs, steeple
Mentioned 2 times: Soldiers, ambulance, ruins of battle, "Cherbourg, 21 miles"
Mentioned 1 time: Hand grenade, restaurant, house, lieutenant, enemies, trench, airplane, bomb, stone wall, "Paris 50 miles," "Paris 150 miles"

It is reasonable to assume that any item mentioned in two or more of the accounts can be accepted. If the item occurs in only one of the four accounts, we cannot be sure that it was not a mistake. With this crude criterion, therefore, we would expect to find in the picture: a church with a steeple and a clock that says ten minutes before two; at least one Negro and several other men, some or all of them soldiers; an ambulance; battle ruins; road sign that says the distance is 21 miles to Cherbourg and that also gives the distance to Paris.

When we check this account against the original picture, we find it correct in all respects but one—the distance to Cherbourg is 50 kilometers.

Notice, however, that we were able to get back to the original picture with some accuracy because we had four independent channels of information. If the channels are not independent but converge at some point and all pass through a single individual, we are not able to eliminate any distortions that this one individual may introduce. Accurate information cannot be restored once it is lost. If several independent channels are not open, we have no way of checking errors.

REFERENCES

Allport, G. W., and Postman, L. *The Psychology of Rumor.* New York: Holt, 1947.

Bavelas, A. "Communication Patterns in Task-Oriented Groups." *Journal Acoust. Soc. Amer.,* 1950, 22, 725-730.

Festinger, L. "Informal Social Communication." In L. Festinger *et al., Theory and Experiment in Social Communication.* Ann Arbor, Michigan: Institute of Social Research, University of Michigan, 1950.

Leavitt, H. J. "Some Effects of Certain Communication Patterns upon Group Performance." *Journal of Abnormal and Social Psychology*, 1951, 46, 38-50.

Loomis, C. P. "Political and Occupational Cleavages—a Hanoverian Village, Germany." *Sociometry*. New York: Beacon House, Inc., 1946, 9, 316-333.

Luce, R. D. "Connectivity and Generalized Cliques in Socio-metric Group Structure." *Psychometrika*, 1950, 15, 169-190.

Luce, R. D., and Perry, A. D. "A Method of Matrix Analysis of Group Structure." *Psychometrika*, 1949, 14, 95-116.

Miller, G. A. "Population, Distance and the Circulation of Information." *American Journal of Psychology*, 1947, 60, 276-284.

Stewart, J. Q. "Empirical Mathematical Rules Concerning the Distribution and Equilibrium of Population." *Geographic Review*, 1947, 37, 461-485.

Zipf, G. K. *Human Behavior and the Principle of Least Effort*. Cambridge, Mass.: Addison-Wesley, 1949.

Alfred Fleishman

HOW TO SABOTAGE A MEETING

Lots of people talk about "communication" as if they know what they're talking about. They don't.

These people usually know more about how to sabotage communication than they do about how to promote it.

Of course, we're all would-be saboteurs. Most of the time, we do this unconsciously; and since sabotage *is* a risky business, sometimes we do succeed in communicating in spite of ourselves, having inadvertently stumbled upon some principle of general semantics—like the notion that the words we use may have a different meaning to the person we're talking to than they do to us, even though we both read the dictionary—diligently.

But there are some people around who have really studied the art of sabotage. They like to attend large gatherings ostensibly devoted to the practice of serious discourse—any meeting will do. Meetings offer them the perfect opportunity to be disruptive. The serious student is advised to study their methods.

If you adhere to the following seven rules, and apply them judiciously, you, too, can be an expert at semantic sabotage.

INTERRUPTION

The secret of breaking up any meeting by using the interruption method lies in your timing.

Let the speaker talk just long enough for you to get a general idea of what he's trying to say. Before he has a chance to conclude, interrupt. Arrange it so that you supply the clincher to *his* argument before he can get a word in edgewise. Even if you don't agree with his point of view, it isn't difficult to twist his words to support whatever different point of view you may be advocating at the moment. Of course, the speaker may insist on plodding on. Let him. This not only gives you a chance to interrupt him again, but, by demonstrating how patient and tolerant you are, wins *you* the support of the audience.

Reprinted from Alfred Fleishman, "How to Sabotage a Meeting," *ETC.* 24, No. 3 (September 1967): 341-44. Reprinted by permission of the International Society for General Semantics.

DIVERSION

The diversion technique begins where the interruption technique leaves off. Changing the subject is the best method of diversion, and the easiest for the beginner to follow. The only thing to remember is CHANGE THE SUBJECT COMPLETELY. You can talk about anything—the latest space shot, civil rights, the "good old days"—just so you change the subject completely.

There are, however, more sophisticated ways of creating a diversion. For instance: if several persons are engaged in a seminar, start talking in semi-hushed tones to the person sitting next to you. Put your hand in front of your mouth to make it even more obvious that you are carrying on a separate conversation. This may earn you some dirty looks, but the main thing is that people's attention is being diverted away from the speaker.

There are a few special techniques to cultivate if you use this device. It is important to be able to pitch your voice at a low enough level so as not to drown out the speaker completely. Yet you must create a "buzz." This takes some practice, but it's worth trying. People will attempt to listen to both you and the speaker. They won't be able to. Their heads will begin to turn and their minds to wander away from what the speaker is trying to say. You've won!

NAME CALLING

Name calling is a more advanced technique. Here, you don't interrupt, you wouldn't dream of creating a diversion. You are completely and totally cooperative. BUT, when the speaker has completed his address or succeeded in making his point, call him a name. It's as simple as that. The name should, of course, cast doubt on his character, or on his ability as a thinker. Suggest that he must be "off his rocker" or "out of his mind." Imply that nobody with a grain of sense could say such things or hold such views.

It isn't necessary to use foul language in your implementation of this technique. In fact, it's better if you keep your remarks "clean," because the effectiveness of this device hinges upon loudness and self-confidence. You want to make sure everybody hears what you are saying, and you want to sound extremely sure of yourself. Only as a last resort should you make a statement such as "I don't want to discuss that woman we both know." The distraught speaker will insist on knowing "what woman." All you have to do now is keep repeating that you don't want to embarrass anybody by going into details. This ploy is practically infallible. People being what they are, many of them will be very interested indeed in knowing all about "that woman." But *you* haven't said anything. Can you help it if other people have "dirty" minds?

CHALLENGING THE SPEAKER'S INTEGRITY

To make this particular method of sabotage work, you must permit the speaker to finish what he has to say—however much it hurts. Your aim is to disarm him. Never raise your voice; for you must appear to be in complete agreement with him. Then pounce:

"Who's *really* making the money out of this?"

"What are you trying to hide?"

"What's in this for you?"

"Why aren't all the facts being brought out in the open?" (You can allow yourself a great deal of moral indignation here.)

This will put the speaker on the defensive all right!

CONTRADICTION

You shouldn't have any difficulty with this technique. All you have to do is sit back, wait until the speaker is finished, and then contradict him. Don't attempt to engage him in debate. Just say authoritatively: "You're wrong."

The speaker will probably try to defend his position. Don't pay any attention to him. Simply shrug your shoulders and repeat your original remark. (He's dead wrong, and you know it.) Never make the fatal mistake of actually arguing with him. And whatever you do, don't let him trap you with specifics.

LAUGHING IT OFF

As demonstrated in the interruption technique, one good way to deflate a speaker is by showing his audience how tolerant you are—by laughing him and his subject off.

Remember, it's within your power to turn any discussion into a farce. *Of course,* you'll stay and listen to what the speaker has to say—patiently and with good-natured amusement. But really, you imply, the whole thing is so ridiculous that if you weren't such a "good Joe," you'd get up and walk out right now.

THE BRUSH-OFF

The brush-off is often used ineffectively. The student should be thoroughly versed in the other techniques before he tries this one. Only the real expert can successfully maneuver a speaker away from the podium by opening his briefcase and starting to rearrange its contents.

The beginner often makes the mistake of thinking that he can employ the same tactics to disrupt a meeting as he uses to get rid of an unwanted guest or client. In a public situation, he can't pick up the phone, dial the golf pro at the Country Club, and ask if he can have a quick lesson. That would not only be impractical, but openly rude. The saboteur has to play by the rules, even if he is playing a different game.

No, if you're a beginner, your best bet is to carry the interruption technique to the point of absurdity. Your first attempts will certainly result in chaos—not necessarily semantic chaos, but chaos nonetheless—and you will have achieved your goal. Cut off communication quick!

Lyman K. Randall

P-A-C AT WORK

1. KNOCK, KNOCK, WHO'S THERE?

When reality knocks at your door, who answers? A whining, complaining little boy or girl? A stern, scolding parent? Or a calm, alert adult? For example, suppose your boss tells you that he wants you to work overtime tonight and you have been planning for several weeks to meet some old friends for dinner immediately after work. Do you (a) turn to one of your colleagues and say, "Why do these things always happen to me, anyway? What's the use in making plans around here? He could have just as easily picked on somebody else." (b) Jump up from your chair and say to your boss, "That's not fair! You have no right to expect me to change my personal plans for this evening when you give me such short notice!" (c) reply to your boss, "That's going to cause a problem for me. You see, I've been planning for several weeks to meet some old friends tonight whom I haven't seen in 3 years. Is it possible to get someone else to work late tonight? Or perhaps I can come in early tomorrow morning. What do you think?"

Perhaps you can remember reacting to similar situations in each of these three different modes of behavior. According to T.A., everyone has three typical modes of behavior. They're called the Parent ego state, the Adult ego state, and the Child ego state. To simplify things, from now on we'll refer to these ego states as Parent, Adult, and Child with capital letters to distinguish them from actual parents, adults and children.

Recognizing your own Parent, Adult, and Child (or P-A-C for short) is the first step in applying T.A. to your daily living. But what are they? Where do they come from? How do you know one from the other when you see it?

In his book, *I'm OK, You're OK*, Dr. Tom Harris describes the experiments of Dr. Wilder Penfield, a Canadian neurosurgeon. Dr. Penfield, using an electrical stimulus, was able to trigger recorded speech and feelings that were stored like tape recordings in the patient's brain. Not only was the memory of an event recalled, but the whole experience was relived by the individual. For example, one individual not only recalled an early experience that involved her walking past a bakery, but

Reprinted from Lyman K. Randall, *P-A-C at Work: An-on-the Job Guide for Answering the Question: "Hey, What's Going on Here?"*, pp. 3-29. Copyright © 1971 by American Airlines. Reprinted by permission of the author and American Airlines.

she also began whistling a tune that she associated with the experience and reported actually smelling the aroma of freshly baked bread. The development of the three ego state concepts was, in part, based on these experiments. The Parent and the Child are permanent recordings in the brain. These tapes are never erased. They can, however, be up-dated by the Adult.

The Child: C

First, let's take a look at the Child. The Child in you is that body of data, recorded and stored in your brain when you were little. It comes from how you responded internally to what you saw and heard in the external world at that time. These recordings are primarily feelings and conclusions about yourself based on these feelings. They include feelings of frustration, inadequacy, and helplessness that were an inevitable part of your childhood. In addition, they contain the early recordings of joy, curiosity, imagination, spontaneity, and the excitement born from new discoveries which were also part of your childhood. For these reasons, the Child is often called the "felt concept of life."

In the example above, it was your Child who answered the knock of reality by pouting and sulking away from your boss after he asked you to work overtime. Your Child can be "hooked" by an event that generates strong feelings. You can spot your Child when you find yourself whining, sulking, throwing a tantrum, or abandoning yourself to the joy of a pleasurable new experience.

The Parent: P

Your Parent is that body of data, also recorded and stored in your brain, that comes from your observations about the way your mother and father (or other important "Big People" in your early life) behaved. It is based on external events that occurred essentially in the first five or six years of your life. It is a mosaic of learnings which you constructed as a little person that is captioned "This is the way the world out there really is!". Because of your smallness and dependency as a little person in a world of "giants," your overriding assumption was that THEY were right. For these reasons, the Parent is often referred to as the "taught concept of life."

Your Parent was the part of you that responded to your boss by lecturing to him about what is or is not a fair and proper way to treat you. Your Parent lectures, moralizes, points its finger righteously or accusingly, teaches, and "lays down the law." You'll know your Parent is in charge when you find your scolding finger pointing, hear yourself lecturing about what's wrong (or right) about today's youth, or discover yourself correcting somebody's grammar or manners.

The Adult: A

Your Adult is that part of you that figures things out by collecting and looking at the facts. You may find it helpful to think of your Adult as your computer which you use to estimate probabilities and to make decisions based on facts. Everyone, even little children, has an Adult which is capable of making assessments about outside reality. For this reason, the Adult is sometimes called the "thought concept of life."

When you told your boss why working overtime would create a problem for you and suggested some alternatives for him to consider, your Adult had taken charge.

Our Three Faces

Since everyone has the three ego states, once you learn to identify your own P-A-C it will be easy for you to recognize the P-A-C in others.

In some ways, our P-A-C's are like three different voices inside us. Our Parent is the voice that says things like: "You must . . . You ought to . . . You shouldn't . . . don't ever . . ." Our Parent tape plays back such old familiar recordings as: "If you want something done right, do it yourself . . . Big boys never cry . . . Idleness is the devil's playmate . . . A penny saved is a penny earned . . . , etc."

Any time you find yourself talking to yourself (either out loud or under your breath) and using the word *YOU*, your Parent is very likely addressing your Child. For example, when you say to yourself, "That was a dumb thing for YOU to do," your Parent is scolding your Child.

Our Child is the voice that says: "I want what I want when I want it . . . Try and make me! . . . Wow! Great! . . . Drop dead! . . . etc." Any time you are experiencing feelings or emotions (happiness, sadness, fear, etc.) your Child is participating in the experience in some way.

Our Adult operates on facts based on what's true today. It is the voice within us which says things like: "What's going on here? . . . *Now* I see why this happened the way it did . . . What part of me came on just a few seconds ago—my Parent? Adult? or Child? . . . Why did I react just the way I did? . . . etc."

You can become acquainted with your own P-A-C by listening to these three different voices inside yourself. You may not always hear distinct words. Sometimes you will be able to decipher messages from the feelings bubbling up inside you. Naturally, you cannot hear the voices or directly experience the feelings occurring within other people. You can, however, become skilled in spotting the P-A-C in others (and yourself) by watching for the kinds of cues [shown in the chart]. The examples in this chart are only a few of the cues to watch for.

As you become more skilled in spotting these P-A-C cues in others, you will also become more aware of some of them in yourself. You can also get some cues from others about how you come across to them by identifying how they react to you. For example, suppose a customer reacts to something you have just said with, "Well, I was only trying to find out where I was supposed to catch my plane!" You might learn something about yourself by replaying what it was you said (or how you said it) immediately prior to the customer's hurting-complaining response. Possibly the customer thought you were "putting him down" or scolding him in some way. It is important to stress that everyone has P-A-C ego states operating. The goal of learning T.A. is to strengthen the Adult in each of us so that we can not only ask, but also answer, questions like: "What part of me is coming on? Are these data true, appropriate, and reasonable for *today's* reality?" To put it another way, T.A. provides us with a means of putting our Adult in the Living Room of today, ready to respond to the problems of daily living that knock on our "front door of life." This does not mean that we are to do away with our Parent and Child. It would be a dull world without them. It does mean, however, that we want to be free enough to be able to examine these two data-tapes.

To the extent that our Parent and Child tapes are archaic and unexamined, we will be dominated by the past. To the extent, however, we are able to learn the truth about how we behave, we will be free. Perhaps this is one of the meanings behind the old saying "Know the truth, and the truth will make you free."

	Parent Ego State	Adult Ego State	Child Ego State
VOICE TONES	Condescending, putting down, criticizing, or accusing	Matter-of-Fact	Full of feeling
WORDS USED	Everyone knows that . . . You should never . . . You should always . . . I can't understand why in the world you would ever . . .	How, What, When, Where, Why Who, Probable	I'm mad at you! . . . Hey, great (. . . or any words that have a high feeling level connected with them.)
POSTURES	Puffed-up, super-correct, very proper	-Attentive, eye-to-eye contact, listening and looking for maximum data.	Slouching, playful, beat-down or burdened, self-conscious.
FACIAL EXPRESSIONS	Frowns, worried or disapproving looks, chin jutted out.	Alert eyes, paying close attention.	Excitement, surprise, down-cast eyes, quivering lip or chin, moist eyes.
BODY GESTURES	Hands on hips, pointing finger in accusation, arms folded across chest	Leaning forward in chair toward other person, moving closer to hear and see better.	Spontaneous activity, wringing hands, pacing, withdrawing into corner or moving away from laughter, raising hand for permission.

180

2. COMING ON STRAIGHT, CROSSED AND CROOKED

Scene #1

Stewardess: "May I see your boarding pass?"

Passenger (In angry tone): "I've already given my ticket to the man in the terminal!"

Scene #2

Employee: "I really would like to get your help in solving my lost time problem."

Supervisor: "OK. Why don't you get a thorough medical examination?"

Employee: "I've thought of that, but I don't have the money now."

Supervisor: "Why don't you try to get more sleep each night?"

Employee: "I've tried that, but my neighbors are too noisy." (etc.)

How many times have you found yourself in situations like the two scenes above? It is common for communication wires between people to get crossed in daily conversations. But why? How do these breakdowns in communication occur? And what can you do to untangle them? T.A. may have some ideas to help you.

In T.A., a *transaction* is an exchange of words and related behavior between two people. For example, when you say, "Good morning, Jim" and he says, "Good morning" back to you, you and Jim have completed a bit of social business which we have defined as a transaction.

When we see each person involved in the exchange as having a Parent, Adult, and Child, we are able to draw an accurate diagram of what happens in the transaction (thus the term, *transactional analysis*). The Parent, Adult, or Child in one person will always be answering the Parent, Adult, or Child in the other person. Any conversation is a series of transactions, one exchange after another. Transactions can be Adult to Adult, Adult to Parent, Adult to Child, Parent to Parent, Parent to Adult, Parent to Child, Child to Parent, etc.

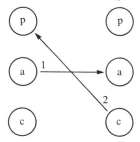

(1) It's time to go.

(2) I'm ready let's go.

(1) You really look tired. May I help you with your baggage?

(2) Whew! I'm exhausted! Thanks.

Examples #1 and #2 above are simple transactions. The arrows indicate who is saying what to whom. In each of these examples, the lines are parallel or uncrossed. As long as the lines in a transaction remain uncrossed, the conversation can go on indefinitely with no breakdown in communication. For this reason this type of exchange is called a complementary transaction.

Scene #1 is an example of a crossed transaction. When we diagram it, the transaction looks like this:

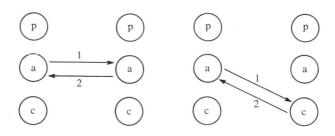

Stewardess	Passenger
(1) "May I see your boarding pass?"	(2) "I've already given my ticket to the man in the terminal!"

In this example the Stewardess is using her Adult to ask the Adult of the passenger, "May I see your boarding pass?" Instead of responding with his Adult with something like "Yes, here it is," the passenger responds angrily with his Child, "I've already given my ticket to the man in the terminal." The passenger has reacted as if the Stewardess has made an unreasonable *demand* on him from her Parent when in reality she has not. The communication about the passenger giving the Stewardess his boarding pass has broken down. The transaction has become crossed. A second rule of communication is: Whenever the subject is abruptly diverted (rather than simply completed), look for a crossed transaction.

In this situation the Stewardess has a choice of response to this crossed transaction. She could scold the passenger with her Parent for being so gruff with her. Or she could react with her Child showing anger or hurt feelings. Or she could use her Adult again and give more information to the Adult of the passenger: "Yes, I'm certain you did, sir. However, the man inside gave you a blue or white piece of paper with your seat number written on it. That's your boarding pass which I'd like to see now." It is probable that the customer will respond with his Adult to this last stewardess comment. Thus the transaction is uncrossed and the business of showing the boarding pass can be completed.

Scene #2 is an example of a duplex transaction. When we diagram it, the transaction looks like this:

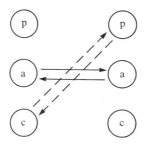

Employee	*Supervisor*
1. "I really would like to get your help in solving my lost time problem."	2. "OK. Why don't you get a thorough medical examination?"
3. "I've thought of that, but I don't have the money now."	4. "Why don't you get more sleep each night?"
5. "I've tried that but my neighbors are too noisy."	6. (etc.)

On the surface this series of transactions appears to involve an employee asking with his Adult for suggestions from his supervisor. And the supervisor, in turn, appears to be replying with ideas from his Adult. There is, however, a second, or hidden, psychological level of communication occurring. At this hidden psychological level the employee is saying, "I'm helpless to solve my own problems so I need a wise person (Parent) like you to solve them for me." The supervisor, in turn, responds on the psychological level with, "Yes I recognize my wisdom and will be happy to give you advice." But then in the 3rd and 5th parts of the transaction, the employee rejects the advice that he appeared to be asking for.

If we look only at the surface or social level of this transaction, it won't make sense to us. It appears contradictory. If, however, we look at the hidden psychological level, we can begin to see that the basic purpose of the transaction was to *reject* advice rather than to receive it. By rejecting the ideas of the supervisor, the employee is able, "to prove" his superiority over the boss in an underhanded or crooked way. This type of transaction is called a duplex transaction because it involves 2 levels of communication, an apparent social level and a hidden psychological level. Duplex transactions are commonly called games.

3. WHERE ARE YOU COMING FROM?

Whether you realize it or not, your behavior toward and reactions to other people are largely based on specific assumptions you make about yourself in relation to others. For most people, these assumptions were made very early in life by their early Adult ego states. They were the result of the young person needing to make some sense from the many hours of confusing and often contradictory data recordings in all three of his ego states—but particularly in his Parent and Child tapes.

These assumptions about yourself in relation to others are called life positions. They can be classified into one of the following four categories:

I'm Not OK and You're OK

(I feel that I am a Not OK person and I want you to know that you are OK with me.)

This is the life position held by most people. It is a conclusion based mostly on early negative or *Not OK feelings* about yourself rather than on a more comprehensive later review of data available in all 3 ego states. It is therefore a "felt decision" rather than a thought-out decision. It is a decision made at a time in your life when you saw and felt a clear distinction between yourself and the BIG PEOPLE around you who could do so many things that you couldn't. Many people continue to make this distinction between themselves and others in their grown-up years.

People in this position often feel low or depressed. Much of their energy is spent in getting away from other people.

I'm OK and You're Not OK

(I feel that I am an OK person and I want you to know that you are Not OK with me.)

This is a distrustful life position. It usually results from a person being beaten or brutalized by grown-ups when he was small. The people who base their lives on it spend much of their energy getting rid of other people.

I'm Not OK and You're Not OK

(I feel that I am a Not OK person and I want you to know that you are Not OK with me.)

This is a despairing life position. From it, life appears hopeless. People in this position use up much of their energy getting nowhere with other people or with their own lives.

I'm OK and You're OK

(I think that I am an OK person and I want you to know that you are OK with me.)

This is a rationally chosen life position. It is an Adult decision. It is made after the individual has had a large number of OK experiences with others and concludes: "*All* persons are important (OK). You and I are important (OK)." Much empirical testing is essential before an individual fully accepts this conclusion. This is the only healthy life position even though an individual who is in it continues to experience some Not OK feelings. (Remember, these feelings are permanently recorded in the Child and cannot be erased.) He however knows himself well enough to figure out what's happening with his Adult. He can therefore get on with others and with living his life (I'm OK and You're OK) rather than surrendering to depression, despair, or the impulse to make the world less Not OK by getting rid of others.

You may find it helpful to visualize these four life positions in the following way:

How you see yourself can be plotted on an axis with "I'm OK" at one end and "I'm Not OK" at the other end. For example:

I'm OK   I'm Not OK
                              (Axis on how I see myself)

Similarly, the way in which you see others can be plotted on a second axis with "You're OK" at one end "You're Not OK" at the other end. For example:

You're OK   You're Not OK
                              (Axis on how I see others)

If one of these is taken as a vertical axis and the other as horizontal, the following Life Position Diagram is formed:

You're OK

A "Getting On With . . ." (Others or Life)	B "Getting Away From . . ." (Others or Life)
C "Getting Rid Of . . ." (Others or Life)	D "Getting Nowhere With . . ." (Others or Life)

I'm OK (left side) I'm Not OK (right side)

You're Not OK

Box A = I'm OK and You're OK	(A potentially common position for people who examine their own experiences with understanding.)
Box B = I'm Not OK and You're OK	(The most common life position, decided before the Adult has had an opportunity to develop.)
Box C = I'm OK and You're Not OK	(An uncommon life position.)
Box D = I'm Not OK and You're Not OK	(An uncommon life position.)

One of these four life positions dominates each person's life. Most people decide as small children that the only life position which seems to make sense (at that time) is "I'm Not OK and You're OK." Taking this position helps them explain the many powerful "Not OK feelings" which they frequently experience in early life. With this position dominating their lives, they spend most of their time and energy "getting away from" others, themselves, and the daily business of taking charge of their own lives. Persons operating from this life position, however, can have occasional "Getting on With Others," "Getting Rid of Others," and "Getting Nowhere with Others" experiences which characterize the other three life positions. But the vast majority of their experiences will be the "Getting Away From"–type which result from the "I'm Not OK–You're OK" dominant position.

Living in an I'm Not OK–You're OK life position is not a pleasant experience. The very small girl or boy also discovers an antidote for the troublesome Not OK feelings. This antidote is stroking: The early rocking of the infant by a grown-up who cares; the holding of a crying little boy with a skinned knee; the physical or verbal attentions paid to the small person with Not OK feelings by a 6 foot tall OK individual.

Strokes are not only an essential antidote for the destructive Not OK feelings that are common to childhood. Stroking is also essential for the physical survival of infants. Studies of high infant death rates in European orphanages revealed that infants who were not touched or held, or stroked, soon became withdrawn and lifeless. If this process of physical deterioration was not reversed by a high quantity of stroking, the infant died.

This need for stroking, or stroke hunger, remains with us even in our grown-up years. Stroking is just as essential today for our psychological well-being as it was for our physical survival as infants. People, however, who live in an "I'm Not OK–You're OK" position sometimes become uncomfortable when others give them strokes. Positive strokes, in particular, make these people very uncomfortable since they believe they don't deserve them. When they receive special attention or a compliment, they discount it by concluding the giver must be after something or must be even more Not OK than themselves. On the other hand, people who are in an I'm OK–You're OK life position use their Adult ego state to obtain these essential strokes from many sources.

4. WORK IS NOT THE ONLY THING THAT OCCURS AT WORK

How many times have you heard, "You're expected to put in 8 hours of work in exchange for 8 hours of pay!" Work, however, is not the only thing that occurs on the job. People have six different ways to structure their time. Whether they are on the job or off makes little difference. These six time-structuring methods apply to all situations. They include (1) withdrawal, (2) rituals, (3) activities or "work," (4) pastimes, (5) games, and (6) authenticity or intimacy. Each of these approaches is related to the life position which you have taken.

The least risky way you can fill your time is *withdrawal*. You withdraw from people and situations when you are physically present by mentally putting yourself in another place or situation. Withdrawal is programmed by your Child as an escape from a boring or threatening present situation. It can also be a way of getting imaginary strokes from imaginary people through daydreams.

Rituals are the next safest way to fill your time and to get *strokes*. They are fixed ways of behaving towards other people which are programmed by your Parent. Rituals are closely related to good manners or "the proper thing to do when you're with others." For example, when you meet someone you know, usually you will say, "Hi! How are you today?" And the other person will likely say in return, "Fine. How are you?" This is a greeting ritual in which you give your friend several word strokes in return for several similar strokes from him. If you have good manners you will probably be a good stroker because you can be depended on to go through with rituals.

A third way you can fill your time is through *activities* which are often called work tasks. Activities are aimed at getting something done. For example, writing an airline ticket, painting a house, writing a letter, or fixing and serving dinner are all activities. Since work is often done with or for other people, it is also a common way of getting or "earning" strokes. Play and recreation are also activities.

Pastimes are a fourth way you can fill your time. Some pastimes are programmed by your Adult to get more information about another person. A common example of this is, "What kind of work do you do?" Other pastimes are programmed by your Parent or your Child to get strokes from others. Examples of these include, "What did you think of the President's speech last night?" and "Have you heard the story about the drunk who . . ." If you have a deficiency of pastimes, you will often feel like a wallflower in social gatherings. Everyone else will be getting lots of strokes except you. Pastimes are usually pleasant and safe ways of exchanging strokes and getting to know people without getting too close to them.

Interpersonal games are a fifth way you can fill your time. Nearly all people play interpersonal games (not to be confused with recreational games) even though they really aren't much fun. Games are programmed by our Not OK Child to help it get strokes and deal with its Not OK feelings. The next section of this handbook will cover games in more detail.

Authenticity or intimacy is the sixth way you can fill your time with other people. Authenticity is programmed by your Adult and occurs when you are in the "I'm OK–You're OK" life position. It is a warm, caring, straight (non-game playing) series of transactions with another person. Authenticity is a means by which people really come together whereas the other five ways of filling time keep you at safe distances from others. In authenticity you are the most vulnerable because you are giving more of yourself away than at any other time.

Your own experience probably tells you that all six of these methods for filling time occur on the job as well as off. The more time you spend with an individual, the more likely you will use all six time-structuring methods. For example, a ticket salesman will probably use only rituals and activities with a customer since he spends so little time with him. On the other hand, a stewardess on a five hour non-stop flight may find that she is engaged in all six time-structuring methods with her passengers.

You can use your job in all six time-structuring ways described above. You can withdraw from relationships by losing yourself in your job. Work can provide you with many opportunities for stroke-exchanging rituals. All jobs are primarily focused on activities designed to get certain things done. Your job also provides you with frequent opportunities for pastimes that help you get to know other people better and exchange recognitions with them. Your job can also serve as a playing field for games. And finally your job can provide you with opportunities for authentic relationships with colleagues and sometimes even customers. Work, therefore, is not the only thing that occurs at work.

5. TRADING STAMPS, GAMES, AND PRIZES

The Not OK feelings which most people experience early in life and record in their Child are not easy to live with. They must therefore learn how to handle these troublesome feelings at an early age. From the examples of important grown-ups around them, they learn how to deal with bothersome Not OK feelings by using Trading Stamps, Rackets, and Games.

What are Trading Stamps? Most people learn early in life that the free expression of their feelings, both the exuberant, positive feelings as well as the negative Not OK feelings, often get them into difficulty. So they learn to save-up their feelings for *later* use very much like people who save trading stamps which can be cashed in later for free prizes.

People save two basic kinds of Trading Stamps when they save-up their feelings: Dirty Stamps represent negative, Not OK feelings such as anger, depression, guilt, frustration, anxiety, and fear. Gold Stamps represent positive OK feelings such as joy, affection, excitement, enthusiasm, and pleasure.

Similar to people who collect S&H green stamps from grocery stores and service stations, people save Dirty Stamps and Gold Stamps for the same reason—to cash in whenever they have sufficient books for a free prize. Free in this case, however, means "free of guilt."

How does this work? Let's watch Mr. Gunther, one of our customers, for a few moments. Mr. Gunther specialized in saving Dirty Anger Stamps. He is a talented stamp collector who manages to find his brand of stamps in many places, including airports. He particularly enjoys the free prizes he gets for redeeming his stamps at our ticket counter. We may find Mr. Gunther cashing in one book of Dirty Stamps for a Free Mad—or two books for a Free Complaint letter to a Vice President—or three books for a Free Blistering Phone Call to the President.

Remember, Free Prize means "free of guilt." Mr. Gunther won't have to pay later for his selected prize with guilt feelings since it was "rightfully" his. After all, anyone who had to put up with all the annoyances that Mr. Gunther did has a *right* to get mad—or to write a complaint letter—or to call the President. In other words, Mr. Gunther's Parent gave permission to his Child to express the angry feelings he had been saving. But this permission is given only after a sufficient number of annoyances were endured to give Mr. Gunther the *right* to be angry.

Although most people seem to save preferred brands of Dirty Stamps, some individuals save Gold Stamps. For example, Miss Hummel is an employee who gives people around her lots of strokes—so she gets lots of strokes from others in return. These give her many good feelings about herself—or Gold Stamps. She may decide to redeem a book of these Gold Stamps for a free new hair-do on her day off—or 3 books for a free weekend on a ranch in Tucson—or 5 books for a free 3 week vacation in Europe. Again, "free" in each of these examples means guilt-free. Miss Hummel has earned the right to do these pleasant things.

If you are a collector of Trading Stamps, remember that your Parent must first "lick" the stamps before your Child can paste them in his book for later use. In other words, your Parent gives your Child both the permission to save the stamp and the permission to cash it in later on.

What are rackets and how are they related to stamp collecting? Rackets are taught by parents or by whomever raised you. If your Child has not taken the I'm OK–You're OK life position, you will find yourself in some kind of bad-feeling racket. Rackets are crooked ways that people go about collecting their favorite brand of Trading Stamps. One way to check-out what your feeling racket might be is to think back to what happened in your home when things got tense. Did your parents respond with anger, confusion, depression, anxiety, fear or with some type of Adult action? If they did not normally respond with Adult action, chances are great that they taught you a feeling racket.

Closely related to trading stamps and rackets are games. Games were popularized a few years ago by Dr. Eric Berne in his best seller, *Games People Play*. Games are special transactions programmed by the Child to help people deal with their Not OK feelings. These special transactions are called games because they require two or more players and always have a payoff at the end.

Game payoffs, which are hidden or under the table, usually come in two basic packages. One is obtaining strokes. The second is getting or giving preferred brands of Dirty Stamps. Because these payoffs are hidden, the Adult part of you does not know exactly what your Child or Parent is up to. This is because all games involve duplex, or double meaning, transactions. (You may want to refer back to Section II to review duplex transactions.)

Why does anyone play games? There are at least six reasons:

(1) Games help your Child to "keep up appearances," but in a dishonest way. For example, games may help you feel that your problems are caused by others' faults instead of your own.

(2) Games help you to keep from facing what you're afraid of, such as responsibility, competition, what others think of you, etc.

(3) Games help you pass the time with people you are close to as well as people with whom you are not close to.

(4) Games help you give and get strokes.

(5) Games help you to maintain your basic life position (such as I'm not as OK as others).

(6) Games help you get close to people without risking getting too close.

Why would anyone's Child "want" to feel NOT OK? No one would unless he was convinced from his early years that he was not as *OK* as others. If he was convinced of that, he will decide to "prove" it in order to justify his feeling that there's no use trying to change for the better. Remember, your Child can feel NOT OK without your Adult realizing it. (If you want to learn more about the specific games people often play, you may decide to buy a paperback copy of Berne's book, *Games People Play*.)

Why is an understanding of trading stamps, rackets, and games important to you? Every customer and employee comes to our work place as a total and complex person. Each one has his own unique P-A-C. He brings his feelings as well as his business or talents. You are also a unique person with your own P-A-C. Whether or not you are able to handle the feelings of your customers or fellow employees in a friendly, concerned, I'm OK–You're OK manner, will depend on how well you can recognize and sort out your feelings.

6. GETTING UNHOOKED FROM THE PAST AND LIVING IN THE PRESENT

At any time in your grown-up years you can make a conscious decision to throw out the old NOT OK position that probably governs the course of your life and replace it with the "I'm OK and You're OK" position. As you may remember, this is the only *healthy* life position. It gets us off the hook of the past and gives us freedom of choice in the present.

But just how do you go about making this decision? Strengthening your Adult is the key. First, your Adult must decide after serious examination that *all* human life is important and valuable. This leads you to respect your own humanity as well as the humanity in others. Simply believing the slogan, "I'm OK–You're OK," does not automatically turn all life into a beautiful rose garden, but it does open up new possibilities.

Of course, you'll be overcome from time to time by the old NOT OK feelings. But if you can use your Adult to reason that "I'm still OK—and so are you," your relationships will remain open, optimistic, and fluid. You won't pin yourself down in advance that everything will automatically turn out rotten.

Through strengthening your Adult, you will be more and more able to recognize your Not OK recordings from the past when they switch on. You can then have your Adult turn them off and get on with the business of living in the present. Sounds easy, doesn't it? It requires, however, hard work. And sometimes it requires the assistance of a professionally trained person.

Strengthening your Adult sufficiently to maintain an I'm OK–You're OK life position requires regular systematic exercise. Your Adult gets this exercise through up-dating your old Parent and Child tapes. This up-dating involves using your Adult to sort out which of the old Parent and Child recordings are still appropriate and valid for you in *today's* living—and which are no longer appropriate or true. By sorting out these old tapes, you can produce new data about yourself which you can now store in your Adult and use for living more fully in the present.

You may ask, "Why is this up-dating so important?" Consider first your old Parent tape. Although many of the recordings on it might have been essential for your early survival, some of them no longer are an appropriate basis for your judgements about today's living. Many of these old Parent recordings generate your own internal resistance to change. They say over and over to you: "Whatever was, is, and ever shall be! World without end. Amen." Other ancient recordings in your Parent may play back these familiar themes: "You don't deserve it. You'll never get it. You'll regret it if you do. You'll live to pay for it!" Although these recordings may have given you stability and a rationale for your experience in early years, they make accomplishing desired changes in your behavior and outlook today very difficult.

How do you up-date these no-longer-appropriate recordings in your Parent? There are several ways. You can learn the Parent cues presented in Section I of this handbook. Then you can put your Adult to work spotting these cues in yourself whenever they occur. It's important to remember that only your Adult can figure things out as they happen *today*. Your Parent can only hear and react in *previously* programmed ways—it can't, however, sort things out and compute them.

We can use certain Adult questions in this process of updating your Parent recordings. These questions include: "Is it now true? Does it apply today? Is it still appropriate? Where did I get that idea? What is the evidence for its validity today?"

Through this process of monitoring your old Parent recordings, you can begin sorting out portions which you want to retain for your daily living today. This becomes your up-dated or OK Parent tape which you will need to sustain an "I'm OK–You're OK" life position. You will also have identified old recordings you will want to turn off whenever they begin to play because they are no longer appropriate or make sense today.

What about up-dating your old Child recordings? Once again, you can begin by putting your Adult in charge of sorting out the rackets, Trading Stamps, and games which you are using to handle your Not OK feelings.

Trackdown is a six step procedure which can help you identify various Dirty Stamps you collect from others.

(1) *First ask yourself, "How do I hurt?"*

It is first essential that you recognize when you are hurting. This hurt can be any Not OK feeling, however small, that you feel. Next you state exactly the word or phrase that describes how you hurt. For example: "I feel stupid . . . or I feel put down . . . or I feel rejected. . . ."

(2) *Next ask yourself, "Which part of me (PAC) hurts?"*

It is not likely that your Adult will hurt. It's more likely, however, that your Child is the part of you that's hurting. Or it's possible that some old Parent tape has been trampled on, thus causing a hurt to enter there before your Parent sent the "ouch" on down to your Child.

(3) *Next ask yourself, "Who did it?"*

Who triggered your hurt? Did you hurt yourself (Damn it! You just goofed again, you stupid so and so!)? Or was it someone else who hurt you (You're disgustingly inefficient!)?

(4) *Next ask yourself, "Which part (PAC) did it?"*

Compute which part (P, A, or C) of the stamp-giver initiated the hurt. If you gave yourself a Dirty Stamp, was it your super-critical Parent beating up again on your Not OK Kid? Or if it was another person, was it his Parent, Adult, or Child that gave you the hurt?

(5) *Next ask yourself, "Why did it happen?"*

Why did you give yourself, or why did the other person give you this hurt? Was it accidental? On purpose? Was there a particular reason the statement was made? What made it hurt?

(6) *Finally, ask yourself, "What do I do differently?"*

Ask yourself, "Instead of collecting this Dirty Stamp, what else can I do right now? What can I do differently next time I meet this person or someone like him? What can I do the next time I meet someone who says or does the same thing?"

At first you may find that trackdown is a slow process. However, with practice you can compute all of these steps without even stopping whatever you're doing.

As you up-date your old Parent and Child tapes through the regular exercise of your Adult, you transfer the authority in your life from your out-dated recordings to your Adult—which now has up-dated Parent and Child data stored in it. You can now use your more flexible and potent Adult to give your OK Kid permission and opportunities to show itself in ways that are fun and appropriate to today's living. It is important to remember that up-dating your Parent and Child tapes is not the same as trying to eliminate your Parent and Child ego states. Life would be colorless and chaotic without them. Up-dating your Child and Parent tapes enables your Adult to take charge of figuring out what happened when old Parent and Child data create problems for you today.

Your little Kid may want magically to keep parents around so that you can feel safe or protected. Almost everyone's Child believes in some kind of magic, even though you may not be aware of it. You can spend your whole life waiting for something big to happen to make your life more interesting or exciting but do nothing to bring it about. This is known as "waiting for Santa Claus." T.A. is not magic nor is it a magical substitute for Santa Claus.

As you are up-dating your Parent and Child tapes, there are several activities which your Adult can carry out that will help you maintain an I'm OK–You're OK position. Remember, these are not magical formulas that guarantee instant OK feelings in relation to your work, your neighbors, and your family. They are, however, tools for you to use in "getting on with" others and the business of taking charge of your life.

When in doubt, leave it out

If you find yourself in a difficult situation and what you are about to say or do doesn't compute very clearly in your Adult, it is better to leave it out.

Exercise your OK Child

Be excited, responsive, and enthusiastic at every opportunity. If at first you can't make it, fake it! Your OK Child may be weak from lack of exercise, and a few forced exercises in expressing OK feelings can help these feelings to become more authentic.

Avoid the Parent of others

Be particularly alert to things that "hook" the Parent in others, then try not to arouse it. Too much playful, OK Child can arouse another person's Parent. Similarly, a NOT OK Child response on your part can also hook another's Parent.

Look for the OK Child in others

If you spot the OK Child in someone else, respond to it. This is the source of hidden gold in transactions with other people. Giving strokes through the use of names, smiling, well-timed humor, and individualized attention brings out the OK Child in others.

Feed your own OK Child

To keep your Child alive and healthy, it must be fed as well as exercised. Plan for ways for getting life sustaining strokes from many people rather than from one or two special persons. Also reserve time each day to have some fun. All work and no play makes your OK Child shrivel-up.

Keep contracts with others

If you say you'll do a certain thing, then live up to that promise. By keeping contracts with others you build reliability, dependability and trust between them and yourself. Being OK is based on reliability and trust. If you devalue others, you also devalue yourself.

After you become more aware of your games and stamp collecting, up-date your Parent and Child tapes, and use selected tools for maintaining an I'm OK–You're OK position, then what? You will be better able to see in your *own* way instead of the way you were taught. You will be free to feel as *you* want to feel, not as your Parent tells you to feel. You will be rid of your bad-feeling rackets since you've replaced them with good feelings. You will have more respect for yourself, and you will be more willing to accept strokes from others. Once your Child starts feeling OK about himself, you can stop listening to old Not OK recordings, stop waiting for Santa Claus, and give your Adult a chance to make your decisions. You can get off the hook of the past and start living in and enjoying the hopeful and exciting present!

SOME SPECIAL STROKES FOR SPECIAL FOLKS

These are some OK people whose ideas and writings have been liberally used in this handbook!

Eric Berne, M.D.: His many books, including *Games People Play,* have helped others (including the author) to learn about transactional analysis.

Frank Ernst, Jr., M.D.: His newsletter, "The Encounterer," contains many helpful clarifications of T.A. theory. The Life Position Diagram contained in this handbook is one of his original contributions to T.A. concepts.

Tom Harris, M.D.: His book, *I'm OK—You're OK,* took transactional analysis theory out of the specialized field of psychotherapy and into everyday experience. He also has encouraged the author at times when such strokes were particularly needed.

Michele Landsberg: Her article, "T.A. A New Way of Understanding Yourself and Others" was the first to take T.A. concepts from the pages of professional journals into the pages of popular magazines. Her article first appeared in the Canadian magazine, *Chatelain.* It then appeared in the October, 1970, issue of *Reader's Digest.*

Larry Mart, L.C.S.W.: His booklet, "Group Treatment and Intimacy" gave the author some of the ideas used in this handbook.

Paul McCormick & Leonard Campos: Their succinct booklet, "Introduce Yourself to Transactional Analysis" gave the author the idea to write this handbook pertaining to work situations. Some of their comments have been liberally used herein.

Section 4

THE AMELIORATION OF
INTERPERSONAL COMMUNICATION

In common usage, the term "amelioration" usually refers to the act of making something better. The amelioration of interpersonal communication consists of saying things and reacting to people so as to produce a better relationship with improved interaction. Amelioration implies just the opposite of alienation. It involves the reduction of distrust with an increase in understanding, whereas alienation stands for an increase in distrust and a decrease in understanding. The readings in this section look at those aspects of communication that might be improved and suggest specific styles of listening and responding to others so as to ameliorate relationships through more effective interpersonal communication.

Schein introduces this section with a concise listing and definition of some of the key dimensions of communication. As you read through these pages, work at developing an image of the components of the communicative process and how they interweave to form a complex basis upon which relationships thrive or dwindle. Reflect, for example, on the implications of who interrupts whom. How does your communicative style affect the way others perceive you? What kinds of double messages do you send? In what ways do your messages get filtered and how do you filter out what others say? Improvement of communicative behavior depends on how well you understand what needs to be changed.

Egan suggests that "listening" may represent the core concept and skill to be developed in the ameliorative process. He explains that "listening means becoming aware of all the cues that the other emits, and this implies an openness to the totality of the communication of the other." Of particular significance is the analysis of Campbell's sources of systematic error in human communication as principles for improving speaking and listening.

Carl Rogers reveals, in "Speaking Personally," some of the things he has learned that have significance for relationships with others. He asserts that only "very rarely do we permit ourselves to *understand* precisely what the meaning of his statement is to him." As with his other "learnings," this one recommends, but doesn't impose, a way of responding to others that can go a long way toward ameliorating relationships.

"Developing Effective Interpersonal Communication" represents an explanation of some theory and how to apply the theory through the development of a number of communication skills. John Wallen analyzes interpersonal relationships in terms of intentions, actions, and effects and lists a variety of statements about you and your reactions that contribute to more effective relationships. He describes "paraphrasing" and "describing feelings" as two major communicative skills for ameliorating communicative relationships. The exercise on communicating feelings should be completed with a group in order to derive the greatest benefit from the experience. Of great importance is practicing "paraphrasing," since it represents a communicative skill with general applicability that can be used often.

Lifton seems to conceive of the importance of communication in the same way that we do when he states that "communication provides the key to the helping process." In the helping process, he suggests, the primary goal is to "assist others in examining their words or behavior to see if they represented what the client wished to communicate." The tools and techniques he describes represent some of the communicative responses that facilitate more effective interpersonal relationships in any context. "Reflecting" is a fundamental way of responding, while questioning, supplying information, clarifying an idea (summarizing points that relate to each other), and silence are techniques central to assisting others to understand. Lifton's analysis of clarifying operations, show-how operations, and security-giving operations is one of the most complete compilations of techniques available in the literature. Developing skill in each type of operation could be a significant step toward amelioration of interpersonal communication.

Elwood Murray, a pioneer in the field of speech communication, introduces the concept of "semantic disorder," then describes how to help prevent such disorders. He urges each of us to take stock of our habits of evaluation to see whether what we are about to say represents an appropriate evaluation of the "facts." He describes a number of specific techniques for keeping ourselves factually oriented. To counter our tendencies toward evaluation in terms of fixed beliefs and preconceptions, he recommends the use of devices such as indexes, dates, *et ceteras*, quotes, and hyphens. A careful study of and a planned acquisition of the skills involved in using these devices and other techniques will expand your abilities to ameliorate interpersonal communication.

"Towards Better Interpersonal Relationships," represents an effort by Bennis and his colleagues to set down their conception of ideal interpersonal relations and what they consider the most effective way to reach those relations. They list and define five personal capacities that lead to good interpersonal relationships. You will want to examine those competencies carefully and make an honest assessment of where you stand with respect to your own abilities in those areas. As they suggest, "People simply do not learn from experience alone; it is experience observed, processed, analyzed, interpreted, and verified that we learn from." So it is with this book. With your experience you have the opportunity to observe with meaning, analyze with significance, interpret with understanding, and verify by doing. Therein lies the avenue to improved interpersonal skills that lead to better interpersonal communication.

Edgar H. Schein

COMMUNICATION PROCESSES

One of the most important processes in organizations, and one of the easiest to observe, is how the members communicate with each other, particularly in face-to-face situations. Many formulations of communication depict it as a simple problem of transfer of information from one person to another. But, as all of us know, the process is anything but simple, and the information transferred is often highly variable and highly complex. We communicate facts, feelings, perceptions, innuendos, and various other things all in the same "simple" message. We communicate not only through the spoken and written word but through gesture, physical posture, tone of voice, timing of when we speak, what we do not say, and so on. . . .

WHO COMMUNICATES? HOW OFTEN? FOR HOW LONG?

The easiest analysis of communication is to focus only on the *relative frequency* and *duration* of communication acts. Thus, if the observer wishes to study the communication behavior of a group or committee, he can list the names of all the members and put a check mark next to a name each time that person says something. He can measure duration by putting down a checkmark every few seconds as long as the speaker continues.

After some period of time the chart can be summarized to show who has talked, how often, and how much of the total available time he has used. One can also determine who used short communications and who spoke for long periods. If one wanted to analyze written communications, an analogous chart could be set up to determine who sends, how often he sends, and how long the message. . . .

WHO COMMUNICATES TO WHOM?

The next level of complexity of observation would be to determine who talks or writes to whom. Such observation is not difficult with written communications if they are addressed, but it can be quite tricky in a group situation since people often are not very explicit about whom they are directing themselves to. The observer may have to watch the speaker's eyes to see whom he is looking at when he is talking, or he may observe bodily posture for similar cues. . . .

WHO TALKS AFTER WHOM? WHO INTERRUPTS WHOM?

Closely related to the issue of who talks to whom is the matter of who triggers whom and in what ways. I have noted in observing groups that there are clear patterns of triggering. Whenever Joe speaks the odds are pretty good that Pete will be the next to speak even if the remarks were not initially directed to him. . . .

Let us now turn to the other kind of behavior mentioned in the heading: who interrupts whom. The importance of observing this type of communication behavior derives from the fact that it gives us clues as to how members perceive their own status or power in the group relative to the status or power of other members. It is a matter of common observation, and has been documented in careful studies of deference, that the person of higher rank, status, or power feels free to interrupt someone of lower rank. We generally let the boss finish his sentences more often than he lets us finish ours. . . .

COMMUNICATION STYLE

Communication style is intended to refer to a whole range of things such as whether the person is assertive, questioning, pedantic, or humorous; whether his tone of voice is loud, soft, grating, or melodious; whether he accompanies his words with gestures, and so on. . . .

For example, I may notice that a person talks very loudly and assertively, causing others gradually to "tune him out," yet he seems to be quite unaware that this is happening. He may even become aware of his declining influence in the group, and yet remain unaware of what has caused this decline. He does not hear himself as loud and assertive. The other members of the group who are no longer paying attention to him are also in a trap. They may not be paying attention because of the communication style used by the speaker and because they erroneously feel that it is the content of what he is saying which is failing to hold their interest. Communication in this situation cannot improve until both parties to the problem gain some insight into what they are doing and why they are doing it (e.g., what cues they are sending and are reacting to). . . .

GESTURAL COMMUNICATION (KINESICS)

As anthropologists and linguists have known for some time, bodily posture, gestures, facial expressions, and other nonverbal behavior can and do become patterned according to the culture in which the person grew up. To the extent that they are patterned and have symbolic meanings, they can be understood just as clearly as verbal or written communication. Certain gestures, for example, reflect ethnic background. It has been shown by careful analysis of films of people in spontaneous interaction that some groups (e.g., first-generation Jewish immigrants) tend to accompany assertive words with forward reaching one-handed gestures, often described as "buttonholing." First-generation Italians, in contrast, tend to use both hands in gesturing and to rotate them outwards rather than pointing toward the listener. . . .

LEVELS OF COMMUNICATION

So far I have discussed more or less manifest and easily observable communication events. In order to make some sense of these events and to understand more fully how members of any encounter react to each other, it is important to analyze less easily observable events. As background for this discussion some psychological theory about the nature of communication is also relevant.

As most of us know from observation of our own behavior, not only do we tend to react to the manifest content of what another person says to us, but we interpret what he says and use various subtle clues to get at the real meaning of the message. Often the same message carries more than one meaning, both a manifest and a latent meaning. Occasionally these meanings tend to contradict each other. Simple examples would be the person who issues an invitation with the statement "Come over to our house anytime," but leaves it sufficiently ambiguous through his tone of voice to make you realize that he does not really want you to come but is merely being polite. . . .

2 Concealed self	1 Open self
4 Unknown self	3 Blind self

FIGURE 1. *The parts of a person.*

Double messages of this kind do not pose unusual difficulties because the sender is aware of them and can clarify misunderstandings. Greater difficulty arises from double messages which reflect parts of the person of which he is unaware. To illustrate what is meant it is useful to think of the person as having several parts as depicted in Figure 1. Quadrant 1 in the figure represents those areas of the person of which he himself is aware and which he is willing to share with others: the "open self." Quadrant 2 represents those parts of himself of which he is aware, but which he is consciously and deliberately trying to conceal from others. . . .

Quadrant 3 in the figure is the key one for this discussion. The "blind area" of the self refers to those things which we unconsciously conceal from ourselves yet which are part of us and which are communicated to others. "I am *not* angry" says the boss in loud tones, purple-faced, as he slams his fist on the table. "These meetings are quite relaxing for me" says the executive as his hand trembles, his voice cracks, and he either has a third martini or tries unobtrusively to slip a tranquilizer into his mouth. "I do not care about the opinions of others," says the manager, but then he gets very upset if others do not notice him or his work. . . .

Quadrant 4 consists of those parts of the person of which neither he nor others are aware. Examples would be truly unconscious and deeply repressed feelings and impulses, hidden talents or skills, potentialities, and so on. For our purposes this area is irrelevant. . . .

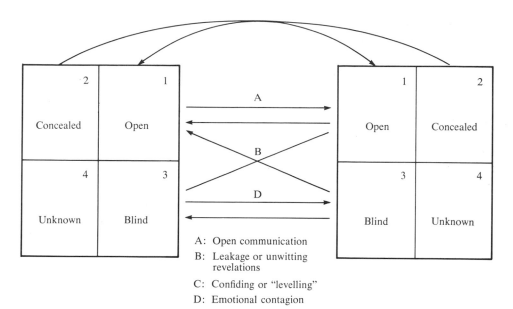

FIGURE 2. *Types of messages in a two-person communication situation.*

Let us now consider two people in interaction with each other (Figure 2) and analyze the implications of the different kinds of messages and different levels of communication which occur. Most communication occurs between the two open selves of the persons (Arrow A), and most popularized analyses of the communication process confine themselves to this level.

A second level of communication is the signals or meanings which we pick up from a person's blind self and which he is unaware of sending (Arrows B).

A third level of communication occurs when we deliberately reveal something which we ordinarily tend to conceal (Arrow C). Ordinarily we think of this as "confiding" in someone or "leveling" if we are sharing reactions or feelings generated by immediate events.

Finally, there is a less common but no less important level of communication represented by Arrow D which might best be labeled "emotional contagion." One person influences the feelings of another without either one's being consciously aware of the origin of the feeling. . . .

Once one recognizes several levels of communication, one can open up communication channels which ordinarily are not used. Once the participants in an interpersonal situation obtain some insight into their own communication behavior, it is possible for them to examine rationally the pros and cons of opening more of the Arrow C or "confiding" kind of channel. Specifically, they can examine whether or not effectiveness of the group would be increased if more members shared their private feelings, particularly feelings pertaining to other members and to the work situation. . . .

FILTERING

The final, and perhaps most difficult, complexity to consider in the communication process is that both the sender and the receiver use a number of filters in selecting what they will send and what they will receive. I am not implying conscious censorship, though this occurs also. Rather, I am implying that all of us select what we say, how we say it, and when we say it in terms of a complex set of decision rules which we have learned over a lifetime and which reflect a number of specific factors:

a) *Self-image.* Both the sender and the receiver have an image or concept of themselves and feelings of self-worth or self-esteem. What their self-concept is at any given time and what value they attach to themselves in a given situation will, in part, determine their communication. . . .

b) *Image of the Other Person or Persons.* Both the sender and the receiver have an image or concept of the others in the situation and attach certain values to these others as people. These images of the "other" will also, in part, determine communication. . . .

c) *Definition of the Situation.* Both the sender and the receiver have a certain picture of the situation they are jointly operating in. Is it a meeting to solve a specific problem? Is it an informal bull session? . . .

d) *Motives, Feelings, Intentions, Attitudes.* Another set of filters on the communication process both for sender and listener are the various needs and motives they bring to the situation, their intentions, and their attitudes toward others. . . .

e) *Expectations.* The final category of psychological factors which create filters is our expectations of ourselves and of others in the situation, based either on actual experience or on preconceptions and stereotypes. . . .

The Circular Process and Self-fulfilling Prophecies

The various factors described above under the category of filtering make it possible for communications to break down in a particularly dangerous manner. If expectations are strong on the part of both the sender and the receiver, it is possible for each to interpret the cues from the other in such a way that both confirm their stereotypes and thus "lock" each other into roles from which it is difficult to escape. . . .

SUMMARY

In the previous sections I have examined various facets of the communication process. Starting with relatively overt processes like who talks, who talks to whom, who interrupts whom, and what style of communication is used, I then reviewed more subtle communication issues like the meaning implicit in nonverbal communication, the role of different levels of communication stemming from our blind spots and tendencies to conceal certain things about ourselves, and the problems stemming from our tendencies to filter in the role of both sender and receiver.

Gerard Egan

LISTENING: THE SINE QUA NON OF
SUPPORTIVE BEHAVIOR

TOTAL LISTENING

For our purposes, listening means becoming aware of all the cues that the other emits, and this implies an openness to the totality of the communication of the other. . . . Listening, then, demands work, and the work involved is difficult enough that the effort will not be readily expended unless the listener has a deep respect for the total communication process.

One does not listen with just his ears: he listens with his eyes and with his sense of touch, he listens by becoming aware of the feelings and emotions that arise within himself because of his contact with others (that is, his own emotional resonance is another "ear"), he listens with his mind, his heart, and his imagination. He listens to the words of others, but he also listens to the messages that are buried in the words or encoded in all the cues that surround the words. As Berne (1961) suggests, he listens to the voice, the demeanor, the vocabulary, and the gestures of the other, or, as Haley (1959) would have it, to the context, the verbal messages, the linguistic patterns, and the bodily movements of the other. He listens to the sounds and to the silences. He listens not only to the message but also to the context, or, in Gestalt terms, he listens to both the figure and the ground and to the way these two interact. He is aware of what Murphy (1964) calls the "world of blushing, blanching, sighing, hinting, and averting the eyes"; like Smith (1966) he is aware that "people interact not only through words but also through spatial relations . . . through temporal relations . . . and . . . through gestures and touch and many other media [p. 3]."

Weick (1968) thinks that nonverbal aspects of communication are generally overlooked, much to the detriment of the communication process:

> Observers who are accustomed to analyzing speech behavior in naturalistic settings may regard nonverbal actions as a redundant source of information. This point of view neglects the fact that humans spend a very small portion of their interactional time vocalizing . . . [p. 381].

Although nonverbal behavior holds promise for observational research because of its visibility, naturalness, and discriminability, it can also be too subtle to record unless the observer has been trained to be sensitive to it. That persons are often unaware of the rich nonverbal language is not surprising, since much of it occurs unconsciously (Scheflen, 1965, p. 34). Jecker *et al.* (1964) found that teachers who were untrained in the analysis of nonverbal behavior could not predict, from filmed facial cues, whether a student had comprehended a lesson in algebra [p. 382].

We are perhaps too ideationally oriented and have a set to bypass nonideational cues. Tomkins (1962) has suggested that the face is the "primary site of affect": "the centrality of the face in affective experience may also be seen in the relationship between the hand and the face. The hand acts as if the face is the site of feeling (p. 210)." The relationship of hand to face, then, is an important source of information concerning the feeling states of the other: "It is our argument that human beings slap, hide, stimulate, support, caress, inhibit, or reassure their faces with their hands because they correctly localize the face as the primary site of their concern [p. 212]." Others have studied the face as a rich source of communication (e.g., Ekman, 1965; Haggard & Isaacs, 1966; Leventhal & Sharp, 1965; Levitt, 1964). Exline and various associates (Exline, 1963; Exline, Gray, & Schuette, 1965; Exline & Winters, 1965) have examined the phenomenon of eye contact and glances exchanged, finding them important channels for communicating such effective information as liking and various forms of interpersonal discomfort. The communication potential of both posture (Scheflen, 1964) and body movements (e.g., Katz, 1964; Mahl, Danet, & Norton, 1959; Spiegel & Machotka, 1965; Werner & Wapner, 1953) is also an area of serious study. . . .

The Nonselective Character of Total Listening

Total listening is, in a sense, nonselective: it encompasses all the cues emitted by the other, even those that the other would rather conceal and those the listener would rather not hear. For instance, the weight of an obviously overweight person is a cue to be reckoned with, for through it the other is saying something to those with whom he interacts. The message may be "I am frustrated" or "I don't care about others" or merely "I have poor self-control," but it is a message that should not be overlooked. . . . Good listening demands both subjectivity—that is, engagement with the other—and objectivity—that is, disengagement from the other—in order to pick up both postively and negatively valenced cues. The good listener is sensitive to what is and not just to what should be or to how I would like things to be.

Active Listening

It becomes quite apparent that the good listener is an active listener, one truly engaged in the communication process, one who goes out of himself in search of significant cues emitted by others. Listening, then, is facilitated if the listener is actively interested in others. Newcomb's (1953) "strain toward symmetry" principle leads to the prediction: the more intense one person's concern for another, the greater is the likelihood that he will be sensitive to the other's orientations toward objects in the environment. Certain studies do show that liking another person increases sensitivity toward him. Eisman and Levy (1960) showed that lipreading was more accurate the more the reader liked the communicator. Suchman (1956) discovered that people who were more favorable toward others were more accurate in estimating the feelings of these others. . . .

The person who is an active listener is much less likely to stereotype others or to become guilty of univocal listening. Perhaps an analogy would make this a bit clearer. Everytime Brahms' Second Symphony is played, the untrained ear hears only the Second Symphony; it is quite a univocal experience. The individuality of different orchestras and different conductors and the nuances of different tempos and accents are all missed. However, while there is only one Second Symphony, it can be played with quite different—and distinguishable—nuances. Similarly, John Doe is only John Doe, but John Doe, too, has different nuances of orchestration at different times, and these nuances will be missed by the untrained, passive listener who finds it more comfortable to deal with him as a stereotype in univocal terms. The active, searching listener, who is open to all the nuances of John Doe, will more likely pick up many of these cues. This openness to nuance, however, does not imply that the good listener is skilled in analyzing the other, for analysis often means reducing the other to a whole series of stereotypes, and sometimes this mistake is worse than the first.

All of Rogers's works (e.g., 1942, 1951, 1961, 1967) form a magnificent treatise on total listening:

> I also find the relationship is significant to the extent that I feel a continuing desire to understand — a sensitive empathy with each of the client's feelings and communications as they seem to him at that moment. Acceptance does not mean much until it involves understanding. It is only as I *understand* the feelings and thoughts which seem so horrible to you, or so weak, or so sentimental, or so bizarre — it is only as I see them as you see them, and accept them and you, that you feel really free to explore all the hidden nooks and frightening crannies of your inner and often buried experience [1961, p. 34].

OBSTACLES TO EFFECTIVE LISTENING

Alienation from Communication

Against the background of what it means to be a good listener, it will be helpful to review some of the obstacles that arise to prevent effective listening in the group. Goffman (1957) discusses three kinds of preoccupation that disturb the communication process. . . .

External preoccupation is the first kind of alienation: the individual neglects the prescribed focus of attention, giving his main concern to something unconnected with the other group members in their capacity as fellow participants. He is listening to something that is outside the group in some way. . . .

Self-consciousness is a second cause of alienation. Self-consciousness results from one's preoccupation with himself as an interactant and this prevents him from giving himself entirely to the topic of conversation. Whitman (1964) discusses this phenomenon in terms of perceptual defense:

> The extreme type of perceptual defense is autistic perception. Here there is really no perception at all. Very often you see somebody in the group who has a dreamy look in his eyes or perhaps even listens interestedly, but a few minutes later will say, "Well, I've been thinking about what was said to me (ten minutes ago!) an I have thought of this point. . . ." This is the person who most often is responsible for contributing a thud or dud to the group discussion, because his remark is connected to his own ruminations but not to the thread of group discussion [p. 321].

The third kind of alienation, according to Goffman, is *interaction-consciousness*. The participant is so worried about how the interaction itself is progressing that he constricts his ability to follow the topic of conversation. . . . The victim of interaction-consciousness is really so deeply involved with his personal concerns that his awareness of what others are saying and of what is happening in the group is constricted, while the interaction-involved participant is hearing more than just the conversation, for he is picking up communication cues from a variety of sources.

"Message Anxiety" as an Obstacle to Listening

Research indicates that the comprehensibility of a message is unfavorably influenced when the content itself is anxiety-arousing. Nunnally (1961) calls this situation "message anxiety." Gynther (1957) found that message anxiety lowered the communicative efficiency of the speaker. Kasl and Mahl (1965) discovered that it led to speaker anxiety and flustered speech, while Geer (1966) found that it produced speaker anxiety, slowed speech, and silences. Message anxiety, then, is an obstacle to effective listening in two ways: (1) it makes the speaker himself less comprehensible, so that the listener has to fill in the gaps, and (2) it is hypothesized that the speaker communicates his own anxiety plus the anxiety of the message to the listener, and the resultant listener anxiety further distorts the message. . . . This means that both the speaker and the listener must be aware of possible communication distortions and try to minimize them. High visibility would be very helpful here; that is, if the speaker were to admit that he finds the content of the message quite disturbing, this would be a cue for the listener to listen more intently and become more aware of the anxieties that are possibly being generated within himself.

Campbell: Human Error in the Communication Process

Campbell (1958), in studying the communication process, discovered certain sources of systematic error, an understanding of which is extremely useful to anyone interested in human interaction. Both speaker and listener can profit from Campbell's findings, for these findings can be cast in terms of principles for improving the purpose of speaking (output) and the process of listening (input).

(1) *Length of the speaker's remarks.* If the only recorder present to take down a speaker's remarks is the listener himself, then both the speaker and the listener should realize that a communications leakage takes place between output and input. There is a good chance, according to Campbell, that the average listener will tend to shorten, simplify, and eliminate detail from the actual output of the speaker. The longer the speaker's remarks, the greater the leakage. Thus, if the speaker really wants to get his remarks across, he will take into account the natural leakage of the listening process and not make an unnecessarily long speech. There is an important lesson here for sensitivity groups. In such groups, there is usually little reason for anyone to speak at considerable length. Extended speeches are out of place both because they cut down on interaction and involvement and because they entail too much leakage. Extended history, for example, has less impact than compact story. An active, concerned listener will interrupt longer discourses precisely because he does want to listen, assimilate, and interact. On the relatively rare occasions on which a participant does speak at some length in the group, he must realize that his listeners are not assimilating all the facts that he is retailing, but

are rather receiving a total impact from his remarks. If he speaks at length, it must be because total impact is more important than individual facts.

(2) *The middle of the message.* ". . . The middle of the message will be least well retained [p. 343]." The concerned listener must make greater efforts to retain what is said as remarks lengthen, but the concerned speaker, realizing this, will try to eliminate the middle, by keeping his remarks short enough so that they have only a beginning and an end.

(3) *"Rounding off" the message.* The listener tends to "round off" what he hears, "dividing the content into clear-cut 'entities,' reducing gradations both by exaggerating some differences and losing others [p. 344]." This seems to be a function, at least in part, of a kind of egocentricity with which every listener is afflicted: he tailors messages to fit his own needs. The good listener, then, has to take pains not to ignore subtle differences in what is said, even though these differences go contrary to opinions that he himself holds. Also, the good speaker will speak frankly, honestly, and plainly, making shadings of meaning as clear as possible. When a speaker becomes too subtle, when shadings of meaning begin to proliferate, this may mean that the speaker is unsure of himself or afraid of those to whom he is speaking. If either is the case, he should be honest enough to say so and let his message be interpreted in the light of his own misgivings.

(4) *The past haunting imperfectly transmitted messages.* "An imperfectly transmitted message will be distorted in the direction of important past messages, both *rewarding* and *punishing* past messages [p. 350]." Perhaps another way of putting this is that a listener is influenced in his listening by the way he has been reinforced by communications in the past. . . . Obviously, the good listener, being active, will try to minimize this source of error by having the speaker clarify the message. But it is surprising how many participants, for one reason or another, allow imperfectly transmitted messages to go by without challenge. Also, a good listener will try to be aware of what the speaker is actually saying in light of previous emotional experiences he has had with the speaker. If the participant is honest enough to keep his relationship with the other members out in the open, there should be less tendency for him to distort messages for emotional reasons.

(5) *The reductive nature of listening.* The "most pervasive of the systematic biases [p. 346]" is the tendency for the listener to modify a new message so that it becomes more like previous messages. Obviously, if the speakers were never to say anything new, the listener would not be burdened with, and have to cope with, anything new. Therefore, the speaker who rarely says something new is contributing to this bias. But the good listener is one who can consistently break away from this bias. To do so, however, he must be in affective contact with the speaker, and he must allow the speaker the freedom to change. . . .

(6) *Hearing what one expects to hear.* In general, according to Campbell's findings, listeners will modify messages so that they conform to the meaning expected by the listeners. The poor listener, then, either does not listen or stops listening halfway through a message, and he does so because he "knows" what the speaker is going to say. This is listening at its worst. Again, it is casting the speaker into a univocal mold, thus stripping him of his freedom. Too much listening is Kantian listening or computer listening. The listener has preset categories, and whatever is heard must fit into these molds or be handled by these banks. Whatever cannot be received into his computer banks must be shunted off and excluded. And yet, Collins

and Guetzkow (1964), in reviewing the literature on group decision-making processes, find that "the most important part of conference communication may occur when another member says something that we do not expect and thus offers us a perspective or possible solution which would not have occurred to us while working alone [p. 184]." Poor listening is poor business practice as well as poor human relations. The intelligent speaker, realizing the human tendency to stereotype, truncate, and not allow for the possibility of change, will emphasize the fact that what he is saying is different from what he has said before, that he has changed or moved away from a previously held position (if this is the case), in order to break through his listeners' natural stereotyping process. Finally, I would hypothesize that those who are uncomfortable with their own freedom or with the freedom of others tend to constrict the messages of others.

(7) *"You agree with me."* The listener tends to modify messages so that they are in better agreement with his own opinions and attitudes. Although such a tendency is nothing more than a concrete specification of the ancient scholastic principle "whatever is received is received according to the state, condition, or bias of the receiver," and, as such, is in no way new, empirical data manifest just how pervasive such a principle is in man's practical life. Thus, to a large extent, we hear what we want to hear. The sensitive listener, however, addicted as he is to what is, constantly fights this natural tendency in order to hear what is actually being said. This means that to be a good listener one must drop, or at least relax, his defenses a bit in order to be willing to explore the new.

(8) *Black-or-white listening.* "There is a tendency to distort coding assignments in the direction of an affective or evaluative coding. The most natural coding of any input by the human operator seems to be of the general nature of 'like' versus 'dislike,' 'approach' versus 'avoid,' 'good' versus 'bad,' 'beautiful' versus 'ugly,' etc. The general finding of psychologists is that whatever assignment is given tends to be distorted in the direction of this evaluative assignment. This is shown repeatedly as a 'halo' effect, or general factor in rating assignments [p. 357]." This is a reflection of the either-black-or-white tendency in man. Not only is everything a subject of evaluation, but things tend to end up in just two categories, good or bad. It seems almost natural for man to listen to messages in evaluative terms, and it is much simpler to hear a communication as bad or good in its entirety rather than to expend the effort that differential evaluation of a message would demand. This basic tendency to listen to communications in evaluative terms prevents the listener from assimilating other aspects of the message; creative aspects of the message are lost in its badness or deficiencies are swallowed up in its goodness. If the speaker realizes that his message might strike others as immediately good or bad, then he should build a caution against this into the message itself, urging listeners to suspend, if possible, this evaluative propensity.

(9) *The pressures of the group and "filtered" listening.* "When a group of persons are exposed to a message stimulus and asked to state its meaning (size, degree of movement, amount of prejudice, etc.), they will distort their individual interpretations in the direction of their fellows [p. 361]." The average listener tends to listen, at least to some extent, through the group; that is, he filters what is said through the complex interactional and attitudinal patterns that comprise one aspect of the group culture. Although such a process can be advantageous at times—for instance, in group decision-making situations: "The social weighting given to the

majority opinion (i.e., conformity) frequently causes the better alternatives to be chosen [Collins & Guetzkow, 1964, p. 55]."

REFERENCES

Berne, E. *Transactional Analysis — Psychotherapy.* New York: Grove Press, 1961.

Campbell, D. T. "Systematic Error on the Part of Human Links in Communication Systems." *Information and Control,* 1958, 1, 334-369.

Collins, B. E., and Guetzkow, H. *A Social Psychology of Group Processes for Decision-Making.* New York: Wiley, 1964.

Ekman, P. "Differential Communication of Affect by Head and Body Cues." *Journal of Personality and Social Psychology,* 1965, 2, 726-735.

Eisman, B., and Levy, J. "The Influence of Certain Communicative Characteristics on Lip Reading Efficiency." *Journal of Social Psychology,* 1960, 51, 419-425.

Exline, R. V. "Explorations in the Process of Person Perception: Visual Interaction in Relation to Competition, Sex, and Need for Affiliation." *Journal of Personality,* 1963, 31, 1-20.

Exline, R. V., Gray, D., and Schuette, D. "The Incidence of Mutual Glances in Dyads as a Form of Communication: Avoidance as a Function of Interview Content and Sex of Interviewee." *Journal of Personality and Social Psychology,* 1965, 1, 201-209.

Exline, R.V., and Winters, L. C. "Affective Relations and Mutual Glances in Dyads." In S. S. Tomkins and C. E. Izard (Eds.), *Affect, Cognition, and Personality.* New York: Springer, 1965. Pp. 319-350.

Geer, J. H. "Effect of Fear Arousal upon Task Performance and Verbal Behavior." *Journal of Abnormal and Social Psychology,* 1966, 71, 119-123.

Goffman, E. "Alienation from Interaction." *Human Relations,* 1957, 10, 47-60.

Gynther, R. A. "The Effects of Anxiety and of Situational Stress on Communication Efficiency." *Journal of Abnormal and Social Psychology,* 1957, 54, 274-276.

Haggard, E. A., and Isaacs, K. S. "Micromomentary Facial Expressions as Indicators of Ego Mechanisms in Psychotherapy." In L. A. Gottschalk and A. H. Auerbach (Eds.), *Methods of Research in Psychotherapy.* New York: Appleton-Century-Crofts, 1966. Pp. 154-165.

Haley, J. "An Interactional Description of Schizophrenia." *Psychiatry,* 1959, 22, 321-332.

Jecker, J., Macoby, N., Breitrose, H. S., and Rose, E. O. "Teacher Accuracy in Assessing Cognitive Visual Feedback from Students." *Journal of Applied Psychology,* 1964, 48, 393-397.

Kasl, S. V., and Mahl, G. F. "The Relationship of Disturbances and Hesitations in Spontaneous Speech to Anxiety." *Journal of Personality and Social Psychology,* 1965, 1, 425-433.

Katz, E. W. "A Content-Analytic Method for Studying Interpersonal Behavior." Unpublished technical report No. 19, University of Illinois, 1964.

Leventhal, H., and Sharp, E. "Facial Expressions as Indicators of Distress." In S. S. Tomkins and C. E. Izard (Eds.), *Affect, Cognition, and Personality.* New York: Springer, 1965. Pp. 296-318.

Levitt, E. A. "The Relationship between Abilities to Express Emotional Meanings, Vocally and Facially." In J. Davitz (Ed.), *The Communication of Emotional Meaning.* New York: McGraw-Hill, 1964. Pp. 87-100.

Mahl, G. F., Danet, B., and Norton, N. "Reflections of Major Personality Characteristics in Gestures and Body Movement." Paper presented at the meeting of the American Psychological Association, 1959.

Murphy, G. "Communications and Mental Health." *Psychiatry*, 1959, 22, 321-332.

Newcomb, T. M. "An Approach to the Study of Communicative Acts." *Psychological Review*, 1953, 60, 393-404.

Rogers, C. R. *Counseling and Psychotherapy*, Boston: Houghton Mifflin, 1942.

Rogers, C. R. *Client-Centered Therapy*. Boston: Houghton Mifflin, 1951.

Rogers, C. R. *On Becoming a Person*. Boston: Houghton Mifflin, 1961a.

Rogers, C. R. "The Process Equation of Psychotherapy." *American Journal of Psychotherapy*, 1961b, 15, 27-45.

Rogers, C. R. "The Process of the Basic Encounter Group." In J. F. T. Bugental (Ed.), *Challenges of Humanistic Psychology*. New York: McGraw-Hill, 1967. Pp. 261-276.

Rogers, C. R. (Ed.) *The Therapeutic Relationship and its Impact: A Study of Psychotherapy with Schizophrenics*. Madison: The University of Wisconsin Press, 1967.

Scheflen, A. E. "The Significance of Posture in Communication Systems." *Psychiatry*, 1964, 27, 316-331.

Scheflen, A. E. "Communication Systems such as Psychotherapy." In J. H. Masserman (Ed.), *Current Psychiatric Therapies*. Vol. 5 New York: Grune and Stratton, 1965. Pp. 33-41.

Smith, A. G. "Introduction: Communication and Culture." In A. G. Smith (Ed.), *Communication and Culture*. New York: Holt, Rinehart and Winston, 1966.

Spiegel, J. P., and Machotka, P. "A Program for Somatotactical Testing." Unpublished manuscript, Harvard University, 1965.

Suchman, J. R. "Social Sensitivity in the Small Task-Oriented Group." *Journal of Abnormal and Social Psychology*, 1956, 52, 75-83.

Tomkins, S. S. *Affect, Imagery, and Consciousness:* The Positive Effects. Vol. 1. New York: Springer, 1962.

Weick, K. E. "Systematic Observational Methods." In G. Lindzey and E. Aronson (Eds.), *The Handbook of Social Psychology*. (2nd edition) Vol. 2. Reading, Mass.: Addison-Wesley, 1968. Pp. 357-451.

Werner, H., and Wapner, S. "Changes in Psychological Distance under Conditions of Danger." *Journal of Personality,* 1953, 24, 153-167.

Whitman, R. M. "Psychodynamic Principles Underlying T-Group Processes." In L. P. Bradford, J. R. Gibb, and K. D. Benne (Eds.), *T-Group Theory and Laboratory Method*. New York: Wiley, 1964. Pp. 310-335.

Carl R. Rogers

SOME SIGNIFICANT LEARNINGS

I might start off these several statements of significant learnings with a negative item. *In my relationships with persons I have found that it does not help, in the long run, to act as though I were something that I am not.* It does not help to act calm and pleasant when actually I am angry and critical. It does not help to act as though I know the answers when I do not. It does not help to act as though I were a loving person if actually, at the moment, I am hostile. It does not help for me to act as though I were full of assurance, if actually I am frightened and unsure. Even on a very simple level I have found that this statement seems to hold. It does not help for me to act as though I were well when I feel ill.

What I am saying here, put in another way, is that I have not found it to be helpful or effective in my relationships with other people to try to maintain a façade; to act in one way on the surface when I am experiencing something quite different underneath. It does not, I believe, make me helpful in my attempts to build up constructive relationships with other individuals. I would want to make it clear that while I feel I have learned this to be true, I have by no means adequately profited from it. In fact, it seems to me that most of the mistakes I make in personal relationships, most of the times in which I fail to be of help to other individuals, can be accounted for in terms of the fact that I have, for some defensive reason, behaved in one way at a surface level, while in reality my feelings run in a contrary direction.

A second learning might be stated as follows—*I find I am more effective when I can listen acceptantly to myself, and can be myself.* I feel that over the years I have learned to become more adequate in listening to *myself;* so that I know, some-what more adequately than I used to, what I am feeling at any given moment—to be able to realize I *am* angry, or that I *do* feel rejecting toward this person; or that I feel very full of warmth and affection for this individual; or that I am bored and uninterested in what is going on; or that I am eager to understand this individual or that I am anxious and fearful in my relationship to this person. All of these diverse attitudes are feelings which I think I can listen to in myself. One way of putting this is that I feel I have become more adequate in letting myself *be* what I *am*. It becomes easier for me to accept myself as a decidedly imperfect person, who by no means functions at all times in the way in which I would like to function.

This must seem to some like a very strange direction in which to move. It seems to me to have value because the curious paradox is that when I accept myself as I am, then I change. I believe that I have learned this from my clients as well as within my own experience—that we cannot change, we cannot move away from what we are, until we thoroughly *accept* what we are. Then change seems to come about almost unnoticed.

Another result which seems to grow out of being myself is that relationships then become real. Real relationships have an exciting way of being vital and meaningful. If I can accept the fact that I am annoyed at or bored by this client or this student, then I am also much more likely to be able to accept his feelings in response. I can also accept the changed experience and the changed feelings which are then likely to occur in me and in him. Real relationships tend to change rather than to remain static.

So I find it effective to let myself be what I am in my attitudes; to know when I have reached my limit of endurance or of tolerance, and to accept that as a fact; to know when I desire to mold or manipulate people, and to accept that as a fact in myself. I would like to be as acceptant of these feelings as of feelings of warmth, interest, permissiveness, kindness, understanding, which are also a very real part of me. It is when I do accept all these attitudes as a fact, as a part of me, that my relationship with the other person then becomes what it is, and is able to grow and change most readily.

I come now to a central learning which has had a great deal of significance for me. I can state this learning as follows: *I have found it of enormous value when I can permit myself to understand another person.* The way in which I have worded this statement may seem strange to you. Is it necessary to *permit* oneself to understand another? I think that it is. Our first reaction to most of the statements which we hear from other people is an immediate evaluation, or judgment, rather than an understanding of it. When someone expresses some feeling or attitude or belief, our tendency is, almost immediately, to feel "That's right"; or "That's stupid"; "That's abnormal"; "That's unreasonable"; "That's incorrect"; "That's not nice." Very rarely do we permit ourselves to *understand* precisely what the meaning of his statement is to him. I believe this is because understanding is risky. If I let myself really understand another person, I might be changed by that understanding. And we all fear change. So as I say, it is not an easy thing to permit oneself to understand an individual, to enter thoroughly and completely and empathically into his frame of reference. It is also a rare thing.

To understand is enriching in a double way. I find when I am working with clients in distress, that to understand the bizarre world of a psychotic individual, or to understand and sense the attitudes of a person who feels that life is too tragic to bear, or to understand a man who feels that he is a worthless and inferior individual—each of these understandings somehow enriches me. I learn from these experiences in ways that change me, that make me a different and, I think, a more responsive person. Even more important perhaps, is the fact that my understanding of these individuals permits them to change. It permits them to accept their own fears and bizarre thoughts and tragic feelings and discouragements, as well as their moments of courage and kindness and love and sensitivity. And it is their experience as well as mine that when someone fully understands those feelings, this enables them to accept those feelings in themselves. Then they find both the feelings and themselves changing. Whether it is understanding a woman who feels that very literally she has a hook in her head by which others lead her about, or understanding a man who feels that no one is as lonely, no one is as separated from others as he, I find these understandings to be of value to me. But also, and even more importantly, to be understood has a very positive value to these individuals.

Here is another learning which has had importance for me. *I have found it enriching to open channels whereby others can communicate their feelings, their private perceptual worlds, to me.* Because understanding is rewarding, I would like to reduce the barriers between others and me, so that they can, if they wish, reveal themselves more fully.

In the therapeutic relationship there are a number of ways by which I can make it easier for the client to communicate himself. I can by my own attitudes create a safety in the relationship which makes such communication more possible. A sensitiveness of understanding which sees him as he is to himself, and accepts him as having those perceptions and feelings, helps too.

But as a teacher also I have found that I am enriched when I can open channels through which others can share themselves with me. So I try, often not too successfully, to create a climate in the classroom where feelings can be expressed, where people can differ—with each other and with the instructor. I have also frequently asked for "reaction sheets" from students—in which they can express themselves individually and personally regarding the course. They can tell of the way it is or is not meeting their needs, they can express their feelings regarding the instructor, or can tell of the personal difficulties they are having in relation to the course. These reaction sheets have no relation whatsoever to their grade. Sometimes the same sessions of a course are experienced in diametrically opposite ways. One student says, "My feeling is one of indefinable revulsion with the tone of this class." Another, a foreign student, speaking of the same week of the same course says, "Our class follows the best, fruitful and scientific way of learning. But for people who have been taught for a long, long time, as we have, by the lecture type, authoritative method, this new procedure is ununderstandable. People like us are conditioned to hear the instructor, to keep passively our notes and memorize his reading assignments for the exams. There is no need to say that it takes long time for people to get rid of their habits regardless of whether or not their habits are sterile, infertile and barren." To open myself to these sharply different feelings has been a deeply rewarding thing.

I have found the same thing true in groups where I am the administrator, or perceived as the leader. I wish to reduce the need for fear or defensiveness, so that people can communicate their feelings freely. This has been most exciting, and has led me to a whole new view of what administration can be. But I cannot expand on that here.

There is another very important learning which has come to me in my counseling work. I can voice this learning very briefly. *I have found it highly rewarding when I can accept another person.*

I have found that truly to accept another person and his feelings is by no means an easy thing, any more than is understanding. Can I really permit another person to feel hostile toward me? Can I accept his anger as a real and legitimate part of himself? Can I accept him when he views life and its problems in a way quite different from mine? Can I accept him when he feels very positively toward me, admiring me and wanting to model himself after me? All this is involved in acceptance, and it does not come easy. I believe that it is an increasingly common pattern in our culture for each one of us to believe, "Every other person must feel and think and believe the same as I do." We find it very hard to permit our children or our parents or our spouses to feel differently than we do about particular issues or problems. We cannot permit our clients or our students to differ from us or to utilize their experience in their own individual ways. On a national scale, we cannot permit another nation to think or feel differently than we do. Yet it has come to seem to me that this separateness of individuals, the right of each individual to utilize his experience in his own way and to discover his own meanings in it,— this is one of the most priceless potentialities of life. Each person is an island unto himself, in a very real sense; and he can only build bridges to other islands if he is first of all willing to be himself and permitted to be himself. So I find that when I can accept another person, which means specifically accepting the feelings and attitudes and beliefs that he has as a real and vital part of him, then I am assisting him to become a person: and there seems to me great value in this.

The next learning I want to state may be difficult to communicate. It is this. *The more I am open to the realities in me and in the other person, the less do I find myself wishing to rush in to "fix things."* As I try to listen to myself and the experiencing going on in me, and the more I try to extend that same listening attitude to another person, the more respect I feel for the complex processes of life. So I become less and less inclined to hurry in to fix things, to set goals, to mold people, to manipulate and push them in the way that I would like them to go. I am much more content simply to be myself and to let another person be himself. I know very well that this must seem like a strange, almost an Oriental point of view. What is life for if we are not going to do things to people? What is life for if we are not going to mold them to our purposes? What is life for if we are not going to teach them the things that *we* think they should learn? What is life for if we are not going to make them think and feel as we do? How can anyone hold such an inactive point of view as the one I am expressing? I am sure that attitudes such as these must be a part of the reaction of many of you.

Yet the paradoxical aspect of my experience is that the more I am simply willing to be myself, in all this complexity of life and the more I am willing to understand and accept the realities in myself and in the other person, the more change seems to be stirred up. It is a very paradoxical thing—that to the degree that each one of us is willing to be himself, then he finds not only himself changing; but he finds that other people to whom he relates are also changing. At least this is a very vivid part of my experience, and one of the deepest things I think I have learned in my personal and professional life.

Let me turn now to some other learnings which are less concerned with relationships, and have more to do with my own actions and values. The first of these is very brief. *I can trust my experience.*

One of the basic things which I was a long time in realizing, and which I am still learning, is that when an activity *feels* as though it is valuable or worth doing, it *is* worth doing. Put another way, I have learned that my total organismic sensing of a situation is more trustworthy than my intellect.

All of my professional life I have been going in directions which others thought were foolish, and about which I have had many doubts myself. But I have never regretted moving in directions which "felt right," even though I have often felt lonely or foolish at the time.

I have found that when I have trusted some inner non-intellectual sensing, I have discovered wisdom in the move. In fact I have found that when I have followed one of these unconventional paths because it felt right or true, then in five or ten years many of my colleagues have joined me, and I no longer need to feel alone in it.

As I gradually come to trust my total reactions more deeply, I find that I can use them to guide my thinking. I have come to have more respect for those vague thoughts which occur in me from time to time, which *feel* as though they were significant. I am inclined to think that these unclear thoughts or hunches will lead me to important areas. I think of it as trusting the totality of my experience, which I have learned to suspect is wiser than my intellect. It is fallible I am sure, but I believe it to be less fallible than my conscious mind alone. My attitude is very well expressed by Max Weber, the artist, when he says. "In carrying on my own humble creative effort, I depend greatly upon that which I do not yet know, and upon that which I have not yet done."

Very closely related to this learning is a corollary that, *evaluation by others is not a guide for me.* The judgments of others, while they are to be listened to, and taken into account for what they are, can never be a guide for me. This has been a hard thing to learn. I remember how shaken I was, in the early days, when a scholarly thoughtful man who seemed to me a much more competent and knowledgeable psychologist than I, told me what a mistake I was making by getting interested in psychotherapy. It could never lead anywhere, and as a psychologist I would not even have the opportunity to practice it.

In later years it has sometimes jolted me a bit to learn that I am, in the eyes of some others, a fraud, a person practicing medicine without a license, the author of a very superficial and damaging sort of therapy, a power seeker, a mystic, etc. And I have been equally disturbed by equally extreme praise. But I have not been too much concerned because I have come to feel that only one person (at least in my lifetime, and perhaps ever) can know whether what I am doing is honest, thorough, open, and sound, or false and defensive and unsound, and I am that person. I am happy to get all sorts of evidence regarding what I am doing and criticism (both friendly and hostile) and praise (both sincere and fawning) are a part of such evidence. But to weigh this evidence and to determine its meaning and usefulness is a task I cannot relinquish to anyone else. . . .

Somewhere here I want to bring in a learning which has been most rewarding, because it makes me feel so deeply akin to others. I can word it this way. *What is most personal is most general.* There have been times when in talking with students or staff, or in my writing, I have expressed myself in ways so personal that I have felt I was expressing an attitude which it was probable no one else could understand, because it was so uniquely my own. Two written examples of this are the Preface to *Client-Centered Therapy* (regarded as most unsuitable by the publishers), and an article on "Persons or Science." In these instances I have almost invariably found that the very feeling which has seemed to me most private, most personal, and hence most incomprehensible by others, has turned out to be an expression for which there is a resonance in many other people. It has led me to believe that what is most personal and unique in each one of us is probably the very element which would, if it were shared or expressed, speak most deeply to others. This has helped me to understand artists and poets as people who have dared to express the unique in themselves.

There is one deep learning which is perhaps basic to all of the things I have said thus far. It has been forced upon me by more than twenty-five years of trying to be helpful to individuals in personal distress. It is simply this. *It has been my experience that persons have a basically positive direction.* In my deepest contacts with individuals in therapy, even those whose troubles are most disturbing, whose behavior has been most anti-social, whose feelings seem most abnormal, I find this to be true. When I can sensitively understand the feelings which they are expressing, when I am able to accept them as separate persons in their own right, then I find that they tend to move in certain directions. And what are these directions in which they tend to move? The words which I believe are most truly descriptive are words such as positive, constructive, moving toward self-actualization, growing toward maturity, growing toward socialization. I have come to feel that the more fully the individual is understood and accepted, the more he tends to drop the false fronts with which he has been meeting life, and the more he tends to move in a direction which is forward.

I would not want to be misunderstood on this. I do not have a Pollyanna view of human nature. I am quite aware that out of defensiveness and inner fear individuals can and do behave in ways which are incredibly cruel, horribly destructive, immature, regressive, anti-social, hurtful. Yet one of the most refreshing and invigorating parts of my experience is to work with such individuals and to discover the strongly positive directional tendencies which exist in them, as in all of us, at the deepest levels.

Let me bring this long list to a close with one final learning which can be stated very briefly. *Life, at its best, is a flowing, changing process in which nothing is fixed.* In my clients and in myself I find that when life is richest and most rewarding it is a flowing process. To experience this is both fascinating and a little frightening. I find I am at my best when I can let the flow of my experience carry me, in a direction which appears to be forward, toward goals of which I am but dimly aware. In thus floating with the complex stream of my experiencing, and in trying to understand its ever-changing complexity, it should be evident that there are no fixed points. When I am thus able to be in process, it is clear that there can be no closed system of beliefs, no unchanging set of principles which I hold. Life is guided by a changing understanding of and interpretation of my experience. It is always in process of becoming.

I trust it is clear now why there is no philosophy or belief or set of principles which I could encourage or persuade others to have or hold. I can only try to live by *my* interpretation of the current meaning of *my* experience, and try to give others the permission and freedom to develop their own inward freedom and thus their own meaningful interpretation of their own experience.

If there is such a thing as truth, this free individual process of search should, I believe, converge toward it. And in a limited way, this is also what I seem to have experienced.

John L. Wallen

DEVELOPING EFFECTIVE
INTERPERSONAL COMMUNICATION

1. THE INTERPERSONAL GAP

You cannot have your own way all the time. Your best intentions will sometimes end in disaster, while, at other times, you will receive credit for desirable outcomes you didn't intend. In short, what you accomplish is not always what you hoped.

The most basic and recurring problem in social life is the relation between what you intend and the effect of your actions on others. The key terms we use in attempting to make sense of interpersonal relations are "intentions," "actions" and "effect." "Interpersonal gap" refers to the degree of congruence between one person's intentions and the effect produced in the other. If the effect is what was intended, the gap has been bridged. If the effect is the opposite of what was intended, the gap has become greater.

Let us look more closely at the three terms.

The word *"intentions"* means the wishes, wants, hopes, desires, fears that give rise to actions. Underlying motives of which you may be unaware are not being referred to.

It is a fact that people may say after an action has produced some result, "That wasn't what I meant to do. That outcome wasn't what I intended." Or, "Yes, that's what I hoped would happen." We look at the social outcome and decide whether it is what we intended. Apparently, we can compare what we wished to happen with the outcome and determine whether they match.

Here are some examples of interpersonal intentions.

> "I want him to like me."
> "I want him to obey me."
> "I want him to realize that I know a great deal about this subject."
> "I don't want her to know that I am angry with her."
> "I don't want to talk with him."
> "I wish he would tell me what to do."

Intentions may also be mixed.

> "I want him to know I like him, but I don't want to be embarrassed."

Materials prepared by John L. Wallen. Reprinted by permission of Northwest Regional Educational Laboratory.

"I want him to tell me I'm doing a good job, but I don't want to ask for
it."

"I would like him to know how angry it makes me when he does that, but
I don't want to lose his friendship."

Intentions are private and are known directly only to the one who experiences
them. I know my own intentions, but I must infer yours. You know your own intentions, but you must infer mine.

"Effect" refers to a person's inner response to the actions of another. We may
describe the other's effect by openly stating what feelings are aroused by his actions.
However, we are often unaware of our feelings as feelings. When this happens our
feelings influence how we see the other and we label him or his actions in a way
that expresses our feelings even though we may be unaware of them.

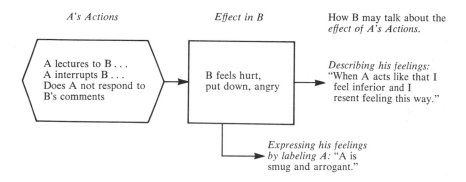

Here are some other examples showing how the same effect may be talked
about as a description of one's own feeling or by labeling the other as an indirect
way of expressing one's feeling.

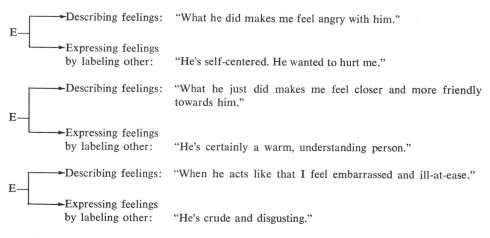

In contrast to interpersonal intentions and effects which are private, actions are
public and observable. They may be verbal ("good morning!") or nonverbal (look-

ing away when passing another), brief (a touch on the shoulder) or extended (taking a person out to dinner).

Interpersonal actions are communicative. They include attempts by the sender to convey a message, *whether or not it is received,* as well as actions that the receiver responds to as messages, *whether or not the sender intended them that way.*

The diagram shows a schematic summary of the interpersonal gap. The interpersonal gap, thus, contains two transformations. These steps are referred to as coding and decoding operations. A's actions are a coded expression of his inner

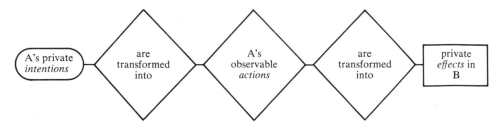

Summary of Interpersonal Gap

state. B's inner response is a result of the way he decodes A's actions. If B decodes A's behavior in the same way that A has coded it, A will have produced the effect he intended.

To be specific, let's imagine that I feel warm and friendly toward you. I pat you on the shoulder. The pat, thus, is an action code for my friendly feeling. You decode this, however, as an act of condescension. The effect of my behavior, then, is that you feel put down, inferior and annoyed with me. My system of coding does not match your system of decoding and the interpersonal gap, consequently, is difficult to bridge.

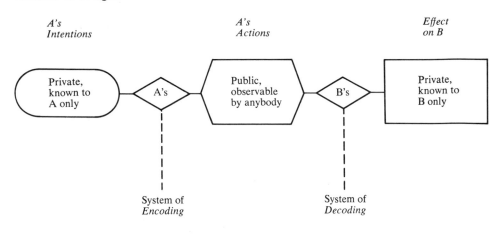

The Interpersonal Gap

We can now draw a more complete picture of the interpersonal gap.

You may be unaware of the ways you code your intentions and decide others' actions. In fact, you may have been unaware that you do. One of the important objectives of this study of interpersonal relations is to help you become aware of the silent assumptions that influence how you code and decode.

If you are aware of your encoding operation, you can accurately describe how you typically act when you feel angry, affectionate, threatened, uneasy, etc.

If you are aware of your method of decoding behavior of others, you can describe accurately the kinds of distortions or misreadings of others you typically make. Some people, for example, respond to gestures of affection as if they were attempts to limit their autonomy. Some respond to offers of help as if they were being put down. Some misread enthusiasm as anger.

Because different people use different codes, actions have no unique and constant meaning, but are interchangeable. As the diagram shows, an action may express different intentions, the same intention may give rise to different actions, different actions may produce the same effect, and different effects may be produced by the same kind of action.

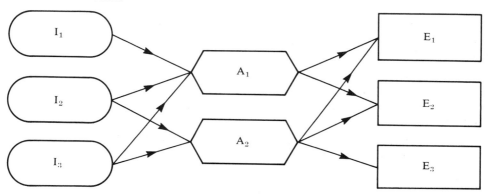

The same intention may be expressed by different actions.

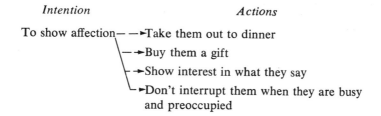

Different intentions may be expressed by the same action.

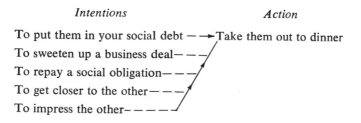

The same action may lead to different effects.

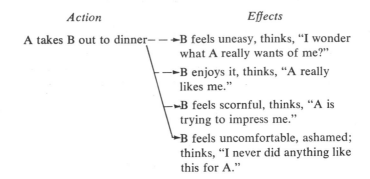

Action

A takes B out to dinner

Effects

B feels uneasy, thinks, "I wonder what A really wants of me?"

B enjoys it, thinks, "A really likes me."

B feels scornful, thinks, "A is trying to impress me."

B feels uncomfortable, ashamed; thinks, "I never did anything like this for A."

Different actions may lead to the same effect.

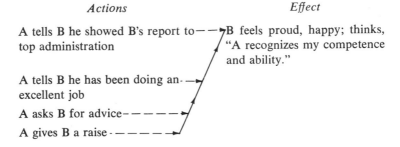

Actions

A tells B he showed B's report to top administration

A tells B he has been doing an excellent job

A asks B for advice

A gives B a raise

Effect

B feels proud, happy; thinks, "A recognizes my competence and ability."

It should be obvious that when you and I interact, each of us views his own and the other's actions in a different frame of reference. Each of us sees his own actions in the light of his own intentions, but we see the other's actions in the light of the effect they have on us. This is the *principle of partial information*—each party to an interaction has different and partial information about the interpersonal gap.

Bridging the interpersonal gap requires that each person understand how the other sees the interaction.

Example:

Jane hadn't seen Tom Laird since they taught together at Brookwood School. When she found that she would be attending a conference in Tom's city she wrote to ask if she could visit him. Tom and his wife, Marge, whom Jane had never met, invited her to stay with them for the three days of the conference.

After dinner the first night Jane was the one who suggested that they clean up the dishes so they could settle down for an evening of talk. She was feeling warm and friendly to both of the Lairds and so grateful for their hospitality that she wanted to show them in some way. As she began carrying the dishes to the kitchen, Marge and Tom at first protested but when she continued cleaning up they began to help. In the kitchen, Jane took over only allowing Marge and Tom to help in little ways and to tell her where to find or store things.

When they had finished in the kitchen, Jane commented, "There now, that didn't take long and everything's spic and span." Marge responded, "It was very helpful of you. Thank you."

When Tom and Marge were preparing for bed later that evening, Tom was startled to hear Marge burst out with, "I was so humiliated. I just resent her so much I can hardly stand it."

"You mean Jane? What did she do that upset you so?"

"The way she took over. She's certainly a pushy, dominating person. To come into my home as a visitor and then the moment dinner is over organize the whole cleanup. It's easy to tell that she thinks I'm not a very good housekeeper. At first I felt inadequate and then I felt angry. I'll keep house any way I like. Who is she to show me up? After all she's a guest and you'd think she'd be grateful for our putting her up."

"Aw, c'mon, Marge, Jane was just trying to be helpful."

"Well, it wasn't helpful. It was humiliating. It's going to be hard for me to be nice to her for three days."

The following is a diagram of the interpersonal gap for the interaction between Jane and Marge.

JANE   MARGE

Interaction

Note the gap between Jane's intention and Marge's inference about Jane's intention. They do not match. In fact, they are almost opposites.

Note the gap between the effect of Jane's action on Marge and Jane's inference about the effect on Marge. Again they are almost opposite.

However, within each person the situation is balanced. Jane's intention is congruent with the effect she believes occurred in Marge. Likewise, the inferences Marge makes about Jane fit with her feelings as a result of Jane's action.

The action code that Jane used to convey her friendly feelings was decoded quite differently by Marge.

Why did Marge tell Jane she had been helpful if she really resented it?

2. CONSTRUCTIVE OPENNESS

Rarely do two persons talk openly about their reactions to each other's actions. Most of us withhold our feelings about the other (even in relations that are very important or dear to us) because we fear hurting the other, making him angry, or being rejected by him. Because we don't know how to be constructively open we say nothing. The other continues totally unaware of our reaction to his actions. Likewise, we continue ignorant of the effect our actions produce in him. As a result many relationships that could be productive and enjoyable gradually founder and sink under the accumulated load of tiny annoyances, hurt feelings and misunderstandings that were never talked about openly.

The following points increase the probability that openness will improve a relationship rather than harm it.

1. *Openness must stem from a desire to improve your relationship with the other.* Openness is not an end in itself but a means to an end. We are not open with people about whom we do not care. When attempting to elicit an open sharing of reactions to each other, try to convey that this encounter indicated that you value your relation with the other and wish to improve it *because* it is important.

2. *Aim at creating a shared understanding of your relationship.* You wish to know how the other perceives and feels about your actions. You wish him to know how you perceive and feel about his actions. (See "The Interpersonal Gap.") Each of you, thus will view the relationship from more nearly the same viewpoint.

3. *Recognize that openness involves risk-taking.* You cannot receive a maximum guarantee with minimum risk. Your willingness to risk your self-esteem, being rejected or hurt by the other, etc. depends upon the importance of the relationship to you. Likewise, you cannot ask that the other guarantee not to become angry or feel hurt by your comments. The important point is that you are willing to risk his being himself—whatever he feels—in the effort to make the encounter into a learning situation for both of you.

4. Although *the discussion* may become intense, spirited, angry, or tearful, it *should be noncoercive and not an attempt to get the other to change.* Each should use the information as he sees fit. The attitude should not be "Who's wrong and who's right?" but "What can each of us learn from this discussion that will make our working together more productive and more satisfying?"

   As a result of the discussion one, both or neither of you, may act differently in the future. Each, however, will act with fuller awareness of the effect of his actions on the other as well as with more understanding of the other's intentions. Any change, thus, will be self-chosen rather than to placate or submit to the other.

THE MOST HELPFUL KINDS OF STATEMENTS ABOUT YOURSELF AND YOUR REACTIONS ARE . . .

1. *Behavior descriptions:* reporting the specific acts of the other that affect you.
   "You cut in before I had finished my sentence."

2. *Describing your own feelings:*
   "I feel blue." "I like what you just said."
   You should try to describe your feelings in such a way that they are seen as temporary and capable of change rather than as permanent attitudes. For example, "At this point I'm very annoyed with you . . ." rather than "I dislike you and I always will."

3. *Timing is important.* Reactions should be shared as close to the behavior that aroused them as possible so that the other will know exactly what behavior is being discussed. For example, behavior during the encounter itself can be commented on. E.g., "What you just said is the kind of remark that makes me feel pushed away."
   Disturbing situations should be discussed as they occur rather than saving up massive accumulations of hurt feelings and annoyance and dumping them on top of the other all at one time.

4. Statements are more helpful if they are . . .
   a. *Specific* rather than general. "You bumped my cup." rather than "You never watch where you're going."
   b. *Tentative* rather than absolute. "You seem unconcerned about Jimmy."
   c. *Informing* rather than ordering. "I hadn't finished yet." rather than "Stop interrupting me."

5. Use perception-checking responses to insure that you are not making false assumptions about the other's feelings. "I thought you weren't interested in trying to understand my idea. Was I wrong?" "Did my last statement bother you?"
   Paraphrase the other's comments about you to make sure you understand them as he intends them. Check to make sure the other understands your comments in the way you intend them. (see exercise on paraphrasing)

6. The least helpful kinds of statements are those that sound as if they are information about the other person but are really expression of your own feelings coming out as . . .
   a. *judgments* about the other. "You never pay attention."
   b. *labelling* traits or name-calling. "You're a phony." "You're too rude."
   c. *accusations* — imputing undesirable motives to the other. "You enjoy putting people down." "You always have to be in the center of attention."
   d. *commands* and orders. "Stop laughing." "Don't talk so much."

e. *sarcasm*. "You always look on the bright side of things, don't you?" (when the opposite is meant).

3. EMOTIONS AS PROBLEMS

The way we deal with emotion is the most frequent source of difficulty in our relations with others. Although each of us continually experiences feelings about others and about himself, most of us have not yet learned to accept and use our emotions constructively. We not only are uncomfortable when others express strong feelings, but most of us do not even recognize, much less accept, many of our own feelings.

We know, intellectually, that it is natural to have feelings. We know that the capacity to feel is as much a part of being a person as is the capacity to think and reason. We are aware of incompleteness in the one who seems only to *think about* life and does not seem to feel—to care about, enjoy, be angered and hurt by what goes on around him. We know all this, and yet we feel that feelings are disruptive, the source of obstacles and problems in living and working with others.

It is not our feelings that are the source of difficulty in our relations with others but the way we deal with them or our failure to use them.

Because of our negative attitude toward emotions, because of our fear of and discomfort with our feelings, we spend much effort trying, in one way or another, to deny or ignore them. Look around you and observe how you and others deal with feelings. Make your own observations and see if they support or contradict the point that our usual response is some variation of, "Don't feel that way."

To the person expressing disappointment, discouragement or depression we say things like, "Cheer up!" "Don't let it get you down." "There's no use crying over spilt milk." "Things will get better." In short, "Don't feel that way." To the sorrowing or hurting person we advise, "Don't cry. Put your mind on something pleasant." We tell the angry person, "Simmer down. There's no point in getting angry. Let's be objective." To the person expressing joy and satisfaction in something he has done we caution, "Better watch out. Pride goeth before a fall." In our various group meetings we counsel each other, "Let's keep feelings out of this. Let's be rational."

In general, the closer the feelings are to the here and now—to you and me in this present moment—the more difficult they are to discuss openly. The scale on p. 227 implies many more subdivisions than shown. For example, it implies that I am more comfortable telling you that I was angry with you a year ago than that I was angry with you last week. The former topic is much more distant. Likewise, I can more easily tell you of last week's anger than of my annoyance with you yesterday.

This scale doesn't mean that people do not get angry in the present or even that they do not act angry, only that to describe one's present anger openly is more difficult than to discuss one's past anger.

The important question is, does it matter whether we discuss our feelings as we are having them? The answer is definitely yes. Feelings that we try to bury inside ourselves do not disappear. They tend to stay stored up inside until, sooner or later, they find a way to come out. The problem is that when they have been bottled up too long they come out in inappropriately strong ways or focused on the wrong target. Instead of telling your spouse you feel angry when you are repeatedly interrupted, you're apt to yell, "Shut up," at the kids. The age old ideas of "getting

DISCUSSING FEELINGS

Another sign of the difficulty we all experience with feelings is that the more distant and remote the feelings, the more comfortable we are in discussing them. Try to pay attention to yourself and others when talking about feelings and ask, "How distant are these things?" You will find relatively few discussions of feelings that someone is having "right here" and "right now" in comparison with the number of discussions about feelings they had somewhere else (there), at a time in the past (then). Do you find that you talk more easily about feelings you had in the past than about feelings you have right now? Do you find that you talk more easily about feelings toward somebody else than about your feelings toward persons who are present? As you observe yourself and others discussing feelings, see whether the following scale roughly represents what you find.

Scale of Difficulty in Discussing Feelings

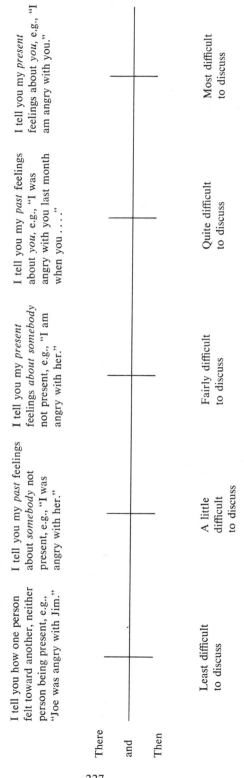

I tell you how one person felt toward another, neither person being present, e.g., "Joe was angry with Jim."

I tell you my *past* feelings about *somebody* not present, e.g., "I was angry with her."

I tell you my *present* feelings *about somebody* not present, e.g., "I am angry with her."

I tell you my *past* feelings about *you*, e.g., "I was angry with you last month when you . . . ."

I tell you my *present* feelings about *you*, e.g., "I am angry with you."

There and Then

Here and Now

Least difficult to discuss

A little difficult to discuss

Fairly difficult to discuss

Quite difficult to discuss

Most difficult to discuss

things off your chest," or "always get to the heart of a problem," are scientifically sound. Of course, there are some times when feelings cannot be dealt with appropriately at the moment. But, rather than assuming it's not appropriate, consider whether it is or not. More often than not, it is probably not only right, it is extremely important.

4. DESCRIPTION OF FEELINGS: A BASIC COMMUNICATION SKILL FOR IMPROVING INTERPERSONAL RELATIONSHIPS

A. The Problem

To communicate your own feelings accurately or to understand those of others is difficult.

First, expressions of emotion take many different forms. Feelings can express themselves in bodily changes, in actions and in words. (See the diagram.)

Second, any specific expression of feeling may come from very different feelings. A blush, for example, may indicate the person is feeling pleased, but it may also indicate that he feels annoyed, embarrassed or uneasy.

Likewise, a specific feeling does not always get expressed in the same way. For example, a child's feeling of affection for his teacher may lead him to blush when she stands near his desk, to touch her as he passes her, to watch her as she walks around the room, to tell her "You're nice," to bring his pet turtle to show her, etc.; different forms of expression indicate the child's feeling of affection.

Communication of feelings, thus, is often inaccurate or even misleading. What looks like an expression of anger, for example, often turns out to result from hurt feelings or from fear.

A further obstacle to the accurate communication of feelings is that your perception of what another is feeling is based on so many different kinds of information. When somebody speaks, you notice more than just the words he says. You note his gestures, voice tone, posture, facial expression, etc. In addition, you are aware of the immediate present situation—the context in which the interaction is occurring. You are aware of whether somebody is watching, for example. Therefore, you make assumptions about how the situation influences what the other is feeling. Beyond all of this you also have expectations based on your past experiences with the other individual.

You make inferences from all of this information—words, nonverbal cues, the situational context, your expectations of the other. These inferences are influenced by your own current emotional state. What you perceive the other to be feeling, then, often depends more upon what you are feeling than upon the other person's actions or words. For example, if you are feeling guilty about something, you may perceive others as angry with you. If you are feeling depressed and discouraged about yourself, others may seem to be expressing disapproval of you.

Communicating your own and understanding the feelings of others is an extremely difficult task. And, yet, if you wish others to respond to you as a person, you must help them understand how you feel. Likewise, if you are concerned about the other as a person and about your relationship with him, you must try to understand his emotional reactions.

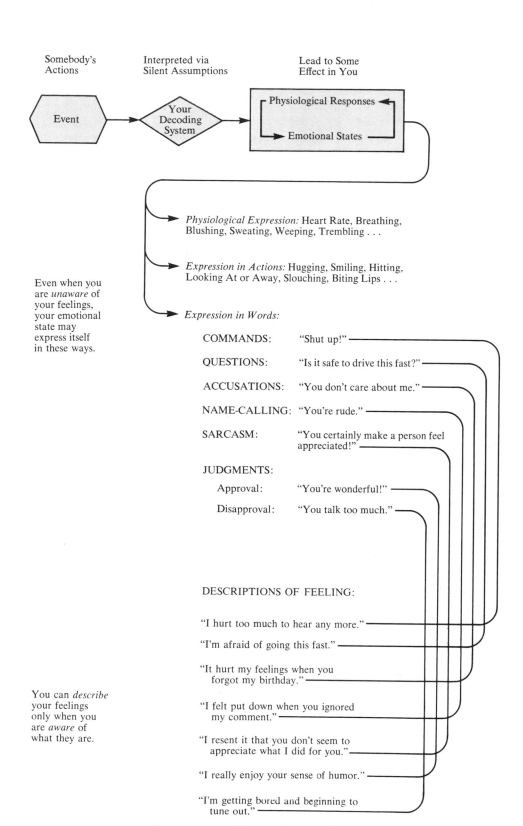

Somebody's Actions | Interpreted via Silent Assumptions | Lead to Some Effect in You

Event → Your Decoding System →

Physiological Responses
Emotional States

Even when you are *unaware* of your feelings, your emotional state may express itself in these ways.

Physiological Expression: Heart Rate, Breathing, Blushing, Sweating, Weeping, Trembling . . .

Expression in Actions: Hugging, Smiling, Hitting, Looking At or Away, Slouching, Biting Lips . . .

Expression in Words:

COMMANDS: "Shut up!"

QUESTIONS: "Is it safe to drive this fast?"

ACCUSATIONS: "You don't care about me."

NAME-CALLING: "You're rude."

SARCASM: "You certainly make a person feel appreciated!"

JUDGMENTS:

Approval: "You're wonderful!"

Disapproval: "You talk too much."

DESCRIPTIONS OF FEELING:

"I hurt too much to hear any more."

"I'm afraid of going this fast."

"It hurt my feelings when you forgot my birthday."

"I felt put down when you ignored my comment."

"I resent it that you don't seem to appreciate what I did for you."

"I really enjoy your sense of humor."

"I'm getting bored and beginning to tune out."

You can *describe* your feelings only when you are *aware* of what they are.

How Emotional States Express Themselves

229

B. The Skill

Although we usually try to describe our *ideas* clearly and accurately, we often do not try to describe our *feelings* clearly. Feelings get expressed in many different ways, but we do not usually attempt to identify the feeling itself.

One way to describe a feeling is to identify or name it. "I feel angry." "I feel embarrassed." "I feel comfortable with you." However, we do not have enough names of labels to encompass the broad range of human emotions, and so we invent other ways to describe our feelings, such as the use of similes. "I feel like a tiny frog in a huge pond." A girl, whose friendly overture had just been rebuffed, said, "I feel like I have just had an arm amputated."

A third way to describe a feeling is to report what kind of action the feeling urges you to do. "I feel like hugging and hugging you." "I'd like to slap you." "I wish I could walk off and leave you."

In addition, many figures of speech serve as descriptions of feeling. "I just swallowed a bushel of spring sunshine."

C. Describing Your Own Feelings

When describing your feelings, try to make clear what feelings you are experiencing by identifying them. The statement must (1) refer to "I," "me," or "my," and (2) specify some kind of feeling by name, simile, action urge or other figure of speech.

The following examples show the relation between two kinds of expressions of feeling, (1) those that describe what the speaker is feeling, and (2) those that do not. Notice that expressions of feeling which describe the speaker's emotional state are more precise, less capable of misinterpretation and, thus, convey more accurately what feelings are affecting the speaker.

Expressing feeling by describing your emotional state	Expressing feeling without describing your emotional state
"I feel embarrassed." "I feel pleased." "I feel annoyed."	Blushing and say nothing.
"I feel angry!" "I'm worried about this." "I feel hurt by what you said."	Suddenly becoming silent in the midst of a conversation.
"I enjoy her sense of humor." "I respect her abilities and competence." "I love her but I feel I shouldn't say so."	"She's a wonderful person."
"I hurt too much to hear any more." "I feel angry at myself." "I'm angry with you."	"Shut up!!!"

Because emotional states express themselves simultaneously in words, in actions and in physiological changes, a person may convey contradictory messages about what he is feeling. For example, his actions (a smile or laugh) may contradict his words (that he is angry). The clearest emotional communication occurs when the speaker's description of what he is feeling matches and, thus, amplifies what is being conveyed by his actions and other nonverbal expressions of feeling.

The aim in describing your own feelings is to start a dialogue that will improve your relationship with the other person. After all, others need to know how you feel if they are to take your feelings into account. Negative feelings are indicator signals that something may be going wrong in a relationship with another person. To ignore negative feelings is like ignoring a warning light that indicates an electrical circuit is overloaded. Negative feelings are a signal that the two of you need to check for misunderstanding and faulty communication.

After discussing how each sees the situation or your relationship, you may discover that your feelings resulted from false perceptions of the situation and of the other person's motives. In this case, your feelings would probably change. However, the other may discover that his actions are arousing feelings in you that he wasn't aware of—feelings that others beside you might experience in response to his behavior—and *he* may change.

In short, describing your feelings should not be an effort to coerce the other into changing so that you won't feel as you do. Rather, you report your inner state as just one more piece of information that is necessary if the two of you are to understand and improve your relationship.

D. *Perception Check*

You describe what you perceive to be the other's inner state in order to check whether you understand what he feels. That is, you test to see whether you have decoded his *expressions* of feeling accurately. You transform his *expressions* of feeling into a tentative *description* of his feeling. A good perception check conveys this message, "I want to understand your feelings—is this (making a description of his feelings) the way you feel?"

Examples:

"I get the impression you are angry with me. Are you?"
(NOT: "Why are you so angry with me?" This is mind reading, not perception checking.)
"Am I right that you feel disappointed that nobody commented on your suggestion?"
"I'm not sure whether your expression means that my comment hurt your feelings, irritated or confused you."

Note that a perception check *describes* the other's feelings, and *does not express disapproval or approval*. It merely conveys, "This is how I understand your feelings. Am I accurate?"

5. PARAPHRASING: A BASIC COMMUNICATION SKILL FOR IMPROVING INTERPERSONAL RELATIONSHIPS

A. *The Problem*

Tell somebody your phone number and he will usually repeat it to make sure he heard it correctly. However, if you make a complicated statement, most people will express agreement or disagreement without trying to insure that they are responding to what you intended. Most people seem to assume that what they understand from a satement is what the other intended.

How do you check to make sure that you understand another person's ideas, information or suggestions as he intended them? How do you know his remark means the same to you as it does to him?

Of course, you can get the other person to clarify his remark by asking, "What do you mean?" or, "Tell me more," or by saying, "I don't understand." However, after he has elaborated, you still face the same question, "Am I understanding his idea as he intended it to be understood?" Your feeling of certainty is no evidence that you do in fact understand.

B. *The Skill*

If you state in your own way what his remark conveys to you, the other can begin to determine whether his message is coming through as he intended. Then, if he thinks you misunderstand, he can speak directly to the specific misunderstanding you have revealed. The term PARAPHRASE can be used for ANY MEANS OF SHOWING THE OTHER PERSON WHAT HIS IDEA OR SUGGESTION MEANS TO YOU.

Paraphrasing, then, is any way of revealing your understanding of the other person's comment in order to test your understanding.

An additional benefit of paraphrasing is that it lets the other know that you are interested in him. It is evidence that you do want to understand what he means.

If you can satisfy the other that you really do understand *his* point, he will probably be more willing to attempt to understand your views.

Paraphrasing, thus, is crucial in attempting to bridge the interpersonal gap. (1) It increases the accuracy of communication, and thus the degree of mutual or shared understanding. (2) The act of paraphrasing itself conveys feeling... your interest in the other, your concern to see how he views things.

C. *Learning to Paraphrase*

People sometimes think of paraphrasing as merely putting the other person's ideas in another way. They try to say the same thing with different words. Such word-swapping may result merely in the illusion of mutual understanding. See the following example:

Sarah: Jim should never have become a teacher.
Fred: You mean teaching isn't the right job for him?
Sarah: Exactly! Teaching is not the right job for Jim.

Instead of trying to reword Sarah's statement, Fred might have asked himself, "What does Sarah's statement mean to me?" In that case the interchange might have sounded like this:

Sarah: Jim should never have become a teacher.
Fred: You mean he is too harsh on the children . . . maybe even cruel?
Sarah: Oh, no. I meant that he has such expensive tastes that he can't ever earn
       enough as a teacher.

Fred: Oh, I see. You think he should have gone into a field that would have insured him a higher standard of living?

Sarah: Exactly! Teaching is not the right job for Jim.

Effective paraphrasing is not a trick or a verbal gimmick. It comes from an attitude, a desire to know what the other means. And to satisfy this desire you reveal the meaning his comment had for you so that the other can check whether it matches the meaning he intended to convey.

If the other's statement was general, it may convey something *specific* to you.

Larry: I think this is a very poor textbook.

You: Poor? You mean it has too many inaccuracies?

Larry: No, the text is accurate, but the book comes apart too easily.

Possibly the other's comment suggests an *example* to you.

Laura: This text has too many omissions; we shouldn't adopt it.

You: Do you mean, for example, that it contains nothing about the Negro's role in the development of America?

Laura: Yes, that's one example. It also lacks any discussion of the development of the arts in America.

If the speaker's comment was very specific, it may convey a *more general* idea to you.

Ralph: Do you have 25 pencils I can borrow for my class?

You: Do you just want something for them to write with? I have about 15 ballpoint pens and 10 or 11 pencils.

Ralph: Great. Anything which writes will do.

Sometimes the other's idea will suggest its *inverse* or *opposite* to you.

Stanley: I think the Teacher's Union acts so irresponsibly because the administration has ignored them so long.

You: Do you think the T.U. would be less militant now if the administration had consulted with them in the past?

Stanley: Certainly. I think the T.U. is being forced to more and more desperate measures.

To develop your skill in understanding others, try different ways of conveying your interest in understanding what they mean and revealing what the other's statements mean to you. Find out what kinds of response are helpful ways of paraphrasing for you.

The next time someone is angry with you or is criticizing you, try to paraphrase until you can demonstrate that you understand what he is trying to convey as he intends it. What effect does this have on your feelings and on his?

Walter M. Lifton

THE TOOLS AND TECHNIQUES
INVOLVED IN THE HELPING
PROCESS

Before examining some of the more basic techniques it is important to have a prior understanding of the way communication provides the key to the helping process. Essentially the major problem in our society is a breakdown in communication. Not only do people have trouble understanding each other, but frequently a person is not sure of himself. Actually this book, itself, is limited to only that help which can be provided through the use of words. The first and hardest lesson for the beginner to learn is that you cannot assume that the other person meant what *you* assumed his words to mean. Not only do words frequently have a variety of meanings, but the way in which they were said can vastly alter their intent. Shakespeare understood this well when he had one of his characters say, "The lady doth protest too much, methinks." One of the skills most desired by maturing youth is to know whether a girl really means no, when she says it. To review then, words are defined with a variety of meanings in the dictionary, they change meaning according to the setting, and they can reflect the exact reverse of their stated meanings. To further complicate the issue, people use ideas to express feelings that are important to them. It is almost as if words were a car, with the feelings being its passenger, and with the passenger being more vital than the car itself. The major problem, then, is to see how one can learn what the other person is trying to convey. Until you understand the feelings you cannot begin to help him (or them) face the issue to be solved.

The first place anyone can start is with his own experience. "What could the words I hear possibly mean?" Having explored the range of possible alternatives, a person next tries to examine the context in which the words occurred to select the most likely meaning. He still cannot be sure that his own needs are not causing him to distort what he has heard so that ultimately all he can do is to check if his idea is what the other person actually meant.

This attempt at precision of meaning is really the very heart of the helping process in which several things are going on at once. To clarify the relationship in the helping process, the person being helped will be called the client. For the client who hears from another his idea exactly as he meant it, there is the wonderful feeling of being understood, of not being alone in the world, and of having someone else available who can help him see if he is getting across to others the things he desires. For the client who sees someone else trying to understand, but who finds that his words do not seem to convey the exact meaning he desires, there is still the opportunity to try to redefine himself. In this process of redefinition—this attempt to clear away ambiguity—frequently the speaker becomes clearer not only in what he wants to say, but also in what his true feelings really are.

The skilled group worker needs more than a text to train his sensitivities to hearing and responding to others. The group leader not only needs to have knowledge of others, but also has to be sure his own house is in order. We do not hear others say things which, if we recognize them in others, would force us to see unacceptable things in ourselves. The more we need to block out from hearing, the less we can help others. . . .

The primary goal in the helping process is to assist others in examining their words or behavior to see if they represented what the client wished to communicate. With this as our goal let's explore some tools which help people clarify their thoughts. The process of reflecting back to the client the literal dictionary meaning of what he says is called *"reflection of content."*

When we reflect back to the person what he is *trying* to say, or the latent desires in his words, the process is called *"reflection of feeling."* Reflection of feeling is particularly tricky. If we can help put into words a feeling of which the person was dimly aware, but had not found a clear way to state, he will be helped by this clarifying process. If, however, we pick up feelings which we feel are there but which the client is either not ready to examine or which represent our distortion of his feelings, we may be in for trouble. The attempt to reflect these unconscious needs or to link up past experiences with present behavior is called *"interpretation."* Since any linking of past with present or any predicting of future behavior has to come from the perceiver's own experiences or logic, the success of this technique will be vitally dependent upon its accuracy and the concurrent help given to the person to face frightening or unacceptable ideas. Since interpretation is so dependent upon a vast experience and an ability to judge a person's readiness for threatening material, it is a device best reserved for only the most skilled. . . .

Other more common tools that all of us have had a chance to experience include *questioning, supplying information, clarifying an idea* (summarizing all the points raised that bear on each other), and (probably most important of all) the use of *silence* to allow the other person to think his own thoughts in his own way. These are but a few of the techniques available. . . .

The touchstone of the helping process is, now more than ever, felt to lie in the way the person who is trying to help indicates to another that he really cares about him. It is a relationship that cannot be faked. One way to let others know that you feel what they say is really important is to constantly look at them. To actually understand them you need to see their facial expressions and gestures that go along with their words. For example, try the following experiment yourself.

Knowing that constant eye contact is helpful, try this on a friend: Tell him that you wish to have him help you learn how to convey interest in a client. Ask him to let you know when he feels you are with him and when he feels you are woolgathering. For the first few moments try your hardest to listen to the feelings the client is expressing. Then, while still focusing your eyes on the client's face imagine a scene taking place behind him, and in a sense look right through him to the scene beyond. Return again to a real attempt to listen. This time, however, spend your time thinking of how you would like to answer him. In other words, although you are concerned with his problem, your major attention is on what it means to you. If you are successful in playing these roles you will discover to your dismay that when you are not really listening to what he is trying to express, you are fooling no one but yourself. . . .

The following analysis of what teaching is represents a summary of an excellent article on this subject by Louis Raths. The comments on each heading, however, are the author's interpretation of their applicability to the helping process.

Raths has divided teaching into separate operations. We will specifically examine what he has called the "Clarifying Operations, the Show-How Operations, and the Security-Giving Operations."

CLARIFYING OPERATIONS

I.1 *Clarifying through reflection.*   This has been partially covered by the preceding section.

I.2. *Clarifying through use of a definition or illustration.*   For a person to understand an idea fully he must be able to communicate its meaning to others. Clarification is frequently best achieved by describing an applicable concrete situation. The group seeks to facilitate its understanding by requesting the person to illustrate his idea.

I.3. *Clarifying by pointing up what appear to be apparent inconsistencies.* Notice the word "apparent." What does not make sense to the hearer initially may be seen as related when the speaker draws up the relationship as he sees it. One good illustration of this comes in the popular refrain, "you always hate the one you love." A moment's thought will reveal the fact that it is hard to feel strongly about someone who is unimportant to you.

I.4. *Clarifying similarities and differences.*   Particularly in a group where there may be a tendency to get support by either forcing a single stand or by the operation of cliques, this approach is very important. As a pressure group forces opinion by presenting a united front, helping members of this subgroup examine their stand and pointing up both areas of hidden disagreement as well as consensus, within their group, causes the clique to disintegrate and join the total group. It also points up that the strength of the group can come from difference as well as agreement.

I.5. *Clarifying through questioning underlying assumptions.*   This can be a dangerous tool. If the group by this device rejects any assumptions but those the majority believes in, it can have a threatening and restricting effect. If, however, it is used to help the person or total group define the assumptions they are making so that they can decide if these are beliefs they can really accept, then the approach has positive implications for growth.

I.6. *Clarifying through anticipation of consequences.*   Since the response of others to our actions is a major concern, the degree to which the group helps provide possible results enables the person to determine his course of action. One rather popular way that is used to think through this situation is by having group members act out with a person a scene in which he tries his idea. The others, by their behavior, give him concrete evidence of what the future effects of his approach might be.

I.7. *Clarifying through questioning meaning.* Is this what you mean? or, Do I understand you to say . . . ? The latter implies that the hearer could be misperceiving but wants to understand.

I.8. *Clarifying by examining points of difficulty.* This could apply not only to an idea but also to helping the group examine their own group process. For example, sometimes a group seems at a loss as to what they want to do. Helping them examine the feelings or ideas that seem to be causing trouble is the first step in removing this road block. What's getting in our way? Why are we so upset?

I.9. *Clarifying if a personal statement was meant to show a personal feeling or one that the individual feels all people must hold.* This is one way of helping the group see demands that individual members are making on them. It also points up to the individual demands he is making on others.

I.10. *Clarifying by relating feelings to behavior.* By calling attention to the feelings others are getting from a person's behavior, it helps the person accept responsibility for the way he expresses his emotion. "We all seem to be so angry at each other that we seem unable to let the other person talk."

I.11. *Clarifying through a review of the steps in a person's logic.* This concept is somewhat like I.5. Implicit is the idea that a review of the steps will help a person see the fallacy of the logic involved. Although this approach can sometimes work, it cannot help failing if the motivation for his reasoning will not be more effectively met by an alternative logic which is presently in the client's available repertoire of responses. For example, the group points out to a member that the client is tired when he stays out late with the boys and his health and school work are suffering. The client recognizes the truth of the group's statement, but the logic does not meet his need for peer group approval or the satisfactions he gets when he is out with the fellows.

I.12. *Raising questions of purpose.* What are you trying to prove? This is an attempt to help the person search for and recognize the underlying motivation for his activity. To the degree that he is secure in the group and has a motivation to get an answer, this approach may be helpful. Also, the question must reflect an attempt to help the person rather than being a belligerent challenge of his rights or goals.

I.13. *Seeking origins of an expression or idea.* Since nothing we think or do is unrelated to our past experiences, to the degree that we can integrate a present idea with the concepts that led to its creation, we achieve a fuller realization of the meaning of the idea to us.

THE SHOW-HOW OPERATIONS

II.1. *Through demonstrations.* Although copying movements to learn skills can be a helpful way of learning, the motivation to succeed through being like someone else is really a double-edged sword. The more the individual sees happiness as being achieved by emulating someone else, the more he will try to be like the other person. In the process he will tend to overlook the things that make him different from his idol. He will assume an equivalence in their interests, skills, personality, and goals. Since he can never be the other person, he never achieves a sense of accomplishment that he feels really reflects what he could achieve on his own two feet. Especially in a democracy we seek to preserve the individual's right to his own life. The issue therefore really is: How do we help people incorporate into their own lives the values *we* feel are important? The answer to this is not a simple one. The author takes the stand that society has the responsibility of providing young people with many samples of roles to examine and try. It must then provide a setting in which each person can examine how the parts of each role will be consistent with his unique abilities and goals. . . .

II.2. *Use of resource persons and teaching aids.*   The use of resource people and materials is closely tied to the meaningfulness of these sources of help to the goals of the group. The resource person who comes in to tell others what they should be doing will be useful only to the extent that he is supplying information that the group needs, wants, and is ready to use. The fundamental concept here is the difference between *information* and *advice*. Although many people ask for advice as one way of avoiding responsibility ("He told me to do it, it wasn't really my idea"); advice rarely works. If the adviser tells people exactly what they want to hear, it is experienced as reassuring. At the same time, people then react with the feeling that they already knew the answer and that the resource person had added nothing. If, however, the adviser suggests ideas that clients cannot accept, a dilemma arises. In the event that they take advice that they basically cannot go along with, they experience the feeling that they are not very worthwhile people if anyone can persuade them to actions that violate their own beliefs. There is then a resulting decrease in feelings of personal worth and in their ability to be responsible for their own behavior. On the other hand, if the group decides to ignore the advice of the resource person it makes it difficult for them to again seek his help since by their actions they have demonstrated a lack of faith in the correctness of his advice.

Information as contrasted from advice, then, is provided only when the people seeking a solution which clarifies their problem see need for knowing alternative ways to reach their goal and are willing to accept responsibility for both implementing their decisions and accepting the fruits of their action.

The timing, then, when information is sought by the group, is vitally dependent on what has preceded their request and the clients' security in accepting responsibility for their behavior. Information, volunteered before a group perceives a need for it, actually works as advice, since it implies the direction in which the adviser thinks they ought to be going and his feeling that they ought to be ready to accept responsibility.

II.3. *Exploring alternative methods or ways to solve the problem.*   Our security in feeling able to cope with our environment certainly is a function of the range of techniques we have learned to use in coping with a variety of situations. We facilitate security and growth of the individual when we provide both a secure setting and opportunity for trial behavior. . . .

An example here might be helpful: Little Billy Smith comes home from school crying. He has been beaten up by another youngster. We could solve (?) the problem by taking action against the other child, but Billy will not have learned how he can cope with the next bully. He will have learned that if you go to someone else he will solve your problem for you. Suppose, as just an alternative solution, Billy had discussed this with the coach, and the coach had offered to teach Billy to use judo. Let's imagine that Billy receives one lesson and on his way home he again meets the bully. How will he fight? The way he did in the past. He will use judo lessons only when the feels he can get results that are equal to or better than what he already knew. Incidentally, Billy was willing to try to develop his skills with the coach because he knew that while he was learning the coach would not hurt him. In his lessons he could make mistakes without suffering irreparable damage. The role of the school or therapeutic group is to offer the same opportunities to make mistakes without irreparable damage to the person.

Also involved in this area is the concept of failure. Typically failure has come to mean that the person has not measured up to a preconceived standard. This is but one way of looking at the inability to achieve beyond a certain point. A more helpful way of conceiving failure is that the point of failure provides a concrete measure of all the person has achieved to that point. For example, how can a person discover how high he is able to jump? He keeps raising the cross bar until he reaches the point where he can no longer clear it. This point of failure is both the measure of how high he *can* jump and a concrete point against which to compare his hoped for goal. Too often in our competitive society, we spend so much time in measuring the distance between where we are and where we feel we must go, that we lose sight of what we have already accomplished. If our goal in society is to help each person feel a sense of personal worth, at some point they need to be helped to examine where they are, where they have been, and where they feel they need to go. It is in helping a person reconcile what he is and the bases he has used to decide where he must go, that we are simultaneously providing motivation for learning while we are improving his mental health.

Actually, in a true learning situation the goal of the people or person providing help is to help the individual discover what he possesses as personal tools he can use to solve problems. The ultimate goal of any therapeutic situation is *not* the resolution of the problem. Rather it is an attempt to teach problem-solving techniques.

SECURITY-GIVING OPERATIONS

III.1. *Meeting the need for belonging.* It has been said that all of us determine our personal worth through the eyes of others. Essentially we recognize that since each person wants to feel worthwhile, to the degree that we share things in common, we are sure of mutual acceptance. The fly in the ointment is, however, that while we can achieve acceptance by being a carbon copy of the stereotype, this role does not enable us to be recognized as a unique person. This need for group acceptance is strongest in the adolescent. Picture the typical high school girl of our day dressed in the uniform of the day. It may be leotards, bobby socks, or whatever the group has decided. Suppose this young lady should overhear two boys trying to decide whom to take to a dance. "I don't see what the problem is, Tom, these gals spend so much time together you can't tell one from the other." Young Miss walks away in confusion. What do you have to do and be, not to be considered a square? How different does she dare let herself be without risking group rejection as a queer? Although the example chosen was that of an adolescent, these questions are common to people at all age levels. What are the limits of our society? How can I meet my needs within these limits? And for the mature adult there is added the more difficult question, how can I help others see that the status quo needs changing without losing group membership?

III.2. *Meeting the need for achievement and personal growth.* One way we prove to ourselves that we are worthwhile is by examining our day-to-day accomplishments. If we keep repeating what we could do yesterday, the glow of accomplishment fades. Personal growth then involves a constant reassessment of the reality of the new goals we are setting up for tomorrow. Since we do not achieve in a vacuum, part and parcel of this assessment process is the reaction and support we get from the reactions of others. One of the rather unique characteristics of the group setting is that as we observe other people solve problems and grow, it gives us courage to try solving problems ourselves. Part of it might be from the feeling that if the other person, whom we feel is weaker, can achieve—we can, too. Along with this is the support that comes from knowing that other people are facing similar problems. We are not alone.

III.3. *The need for economic security.* Although a group does not meet this specific need it can be very helpful in assisting the person in sharpening his skills in achieving economic self-sufficiency. Job security in our society is more than just having needed skills. One of the major reasons people lose jobs is their inability to get along with fellow workers and to accept responsibility. Job security rests also on the degree to which the job gratifies basic needs. For some, job satisfaction depends purely on the money they earn. This is not only a status symbol but also a means to gratify needs that cannot be met through their jobs. For other people the conditions under which they work are more vital....

III.4. *Need to be free from fear.* Fear can be a motivating force to solve a problem. It can also be the basis for avoiding situations which realistically are dangerous and beyond the control of an individual. Rather than freedom from fear there ought to be substituted help in facing fear. For example, many of us are aware of the fact that any day some trigger-happy person could fire a bomb which might precipitate the end of the world as we know it. This is a very real possibility. There are many things an individual can do to attempt to modify society so that this no longer will be possible. Immediate solutions are not likely. Living in daily fear could make a person unable to do even those small things which on a combined group basis might solve the problem. In other words at some point, we need to help people live in a society where security and the absence of fear can become a possibility. We need to build up individual security that comes from knowing that each person has used the full extent of his capacity. No more can be demanded of any man.

III.5. *The need for love and affection.* Raths has described this as showing others you are hurt when they are hurt. There is a real question if this is a helpful thing. To the extent that you are truly hurt each time another suffers, the trials and tribulations of the world can soon overwhelm you. As an alternative the development of an empathic attitude might be considered. Instead of sympathizing and identifying with each pain of the other person, you attempt to let him know that you understand how he feels and that you want to help. In your own mind you recognize that *he* is feeling the pain, not you. Unless you are free of the pain you cannot be objective enough to provide him help in looking at his feelings. When the counselor identifies with his client we have two clients instead of one. This augments the problem rather than lessens it.

There are many kinds of love. Many of you are familiar with what has been termed "Mother Love," or the possessive kind of attention that robs the person of his rights and personality. All of us tend to be suspicious of other people. A rather frequent question is "Why are you being so nice to me?" People basically recognize that all behavior is motivated by some need of the individual. Understanding the needs the "loving" person is trying to meet helps the recipient decide if this is helping or hindering his own desires. The more honestly we express our motivations for being concerned about others, the more secure both they and we will feel. In the group this problem is somewhat simplified. Very quickly groups come to realize that they will sink or swim together. The growing awareness of how interdependent they are on each other makes very clear that from what may appear as a selfish basis, each person wants the others well and happy. This is so that the other people can meet your needs which they couldn't do if their abilities were impaired.

Feeling important to others in and of itself demonstrates your value. The security of love works two ways. It proves that there are others who care while at the same time increasing your esteem in your own eyes.

III.6. *The need to be free from guilt.* Feelings of guilt can so immobilize a person that any positive action is impossible. Guilt feelings can be alleviated in several ways. One common method is for an authority to remove guilt by providing you with punishment which will pay for the action that is causing guilt feelings. A common example of this is the little boy who confesses to misbehavior and feels relief when he is spanked since he then considers the score has been settled....

III.7. *Need for acceptance of the other person.* A group soon learns that each person in his turn will ask questions that are very naive in the eyes of others. Accepting the "naive" person's need for information and his right to use the group to clarify his own thinking causes the group members to examine questions, not in terms of their sophistication, but rather in terms of what it means to the person asking.

III.8. *Ways of controlling conflict situations.* Groups develop a sixth sense in judging when a group member is being pressed beyond his ability to cope with the situation. Since taking a problem out of someone else's hands implies a lack of faith in their capacity to handle the problem, group members hesitate to take overt action. Rather than have the person retreat from danger, or remove the danger, group members provide support to the person under attack so that he has additional strength in facing the situation. It is not uncommon for the group to take overt action toward a member who seems to be unfairly treating another. Learning that the way that he treats other group members will affect how the rest of the group will treat him causes each person to carefully consider his effect on others.

These are a few of the characteristics that Raths covers in his article. Although there are many other aspects of teaching, those presented should demonstrate the communal focus of teaching and therapy.

Elwood Murray / Raymond H. Barnard / J. V. Garland

SEMANTIC DISORDERS

OF RABBITS AND MEN

Let us begin by looking at semantic disorders in terms of a contrast between the evaluations of an animal and a human. George Preston, in his *Psychiatry for the Curious,* uses a rabbit as an example. As Preston points out, rabbits have "learned," through thousands of generations of natural selection which eliminated the "unfit," that when danger threatens, the best thing to do is to "freeze"—that is, become immobile. In the field or thicket this works well, for it tends to make the rabbit invisible, and for thousands of years fields and thickets have been the habitat of rabbits. Consequently, rabbits have come to equate immobility with safety. Then comes man with his automobiles and roads. One night, as a rabbit is crossing a road, it is caught in the glare of a car's headlights. Instantly it "freezes" in order to be "safe." It is, of course, run over and killed.

The lesson for us in this lies in noting the "allness" in the reaction of the rabbit. It held an "assumption" that immobility always meant safety. The rabbit has no means of revising its "assumptions" except through generations of the nonsurvival of rabbits who stop in front of cars. Nature has to take the hard way of weeding out that tendency.

Humans, on the other hand, are not bound to that compulsive type of behavior. Humans possess an extracortical layer of brain which animals do not have, and this gives us the capacity to discriminate and adapt indefinitely. We can take automobiles —and even atomic bombs—in our stride, if we will but exercise the nervous capacity we have for adaptation.

If, however, we possess attitudes of "allness" — if we are rigid, dogmatic, "know-it-all" in our outlooks — then we are effectively prevented from using our higher brain areas, and our behavior tends to take on a compulsive character rather like that of the rabbit. In effect, we choke off some of our most powerful nervous energies, and instead of using them to discriminate and adapt — which is the proper survival use of them — we short-circuit them into fighting for blind dogmas.

Back in the days of Hitler it used to be said that a good Nazi was one who felt that he had died a good death if he crossed the street on the green light even though he knew that a truck which had cut through the red light was bearing directly down on him. Such uncritical reactions to signals (and to words) are the stuff of which dictatorship is made. They are the counterpart in the human sphere of the rabbit's "allness" reaction. In the human, however, they are not normal but pathological. Barring the presence of an actual nervous lesion, such as a brain injury of some sort, they are symptoms of what is called a "semantic disorder."

SIGNIFICANCE OF THE WORD "SEMANTIC"

The word "semantic" is one that has been used rather indiscriminately in recent years. Looking it up in a dictionary, we find little more than that it seems to have something to do with words. It has, in a way, but words are only part of the story. More accurately, we would say that it has to do with "significances" or "values." In the case of the Nazi mentioned above, for example, words did not enter into the picture. What happened was simply that he overevaluated the green light and underevaluated other factors (*e.g.*, the truck) in the total situation about him. In other words, he had an inappropriate "*semantic* reaction"—the *values* he attached to the various factors of the situation in which he found himself were inappropriate.

We are now in a position to see more clearly what a "semantic disorder" represents. It represents values which are confused or out of perspective. And the presence of semantic disorders leads, of course, to lack of predictability. (Note the lack of predictability in the rabbit's "belief": "If I remain immobile I shall be safe," and in the Nazi's belief, which may have been something like this: "In crossing on the green light I am obeying the law, and it is good to obey the law.") Since, in our use of speech, we are constantly concerned with the matter of developing a higher degree of predictability in our own evaluations and those of our audience, semantic disorders are important for us to understand. Now, to further our understanding, let us look at some more common examples of semantic disorders.

EXAMPLES OF SEMANTIC DISORDERS

We do not have to look far to find occurrences of semantic disorders, for they are happening all about us. Let us take, for example, the case of an ambitious young executive who is spending the week end with the other junior executives and some of the senior executives at the ranch of the president of a corporation. The president decides that they are to have a mountain-climbing expedition to the top of a near-by peak, and the last man up is to be in disgrace for the rest of the week end. This particular young executive happens to be suffering from a severe heart ailment which the others do not know about. He has not let it be known, for the president has always regarded with contempt subordinates who complained of an ailment of any kind. So the question is, shall he risk death climbing the mountain or risk the contempt, which possibly could cost him his job. A problem of evaluation is involved. We may also call it a semantic problem, even though words are not involved for it is a problem of which is properly the more significant—the irrevocable fact of his heart condition or what his superior thinks of him.

Clearly, proper evaluation should place his health as the prime consideration. All that he would be risking then would be his job and a certain amount of prestige, and that is a lesser risk than life itself, which includes obligations to wife, to children, etc. Suppose, however, that the young executive evaluates the opinions of his fellows and of his superior so highly that he feels he cannot refuse to go on the expedition. He is then seriously misevaluating. If he does it thoughtlessly or impulsively, it is bad enough. If he does it because he feels a compulsion of some sort to "keep up with the gang," then one would say that this represents a semantic disorder of high degree.

Semantic disorders of this kind would appear to be one of the serious sicknesses of our times. Many individuals do not evaluate adequately, but react in compulsive ways (like the rabbit) to various pressures that they let be put upon them. And as they fail to make proper evaluations, they fail in predictability, and unpleasant surprises and even disasters follow as a result. Many individuals, instead of making sound evaluations every step of the way and proceeding with the circumspection that conditions would warrant, fly along at full throttle, so to speak, on the track of their too-limited abstractions and assumptions. Then comes the sudden curve (the aberrant factor whose possibility they left out of account—the unexpected that they failed to allow for), and disaster happens. The tragedy of it is that in our interdependent world they carry many other people with them, and there falls to the better evaluators the burden of cleaning up the wreckage, salvaging what can be salvaged, and paying the bill. For such individuals life is a series of violent oscillations, of high ups and low downs, of fond hopes and disillusioning disasters, instead of the more efficient progressive growth and development which come from our making adequate evaluations all along the line. . . .

CRITICIZING OUR OWN SEMANTIC REACTIONS

What, then, does this imply with respect to our use of speech? It implies, first of all, that we must from time to time stop and take stock of our habits of evaluation to see whether we are letting some "allnesses" creep into our evaluations. And it implies in particular that we need to pause more often before we make an utterance, to see whether what we are about to say represents an appropriate evaluation of the "facts." How often, for example, do we not say impulsively, "Oh, that fellow doesn't know what he's talking about!"—leaving out of account that this is our private evaluation, limited by our prejudices and tastes, and circumscribed by the conditions of our specific experience? How much more appropriate it would be if we were habitually to express ourselves with less dogmatism, taking into account always that others may evaluate quite differently.

All this is not to say that we should go about severely qualifying everything we say, tediously and pedantically trying to point out every consideration involved. On the contrary, it means that we should keep silent more, and live with fact-territory instead of in the airy heights of words. For in silence there is room for the awareness of realities, room for intimate acquaintance with fact-territory. On the other hand, the moment we speak we begin circumscribing and confining realities. Who, for example, has not had the experience of riding through a beautiful countryside with someone who kept up a running commentary on everything he saw. One suspects that he did not see as much as he pretended to, because he was so engrossed in talking about it all. Certain it is, in any case, that he spoiled the drive for those who sought their pleasure in a silent relationship with the beauties about them.

As we become better evaluators, we become less "word-oriented" and more "fact-oriented." We become more mature. We cast off the juvenile habit of puns and glib remarks. We "soften" our evaluations to allow for non-allness and variety. This does not mean that we constantly abandon the grounds on which we stand. On the contrary, we stand our ground, but our ground is large enough to accommodate others too. We find room in our lives not just for ourselves but also for our fellow men. We become more adaptable, more agreeable, better citizens, and better members of society.

LEVELS OF ABSTRACTION

First of all, let us note again that "facts" do not exist in and of themselves; they exist as they are observed and abstracted *by someone*. As the physicist R. D. Carmichael expressed it, "The universe, as known to us, is a joint phenomenon of the observer and the observed." And so in all our human knowledge there is inevitably a degree of uncertainty—we are limited by the capacities of our senses and of the extensions of them, such as microscopes, Geiger counters, etc., which we are able to construct.

Our immediate observations represent first-order abstractions from the energies (heat, light, pressure, etc.) which have impinged on our senses. For example, the image on the retina of our eye as transmitted along the optic nerve to the visual center of the brain, forms our first-order abstraction of the garden scene that we view through the window. (Note that here we have a picture, *not* words.) Now we may abstract further. We may ignore the individuality of each leaf, each flower, each butterfly — indeed, we may leave out billions of discernible characteristics — and simply *say* that the garden contains zinnias, poppies, and hollyhocks. Here we have generalized, leaving out hosts of special characteristics. (If we had drawn a more detailed verbal "map" of our perception of the garden, it would be called a first-order description.) Finally, we may jump to an exceedingly high level of abstraction and say, "Ah, beauty!" Here we have left out almost all special characteristics and details and stated virtually the ultimate in generality. This is convenient because it omits so many pertinent details.

Our mental pictures and our recollections of taste, touch, sound, smell, etc. tend to be close to the original fact-territory of immediate experience. Words, on the other hand, are by their very nature in some degree removed from fact-territory. It is this generality of words which allows for "meanings" and makes them such convenient instruments of communication. And therein also lies the peril of using them—we may forget that they do not tell "all," that they are but "maps" and not the actual "territory."

ORIENTING OURSELVES BY FACT-TERRITORY

Now, in the light of the summary we have just given, it should be clear that it is possible for us to orient ourselves in either of two ways—either predominantly by words, or predominantly by our observations of fact-territory.

To see the contrast between these two orientations even more clearly, let us take as an example two individuals examining a new car. One will stand back looking it over. But instead of silently inspecting the car, he feels the urge to talk about it. So he chatters with the salesman or with whoever else may be at hand: "Say, she's a beauty, all right. I hear she'll do over a hundred. A neighbor of mine, Paul Fredericks, got one last week. He's pleased as a peacock; says he looked 'em all over and there's not another car to compare with her." This man is oriented predominantly by words. Inwardly he may be a rather insecure person, for he seems to put greater value on what others *say* than on his own first-hand evaluations. Note that he approaches the car with *words* at the very beginning; this is a reversal of the proper order of evaluation.

Now let us note how a second individual may approach the car. He has perhaps heard the same talk about this car, but, being conscious of abstracting, he is aware that words, especially in a case like this, are highly tenuous things. What he is after now is the "facts." He has tucked the words away in a far corner of his mind, so that they will not color the first-hand evaluations which he is now setting out to make. He approaches the car with all his senses functioning and focussed. He touches, feels, looks, listens. He tries seats, feels textures, examines materials. He pictures this car in terms of his own driving habits and needs and those of his family. It matters little to him what the advertisers or anyone else has said about the car. He wants to know how it will suit *him* under *his* conditions of using it. It may have the sleekest lines of any car on the market—a point featured in all the national advertising—but the significance of that falls to zero in his eyes if he sees that the hood is so high that his wife will not be able to see over it conveniently when she drives. *After* he has gone over the car and perhaps tried it out on the road, he may make some verbal "maps" to fit the "territory" as he has discovered it to be. This man is oriented predominantly by fact-territory instead of by words. His is the proper order of evaluation: first-order evaluations first, *then* higher-order abstractions to fit them.

The difference between these two orientations is sometimes difficult to see, especially in relation to ourselves. The reason is that we may not have been trained to see it. Indeed, most traditional education tends to overevaluate the verbal. Words are drummed into us, and a premium is put on mere verbal skill. Unfortunately, it is often with the most intelligent and gifted individual that the verbal orientation takes hold the hardest, and he may have more difficulty than others in retraining himself to live closer to fact-territory.

The most effective speakers, however, are fact-oriented. The day of windiness is past. Now people want to sense that a speaker is conscious of non-allness, that he is aware of the limitations of words and of his particular abstractions. If he does not acknowledge the realm of the "unspoken," his words will seem to lack depth and fail to have a ring of authenticity. There is perhaps nothing so fresh and effective in a speech as the indication that the speaker is not parroting a single phrase from anyone else but is presenting simply and directly his own word-map of fact-territory as he has evaluated it.

THE "MAP" IS NOT THE "TERRITORY"

It should be obvious enough that a map is *not* the territory it represents, and that words are *not* the nonverbal actualities for which they stand. Yet our habits of speaking and evaluating often tend to make us ignore this crucial distinction. All too many people tend to react to words as if they *were* actual fact-territory; they tend to *identify in value* the map with the territory. This is a second consideration we need to take into account in orienting ourselves to prevent semantic disorders.

A woman in Youngstown, Ohio, according to newspaper reports, ignored a railroad brakeman's red lantern, drove her car around him, and crashed into the side of a freight train. When she was asked why she did not obey the signal to stop, she replied that she thought it was dangerous to stop in that neighborhood after dark! In other words, she made an utterly uncritical, indiscriminate, "allness" application of the verbal formulation: "dangerous to stop in that neighborhood after dark." She oriented herself more by her verbal belief than by the realities of the situation at hand, to the extent even that she could ignore a circumstance which made it even more dangerous *not* to stop.

Not all cases of identifying beliefs with actualities are quite as obvious as this. Most of them are far more subtle. For example, there is the student who over-evaluates grades. He is likely to be utterly crestfallen when he gets a low grade and tremendously elated when he gets a high one. Yet a grade is *not* the actual work done. It represents, rather, an evaluation of the instructor, a tag which he hangs on certain accomplishments. As against the inner maturing and developing that the student should get out of the course, the tag counts for little. And yet there are many students who would rather have the grade than the growth. They, too, are reversing the natural order of evaluation, wanting window-dressing more than actual goods.

AVOIDING VERBAL IMPASSES

A third consideration in orienting ourselves to prevent semantic disorders involves our understanding how to avoid merely verbalistic arguments. Let us recall, first of all, that a map, chart, diagram, blueprint, etc. may be said to be adequate to the extent that it includes as much detail as is necessary for our purposes at the time and omits what is not necessary. In no case, however, can it give *"all,"* for the actuality will always include far more details than can be shown on the map. Moreover, as the actuality changes, the map has to be brought up to date. All this holds similarly for our word-maps.

Whenever there is a verbal impasse, it is an almost certain sign that someone is standing pat on his particular "map" and refusing to check with "territory." Agreement *is* always possible once we know enough of the "facts" and are willing to face them. It is possible even when we lack facts, if we are willing to admit to ignorance. Agreement becomes impossible only when we cling dogmatically to our abstractions and assume them to say "all" about fact-territory.

The late Alfred Korzybski was fond of telling the story about two professors discussing the ameba. One professor, lacking consciousness of abstracting and being quite dogmatic about words, asserted flatly that the ameba has consciousness. The other professor, equally dogmatic, retorted that it was idiotic to say that the ameba had consciousness—humans, animals, might have consciousness, but certainly not a unicellular organism such as the ameba. Note in this case that each professor was *identifying in value* the word with the actual behavior of the ameba; they were reading certain abstractions into the actions of the creature and insisting that they were *there*, whereas actually the abstractions were but their own nervous constructs. As Korzybski liked to point out, the only ultimate resolution of the argument—so long as each clung to his identifications—was murder.

Suppose, however, that each was conscious of abstracting, aware that words represent constructs of our nervous systems which we may apply or not, as seems appropriate. In that case the discussion would go quite differently. One professor might say, "The actions of the ameba appear to be so and so, as we have both observed. In the light of this, should we not *ascribe* consciousness to the ameba?" And the other might say, "Well, possibly. In any case it would not be exactly the same as what we call 'consciousness' in humans. We might say that the ameba has consciousness of a sort. But really it isn't important, because anything we *say* is certainly not going to change the actual behavior of the creature itself!" And in this case there is not even a quarrel, least of all murder, for the ameba goes its way and the professors observe it silently and refuse to get into a fight over words. In the first instance, the professors, in spite of their scientific training, tended to be word-oriented; they reversed the natural order of evaluation and read a higher-order abstraction into their first-order observations. In the latter, they were fact-oriented; they observed the "territory," and then applied such terminology as seemed appropriate.

This illustration well typifies the verbalistic arguments that we can discover among people in virtually every field today—in politics, economics, medicine, religion, sociology, etc., and even in science. If we have any doubts as to the extent to which people are reversing the natural order of evaluations and putting words ahead of fact-territory, we have only to read the daily papers or listen to speeches and note how indiscriminately and with what absolutistic implications many people use such terms as "private enterprise," "big business," "freedom," "socialism," "appeasement," "monopoly," "bureaucracy," "Wall Street," "undemocratic," etc.

In the complexity of modern issues, a speaker needs consciousness of abstracting more than ever if he is not to tie himself and his listeners into knots of misunderstanding and misevaluations. . . .

THE TRAGEDIES OF "IS"

Perhaps our greatest difficulty in getting ourselves and others to be fact-oriented and to pursue the natural order of evaluation (fact-territory first, *then* words) comes from the very fact that there are pernicious influences buried in the standard forms of our everyday language. For example, the mere remark "It's hot today" presupposes certain assumptions about the character of "reality." We would seem pedantic, of course, if we were to say, "I evaluate this weather as hot," even though that would represent a more appropriate statement. To say "It is hot" objectifies our evaluation and reads into the outside world what is actually only an interpretation inside ourselves. To a visiting native of Liberia, it may not seem hot at all; it may even seem cool. And so if we were to be dogmatic about our statement, we and the Liberian could not "understand" each other.

The more serious difficulties arise when in important matters we insist on ascribing an exterior validity to our own inner evaluations. Consider, for example, the projection and reversal of natural order implied when the Archbishop of Canterbury said in a sermon that there "are" (quotation marks ours) only three kind of people in the world — "Communists, convinced Christians, and amiable nonentities." Here, surely, is something close to the ultimate in dogmatic classification, an ascribing of universality to what is actually only a private evaluation. Nehru of India, for example, is probably only one of millions who would quite rightly take serious exception to being called an "amiable nonentity."

One of the most treacherous shoals in our everyday language appears to be the simple word "*is*." In our glib and uncritical use of it our evaluations may run aground and become stranded in dogmatism. As the philosopher Santayana said: "The little word *is* has its tragedies; it marries and identifies different things with the greatest innocence; and yet no two are ever identical...."

The word "is" appears in a great many different ways, not all of them especially dangerous. The most dangerous, as Santayana suggests, appears to be what is called the *is* of identification. When we say, for example, "That fellow is a rascal!" we inevitably do violence to facts, regardless of what the fellow may have done. For linguistically what we have done is to equate a living individual, who in his totality is made up of countless separate characteristics, with a blanket term of opprobrium. Granted even the worst of the fellow, the word "rascal" can apply to him in only a limited way. For in addition to having committed certain heinous crimes, he may also "be" a father, a considerate husband, a dutiful son, a citizen, a taxpayer, a churchgoer, an ace golfer, a veteran, and so on.

If we but consider this for a moment, we shall begin to see what a treacherous thing the *is* of identification turns out to be. As in the case of the biology professors, we can best make our verbal "maps" fit the "facts" if we take them *as maps* and do not value them the same as living actuality. Instead of saying, "He *is* a rascal!" we may say, "Well, he is known to have done so and so; I would call him a rascal." There is a world of difference between this statement and the preceding one. The first has dogmatism in it; the second has no dogmatism. They imply vastly different attitudes on the part of the individuals who utter them. The first contains "allness"; the second is more limited to the "facts." The first grossly misevaluates the living actuality; the second shows better evaluation. The first may set off an argument; the second will tend to lead to agreement.

And so an important technique for avoiding misevaluations in ourselves and others is to avoid in so far as we possibly can the *is* of identification. If, each time we start to use it uncritically, we will stop and deliberately try to rephrase our sentences, we may soften our own attitudes a great deal—and such softening will make us more mature and considerate individuals.

We cannot, of course, completely avoid the *is* of identification, as one may note from merely reading this book. It is too convenient a communication short cut. What we can do, however, is remain conscious of its treachery; when we hear it or use it ourselves, we can remember the actual *non*-allness behind the superficial implication of "allness" which it suggests.

THE FALLACY OF "EITHER-OR"

The *is* of identification, then, represents a language form which grossly distorts actualities. A second fallacy occurs in the assumption that everything must "be" either one thing or another—the fallacy of "either-or." This is probably one of the most rampant fallacies in the world today. Consider, for example, the words of Mao Tse-tung, leader of Communist China, who wrote in 1949: "The people of China must side either with imperialism or socialism. There must be no exception, no third line of action. Straddling the fence is a futile thing." This is typical "either-or" thinking. Followed out to its inevitable conclusion, it can produce only conflict, for the other fellow must choose to capitulate completely or to be regarded as an "enemy."

The "either-or" fallacy manifests itself again and again in the Communist belief that "all those who are not with us are against us." But it may also crop up in many other forms. There are, for example, individuals in our own country who believe that because we can *say* it verbally, everything must *"be"* either "good" *or* "evil," "true" *or* "false," and so on. It may even crop up in subtle ways that are difficult to detect. According to the famous columnist Walter Lippmann, it has apparently occurred in the thinking of our State Department with respect to the organization of foreign alliances. Here is what Lippmann had to say about it.

> It is in Asia, rather than in Europe, that we are doing ourselves the most harm by trying to bring every non-Communist government into our alliance. When we say, as we like so often to say, that every government must choose between the U.S.S.R. and ourselves, that in this great struggle there can be no middle or neutral, no separate and independent position, we are unwittingly playing the Soviet game.
>
> For all over Asia there is a profound revolution in progress. . . . When we insist on an alliance . . . we become identified with the old regime.
>
> It is, I believe, folly on our part . . . to say that the only alternative to Soviet imperialism is an alliance with the United States. For then, when the old regime of the Farouks and the Qavams is overthrown, we are, so to speak, overthrown with them. We draw upon ourselves the odium of a past that we had no responsibility for.
>
> It would be ever so much wiser to say to the countries of Asia . . . that we will support, and indeed guarantee, their neutrality against Soviet aggression. . . . (From "Today and Tomorrow," *New York Herald Tribune*, August 5, 1952.)

Meanwhile, as we make our way through life we have actually to live by the great variety of reality, which almost never falls into the neat categories of "either-or." And in our speaking we have to avoid the entrapment of an "either-or" type of evaluation; otherwise we inevitably misrepresent actualities and mislead our hearers.

THE FALLACY OF ADDITIVITY

The high-ranking Air Forces general flying over Hiroshima after World War II was asked, "What do you think are the implications of the atomic bomb for warfare in the future?" His answer was: "There's just one simple thing to remember; it's a bigger bomb; it destroys more area and kills more people. For all we've been hearing about it, it's not a magic weapon. It's just a bigger bomb."

The general's answer was an example of what is called "additive thinking." That is, he was not taking into account that consequences of any given happening are likely not just to "add" up but to "multiply," or grow at what we call a "geometrical" rate. For the consequences of the atomic bomb were, of course, far more than simply those of "a bigger bomb." In the years since Hiroshima, we have seen them multiply and affect virtually every aspect not only of warfare but of civilian life—airplanes have had to be redesigned with the atomic bomb in mind, manufacturing facilities have had to be modified, systems of civilian defense changed, and so on.

Now, ... we shall study some specific techniques that we may use to keep ourselves factually oriented, to prevent semantic disorders in ourselves, and to note them in others. To begin with, we shall introduce two new terms—*intension* and *extension*—which conveniently sum up a great deal that we have studied thus far.

INTENSION VERSUS EXTENSION

Alfred Korzybski, in formulating his "general semantics," borrowed two terms from logic and gave them a new significance in the light of our human problems of evaluation. The terms are *intension* (with an *s*, note) and *extension*. The student should learn these words carefully, for they will be used frequently from here on.

As we saw earlier in this chapter, we may orient ourselves predominantly by words, or predominantly by fact-territory. Another and shorter way to say it is simply that we may orient ourselves predominantly by *intension* or predominantly by *extension*. Note that we say "predominantly," for it is not entirely an either-or matter. We have to have some of both. Perhaps the best way for us to picture this is to think of our evaluations as lying along a scale running from an extreme of intension at one end to an extreme of extension at the other.

Now, to translate this into an example, let us say that on an expedition into the mountains we come across a piece of ore. We pick it up and examine it, smell it, feel it, scrutinize it by every means of observation at our command, even to sending away a bit of it to be analyzed—all this silently, without words, and without even thinking in words. This acquaintanceship stands at the extreme of extension. Now let us say that the place where we sent it analyzes it (again by silent, extensional methods), and it turns out to be high-grade uranium ore! We may *now* start to verbalize about it. We can speak of a possible mine, of claims and leases, of our property, of our "wealth," of the "bonanza" we have struck, and so on. In so doing we move toward higher orders of abstraction—toward intension. Once we arrive at the words "wealth," "property," etc. and begin to speculate in terms of them, we are working in what may be considered perhaps the extreme of intension.

Obviously, both intension and extension are necessary. By *ex*tension we make our acquaintance with the world of fact-territory outside us. By *in*tension we produce the higher-order abstractions in terms of which we can rhapsodize, ponder and speculate, and communicate fluently with others.

Yet it should be just as obvious that there is also an *order of importance* involved here. Clearly, *ex*tension should come first, and then *in*tension. We should keep ourselves oriented predominantly by extension. For suppose that on finding the piece of ore we jumped to conclusions and said to ourselves. "Oh! this is uranium for sure! This is going to make me wealthy; I'll be a powerful man!" and then went on to build castles in the air on the basis of our "find." We might be in for a rude shock, for the ore might turn out not to be uranium after all.

This is not to say that we should never speculate. It means that we should speculate only so far as is warranted by the extensional facts. In short, we may go through life in either of two ways: (1) seeing everything in terms of our fixed beliefs and preconceptions and jumping to conclusions at every turn, or (2) silently inspecting and gathering the extensional facts first, and then molding our beliefs and conclusions to fit them. The first represents what is called an *in*tensional orientation, the second an *ex*tensional orientation. The first reverses the proper order of evaluation, the second follows it. The first is "sick" and tends toward nonsurvival for humans; the second is healthy and tends to promote our survival.

Yet huge numbers of people in the world are far more intensionally than extensionally oriented. For example, we have the extensional fact that healthy cows, if they are properly slaughtered and the meat is properly handled, provide an excellent and nourishing food. Yet the Hindu clings to his intensional belief that cows are "sacred" and never to be eaten, even though he die of starvation. We in this country, however, should not be arrogant about our own "practicality," for we have our own more subtle and sophisticated fetishes. Even the character of our traditional education has tended to be much more intensional than extensional.

To counteract our tendency toward excessive intension, Korzybski put forward what he called the "extensional devices," which we may apply in making our evaluations and checking the evaluations of others. If we actually apply them in our own reactions and in checking the reactions of others, we shall have valuable techniques for dealing with semantic disorders. The devices include: indexes, dates, *et ceteras,* quotes, and hyphens. Let us study these now one by one and see how our use of them may avert semantic disorders.

INDEXES

The indexes to which we refer here have to do not with the alphabetical key to the topics in a book but with the little numerical subscripts used by mathematicians. At a fairly high level of abstraction we may speak intensionally, for example, of *person, crime, industry, war,* and so on. Our problem is to extensionalize these terms and bring them closer to first-order facts. One way to do it is, of course, instead of using the word *person* to name a specific person, such as *Adam Q. Combs* or *Abraham Matthews;* or, instead of speaking of *industry* in the abstract, we may make it specific by saying *Bethlehem Steel,* or *United Aircraft.* There is another way, however, which enables us to keep the generality and at the same time remind ourselves of the indefinite number of particulars in the generality. We may simply use subscripts, such as $person_1$, $person_2$, $person_3$, and so on; or $industry_1$, $industry_2$, $industry_3$, and so on.

That is not to say that in every speech we make we shall self-importantly assign indexes to every general term we use. That would make us sound precious and pedantic. We shall, however, be using the indexes in our own evaluations. After some practice with them, we begin to use them unconsciously. The advantage of this is tremendous. It keeps us from working ourselves into verbal impasses; thus, when we talk, say, about "crime," we automatically remind ourselves that people are going to place different interpretations on the word. Moreover, as we use the indexes, we train ourselves to think more extensionally, and thus realistically. Use of the indexes reminds us of similarities *and* differences. It enables us to apply a very limited number of words to the unlimited variety of fact-territory.

Indexes are especially useful if we keep them mentally at hand, so to speak, when we read or listen to others. When someone says, for example, "Education is the key to survival," we instantly remind ourselves that $education_1$ is not $education_2$, and $survival_8$ is not $survival_{10}$, and so on. For one sort of "education" may even have a pernicious, nonsurvival effect. And obviously there are many different survivals—$survival_1$, for example, may be the bare subsistence of an Egyptian fellah whereas survival$_{15}$ may be the gay life of a rich playboy. What kind of "education" for what kind of "survival" do we want?

Use of the indexes—and indeed, this is true of all the extensional devices—enables us to be more critical and discriminating. It sharpens our perceptions and awarenesses. Yet at the same time it "softens" our attitudes and makes us less rigid and dogmatic. It makes us more pliable and adaptable in the unlimited variety of extensional reality that we have to live with.

DATES

The use of dates introduces the time coordinate into our evaluations, and without the time coordinate we almost inevitably misevaluate. Actualities flow and change; if we are to make our maps fit the territory, we must take this into account. Eddie Bangs, for example, who was such an obnoxious brat at the age of ten, has grown up to be a very decent sort of fellow—Eddie Bangs^{1953} *is not* Eddie Bangs^{1943}.

Thus, in addition to indexing our higher-order abstraction, we further extensionalize it by attaching a date. And so when someone glibly says, for example, "War is war!" we may mentally index and date their terms, reminding ourselves that war$_1$^{1916} was quite different from war$_2$^{1941}, which was again still different from war$_3$^{1953}, and so on. Indeed, peace^{1920} was vastly different from peace^{1952}, which turned out to have quite a bit of war in it. (See Figure 1.)

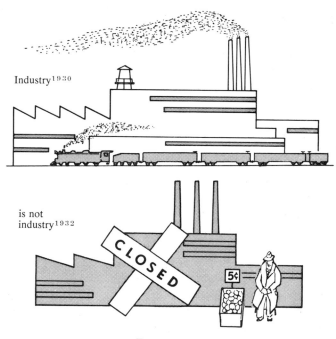

Industry^{1930}

is not
industry^{1932}

FIGURE 1.

Note how these extensional devices keep reminding us of the great complexity and variety of extensional reality. They bring us up short when we tend to float away from the facts and thrust us back into the maelstrom of actualities. They help us to avoid the mere rattling interplay of words and compel us to keep matching our "maps" with the "territory."

ET CETERAS

The reader will already have noticed that we use the abbreviation *etc.* a great deal in this book. We have done this not to avoid enumerations but to indicate that *complex* enumeration is impossible. For, regardless of how many categories we may enumerate, it is always possible to invent more. If we are to say, for example, "Atomic energy is important in war and industry."—using only a period and no *etc.*—we have verbally circumscribed the actuality very tightly indeed. Our problem, let us remember, is to make our "maps" fit the "territory." And so a more appropriate "map" of the extensional actuality would be some such statement as this: "Atomic energy is important in war, industry, chemistry, biophysics, archeology, paleontology, *etc.*"

Again, we do not always have to be explicit in our use of the *et cetera*. We may simply let it be implied in what we say—in speaking, we may even imply it quite eloquently with a gesture. Far from weakening what we say, this actually strengthens it; it makes it less brittle and gives our remarks a broad grounding in the "facts." It makes us, in effect, less dogmatic.

QUOTES

Again, the reader will have noticed that this book employs quotation marks rather liberally. The quotes represent simply a so-called "safety device" to remind us that certain words have highly intensional implications. For example, in this book the word "truth" has been placed in quotation marks. For here is a high-order abstraction indeed, and when we try to extensionalize it we may run into a morass of difficulties. "Truth" for Claudius Brown may not be "truth" at all to Mohammed Ahmad. Indeed, "truth" for Claudius Brown[1940] may even be quite different from "truth" for Claudius Brown[1953].

Note how on page 253 we placed the words "education" and "survival" in quotation marks. This represents a typical use of quotes as an extensional device. Here the quotes immediately remind us of the hidden actual diversity behind the unity of the word.

There are a number of terms which Korzybski recommended should not be used without quotation marks—for example, "know." The mechanisms of so-called "knowing" are obscure; what we feel we "know" we may discover that we are only acquainted with; and what we "know" at one date we may "know" in quite a different way at another date—the psychology major, for example, may "know" about marriage, but it is not the kind of "knowing" he will have after he has been married for a few years. Some other terms which tend to be highly untrustworthy if used without careful qualification and which therefore need quotation marks are: "intelligence," "meaning," "democracy," "belief," "intellect," "emotion," "concrete," "abstract," and so on.

HYPHENS

We happen to have the misfortune of being burdened with a language formulated ages ago, when people's outlooks on the world were far more static and categorical than they are today. Indeed, in the light of present-day scientific knowledge, their views were often extremely naive. Some of these outlooks have become embedded in our language, despite the fact that English is one of the most flexible of languages. Some of the distortion came into our language from the Greek and other ancient languages.

For example, our ancestors 2000 years ago glibly split the whole living individual into two categories—mind and body. And yet neither they nor anyone to this date has been able to show a "mind" without a "body." So deeply, however, has this merely *verbal* split shaped people's ways of evaluating that they find it hard to conceive of a body-mind unity of the living individual, and instead persist in thinking of body *and* mind. Another example is so-called "space" and "time." No one has yet ever observed or produced any "space" without some duration in "time," or any "time" without "space." And yet the split persisted for hundreds of years, even in the thinking of scientific men. Finally Einstein conceived the unity of space-time, and this unified formulation made possible the tremendous development which has grown out of his work. It is at least possible that Einstein's great discoveries and formulations would have been made far earlier had it not been for the artificial splitting by means of words of what in actuality cannot be split.

The examples above have already suggested how we may use the hyphen to bridge the verbal split which does violence to the extensional facts. Again, we shall not always use it explicitly. But we shall do well to keep it permanently present as we make our evaluations. For example, a physician who treats "body" without also taking "mind" into account is actually practicing little more than veterinary medicine. For with humans the "mental" aspect invariably plays a part. Thus a physician is compelled to think in terms of body-mind and not "body" *and* "mind." His thinking has to be not of "psyche" (mind) or "soma" (body) but *psychosomatic*.

The cumulative effect of our deliberately and habitually using the extensional devices is to bring our thinking up to date, so that our evaluations[1953] will be adequate to the extensional facts[1953].

EVALUATE THE FOLLOWING STATEMENTS

1. A reaction that may be "normal" for animals may be quite "abnormal" for humans.
2. "Semantic disorders" have to do with our misuse of words.
3. Individuals who orient themselves predominantly by intension frequently react to the least important as if it were the most important.
4. The extensional devices in effect make us conscious of abstracting, if we apply them in making our evaluations.
5. The conventional notions of "fact," "truth," etc. come into a new perspective when we consider them in the light of consciousness of abstracting.
6. Some current methods of advertising tend to encourage us to confuse levels of abstraction.
7. An individual who is predominantly intensionally oriented is actually suffering from a kind of semantic disorder.
8. There are many assumptions embedded in the standard forms of language which tend to make us misevaluate.
9. We cannot live exclusively by intension or exclusively by extension.
10. Scientists in their work have a predilection for extensional methods.

Warren G. Bennis / Edgar H. Schein
Fred I. Steele / David E. Berlew

TOWARDS BETTER
INTERPERSONAL RELATIONSHIPS

This is our pad
we all have a ball here
we don't have much bread but
bread is really not very important
when you have good relationships

From Suzuki Beane

1. A FRAMEWORK FOR EVALUATING
INTERPERSONAL RELATIONSHIPS

Can we establish a single criterion of goodness or badness which would be relevant for all interpersonal relationships? Consider the following: customer-salesman, psychiatrist-patient, husband-wife, manager-foreman, guard-inmate, lover-mistress, nurse-doctor. Or take the following kinds of relationships: puppy love, friendship, a crush, an affair, rivals, enemies, boyfriends, fraternity brothers, colleagues, cousins, siblings; or conditions like enforced, contractual, clandestine, accidental, "stuffy," informal, creative, chronic, stable. Or take the following settings: bureaucracy, fraternity, family, board of education, classroom. Does goodness mean the same thing for all of these? Obviously not.

We have to ask: "good for what?" As a starting analytic point let us say that all interpersonal relationships are oriented toward some *primary goal,* that is, some goal or function whose presence is necessary for the relationship to exist and whose absence would seriously undermine it. For example, if two friends stop satisfying each others' affiliative needs, the relationship would end. If two research collaborators can no longer do good research together, they will drift to more productive partners or work on their own. When the pupil can no longer learn from the teacher or the teacher thinks he can no longer impart new knowledge, the relationship will draw to a close. Thus, the *raison d' être* of the relationship, the salient reason for its formation, serves as a framework for evaluation.

On this basis we can characterize four distinct types of relationships: *Type A:* a relationship formed for the purpose of fulfilling *itself,* such as love, marriage, friendship. The main transaction in the relationship is "feelings" and for that reason we will refer to Type A as *expressive-emotional.*

A *Type B* relationship exists in order to establish "reality," but of two distinct kinds. The content of the interpersonal transaction for one kind of Type B (1) is information about the "self" or about the relationship. This could include interpersonal "feedback" or reflected appraisals. The content of the interpersonal transaction for the other kind of Type B (2) encompasses information about the environment or a "definition of the situation." The former kind (1) exists in order to understand the relationship and the "self;" the latter (2) exists in order to comprehend social realities. An example of (1) might be a pair of friends who help each other find their identity. The other (2) can often be observed in social groups, say a fraternity, where the norms of the group establish certain social realities: e.g. "what courses or professors are best," "what kind of girls are the best 'dates'," etc. In either case (1) or (2) we refer to Type B as *confirmatory.*

A *Type C* relationship is formed for the purpose of *change* or *influence.* Thus one or both parties to the relationship come together to create a change in each other or the relationship. The change may entail anything from acquiring new behaviors to attitude change. The main transaction between the change-agent and change-target is information about the desired state to be achieved and feedback on how the target is doing. Examples of change are psychiatrist-patient, teacher-student, parent-child, etc.

A *Type D* relationship is formed in order to achieve some goal or task: a conductor and his violin section or a foreman and his workers or collaborators on a research project are all examples of Type D. We will call this type, *instrumental*; the main coin of interpersonal exchange is information *about the task.*

Before continuing our analysis, we should mention that these four types can rarely, if ever, be observed in "pure" form; the purpose of a relationship cannot be so simple or monolithic. A couple, for example, may marry not only for the relationship itself (Type A) but for the same instrumental purpose as well (Type D). We know of two anthropologists whose marriage was based on "love" and the need to work together. And we know of many co-workers, engaged in instrumental activities who permit—even desire—the relationship itself to take priority over the task. Conversely, there are partners in business, often brothers, whose relationship has become increasingly contractual rather than familial. And Type B, confirmatory relationships are, of course, a category of the more general types, particularly Type C, change relationships. In any case, we have never seen a purely "confirmatory" relationship. So we are not dealing with mutually exclusive types, but with overlapping categories with multiple functions. Despite this qualification, we do want to stress for analytical purposes that every relationship is formed—indeed, is caused—in order to realize one primary function.

Now we are in a better position to answer the question raised earlier on: what is a good relationship? Let us now turn to Figure 1. This diagram shows the four types of relationships ordered down the vertical axis. In column (1) we have listed the content of the interpersonal transactions. In column (2) we have listed the various criteria for a good relationship. This is based on our main assertion, only implied until now, that a relationship is considered good to the extent that it fulfills its primary function. Thus, to determine whether a Type A relationship is good, we have to

Primary Function of Interpersonal Relationship: / Defining Characteristics	(1) The Content of the Interpersonal Transaction	(2) Criteria for Good Relationships	(3) Outcomes of Good Relationships	(4) Outcomes of Bad Relationships
Type A: Emotional-Expressive	Feelings	Mutual satisfaction	"Solidarity"	Alienation Ambivalence Hostility
Type B: Confirmatory	Information about self: 1) Interpersonal feedback; reflected appraisals	1) Confirmation	1) Integrated identity Self-actualization — Consensus about Reality	1) Disconfirmation
	Information about environment: 2) Definitions of the situation	2) Consensus	2) Cognitive mastery	2) Anomie
Type C: Change-Influence	Information about desired goal and progress toward achieving goal	Desired change	Growth Termination Internalization	Resistance Interminable dependence
Type D: Instrumental	Information about task	Productivity Creativity	Competence Output	Inadequate Low output

FIGURE 1. *Multiple criteria framework for evaluating interpersonal relationships.*

estimate if it is mutually *satisfying* to the participants; that is: do they have the desired relationship? For Type B there are two kinds of criteria depending on whether or not the exchange concerns the establishing of an interpersonal or self reality or whether or not the relationship was used to apprehend external reality. If (1), then we observe confirmation, some agreement about the relationship. If (2), then we observe consensus, some agreement about the definition of the situation. For Type C the change is the main criterion; for Type D, productivity (or creativity) is the key. *Satisfaction, confirmation* (and *consensus*), *desired change,* and *productivity* are the terms which can be applied to the goodness of a relationship, depending upon its unique function.

2. OUTCOMES OF GOOD AND BAD RELATIONSHIPS

If the primary function of a relationship is fulfilled—what we have been calling a *good* relationship—we can expect a positive outcome; if not, then a negative one. What are the outcomes of good and bad relationships? Columns (3) and (4) list these.

A. For Type A, solidarity is the indicator of a good relationship, and *ambivalence, alienation, or chronic hostility* are the indicators of a bad relationship. Let us say a word or two more about "solidarity," a term which has had the recent misfortune of connoting "togetherness." What we have in mind is closer to Murray's Dionysian couple:

> ... engaged now and again in unpremeditated, serious yet playful, dramatic outbursts of feeling, wild imagination, and vehement interaction, in which one of them—sometimes Adam, sometimes Eve—gave vent to whatever was pressing for expression. Walpurgis was the name they gave to episodes of this insurgent nature ... each of the two psyches, through numberless repetitions, discharged its residual as well as emergent and beneficient dispositions, until nearly every form of sexuality and nearly every possible complementation of dyadic roles had been dramatically enacted ... and all within the compass of an ever mounting trust in the solidarity of their love, evidenced in the Walpurgis episodes by an apparently limitless mutual tolerance of novelty and emotional extravagance.[1]

In our view, then, solidarity encompasses a wide range of complex emotions as well as the capacity for the individuals to risk the confrontation of their emotional vicissitudes; at the same time they must remain together despite and because of their own anxieties and appetites.

B. It might be useful to state with greater clarity than before the two classes of relationships we are grouping in Type B. Both have to do with comprehending reality, one an *interpersonal* reality that develops from the interactions between the participants and serves to define the boundaries of self-hood and of the interpersonal relationship. The "self" is born in the communicative acts and, according to this symbolic-interactionist position, "we begin to see each other as others see us" and begin to "take the role of the other." Thus, the formation, definition, and evaluation of the self emerge from the successive interactions we have with significant others.[2]

The other class of Type B has to do with apprehending some element in the environment, an item "x," let us say, for which we require interpersonal support in order to "understand" it. This is identical to Festinger's idea concerning the attainment of "social reality."[3] He asserts that opinions, attitudes, and beliefs—as differentiated from physical realities, which could be proved or disproved by physical means—need anchorage in a socially valued group. Thus, one powerful motive for people to come together in interpersonal relationships is to "make sense," to order, to develop cognitive mastery over the outside world. As Festinger says: "An opinion, a belief, an attitude is correct, valid, and proper to the extent that it is anchored in a group of people with similar beliefs, opinions, and attitudes."[4]

To this extent we are all "conformists;" that is, all of us need interpersonal evidence to attain cognitive control over our environments.

Let us come back now to the possible outcomes of good and bad Type B relationships. If we consider the interpersonal class, (1), then in a good relationship, an integrated "personal identity" or self-actualization and self-enhancement would emerge as well as a realistic relationship; in the external (2) case, cognitive mastery over some salient aspect of the environment would emerge. In either case *the outcomes of goodness in Type B is the consensus and confirmation regarding the perception of reality.*

This increased perception of reality that comes about through consensus or confirmation—regardless of its *validity*—has a tremendous liberating effect leading to a self-expansiveness and self-acceptance in (1) and a high degree of morale and confidence in (2).

A bad Type B (1) would consist of chronic refutation and dissonance and therefore probably not last. Farber[5] writes movingly of his experience with a patient who refused to confirm him (Farber)—by simply not getting "well;" that is, by not acting like a patient should. We have all experienced and witnessed situations like this where a group or person has denied self or role confirmation to another, consciously or not: students who won't learn, children who won't obey, audiences who won't approve, followers who won't be *influenced,* and friends who won't share or confirm our delusions about self, and in fact, stubbornly transmit cues counter to our own self-image.[6]

A bad Type B (2) exists when the parties to a relationship cannot agree on or make sense about external realities. It is most graphically described in the words of Kafka where even the reader gets fooled into thinking that the Kafkaesque world *is* more eerie and ambiguous than "real life." The fact of the matter is that the *world* is no more or less complicated but *people* cannot arrive at any agreement about it. So it is a world without "norms," without clear-cut references—evolved out of a shared frame of reference—necessary to establish consensus about "reality." The ability to predict future events, the need to reduce uncertainty—all these matters we call "cognitive mastery"—are essential for man's security. It is one of the main reasons (and costs) for interpersonal relationships, for without it, relationships devolve into *anomie,* a disoriented, ambiguous, uncertain world.

There is a special case of a bad outcome for a Type B that bears some attention. Imagine a situation where two or more people come together and confirm their own relationship but seriously distort some aspect of "social reality." Let us take an example from literature. In Thomas Mann's story "The Blood of the Walsungs,"[7] the twin brother and sister seriously misperceive (but agree on) the outside world and withdraw further and further into the nest of their own distortions. The fact that they hold a unique and different view from most people tends to further intensify their alienation, for the only support they can find is restricted. This form of social withdrawal has been observed, for example, among apocalyptic messianic groups.[8]

This distortion of and rejection by the outside world—always linked with libidinal contraction and intensification—leads to a state of affairs Slater calls "social regression.[9]

The tandem alcoholism of the married couple in the movie, "Days of Wine and Roses," as well as the bizarre and autistic games played by George and Martha in Albee's play, *"Who's Afraid of Virginia Woolf?"*[10] are both examples of this phenomenon. Sometimes this type of relationship resembles "solidarity," like the Walpurgis experiences reported above, but they are always different by nature. "Social regression" flourishes only in a social vacuum and when there is a powerful motive to distort external reality. Solidarity can last only if there is some realistic connection with the outside world.

C. A Type C relationship is defined by its pivotal concern with the acquisition or modification of behavior or attitudes, as imparted by a change-agent (A) to some change target (B). It is true that changes occur in the other types of relationship discussed, but only spontaneously and adventitiously. Type C encompasses primarily the class of change-inductions that are planned; for example, it would include primarily relationships resulting in changes due to formal course work (teacher-student or work partner in "lab"), and only incidentally the informal and unplanned kinds of relationships such as those which occur in "bull-session" groups. Type C covers a wide range of relationships, from parent-child to phychiatrist-patient, from coach-pupil to warden-inmate.[11]

In addition to this emphasis on change, growth, and learning, an analysis of Type C further reveals two unique characteristics. First, these relationships are almost always oriented toward termination (graduation, parole, or death). An "interminable" psychoanalysis is considered deplorable, while an "interminable" marriage is considered honorable. Secondly, Type C reveals a special kind of relationship between the change-agent (A) and the target (B) which we refer to as "tilted." In other words we expect A to influence B, to "give to" B, to teach B more—than the otherway around. As a rule students learn from teachers, patients from psychiatrists, pupils from coaches.[12] Thus the interpersonal exchange is slanted and less reciprocal, by definition, than other types. With these preliminary considerations out of the way, let us turn to the indicators of a good and bad Type C relationship.

A good Type C leads to three distinct, but related, outcomes. First, there is consensus between A and B that the desired growth or change or influence has been attained. Second, the relationship has reached a state wherein its continuation, while possibly helpful, will not lead to significant advances. It must end. Third, the client must have internalized the learning process, such that the process of learning begun in the relationship can continue. Thus *growth, termination,* and *internalization* are the indicators of a good Type C relationship.

The reverse of these criteria serves to signify badness. Dissatisfaction with B's rate of progress on the part of either A or B is a common indicator. The frequently heard remark: "I must change my teacher-therapist-coach-trainer; we're not getting anywhere" is an example. Second, the relationship cannot be extended indefinitely. That is, there must be some point at which the hoped-for changes will occur. Without this explicit termination point, both A and B can possibly get trapped in a false dream where the original and primary purpose of the relationship gets sidetracked.[13]

Third, the target must be able to use what he has learned in an autonomous fashion; that is, without undue dependence on the change-agent. Patients who are forever returning to their therapists are not "cured"; acting students who suffer immobilizing stage fright unless their coach is watching from the wings are not "trained." We do not mean to imply that in a good Type C relationship the client has nothing more to learn and never returns for further training; we do mean that the client is relatively free of dependence and has learned how to continue the process on his own.

D. Instrumental relationships, Type D, are formed in order to produce or create: a song, an idea, a car, a formula, a dress. It encompasses the range of relationships involved in those activities which function in order to produce a "good or service."[14] It is ordinarily what people "do for a living"; it is certainly what most people do to earn enough for other types of relationships. As the need for interdependence and collaboration increases—that is to say: as specialization increases—this form of relationship will grow in importance and will call for more searching examination. It may be already the most ubiquitous form of interpersonal relationship in an industrialized society such as ours.

These are two main indicators of a good instrumental relationship; *competence* and *output*. The latter is objectively measured, usually in the form of a productivity rate: stories sold *per* year, pages typed *per* day, articles published *per* year, bolts attached *per* minute, profits earned *per* quarter, etc. Because of the relative ease of measuring output, instrumental relationships are often easier to judge as good or bad.

Less objective than output, but equally important from our point of view, is the way participants engaged in an instrumental relationship manage their work. Decision making, problem solving, coordination, quality of collaboration, energy expenditure: these are some of the elements in the complex factor we refer to as *competence*.[15]

A bad instrumental relationship exists, then, if either competence or output is unsatisfactory relative to certain norms. One would expect that these two factors would be positively correlated, but there is inadequate evidence to make this assertion.[16] . . .

3. THE PERSONAL COMPETENCIES FOR GOOD INTERPERSONAL RELATIONS

Assume that we are dealing with a population of mature adults reasonably motivated for interaction. What are the competencies (or capacities) that would lead to good interpersonal relationships? We are biased toward those capacities that tend to deepen and widen the *emotional interchange* as well as *increase understanding:*

1. *Capacity to Receive and Send Information and Feelings Reliably.* This not only includes the ability to *listen* and *perceive* accurately and fully, but other qualities as well. For example, it includes *sensitivity*, meaning a lowered threshold or heightened alertness to salient interpersonal events; that is, an active and creative awareness, not simply a passive absorption.

2. *Capacity to Evoke the Expression of Feelings.* Most anybody can listen passively to someone; the kind of listening that makes a difference is where the other is unafraid to express a thought, a belief, a feeling ordinarily reserved for autistic reveries or denied to the self. Just as we *maintain* a certain threshold to human ex-

perience, we also communicate our threshold, and quite often "stop" or inhibit the other.[17]

3. *Capacity to Process Information and Feelings Reliably and Creatively.* This means that we can conceptualize and order our interpersonal experience, that we can abstract and play with various combinations of interpersonal exchanges and arrive at some diagnosis. Points one and two have to do with *sensitivity*; this point has to do with adequate *diagnosis*.

4. *Capacity to Implement a Course of Action.* A diagnosis may indicate a certain behavior; say the girl really requires more dominance or the boy needs to be included more but doesn't know how to ask for it. What is required are *action*-skills. Diagnostic sensitivity without remedial action may be no more disastrous than action without diagnosis, but it is often sadder. *Behavioral flexibility plus* diagnostic sensitivity raises the prospects for better interpersonal relations.

5. *Capacity to Learn in Each of the Above Areas.* It is far easier to talk of the *blocks* to learning—and "learning how to learn" in the interpersonal area—than to suggest some positive steps. Nevertheless, let us try. First, the individual must attempt to develop an attitude of "observant participation"; that is, a frame of mind that permits and encourages a constant analysis and interpretation of his interpersonal experiences. People simply do not learn from experience alone; it is experience observed, processed, analyzed, interpreted, and verified that we learn from. This constant scrutiny of one's own and other's behavior causes some stiltedness at first[18] and may interfere with spontaneity, but gaining any new skill causes this initial uneasiness.

This constant review and reflection is difficult, for it asks the individual to consider data that may be not only "new" (i.e., unnoticed until now) but also contradictory to the way the person ordinarily likes to see himself. Socrates once said that "the unexamined life isn't worth living." Modern psychiatry would tell him that the examined life is no fun either.

In any case, learning is simply not possible without continual surveillance and appraisal. And this examination is not possible without the possibility of gaining validating (or disconfirming) data from one's personal environment.

How these capacities are developed; how individuals learn "empathy," or learn to "identify" or learn to listen and perceive more realistically; how individuals learn to make connections, to induce trust, to permit other people to understand them and vice-versa, to develop an observant-participating orientation; how human beings can become more sensitive: these are all questions that deserve better answers than we now have.

We are, almost all of us, equally in the dark on this issue. And society seems reluctant to consider or provide viable methods for satisfying the enormous curiosity about, and the will to enhance, interpersonal relations. Two roads, only, seem available. We have the "how-to-do" approach symbolized by the Sunday rotogravure personality test; on the other hand, we have a long-term bout with psychotherapy, where the person is defined as "ill."

Please do not misunderstand. Psychoanalysis is irreplaceable as a healing force in our society; even "do-it-yourself" personality tests may help to engender curiosity. But certainly a society such as ours which is placing increasing emphasis on interpersonal skills and knowledge requires more institutional avenues for fulfillment than these.[19]

NOTES

1. H. A. Murray, "Vicissitudes of Creativity," in H. H. Anderson (ed.), *Creativity and Its Cultivation*, Interdisciplinary Symposia on Creativity, Michigan State University, 1957-58 (New York: Harper & Bros., 1959), pp. 110-18.

2. For a recent discussion stemming from this tradition of Mead and Cooley see H. D Duncan, *Communication and Social Order* (New York: Bedminister Press, 1962).

3. L. Festinger, "Informal Social Communication," *Psychological Review,* Vol. 57 (1950), pp. 271-82.

4. *Ibid.,* p. 273.

5. L. Farber, "Therapeutic Despair," *Psychiatry,* Vol. 21 (Feb., 1958), pp. 7-20.

6. Recently, some evidence has been gathered which shows the effects of role confirmation and refutation on a group of nurses. (J. E. Berkowitz and N. H. Berkowitz, "Nursing Education and Role Conception," *Nursing Research,* Vol. 9 [1960], "briefs.") It was felt that the patients who responded to treatment were confirming the nurses' role and those patients who did not respond to treatment were refuting the nurses' role. The hypothesis, supported by the data, was: patients who were disconfirmers would not be liked or treated as well by the nursing staff as those patients who were role-confirmers.

7. T. Mann, *Stories of Three Decades* (New York: Knopf, 1936), pp. 279-319.

8. L. Festinger, H. W. Riecken, Jr., and S. Schachter, *When Prophecy Fails* (Minneapolis: University of Minnesota, 1956); also J. A. Hardyck and M. Braden, "Prophecy Fails Again: A Report of a Failure to Replicate," *J. of Abn. Soc. Psychol.,* Vol. 65 (1962), pp. 136-41.

9. P. Slater, "On Social Regression," *American Soc. Review,* Vol. 28 (1963), pp. 339-64.

10. E. Albee, *Who's Afraid of Virginia Woolf?* (New York: Atheneum, 1963).

11. The reader is referred back to the essay introducing Part III where change relationships are treated in detail.

12. We have omitted those exceptional, but highly interesting, cases where B can influence A more than A can influence B. More often than not, these are perverse, given our definition of Type C. Teachers may indeed learn from students, but this is different from exploitation and "stealing ideas." Analysts may "use" counter-transference productively for the patient's ultimate health, but this is different than cashing in on stock tips or sexual exploitation. See Cheever for a literary treatment of an interesting exception to the rule.

13. What often happens in these cases is that both partners in the relationship shift consciously or unconsciously to another type of relationship; the ski-instructor who marries his student, for example, is a switch from C to A. We will return to this point later.

14. Unaccounted for here are those instrumental relationships we associate with the service industries, such as some customer-salesman relationships, cabbie-passenger, receptionist-customer. We have ignored this class of relationships for two reasons. First because this type of relationship rarely involves more than a brief encounter in a transient setting. Second because there is a peculiar lack of reciprocity. The waitress is instrumentally involved with the diner, but he is not involved instrumentally with her—and typically he has only a "service" relationship to her. This is a difficult class of problems for our analytic scheme to handle. Temporary relationships, such as games, vacation trips, etc., are examined brilliantly in a recent essay by M. Miles, "On Temporary Systems," manuscript (New York: Columbia University, 1963); see also A. R. Anderson and O. K. Moore, *Autotelic Folk-Models* (New Haven: Sociology Department, Yale University, 1959).

15. Time and space considerations do not allow for a complete discussion of these issues. They go far beyond the purposes of this essay. The so-called "criterion problem" has perplexed industrial psychologists and students of organizational behavior for some time and we do not aim to settle any issues with this inadequate discussion. For a fuller statement, see W. G. Bennis "Towards a 'Truly' Scientific Management: The Concept of Organization Health," *General Systems Yearbook* (Ann Arbor: Mental Health Research Institute, 1962).

16. C. Argyris, *Interpersonal Competence and Organizational Effectiveness* (Homewood, Ill.: Irwin-Dorsey Press, 1962); R. Likert, *New Patterns of Management* (New York: McGraw-Hill Book Co., Inc., 1961).

17. An unexplored, but important, area for research is the role of the *listener* in interpersonal relations. There are "charismatic listeners" and "dull listeners"; there are listeners who evoke deep, meaningful human encounters and others who foreclose them. Why? We should know more about this.

18. Exposure to almost anyone undergoing the early days of psychoanalysis or a human relations training laboratory, such as those conducted by the National Training Laboratory, is sufficient indication of a spastic, "overserious," rather mannered self-examination. To the outsider it is Theater of the Absurd. The insider sympathizes with what the outsider is missing.

19. The National Training Laboratory in this country and Tavistock Institute in England have developed the methodology of "human relations training" to a genuinely professional level. We feel this is an encouraging sign and will be a development that will increase its momentum in and import on our society. We still await, however, a sound statement on "positive mental health" that will legitimize the idea of *enhancement* as well as cure (E. H. Schein, and W. G. Bennis, *Personal and Organizational Change through Group Methods* [New York: Wiley, 1964]).

Index

272 *Index*

Time-binding, 29
Tomkins, S.S., 204, 209, 210
Touching, 130-31
Transactional Analysis (TA), 177-93

Understanding, 212-13
Undirected communication, 163

Verbal, 25, 29-32, 111, 115, 247-48;
communication, 25; dialogue, 127;
impasses, 247-48; maps, 246, 249;
symbol, 121
Voice tones as cues, 180

Walter, A.A., 45, 50
Wallen, J., 196, 218

Wapner, S., 204, 210
Weick, K.E., 203, 210
Werner, H., 204, 210
Weyl, H., 43, 52
Whitehead, A.N., 27, 35, 52, 54
Whitman, R.M., 205, 210
Whorf, B.L., 35, 53, 57, 85
Wiener, N., 51, 53, 113, 119
Winters, L.C., 203, 209
Withdrawal, 187
Wittgenstein, L., 28, 32, 53, 112, 119
Woodruff, A., 1, 2, 12
Woodworth, R.S., 61, 80, 81, 84
Words as cues, 180

Zipf, G., 169, 173